LIBRARY OF THE HISTORY OF IDEAS
VOLUME XII

Figures on the Horizon

LIBRARY OF THE HISTORY OF IDEAS

ISSN 1050–1053

Series Editor: JOHN W. YOLTON

PREVIOUS VOLUMES

I The History of Ideas: Canon and Variations, *ed. Donald R. Kelley*

II Philosophy, Religion and Science in the Seventeenth and Eighteenth Centuries, *ed. John W. Yolton*

III Race, Class and Gender in Nineteenth-Century Culture, *ed. Maryanne Cline Horowitz*

IV Hume as Philosopher of Society, Politics and History, *ed. Donald Livingston and Marie Martin*

V Essays on the History of Aesthetics, *ed. Peter Kivy*

VI Essays on Political Philosophy, *ed. Patrick Riley*

VII Discovering China: European Interpretations in the Enlightenment, *ed. Julia Ching and Willard G. Oxtoby*

VIII Race, Gender, and Rank: Early Modern Ideas of Humanity, *ed. Maryanne Cline Horowitz*

IX Renaissance Essays, *ed. Paul Oskar Kristeller and Philip P. Wiener*

X Renaissance Essays II, *ed. William J. Connell*

XI The American Enlightenment, *ed. Frank Shuffelton*

FIGURES ON THE HORIZON

Edited by
JERROLD SEIGEL

UNIVERSITY OF ROCHESTER PRESS

Copyright © 1993 JOURNAL OF THE HISTORY OF IDEAS, INC.

All Rights Reserved. Except as permitted under current legislation
no part of this work may be photocopied, stored in a retrieval system,
published, performed in public, adapted, broadcast,
transmitted, recorded or reproduced in any form or by any means,
without the prior permission of the copyright owner

This collection first published 1993

University of Rochester Press
200 Administration Building, University of Rochester
Rochester, New York 14627, USA
and at PO Box 9, Woodbridge, Suffolk IP12 3DF, UK

ISBN 1 878822 30 6

Library of Congress Cataloging-in-Publication Data
Figures on the horizon / edited by Jerrold Seigel.
    p.   cm. – (Library of the history of ideas, ISSN 1050–1053 ;
v. 12)
    Includes bibliographical references.
    ISBN 1–878822–30–6 (alk. paper)
    1. Philosophy, Modern – 20th century. 2. Philosophy, Modern –
19th century.   3. Social sciences – Philosophy. 4. Intellectual life –
History.   I. Seigel, Jerrold E.   II. Series.
B804.F4446   1993
190'.9'04–dc20   93–41061

British Library Cataloguing-in-Publication Data
Figures on the Horizon. – (Library of the
History of Ideas, ISSN 1050–1053;Vol.12)
    I. Seigel, Jerrold   II. Series
    190
    ISBN 1–878822–30–6

This publication is printed on acid-free paper

Printed in the United States of America

TABLE OF CONTENTS

Acknowledgements			vii
Introduction	*Jerrold Seigel*		ix
I.	*Steven Lukes*	The Meanings of "Individualism"	1
II.	*Keith Ansell-Pearson*	Who is the Übermensch? Time, Truth and Woman in Nietzsche	23
III.	*Jerrold Seigel*	Autonomy and Personality in Durkheim: An Essay on Content and Method	46
IV.	*Mark S. Cladis*	Durkheim's Individual in Society: A Sacred Marriage?	71
V.	*Michael Freeden*	J. A. Hobson as a New Liberal Theorist: Some Aspects of his Social Thought until 1914	91
VI.	*Andrew Feffer*	Sociability and Social Conflict in George Herbert Mead's Interactionism, 1900–1919	114
VII.	*Keith R. Burich*	Henry Adams, the Second Law of Thermodynamics, and the Course of History	136
VIII.	*John Farrenkopf*	The Transformation of Spengler's Philosophy of World History	152
IX.	*Walter L. Adamson*	Gramsci's Interpretation of Fascism	175
X.	*Toby Gelfand*	Charcot's Response to Freud's Rebellion	194
XI.	*Pete A. Y. Gunter*	Bergson and Jung	209
XII.	*Peter C. John*	Wittgenstein's "Wonderful Life"	227
XIII.	*Walter Lammi*	Hans-Georg Gadamer's "Correction" of Heidegger	243
XIV.	*David Adams*	Metaphors for Mankind: The Development of Hans Blumenberg's Anthropological Metaphorology	264

ACKNOWLEDGEMENTS

The articles in this volume first appeared in the *Journal of the History of Ideas* as indicated below, by volume, year and pages, in order.

Adams, David, "Metaphors for Mankind: The Development of Hans Blumenberg's Anthropological Metaphorology," 52 (1991) 152–66

Adamson, Walter L., "Gramsci's Interpretation of Fascism," 41 (1980) 615–33

Ansell-Pearson, Keith, "Who is the Übermensch? Time, Truth and Woman in Nietzsche," 53 (1992) 309–31

Burich, Keith R., "Henry Adams, the Second Law of Thermodynamics, and the Course of History," 48 (1987) 467–82

Cladis, Mark S., "Durkheim's Individual in Society: A Sacred Marriage?," 53 (1992) 71–90

Farrenkopf, John, "The Transformation of Spengler's Philosophy of World History," 52 (1991) 463–85

Feffer, Andrew, "Sociability and Social Conflict in George Herbert Mead's Interactionism, 1900–1919," 51 (1990) 233–54

Freeden, Michael, "J. A. Hobson as a New Liberal Theorist: Some Aspects of his Social Thought until 1914," 34 (1973) 421–43

Gelfand, Toby, "Charcot's Response to Freud's Rebellion," 50 (1989) 293–307

Gunter, Pete A. Y., "Bergson and Jung," 43 (1982) 635–52

John, Peter C., "Wittgenstein's 'Wonderful Life'," 49 (1988) 495–510

Lammi, Walter, "Hans-Georg Gadamer's 'Correction' of Heidegger," 52 (1991) 487–507

Lukes, Steven, "The Meanings of 'Individualism'," 32 (1971) 45–66

Seigel, Jerrold, "Autonomy and Personality in Durkheim: An Essay on Content and Method," 48 (1987) 483–507

INTRODUCTION

The history of ideas spans the whole history of civilization, but as a discipline intellectual history has a special relationship to thinking in its own time. This is partly the case because every historical inquiry belongs to its own present and speaks in some way to present needs, but also because writing the history of thought can be a way of taking part in contemporary intellectual life. Since Hegel, some of the greatest historians of ideas have been theorists and philosophers themselves, convinced like him that the task of thought in the present necessarily includes a reconsideration of its own past. Karl Marx's *Capital* began as a historical critique of earlier economic theory (a beginning that finally took on separate existence as *Theories of Surplus Value*), Emile Durkheim supported his kind of sociology by writing the history of both social theory and educational ideas, Ernst Cassirer was both a neo-Kantian philosopher and a historian of thought, Arthur O. Lovejoy, the founder of *The Journal of the History of Ideas* (from which all the essays that follow are reprinted), linked the history of ideas to a more specifically philosophical project, and more recently figures like Michel Foucault and Jacques Derrida have pursued their intellectual goals partly by providing new ways to think about past ideas and their history. Not all historians of ideas are theorists themselves, to be sure, but their reconsideration of thought in the past often brings them up against the work of their contemporaries who are, so that the history of contemporary thought sometimes serves intellectual historians as a form of self-reflection, reminding them of their own participation — however minor — in the world of ideas they study, and explicitly posing questions about their own methods and practices.

From its beginning, *The Journal of the History of Ideas* has given attention to contemporary thinkers and movements. The very first issue, in 1940, contained Crane Brinton's discussion of "The National Socialists' Use of Nietzsche," while subsequent ones provided review-discussions of new works by living thinkers, notably Karl Mannheim's *Man and Society in an Age of Reconstruction* (reviewed by J. H. Randall, Jr., in 1941) and Benedetto Croce's *History as the Story of Liberty* (reviewed by J. Salwyn Schapiro in the same year). Sigmund Freud made his first appearance in 1940, only a year after his death, in George Boas's consideration of "The Mona Lisa in the History of Taste." Brinton's initial analysis of Nazi ideas was followed up in the same year by A. O. Lovejoy's reflections on the relationship between fascism and romanticism in "The Meaning of Romanticism for the

Historian of Ideas," and by two articles on fascist doctrine and the Nazi leadership principle in 1942.

Recent thought was present in the *JHI* from the start, then, but it was never dominant. The fact of war probably made contemporary issues more salient in the early years than they would have been in peacetime, and for most of the journal's history twentieth-century questions have seemed to occupy – at best – only their chronological portion of a space that has had to be shared with classical, medieval, Renaissance, enlightenment and nineteenth-century currents. I think it is right to say that the general spirit of the *JHI*'s attention to recent intellectual history has been one of continuity with earlier eras; seldom have readers found in its pages articles that presume the virtue of twentieth-century attempts to make a sharp break with the cultural past. George Boas's essay on "The Mona Lisa in the History of Taste" referred to above mentioned Freud but not Marcel Duchamp; in half a century the *JHI* has never published an article about the literary and artistic avant-garde. Moreover — and partly as a reflection of this spirit of continuity — the relation between the *JHI* and contemporary thinkers has changed as the landscape of contemporary intellectual life has shifted. Marxism and psychoanalysis have been subjects of interest from the start, but the Frankfurt School version of "critical theory" has been relatively ignored, and self-consciously radical post-1960s currents such as literary theory, deconstruction and feminist theory have been little represented.

If these observations may seem to point to the limits of the *JHI*'s engagement with twentieth-century thinking, perhaps they also suggest certain of its virtues. Difficult as the distinction may be to maintain, the journal's mode of attention to recent thinkers has usually sought to be one of scholarship rather than partisanship. Most of its contributors and editors, asked to state the purpose of historical inquiry, would probably be happy with some version of Marc Bloch's reply: *comprendre*. If that is an answer to which many others might lay claim, still it is distinguishable both from another French-speaking historian whose response was *pour glorifier la patrie*, just as it is different from those — increasingly vocal in our academic life today — for whom history, like literary study, ought to be a form of cultural critique, an attempt to put in question the tradition of Western thought which the founders of this journal never doubted to be a source of nourishment and renewal.

What readers of the collection of essays that follows will find, therefore, is a sustained and diverse example of a kind of scholarship which presupposes that the past — however recent — must be learned from before it can be turned to present uses, and which seeks meaning in the interplay between text and context, on the — perhaps old-fashioned — assumption that thought is the expression of human individuals working in definite situations, rather than the projection of deep unconsious structures or the product of metaphorical strategies. Despite the many things that make the essays that follow all differ from each other, I think it is fair to say that they all belong to this humanistic tradition. This is true even of the one among them which declares its rootedness in the post-modern technique of deconstruction, Keith Ansell-Pearson's exploration of the character of Nietzsche's *Uebermensch*. As suggested above, references to deconstruction have been few and slow to appear in the pages of the *JHI* (the essay in question comes from a very recent volume); that they have begun to have a presence there owes much to the efforts of its editor since 1985, Donald R. Kelley, to open the journal to currents that had not been attracted to it before. But Mr Ansell-Pearson's essay owes to deconstruction above all its awareness of the metaphorical, poetic quality of Nietzsche's main notions, and of how his writings systematically call into question their own presumed claim to philosophical authority; in its readings of Nietzsche's texts it is scrupulously devoted to careful exposition, not the playful subversion in which much "deconstructive" interpretation revels.

Certain themes run through many of the assembled essays, a major one being the relationship between society and the individual in modern thinking. For this reason it seems appropriate to begin the volume with Steven Lukes's synoptic survey of "The Meanings of Individualism," even though much of his focus is on the nineteenth century, when many of the terms of discussion for modern individualism were first established. Lukes devotes his attention to the different "traditions of use" within which individualism was mainly discussed in four national contexts. In France, where recurring revolution made the social order seem most fragile, individualism very often took on a negative guise, condemned both by conservatives for its disruption of community and tradition, and by socialists who equated it with egotism and domination, and suspect even to liberals who either (like Tocqueville) saw it as undermining public spirit and social cohesion or (like later figures) as threatening the establishment of a pluralist social order. (Had Lukes been writing closer to our own time he would perhaps have had something to say about how these traditions relate to the recent neo-individualist currents in France.) Germany and the United States were the places where this negative image was most often countered by others, in the first because it stood for the project of self-realization that was still an unachieved national goal and for the romantic qualities of genius and originality, and in the second because of its association with expanding capitalism and liberal democracy. All the same, figures like Jacob Burckhardt in Germany combined the dominant notion with other, more troubled senses of the term, and in America the celebration of individualism meant something different in the mouth of Walt Whitman than it did in the speeches of Herbert Hoover or the novels of Ayn Rand. Characteristically, England was the country where the positive and negative traditions intermingled most, as both French and German usages were imported, and as individualism was considered by friends or enemies of nonconformist religion, capitalist self-reliance, cultural tradition and collectivist politics. By looking carefully at the different meanings of a single term, and distinguishing so clearly between the different contexts within which its sense was determined, Lukes was conducting an investigation akin to ones that more recent writers have pursued more self-consciously when they attempt to identify different "languages of political discourse."

Keith Ansell-Pearson's answer to the question "Who is the Übermensch?" proposes a reading of Nietzsche that resolves the apparent contradiction between Zarathustra's prophecy of a future, higher state for human life and Nietzsche's general rejection of all claims to subordinate the present to the future, as well as his celebration of the past in the doctrine of the eternal return. The resolution requires taking the *Übermensch* not as a doctrine, but as a metaphor or figure, a sign for the form of life which no longer looks to the future as a redemption from the present, but whose will is a joyful affirmation of all that life is, including the whole of the past, recognized as necessary for us to become what we are. In this metaphorical existence philosophy loses its claims to authority, as it descends like Zarathustra from the heights and "opens up the discourse of philosophy to a free play of signs in which new and more complex hybrid identities can be created." One form of this hybrid is the union of male and female qualities, adumbrated in some of Nietzsche's female figures, metaphors for "life understood as eternal pregnancy and fecundity," and the riposte in Nietzche's own writings to some of his well-known misogynistic pronouncements. If we relate to our lives like women who bear new life within themselves, then we (Nietzsche's readers) may come to see ourselves as pregnant with the *Übermensch*, with the form of life that will cure our apparent sickness by revealing it as the condition out of which can emerge an affirmative will that at once lives in the present and overcomes it. Nietzsche's teaching aimed to make us recognize our own unique selves as the source of this positive relationship to life, to bring us toward the autonomy that Zarathustra stood for but could not deliver or legislate; when we reach this state then the prophet will return to live among us. Ansell-Pearson's reading of Nietzsche seems to me far more persuasive than those that posit some kind of contradiction between Zarathustra's prophecy of the *Übermensch* and the doctrine of the eternal return; his imaginative use of deconstructive ideas does not subvert Nietzsche but affirms the poetic quality of his thinking on which he often remarked. And the view of the *Übermensch* that emerges suggests that Nietzsche's thinking had its roots in the German tradition whose approach to individualism Steven Lukes defines in terms of the self-realization and coming to be of a form of life which escapes clear definition while constantly affirming its own uniqueness and originality.

That the question of individualism appeared in different terms in the French context will be apparent in the two essays that follow; both deal with Emile Durkheim, but come to different conclusions about him. The first, by the editor of this volume, finds Durkheim's sense of the relationship between society and the individual to be close to the one posited by Lukes. Although as a liberal Durkheim sought to defend modern individualism against those who desired a return to an earlier social order, and remained an upholder of individual rights throughout his life, his ambivalence about individualism was clear throughout his career, deepening as time went on. His early attempt to reconcile individualism with social membership by presenting modern society as the source of liberation from the bonds of collective obligation and tradition yielded in his later writings to a tenser, more conflicted view of this relationship, along with an attempt to claim that the autonomy he had once linked to the opening modernity created for individual difference arose instead out of the universal qualities all people shared. Throughout his career Durkheim sought simultaneously to validate individualism and to set limits to it, but at each successive stage his previous solution appeared to him insufficiently severe in preventing modern individualism from legitimizing the egotism to which it was kin. The essay seeks the roots of this pattern in Durkheim's early experience in his family, which was shaped by the nature of French society and the educational policies of the state; it is the only one of the pieces reprinted here which tries to understand a thinker's work in terms of his personal psychology.

By contrast, Mark Cladis argues for the success of Durkheim's attempt to reconcile society and the individual. Durkheim's opposition to egotism was managed in such a way that it did not overflow into a hostility toward the individual, and "at his best" Durkheim provided a way to challenge and overcome the Cartesian dichotomy between subject and object. Durkheim's theory of the social nature of knowledge was undertaken as a way to overcome the defects of existing epistemologies, both empiricist and idealist, positing the individual formed within social relations as the being able to give coherent logical shape to experience. Religion, as the way of thinking characteristic of collective existence, provided the first form of this knowledge. Although Durkheim made logical categories dependent on social experience, he did not deny that the germs of logical thinking were to be found in individual natures too. In a subtle and suggestive reading of Durkheim's essay on "The Dualism of Human Nature and its Social Conditions," Cladis argues that the dichotomies between individual and social existence Durkheim discussed there were not absolute, and tries to show how to think about them in more flexible, less exclusive ways. If the interpretive strategy of the previous essay is developmental and relies on psychology, here the basic approach is from the side of theory and seeks to distill the best elements from Durkheim's thinking. If the editor is right then Durkheim tried but failed to extricate himself from the tense field of relations between the individual and society outlined for his country by Lukes; if Cladis is right then he succeeded.

The different tonality taken on by these and related issues in England and the United States is suggested by the two following essays, both of which deal with late nineteenth-century liberals who like Durkheim sought to bring liberalism closer to doctrines of social reform. In the first Michael Freeden examines the attempt by J. A. Hobson (whom most of us probably know first of all as a pioneering analyst of imperialism) to present a theory of this new liberalism. Hobson drew on varied sources, including both John Ruskin's critique of laisser-faire economics and Darwinian evolutionary theory, in order to present a revised liberalism that would make "the conscious play of organized human intelligence" operative in society. His thinking was dialectical in its attempt to describe a passage from primitive collectivism through intense individualism to a state where individuals would become aware of their own place within a society of interconnectedness. Social inequities were inefficient and in the end narrowed the grounds of individual development, while society had to be brought to the recognition that "an area of individual liberty is conducive to the health of the collective life." In place of John Stuart Mill's distinction between "self-regarding" and "other-regarding" actions, Hobson offered a more complex theory of the interaction or "feedback" between individual and social development, based on "a just apprehension of the social" — a goal, one might add, very close to Durkheim's. Freeden suggests that Hobson's redistributive liberalism found its nearest practical expression in the Liberal Party's famous budget of 1909, but he admits that what Hobson tried to present as a reconciliation of individual and social claims sometimes appeared as a vacillation between them.

Whether progressive liberals could in fact succeed in harmonizing individualism with social reform is the question posed somewhat more tartly by Andrew Feffer in regard to the writings and career of the American social psychologist and reformer George Herbert Mead. Mead's attempt to show that social reciprocity was a natural part of human character moved beyond the Darwinian strategy of collective survival appealed to by John Dewey (and by Hobson) to draw on the *Völkerpsychologie* of Wilhelm Wundt (whose works Durkheim had also studied early in his career), in particular Wundt's derivation of language from primitive gestures. Because human speakers were able to develop their expressive capacity only in interaction with respondents, each person's ability to speak depended on the presence of others who would reflect it back on her or him. Individual development therefore depended not just on cooperation with others, but on a recognition of their autonomy. Using these ideas Mead rooted the social needs of individuals more deeply in the conditions of their own achievement of self-consciousness and subjective development than earlier thinkers had. But the theory did not serve Mead very well when he sought to be guided by it in his practical work of mediating conflicts between employers and workers in early twentieth-century Chicago. There his assumption that social interaction depended on cooperation made it impossible to intervene effectively on behalf of workers — or teachers — engaged in struggle with opponents whose power and resources significantly outweighed theirs. Mead's and Dewey's rejection of struggle in the name of cooperation and responsibility made them blunt the claims of the disadvantaged people whose causes they hoped to further, leading them "simultaneously to embrace and deny utopian advocacy."

One of the fields where these issues about modern society and individuality have been fought out is in the understanding of history, which is the subject of the next three essays. In the first, Keith R. Burich argues that Henry Adams's well-known invocation of the second law of thermodynamics as a touchstone for understanding the course of history had a more subtle intention than his interpreters have thought. The law was not a simple metaphor for the underlying disorder and meaninglessness of the historical process. Presenting a revealing account of how scientists discussed the law in Adams's time, and evidence for his awareness of what they were saying, Burich shows that Adams looked to the law to underpin his conviction that attempts to achieve stable, unchanging forms of order in human life were self-defeating because they sought to monopolize and consume the energies that flowed out of individual difference and autonomy. Society might try to enlist individual energies for its great crusades and massive projects, but in doing so it would finally lose contact with the source of its own vitality. The great symbol of the Virgin, presiding over medieval life, stood both for unity and multiplicity, but what made her so powerful and attractive was that her sympathies "lay with man's constant rebellion against the laws of science, society and religion." That history had no predetermined direction did not mean that it was mere chaos, but instead that it was the story of individual energies in recurring revolt against overbearing forms of social order, outwitting society to discover new modes of free expression. Adams's view of history was not a pessimistic affirmation of disorder, but a protest against collectivism and uniformity.

Another turn-of-the-century historical theorist famous for his pessimism, Oswald Spengler, is the subject of John Farrenkopf's contribution. The hitherto unrecognized change in Spengler's thinking described here constituted on one level a departure from pessimism, since it led Spengler to move away from his earlier relativism and to posit a universal meaning in history. Whereas *The Decline of the West* had described the differing civilizations of the past as separate and autonomous, with each one following out its own individual destiny, Spengler's later (more scattered and speculative) writings spoke of these individual cultures in terms of interaction and posited a general pattern of development which all in some way followed. But in the end this new historical vision was even more pessimistic than Spengler's earlier one. Beginning from a practical weakness in the face of nature, human societies moved toward a Promethean domination of nature which brought, along with new forms of power, many dangerous consequences. Chief among these was a spoliation of nature that led on to a world ecological crisis, as the human domination over nature undermined the basis of civilization itself. Man was therefore an ephemeral species, caught in a tragic spiral that bore him upward, but toward an apocalyptic *finale*. In this new guise, Spengler seems to emerge as a more modern figure than those who know him only from *The Decline of the West* have supposed, even as one who has something important to say today.

Coming to terms with pessimism is also one of the problems that Antonio Gramsci had to face in his attempt to understand the nature of Italian fascism. As Walter Adamson makes clear, it was in his attempt to comprehend fascism that Gramsci came to many of his most characteristic and influential notions, including his idea of hegemony and his recognition that the importance of "civil society" in the West made it impossible to expect a Leninist seizure of power there. From the start Gramsci's views of fascism transcended Marxist categories, seeing in the movement even before its triumph in 1922 the signs of an elemental crisis of the Italian nation and state. But for a while he still looked to the proletariat for redemption from that crisis. It was as his confidence in the workers' ability to play this role waned that Gramsci began to understand fascism in terms of the character of the Risorgimento and the political system it established, moving ever farther from the view of the fascist movement that made it simply an agent of the bourgeoisie. From this point his notion of hegemony developed, as he reflected on the reality of non-state forms of power, followed soon by his ideas of "Caeserism" and "passive revolution." Subtle as Gramsci's analysis became, Adamson thinks it was always limited by his inability to envision a psychological dimension of fascist domination, and he notes that Gramsci's developing ideas about the separate spheres of economics and politics left him with the most critical question of all for Marxists — how far does the autonomy of politics extend?

The psychological focus that Gramsci's Marxist perspective placed at the margins was central for the four figures whose relations are examined in the next two essays: Sigmund Freud, Jean-Martin Charcot, Henri Bergson and Carl Gustav Jung. That Freud was deeply affected by his study with Charcot in Paris, and that the views of the two finally diverged sharply, has long been understood, but Toby Gelfand outlines a revealing and hitherto unknown chapter in their relationship. Freud translated his former teacher's "Tuesday Lectures" (*Leçons de Mardi*) into German, an act of homage that was laced with rebellion, because Freud included footnotes in which he stated his disagreement with Charcot's views. Whereas Charcot upheld theories that drew on biological notions of degeneration and family susceptibility to explain nevous diseases, Freud in 1892 was already looking to explanations based on the experience of particular individuals. His views had not yet developed to the later point of associating neuroses with fantasy life and the operation of repressed wishes, but still focused on actual experience of the sort he would soon codify in his famous — and later abandoned — "seduction hypothesis." Charcot wrote Freud a letter thanking him for the translation but — as Gelfand shows for the first time — firmly reasserting his views. It was a polite and quiet exchange, but one that revealed the already clear divergence between two traditions of psychological understanding.

Just as Charcot's reply to Freud has remained unknown, so for the most part has the debt that Freud's onetime disciple Jung owed to Charcot's countryman Bergson. Pete A. Y. Gunter shows that Bergson's notion that human freedom and creativity resided in a deep self removed from conscious life and from material limitation was of great importance to Jung at the moment when he was evolving a notion of *libido* whose energies were not sexual as Freud posited but broadly spiritual. Even Jung's notions of a collective unconscious and of the archetypes that could be found in it owed something to Bergson's ideas about the way *elan vital* came to be differentiated, and the innate intuitions of living beings. Gunter suggests however that Jung's interest in Bergson may not have gone deep enough, since Bergson possessed ways of thinking about creativity that were more promising than Jung's.

The last three essays in our collection deal with German-speaking philosophers, two still alive at this writing, and all of them important figures in contemporary debates about culture and how it ought to be interpreted. Peter C. John approaches Ludwig Wittgenstein by way of

xviii INTRODUCTION

the importance he attached to his own experience of a recurring sense of wonder — evoked in his otherwise puzzling deathbed declaration that he had had "a wonderful life." He meant, John suggests, that his life had literally been full of wonder, especially wonder in face of the inexplicable circumstance that anything at all exists. His career was a constant fight against the means we human beings employ to undermine our own capacity to wonder, and his ideas about the limits of science and the nature of mathematics were partly expressions of that struggle. It was this sense of wonder that tied Wittgenstein to religious experience despite his lack of explicit belief, and which underlay his orientation toward the ethical value of existence. Many examples show how this sense operated in his daily life, and it nourished a quality that fed both the independence and the eccentricity of his philosophical stance, namely his remarkable and childlike ability to look at everything as if for the first time.

Another philospher who placed the wonder that anything exists at the center of his philosphical project was Martin Heidegger, whose work provided an important starting point for both Hans-Georg Gadamer and Hans Blumenberg. Both have developed strategies of cultural interpretation that owe much to Heidegger, but each differs from him in some important ways. Walter Lammi clarifies this complex of debt and independence in Gadamer's case by showing how Gadamer retains elements both of Husserl's phenomenology, and of enlightenment rationality which Heidegger renounced. Gadamer follows Heidegger in rejecting the Cartesian notion of a pure subject who penetrates the objective world, and also in regarding the work of art as an "event" in which Truth becomes manifest in the world, rather than as the act of an individual maker. In Heidegger's hands however these moves implied a break with the western philosophical tradition, and with the notion of continuous history, in the name of a notion of Being whose ultimate possibility lay in what put it outside historical existence — its potential for death. Gadamer however made remembrance rather than the future primary, looking to history as exemplary of the kind of knowledge that opens human understanding to Being, a knowledge informed by Husserl's notion that the objects which exist for us are always constituted partly by our intentions in regard to them, and whose form of growth involved the combination or "fusion" of our present horizon of understanding with that of other historical moments. Whereas Heidegger posited revelation as the foundation of all experience, Gadamer makes experience open to revelation, but along a path where reason and commonsense first prepare the way.

David Adams locates Hans Blumenberg's theory of metaphor in a somewhat similar position, between Heidegger's anti-Enlightenment orientation toward the understanding of a Being that is prior to all culture, and the affirmation of culture associated with an enlightenment (specifically neo-Kantian) attempt to posit a meaningful shape for history. Human culture always takes its rise from an experience of deficiency of meaning; compared to animals human beings are instinctually impoverished and cannot respond directly to the world. In this situation man "comprehends himself only by way of what he is not," a condition that makes all human knowledge originate in metaphor — that is, by way of comparison with something else. Rhetoric is therefore the primary realm in which the human questioning of the world takes place, and reason's attempt to insert itself there always leads to a failure to answer the fundamental questions it poses, so that rhetoric is always able to reassert its primacy.

Because man's constitution is in this way fundamentally metaphorical, a barrier always separates us from the kind of inner knowledge of *Sein* and *Dasein* Heidegger sought. Difficult as it must be, the task of culture is to teach us the necessity of leaving our desire for certain kinds of knowledge unsatisfied. We carry out this task when we recognize that myth is a rational response to the indeterminacy and ambiguity we find in the world, and that therefore the antithesis between myth and reason needs to be called into question. Even the account just given, which presents itself as an answer to questions arising from reason, is actually a mythical one, showing how culture grows as a continual response to our need for such stories. Each manifestation of culture is useful as a way of distancing us from the hidden starting point of our life, the basic "lack" (*Mangel*) which threatens our existence. Although this means that every cultural epoch has its own legitimacy (a point Blumenberg argued explicitly in his mammoth exposition of *The Legitimacy of the Modern Age*), there is a danger in the modern projects which seek to answer the big questions outside the realm of metaphor. (One thinks of Wittgenstein's objection to those modern projects which seek to weaken our sense of wonder in the face of existence.) Like Heidegger, Blumenberg sought ways to forget certain philosophical questions, not however to replace them with a supposedly direct relationship to Being, but in order to replace them with "many smaller questions and possibilities, old and new."

Gadamer and Blumenberg are fit figures with which to conclude this selection of essays from *The Journal of the History of Ideas* because they provide contemporary justifications for the attitude toward recent intellectual history which has reigned in its pages, an attitude of scholarship rather than partisanship, and one that approaches our intellectual present with a sense that its continuity with the past can still be maintained.

I

THE MEANINGS OF "INDIVIDUALISM"

By Steven Lukes

We shall begin with the fact that the same word, or the same concept in most cases, means very different things when used by differently situated persons.[1]

"The term 'individualism'," wrote Max Weber, "embraces the utmost heterogeneity of meanings," adding that "a thorough, historically-oriented conceptual analysis would at the present time be of the highest value to scholarship."[2] His words remain true. "Individualism" is still used in a great many ways, in many different contexts and with an exceptional lack of precision. Moreover, it has played a major role in the history of ideas, and of ideologies, in modern Europe and America. The present study seeks to contribute to the analysis Weber desired. But clearly, what is still needed is to carry the analytical task further: to isolate the various distinct unit-ideas (and intellectual traditions) which the word has conflated—unit-ideas whose logical and conceptual relations to one another are by no means clear.[3]

Like "socialism" and "communism," "individualism" is a nineteenth-century expression. In seeking to identify its various distinct traditions of use, I shall concentrate on its nineteenth-century history, for this is what chiefly determined its twentieth-century meanings. My main purpose is to indicate both the variety and the directions of the main paths traced during the term's rich semantic history. The interest of such an account is, however, neither merely semantic nor merely historical. The meanings of words generally incapsulate ideas, even theories. Accordingly, where semantic divergences systematically tend to follow social and cultural (in this case national) lines, to explain those divergences becomes a challenging problem in the sociology of knowledge.

(i) *France*. The first uses of the term, in its French form "*individualisme*," grew out of the general European reaction to the French Revolution and to its alleged source, the thought of the Enlightenment.[4] Conservative thought in the early nineteenth century was virtually unanimous in condemning the appeal to the reason,

---

[1]K. Mannheim, *Ideology and Utopia* (London, 1960), 245. In what follows I am particularly indebted to the studies by Koebner, Swart, and Arieli, cited *infra*.

[2]M. Weber, *The Protestant Ethic and the Spirit of Capitalism*, (1904-5), tr. T. Parsons (London, 1930), 222 (amended translation: S. L.).

[3]Cf. my article on "Individualism" in *Dictionary of the History of Ideas* (New York, 1972)

[4]H. Peyre, "The Influence of Eighteenth Century Ideas on the French Revolution," *JHI*, X (1949), 63-87; W. F. Church (ed.), *The Influence of the Enlightenment on the French Revolution* (Boston, 1964).

1

interests, and rights of the individual; as Burke had said: "Individuals pass like shadows; but the commonwealth is fixed and stable."[5] The Revolution was proof that ideas exalting the individual imperilled the stability of the commonwealth, dissolving it into "an unsocial, uncivil, unconnected chaos of elementary principles."[6] Conservative thinkers, above all in France and Germany, shared Burke's scorn for the individual's "private stock of reason" and his fear lest "the commonwealth itself would, in a few generations, crumble away, be disconnected into the dust and powder of individuality, and at length dispersed to all the winds of heaven," as well as his certainty that "Society requires" that "the inclinations of men should frequently be thwarted, their will controlled, and their passions brought into subjection."[7]

These sentiments were found at their most extreme among the theocratic Catholic reactionaries in France. According to Joseph de Maistre, the social order had been "shattered to its foundations because there was too much liberty in Europe and not enough Religion"; everywhere authority was weakening and there was a frightening growth of "individual opinion [*l'esprit particulier*]."[8] The individual's reason was "of its nature the mortal enemy of all association": its exercise spelt spiritual and civil anarchy. Infallibility was an essential condition of the maintenance of society, and indeed government was "a true religion," with "its dogmas, its mysteries, its priests; to submit it to individual discussion is to destroy it."[9] In the earliest known use of the word, de Maistre spoke in 1820 of "this deep and frightening division of minds, this infinite fragmentation of all doctrines, political protestantism carried to the most absolute individualism."[10]

The theocrats agreed in giving to "society" the same exclusive emphasis that they accused the eighteenth-century *philosophes* of giving to "the individual." Society for de Maistre was God-given and natural, and he wished the individual's mind to lose itself in that of the nation "as a river which flows into the ocean still exists in the mass of the water, but without name and distinct reality"[11]; while for

[5]"Speech on the Economic Reform" (1780), *Works* (London, 1906), II, 357.
[6]*Reflections on the Revolution in France* (1790) (London, 1910), 94.
[7]*Ibid.*, 84, 93, 57. Cf. D. Bagge, *Les Idées Politiques en France sous la Restauration* (Paris, 1952); K. Mannheim, "Conservative Thought," *Essays in Sociology and Social Psychology* (London, 1953).
[8]J. de Maistre, *Du Pape* (1821), bk. III, ch. II, *Oeuvres Complètes* (Lyon, 1884-7), II, 342, 346.
[9]J. de Maistre, *Etude sur la Souveraineté* (1884), bk. I, ch. X, *Oeuvres Complètes*, I, 375-6. [10]"Extrait d'une Conversation," *Oeuvres Complètes*, XIV, 286.
[11]*Etude sur la Souvenaineté* (1884) bk. I. ch. X, *Oeuvres Complètes*, I, 326.

de Bonald "man only exists for society and society only educates him for itself."[12] The ideas of the *philosophes* were, they thought, not merely false; they were wicked and dangerous. According to Lamennais, they proclaimed the individual as sovereign over himself in the most absolute sense:

His reason—that is his law, his truth, his justice. To seek to impose on him an obligation he has not previously imposed on himself by his own thought and will is to violate the most sacred of his rights . . . . Hence, no legislation, no power is possible, and the same doctrine which produces anarchy in men's minds further produces an irremediable political anarchy, and overturns the very bases of human society.

Were such principles to prevail, "what could one foresee but troubles, disorders, calamities without end, and universal dissolution?" Man, Lamennais argued, "lives only in society" and "institutions, laws, governments draw all their strength from a certain concourse of thoughts and wills." "What," he asked, "is power without obedience? What is law without duty?" and he answered:

Individualism which destroys the very idea of obedience and of duty, thereby destroying both power and law; and what then remains but a terrifying confusion of interests, passions, and diverse opinions?[13]

It was the disciple of Claude Henri de Saint-Simon,[14] who were the first to use "*individualisme*" systematically, in the mid-1820's.[15] Saint-Simonism shared the ideas of the counter-revolutionary reactionaries—their critique of the Enlightenment's glorification of the individual, their horror of social atomization and anarchy, as well as their desire for an organic, stable, hierarchically organized, harmonious social order. But it applied these ideas in a historically progressive direction: that social order was not to be the ecclesiastical and feudal order of the past, but the industrial order of the future. Indeed, the proselytizing Saint-Simonians systematized their master's ideas into an activist and extremely influential secular religion, an ideological force serving as a kind of Protestant ethic for the expanding capitalism of the Catholic countries in nineteenth-century Europe.

History for the Saint-Simonians was a cycle of "critical" and "organic" periods. The former were "filled with disorder; they destroy former social relations, and everywhere tend towards egoism"; the latter were unified, organized, and stable (the previous instances in

---

[12]L. de Bonald, *Théorie du Pouvoir* (1796), Preface, *Oeuvres* (Paris, 1854), I, 103.

[13]F. de Lamennais, *Des Progrès de la Révolution et de la Guerre contre l'Eglise* (1829), ch. I, *Oeuvres Complètes* (Paris, 1836-7), IX, 17-18.

[14]Cf. my chapter on Saint-Simon in T. Raison (ed.), *Founding Fathers of Social Science* (London, 1969).   [15]Cf. *Le Producteur*, Vols. I-IV, *passim*.

Europe being the ancient polytheistic preclassical society and the Christian Middle Ages). The modern critical period, originating with the Reformation was, the Saint-Simonians believed, the penultimate stage of human progress, heralding a future organic era of "universal association" in which "the organization of the future will be final because only then will society be formed directly for progress." They used *"individualisme"* to refer to the pernicious and "negative" ideas underlying the evils of the modern critical epoch, whose "disorder, atheism, individualism, and egoism" they contrasted with the prospect of "order, religion, association, and devotion." The "philosophers of the eighteenth century"—men such as Helvetius, with his doctrine of "enlightened self-interest," Locke, Reid, Condillac, Kant, and the "atheist d'Holbach, the deist Voltaire, and Rousseau"—all these "defenders of individualism" refused to "go back to a source higher than individual conscience." They "considered the individual as the center" and "preached egoism," providing an ideological justification for the prevailing anarchy, especially in the economic and political spheres. The "doctrine of individualism" with its two "sad deities . . . two creatures of reason—conscience and public opinion" led to "one political result: opposition to any attempt at organization from a center of direction for the moral interests of mankind, to hatred of power."[16]

Partly perhaps because of the extraordinarily pervasive influence of Saint-Simonian ideas, *"individualisme"* came to be very widely used in the nineteenth century. In France, it usually carried, and indeed still carries, a pejorative connotation, a strong suggestion that to concentrate on the individual is to harm the superior interests of society. The latest edition of the Dictionary of the *Académie Française*[17] defines it simply as "subordination of the general interest to the individual's interest," and one recent writer, noting its naturally pejorative sense, has remarked on its "tinge of *'ubris,'* of *'démesuré'* " which "does not exist in English,"[18] while another observes that in France "until the present day the term individualism has retained much of its former, unfavorable connotations."[19] It is true that there was a group of French revolutionary republican *Carbonari* in the 1820's who proudly called themselves the "Société d'Individualistes," and that various individual thinkers adopted the label, among them Proudhon—though

---

[16]*The Doctrine of Saint-Simon: An Exposition, First Year 1828-9* (1830) tr. G. Iggers (Boston, 1958), 28, 70, 247, 178-80, 182.   [17]Paris, 1932-5.

[18]L. Moulin, "On the Evolution of the Meaning of the Word 'Individualism'," *International Social Science Bulletin*, VII (1955), 185.

[19]K. W. Swart, " 'Individualism' in the Mid-Nineteenth Century (1826-60)," *JHI*, XXIII (1962), 84.

THE MEANINGS OF "INDIVIDUALISM"

even Proudhon saw society as "a *sui generis* being" and argued that "outside the group there are only abstractions and phantoms."[20] From the mid-nineteenth century, liberal Protestants and eventually a few *laissez-faire* liberals started to call themselves individualists and one wrote a comprehensive history of "economic and social individualism," incorporating a variety of French thinkers[21]—yet the tone was always one of defensive paradox. Few have welcomed the epithet, and many, from Balzac onwards,[22] stressed the opposition between *"individualisme,"* implying anarchy and social atomization, and *"individualité,"* implying personal independence and self-realization. For the Swiss theologian Alexandre Vinet, these were "two sworn enemies; the first an obstacle and negation of any society; the latter a principle to which society owes all its savor, life and reality." The "progress of individualism" meant "the relaxation of social unity because of the increasingly pronounced predominance of egoism," while the "gradual extinction of individuality" meant "the increasingly strong inclination for minds ... to surrender themselves to what is known as public opinion or the spirit of the age."[23] In general, *"individualisme"* in French thought points to the sources of social dissolution, though there have been wide divergences concerning the nature of those sources and of the social order they are held to threaten, as well as in the historical frameworks within which they are conceptualized.

For some, individualism resides in dangerous ideas, for others it is social or economic anarchy, a lack of the requisite institutions and norms, for yet others it is the prevalence of self-interested attitudes among individuals. For men of the right, from de Maistre to Charles Maurras, it is all that undermines a traditional, hierarchical social order. Thus Louis Veuillot, the militant Catholic propagandist, wrote in 1843 that "France has need of religion" which would bring "harmony, union, patriotism, confidence, morality ...":

The evil which plagues France is not unknown; everyone agrees in giving it the same name: *individualism.*

It is not difficult to see that a country where individualism reigns is no longer in the normal conditions of society, since society is the union of minds and interests, and individualism is division carried to the infinite degree.

---

[20]P. J. Proudhon, *Lettres sur la Philosophie du Progrès* (1853), Letter I, pts V and IV, *Oeuvres Complètes,* new ed. (Paris, 1868–76), XX, 39–40, 36.

[21]A. Schatz, *L'Individualisme Economique et Sociale* (Paris, 1907). *Cf.* H.-L. Follin, "Quelle est la Véritable Définition de L'Individualisme," *Journal des Economistes* (April 15, 1899).

[22]Swart, *art. cit.,* 84.

[23]Quoted *ibid.,* 84–5. *Cf.* Arieli, *Individualism and Nationalism in American Ideology* (Cambridge, Mass., 1964), ch. X.

6 STEVEN LUKES

All for each, each for all, that is society; each for himself, and thus each against all, that is individualism.[24]

Similarly, during the Dreyfus Affair, Ferdinand Brunetière, the strongly *anti-Dreyfusard* literary historian, defended the army and the social order, which he saw as threatened by "individualism" and "anarchy," and poured scorn on those intellectuals who had presumed to doubt the justice of Dreyfus's trial. Individualism, he wrote, was

the great sickness of the present time.... Each of us has confidence only in himself, sets himself up as the sovereign judge of everything ... when intellectualism and individualism reach this degree of self-infatuation, one must expect them to be or become nothing other than *anarchy*....[25]

Among socialists, individualism has typically been contrasted with an ideal, cooperative social order, variously described as "association," "harmony," "socialism," and "communism"; the term here refers to the economic doctrine of *laissez-faire* and to the anarchy, social atomization, and exploitation produced by industrial capitalism. Pierre Leroux, aiming at a new humanitarian and libertarian socialism, used it to mean the principle, proclaimed by political economy, of "everyone for himself, and ... all for riches, nothing for the poor," which atomized society and made men into "rapacious wolves"[26]; "society," he maintained, "is entering a new era in which the general tendency of the laws will no longer have individualism as its end, but association."[27] For Constantin Pecqueur, "the remedy lies in association precisely because the abuse springs from individualism"[28] and the utopian Etienne Cabet wrote that

Two great systems have divided and polarized Humanity ever since the beginning of the world: that of Individualism (or egoism, or personal interest), and that of Communism (or association, or the general interest, or the public interest).[29]

Likewise, the conspiratorial revolutionary Auguste Blanqui asserted that "Communism is the protector of the individual, individualism his extermination."[30]

Other socialists used the term in more complex ways. Louis Blanc saw individualism as a major cultural principle, encompassing Protes-

[24]L. Veuillot, "Lettre à M. Villemain" (August, 1843), *Mélanges Religieux, Historiques, Politiques et Littéraires* (1842–56) (Paris, 1856–60), lère série, I, 132–3.

[25]F. Brunetière, "Après le Procès," *Revue des Deux Mondes*, LXVII (15 March 1898), 445. *Cf.* my article: "Durkheim's 'Individualism and the Intellectuals'," *Political Studies*, XVII (1969), 14–19.   [26](1832 and 1833), quoted in Arieli, *op. cit.*, 233.

[27](1841), quoted in J. Dubois, *Le Vocabulaire Politique et Sociale en France de 1869 à 1872* (Paris, 1962), 220.

[28](1840) quoted *ibid.*, 322.   [29](1845) quoted *ibid.*   [30](1869) quoted *ibid.*, 267.

THE MEANINGS OF "INDIVIDUALISM"

tantism, the Bourgeoisie, and the Enlightenment, bringing a historically necessary, though false and incomplete, freedom. Its progressive
aspect was a new self-assertion, a new independence of traditional
structures and rejection of Authority in the religious, economic, and
intellectual spheres; but it needed to be transcended and completed,
pointing towards a future age of socialist Fraternity. In Blanc's own
words:

Three great principles divide the world and history: Authority, Individualism, and Fraternity.

The principle of individualism is that which, taking man out of society,
makes him sole judge of what surrounds him and of himself, gives him a
heightened sense of his rights without showing him his duties, abandons
him to his own powers, and, for the whole of government, proclaims *laisser-
faire*.

Individualism, inaugurated by Luther, has developed with an irresistible force, and, dissociated from the religious factor ... it governs
the present; it is the spiritual principle of things.

... individualism is important in having achieved a vast progress. To
provide breathing-space and scope to human thought repressed for so long,
to intoxicate it with pride and audacity; to submit to the judgment of every
mind the totality of traditions, centuries, their achievements, their beliefs; to place man in an isolation full of anxieties, full of perils, but sometimes also full of majesty, and to enable him to resolve personally, in the
midst of an immense struggle, in the uproar of a universal debate, the problem of his happiness and his destiny ...—this is by no means an achievement without grandeur, and it is the achievement of individualism. One
must therefore speak of it with respect and as a necessary transition.[31]

Again, the disciples of Charles Fourier denied any basic opposition between individualism and socialism,[32] while at the end of the century,
Jean Jaurès argued that "socialism is the logical completion of individualism,"[33] a formula echoed by Emile Durkheim, who saw a kind
of centralized guild socialism as a means of "completing, extending,
and organizing individualism."[34] For all these socialist thinkers,
individualism signified the autonomy, freedom, and sacredness of the
individual—values which had hitherto taken a negative, oppressive,
and anarchic form but could henceforth only be preserved within a
cooperative and rationally-organized social order.

[31]From his *Histoire de la Révolution Française* (1846), quoted in R. Koebner, "Zur
Begriffbildung der Kulturgeschichte: II: Zur Geschichte des Begriffs 'Individualismus'
(Jacob Burckhardt, Wilhelm von Humboldt und die französische Soziologie)," *Histor-
ische Zeitschrift*, CXLIX (1934), 269. [32]Swart, *art. cit.*, 85.

[33]J. Jaurès, "Socialisme et Liberté," *Revue de Paris*, XXIII (Dec. 1898), 499.

[34]E. Durkheim, "Individualism and the Intellectuals" (1898), tr. S. and J. Lukes,
Political Studies, XVII (1969), 29. *Cf.* Lukes, "Durkheim's 'Individualism and the
Intellectuals'," *loc. cit.*

STEVEN LUKES

French liberals also spoke of individualism, but they characteristically saw it as a threat to a pluralist social order, with minimum state intervention and maximum political liberty. Benjamin Constant, perhaps the most eloquent exponent of classical liberalism, was clearly groping for the word when he observed that "when all are isolated by egoism, there is nothing but dust, and at the advent of a storm, nothing but mire."[35] It was, however, that aristocratic observer of early nineteenth-century America, Alexis de Tocqueville, who developed its most distinctive and influential liberal meaning in France. For Tocqueville, individualism was the natural product of democracy ("Individualism is of democratic origin and threatens to develop insofar as conditions are equalized"), involving the apathetic withdrawal of individuals from public life into a private sphere and their isolation from one another, with a consequent weakening of social bonds. Such a development, Tocqueville thought, offered dangerous scope for the unchecked growth of the political power of the state.

More specifically, "individualism"—a "recent expression to which a new idea has given birth"—was "a deliberate and peaceful sentiment which disposes each citizen to isolate himself from the mass of his fellows and to draw apart with his family and friends," abandoning "the wider society to itself." At first, it "saps only the virtues of public life; but, in the long run, it attacks and destroys all others and is eventually absorbed into pure egoism." In contrast to aristocratic society, in which men were "linked closely to something beyond them and are often disposed to forget themselves" and which "formed of all the citizens a long chain reaching from the peasant to the king," democracy "breaks the chain and sets each link apart," and "the bond of human affections extends and relaxes." With increasing social mobility, the continuity of the generations is destroyed; as classes become fused, "their members become indifferent and as if strangers to one another"; and as individuals become increasingly self-sufficient, "they become accustomed to considering themselves always in isolation, they freely imagine that their destiny is entirely in their own hands." Democracy, Tocqueville concluded, "not only makes each man forget his forefathers, but it conceals from him his descendants and separates him from his contemporaries; it ceaselessly throws him back on himself alone and threatens finally to confine him entirely in the solitude of his own heart."[36]

Individualism for Tocqueville thus sprang from the lack of intermediary groups to provide a framework for the individual and protec-

[35]Quoted in H. Marion, "Individualisme," *La Grande Encyclopédie* (Paris, n.d.), Vol. XX.

[36]A. de Tocqueville, *De la Démocratie en Amérique* (1835) bk. II, pt. II, ch. II, *Oeuvres Complètes*, ed. J. P. Mayer (Paris, 1951-), I, II, 104–6.

THE MEANINGS OF "INDIVIDUALISM"

tion against the State. (As for the Americans, they only avoided its destructive consequences because of their free institutions and active citizenship: they conquered individualism with liberty.) It was, moreover, a peculiarly modern evil: "Our fathers," Tocqueville wrote, "did not have the word 'individualism,' which we have coined for our own use, because in their time there was indeed no individual who did not belong to a group and who could be considered as absolutely alone."[37]

No less diverse than these conceptions of the sources and the dangers of individualism have been the historical frameworks within which French thinkers have placed it. It is variously traced to the Reformation, the Renaissance, the Enlightenment, the Revolution, to the decline of the aristocracy or the Church or traditional religion, to the Industrial Revolution, to the growth of capitalism or democracy, but, as we have seen, there is wide agreement in seeing it as an evil and a threat to social cohesion. Perhaps the role of *"individualisme"* in French thought is partly due to the very success of "individualist" legislation at the time of the Revolution,[38] the elimination of intermediary groups and bodies in the society, and the ensuing political and administrative centralization of the country. The basis for this had been laid, as Tocqueville observed, in the municipal and fiscal policies of the French Kings in the seventeenth and eighteenth centuries, which had systematically prevented the growth of spontaneous, organized activities and informal groupings.[39] One can even reasonably postulate that the lack of such activities and groupings is a basic and distinctive French cultural trait.[40]

However that may be, the mainstream of French thought, above all in the nineteenth century, has expressed by *"individualisme"* what Durkheim identified by the twin concepts of "anomie" and "egoism"[41] —the social, moral, and political isolation of individuals, their dissociation from social purposes and social regulation, the breakdown of social solidarity. General de Gaulle was using it in its paradigm French sense when, in his New Year's broadcast to the nation on 31 December 1968, recalling the *Evènements* of May, he observed:

> At the same time, it is necessary that we surmount the moral malaise which—above all among us by reason of our individualism—is inherent in modern mechanical and materialist civilization. Otherwise, the fanatics of destruction, the doctrinaires of negation, the specialists in demagogy, will once more have a good opportunity to exploit bitterness in order to provoke agita-

---

[37]*L'Ancien Régime et la Révolution* (1856), bk. II, ch. IX, *ibid.*, II, 1, p. 158.

[38]R. R. Palmer, "Man and Citizen: Applications of Individualism in the French Revolution," *Essays in Political Theory* (Ithaca, N.Y., 1948).

[39]*L'Ancien Régime et la Révolution*, bk. II, chs. 3, 6, 9, 12.

[40]M. Crozier, *The Bureaucratic Phenomenon* (London, 1964), esp. ch. 8.

[41]*Suicide* (1897), trans. J. A. Spaulding and G. Simpson (Glencoe, Ill., 1951).

10 STEVEN LUKES

tion, while their sterility, which they have the derisory insolence to call revolution, can lead to nothing else than the dissolution of everything into nothingness, or else to the loss of everything under the grinding oppression of totalitarianism.[42]

Despite wide divergences in views about the causes of social dissolution and the nature of an acceptable or desirable social order, the underlying perspective conveyed by the term is unmistakable.

(ii) *Germany*. This characteristically French meaning was certainly subject to cultural diffusion beyond the borders of France. It was, for instance, adopted by Friedrich List, precursor of the German Historical School of economics and advocate of economic nationalism, who used it in the sense developed by the Saint-Simonians and the socialists. List's major work, *The National System of Political Economy*,[43] written in Paris, stressed the organic nature of society and the economy, and the historical and national framework of economic activity; and it attacked the classical economists for abstracting economic life from its social context. Thus List accused classical economics, which supported free trade and *laissez-faire*, of *"Kosmopolitismus," "Materialismus," "Partikularismus,"* and, above all, of *"Individualismus"*—sacrificing the welfare of the national community to the individual acquisition of wealth.

There is, however, quite distinct from this French use of the term, another use whose characteristic reference is German. This is the Romantic idea of "individuality" (*Individualität*), the notion of individual uniqueness, originality, self-realization—what the Romantics called *"Eigentümlichkeit"*—in contrast to the rational, universal, and uniform standards of the Enlightenment, which they saw as "quantitative," "abstract," and therefore sterile. The Romantics themselves did not use the term *"Individualismus,"* but it came to be used in this sense from the 1840's when a German liberal, Karl Brüggemann, contrasted with its negative French meaning, as found in List, that of a desirable and characteristically German "infinite" and "wholesouled" individualism, signifying "the infinite self-confidence of the individual aiming to be personally free in morals and in truth."[44]

Thereafter, the term soon became, in this, chiefly German, use, virtually synonymous with the idea of individuality, which had originated in the writings of Wilhelm von Humboldt, Novalis, Friedrich Schlegel, and Friedrich Schleiermacher. Thus Georg Simmel wrote of the "new individualism" which he opposed to "eighteenth-century individualism" with its "notion of atomized and basically undif-

---

[42]*Le Monde*, 2 Jan. 1969.   [43](1841) tr. (London, 1928).
[44]K. H. Brüggemann, *Dr. Lists nationales System der politischen Ökonomie* (Berlin, 1842) quoted in Koebner, *art. cit.*, 282.

ferentiated individuals"; the new, German, individualism was "the individualism of difference, with the deepening of individuality to the point of the individual's incomparability, to which he is 'called' both in his nature and in his achievement." The individual became "this specific, irreplaceable, given individual" and was "*called* or destined to realize his own incomparable image." The "new individualism," Simmel wrote, "might be called qualitative, in contrast with the quantitative individualism of the eighteenth century. Or it might be labeled the individualism of uniqueness *(Einzigkeit)* as against that of singleness *(Einzelheit)*. At any rate, Romanticism was perhaps the broadest channel through which it reached the consciousness of the nineteenth century. Goethe had created its artistic, and Schleiermacher its metaphysical basis: Romanticism supplied its sentimental experiential foundation."[45]

The German idea of individuality has had a remarkable history. Having begun as a cult of individual genius and originality, especially as applied to the artist, stressing the conflict between individual and society and the supreme value of subjectivity, solitude, and introspection, it developed along various lines. In one direction, it led to an uninhibited quest for eccentricity and to the purest egoism and social nihilism. This development found perhaps its most extreme expression in the thought of Max Stirner, whose "individualism" amounted to an amoral and anti-intellectualistic vision of freely cooperating and self-assertive egoists. For Stirner,

I, the egoist, have not at heart the welfare of this "human society." I sacrifice nothing to it. I only utilize it: but to be able to utilize it completely I must transform it rather into my property and my creature—i.e., I must annihilate it and form in its place the Union of Egoists.[46]

The main development, however, of the idea of individuality was in the direction of a characteristically German *Weltanschauung,* or cosmology, a total view of the (natural and social) world, fundamentally in conflict with the essentially humanist and rationalist thought typical of the rest of Western civilization. In a justly famous essay, Ernst Troeltsch contrasted the two systems of thought, the "west-European" and the German: on the one side, "an eternal, rational, and

[45]G. Simmel, "Individual and Society in Eighteenth- and Nineteenth-Century Views of Life: an Example of Philosophical Sociology" (1917) tr. in *The Sociology of Georg Simmel,* tr. and ed. K. H. Wolff (Glencoe, Ill., 1950), 78–83. *Cf.* L. Furst, *Romanticism in Perspective* (London, 1969), pt. I: "Individualism."

[46]M. Stirner, *The Ego and its Own: The Case of the Individual against Authority* (1844) tr. S. T. Byington (London and New York, 1907), quoted in G. Woodcock, *Anarchism* (London, 1963), 93. Cf. V. Basch, *L'Individualisme Anarchiste: Max Stirner* (Paris, 1904).

12   STEVEN LUKES

divinely ordained system of Order, embracing both morality and law";
on the other, "individual, living, and perpetually new incarnations of
an historically creative Mind." Thus,

> Those who believe in an eternal and divine Law of Nature, the Equality of
> man, and a sense of Unity pervading mankind, and who find the essence of
> Humanity in these things, cannot but regard the German doctrine as a curious
> mixture of mysticism and brutality. Those who take an opposite view—who
> see in history an ever-moving stream, which throws up unique individual-
> ities as it moves, and is always shaping individual structures on the basis of a
> law which is always new—are bound to consider the west-European world of
> ideas as a world of cold rationalism and equalitarian atomism, a world of
> superficiality and Pharisaism.[47]

Friedrich Meinecke summed up the revolution in thought which
he saw Romanticism as bringing to Western civilization in the following way:

> Out of this deepening individualism of uniqueness, there henceforth arose
> everywhere in Germany, in various different forms, a new and more living
> image of the State, and also a new picture of the world. The whole world now
> appeared to be filled with individuality, each individuality, whether personal
> or supra-personal, governed by its own characteristic principle of life, and
> both Nature and History constituting what Friedrich Schlegel called an "abyss
> of individuality".... Individuality everywhere, the identity of mind and na-
> ture, and through this identity an invisible but strong bond unifying the other-
> wise boundless diversity and abundance of individual phenomena—these were
> the new and powerful ideas which now burst forth in Germany in so many
> different ways.[48]

In particular, the personal "individualism" of the early Romantics
very soon became transformed into an organic and nationalistic theory
of community, each unique and self-sufficient, according to which, as
one recent scholar has said, the individual was "fated to merge with
and become rooted in nature and the Volk" and would thus be "able to
find his self-expression and his individuality."[49] Moreover, individuality was ascribed no longer merely to persons, but to supra-personal
forces, especially the nation or the state. Meinecke paints a vivid
picture of this transformation:

> This new sense for what was individual resembled a fire which was capable of
> consuming, not all at once, but gradually, every sphere of life. At first, it seized

---

[47]E. Troeltsch, "The Ideas of Natural Law and Humanity in World Politics"
(1922), O. Gierke, *Natural Law and the Theory of Society, 1500-1800*, tr. E. Barker
(Boston, 1957), 204.

[48]F. Meinecke, *Die Idee der Staatsräson* (1924), *Werke* (Munich, 1957–62), I, 425.

[49]G. L. Mosse, *The Crisis of German Ideology* (London, 1966), 15. *Cf.* Mannheim's
attempt to explain the conservative direction taken by Romanticism in Mannheim,
"Conservative Thought," *loc. cit.*

only the flimsiest and most inflammable materials—the subjective life of the individual, the world of art and poetry; but then it went on to consume heavier substances, above all the state.[50]

The same progression from the individuality of the person to that of the nation or state occurred in countless German thinkers of the early nineteenth century—notably, in Fichte, Schelling, Schleiermacher, and even, in a sense, Hegel. The state and society were no longer regarded as rational constructions, the result of contractual arrangements between individuals in the manner of the Enlightenment; they were "super-personal creative forces, which build from time to time out of the material of particular individuals, a spiritual Whole, and on the basis of that Whole proceed from time to time to create the particular political and social institutions which embody and incarnate its significance."[51] As Simmel wrote, the "total organism" of society "shifts, so to speak into a location high above [individuals]" and, accordingly, "this individualism, which restricts freedom to a purely inward sense of the term, easily acquires an antiliberal tendency"; it is "the complete antithesis of eighteenth-century individualism which . . . could not even conceive the idea of a collective as an organism that unifies heterogeneous elements."[52]

While the characteristically French sense of "individualism" is negative, signifying individual isolation and social dissolution, the characteristically German sense is thus positive, signifying individual self-fulfillment and (except among the earliest Romantics) the organic unity of individual and society. The distinction was drawn with particular force by Thomas Mann, in a passage written at the close of the First World War, which argues that German life reconciles the individual and society, freedom and obligation:

It remains the uniqueness of German individualism that it is entirely compatible with ethical socialism, which is called "state socialism" but which is quite distinct from the philosophy of the rights of man and Marxism. For it is only the individualism of the Enlightenment, the liberal individualism of the West, which is incompatible with the social principle.

The German variety, Mann thought, "includes the freedom of the individual." To "reject the individualistic Enlightenment does not amount to a demand for the submergence of the individual in society and the state": the German theory of organic community protected freedom, whereas ideas deriving from the Enlightenment (among which Mann included Marxism) led to Jacobinism, state absolutism, political tyranny. "Organism" was a word that is "true to life," for "an organism is more than the sum of its parts, and that more is its spirit,

---

[50]*Op. cit.*426.   [51]Troeltsch, *loc. cit.*, 210–11.   [52]*Loc. cit.*, 82.

14 STEVEN LUKES

its life."[53] Here one can see that individualism does not, as with the French, endanger social solidarity; it is its supreme realization.

(iii) *Burckhardt.* A striking and influential synthesis of French and German meanings of "individualism" is to be found (appropriately enough) in the work of the Swiss historian, Jacob Burckhardt. A central theme of Burckhardt's *The Civilization of the Renaissance in Italy*[54] was the growth of "individualism." Summing up the "principal features in the Italian character of that time," Burckhardt maintained that its "fundamental vice ... was at the same time a condition of its greatness, namely, excessive individualism."[55] The second part of the work is entitled "The Development of the Individual" and, in general, Burckhardt treated the Italians of the Renaissance as a people "who have emerged from the half-conscious life of the race and become themselves individuals."[56]

Schematically, one can say that Burckhardt's use of "individualism" combines the notion of the aggressive self-assertion of individuals freed from an externally given framework of authority (as found in Louis Blanc) and that of the individual's withdrawal from society into a private existence (as in Tocqueville) with the early Romantic idea, most clearly expressed by Humboldt, of the full and harmonious development of the individual personality, seen as representing humanity and pointing towards its highest cultural development. The Italian of the Renaissance was for Burckhardt "the firstborn among the sons of modern Europe"[57] in virtue of the autonomy of his morality, his cultivation of privacy, and the individuality of his character.

"The individual," Burckhardt wrote,

first inwardly casts off the authority of a State which, as a fact, is in most cases tyrannical and illegitimate, and what he thinks and does is now, rightly or wrongly, called treason. The sight of victorious egotism in others drives him to defend his own right by his own arm.... In face of all objective facts, of laws and restraints of whatever kind, he retains the feeling of his own sovereignty, and in each single instance forms his decision independently, according as honor or interest, passion or calculation, revenge or renunciation, gain the upper hand in his own mind.[58]

As to privacy, Burckhardt wrote of "the different tendencies and manifestations of private life ... thriving in the fullest vigour and variety" and cited "Agnolo Pandolfini (d. 1446), whose work on domestic economy is the first complete programme of a developed private life." "The private man," he argued, "indifferent to politics, and busied partly with serious pursuits, partly with the interests of a *dilettante,*

[53]T. Mann, *Betrachtungen eines Unpolitischen* (Berlin, 1918), 267.
[54](1860) tr. S.G.C. Middlemore (London, 1955). *Cf.* Koebner, *art. cit.*
[55]*Ibid.*, 279.   [56]*Ibid.*, 200.   [57]*Ibid.*, 80.   [58]*Ibid.*, 279.

seems to have been first fully formed in these despotisms of the fourteenth century."[59] Finally, he identified the "impulse to the highest individual development" and saw Italy at the close of the thirteenth century as beginning to "swarm with individuality; the ban upon human personality was dissolved; and a thousand figures meet us each in his own special shape and dress." Dante, "through the wealth of individuality which he set forth," was "the most national herald of his time"; much of Burckhardt's book treats of "this unfolding of the treasures of human nature in literature and art." An acute and practised eye could trace

the increase in the number of complete men during the fifteenth century. Whether they had before them as a conscious object the harmonious development of their spiritual and material existence, is hard to say, but several of them attained it, so far as is consistent with the imperfection of all that is earthly.[60]

It is worth adding that for Burckhardt this growth of individualism was, as for so many philosophers of history, no accident but a "historical necessity." Transmitted by Italian culture, and infusing the other nations of Europe, it

has constituted since then the higher atmosphere which they breathe. In itself it is neither good nor bad, but necessary; within it has grown up a modern standard of good and evil—a sense of moral responsibility—which is essentially different from that which was familiar to the Middle Ages.[61]

(iv) *America.* It was in the United States that "individualism" primarily came to celebrate capitalism and liberal democracy. It became a symbolic catchword of immense ideological significance, expressing all that has at various times been implied in the philosophy of natural rights, the belief in free enterprise, and the American Dream. It expressed, in fact, the operative ideals of nineteenth- and early twentieth-century America (and indeed continues to play a major ideological role), advancing a set of universal claims seen as incompatible with the parallel claims of the socialism and communism of the Old World. It referred, not to the sources of social dissolution or the painful transition to a future harmonious social order, nor to the cultivation of uniqueness or the organic community, but rather to the actual or imminent realization of the final stage of human progress in a spontaneously cohesive society of equal individual rights, limited government, *laissez-faire,* natural justice and equal opportunity, and individual freedom, moral development, and dignity. Naturally it carried widely varying connotations in differing contexts and at different times.

[59]*Ibid.*, 82–3.   [60]*Ibid.*, 81–4.   [61]*Ibid.*, 279.

16   STEVEN LUKES

It was imported, in the negative French sense, *via* the writings of various Europeans, among them the socialists, as well as Tocqueville, List, and the Saint-Simonian Michel Chevalier, whose *Lettres sur l'Amérique du Nord* (1836) contrasted the anarchic individualism of the Yankees with the more socially inclined and organizable French. Already in 1839, an article in the *United States Magazine and Democratic Review* identified it positively with national values and ideals seen in evolutionary and universal terms. The course of civilization

is the progress of man from a state of savage individualism to that of an individualism more elevated, moral and refined.... The last order of civilization, which is democratic, received its first permanent existence in this country.... The peculiar duty of this country has been to exemplify and embody a civilization in which the rights, freedom, and mental and moral growth of individual men should be made the highest end of all social restrictions and laws.[62]

This abrupt change in the evaluative significance of the term is strikingly illustrated in one of the earliest American discussions of Tocqueville's *Democracy in America* by a Transcendentalist writer in the *Boston Quarterly Review.* The writer, inaccurately but significantly, expounded Tocqueville's concept of individualism as expressing "that strong confidence in self, or reliance upon one's own exertion and resources" and as "the strife of all our citizens for wealth and distinction of *their own*, and their contempt of reflected honors." "Individualism," he continued, "has its immutable laws ... which ... when allowed to operate without let or hindrance ... must in the end assimilate the species, and evolve all the glorious phenomena of original and eternal *order*;—that order which exists in man himself, and alone vivifies and sustains him."[63]

"Individualism" had, by the end of the Civil War, acquired an important place in the vocabulary of American ideology. Indeed, even those who criticized American society, from New England Transcendentalists to the Single Taxers and the Populists, often did so in the name of individualism. The term acquired differing layers of meaning under the successive influences of New England Puritanism, the Jeffersonian tradition, and natural rights philosophy; Unitarianism, Transcendentalism, and evangelicalism; the need of the North to develop an ideological defence against the challenge of the South; the immensely popular evolutionary and *laissez-faire* ideas of Herbert Spencer and the growth of Social Darwinism; and the permanent and

[62]"The Course of Civilization," *United States Magazine and Democratic Review,* 6 (1839), 208ff, 211, quoted in Arieli, *op. cit.*, 191-2.
[63]"Catholicism," *Boston Quarterly Review* (1841), 320ff, quoted in Arieli, *op. cit.*, 199.

THE MEANINGS OF "INDIVIDUALISM" 17

continuing impetus of alternative, European-born ideologies. The course of this development has been admirably traced in Yehoshua Arieli's book, *Individualism and Nationalism in American Ideology*,[64] which rightly treats the American version of "individualism" as a symbol of national identification. As Arieli concludes,

Individualism supplied the nation with a rationalization of its characteristic attitudes, behaviour patterns and aspirations. It endowed the past, the present and the future with the perspective of unity and progress. It explained the peculiar social and political organization of the nation—unity in spite of heterogeneity—and it pointed towards an ideal of social organization in harmony with American experience. Above all, individualism expressed the universalism and idealism most characteristic of the national consciousness. This concept evolved in contradistinction to socialism, the universal and messianic character of which it shared.[65]

It can, indeed, be argued that the lack of a real socialist tradition in America is in part a function of the very pervasiveness of the ideology of individualism.

Certainly, a perusal of the various American uses of the term reveals a quite distinctive range of connotations. For Emerson, contemplating the failure of Brook Farm, individualism, which he endowed with an exalted moral and religious significance, had "never been tried"[66]; it was the route to perfection—a spontaneous social order of self-determined, self-reliant and fully developed individuals. "The union," he wrote, "is only perfect when all the uniters are isolated.... Each man, if he attempts to join himself to others, is on all sides cramped and diminished.... The Union must be ideal in actual individualism."[67] Society was tending towards a morally superior voluntary social order, a "free and just commonwealth" in which "property rushes from the idle and imbecile to the industrious, brave and persevering."[68] For the historian John William Draper, writing immediately after the Civil War, in celebration of the social system of the North, its

population was in a state of unceasing activity; there was a corporeal and mental restlessness. Magnificent cities in all directions were arising; the country was intersected with canals, railroads ... companies for banking, manufacturing, commercial purposes, were often concentrating many millions of capital. There were all kinds of associations ... churches, hospitals, schools abounded. The foreign commerce at length rivaled that of the most powerful nations of Europe. This wonderful spectacle of social de-

---

[64]See note 23 above.   [65]*Op. cit.*, 345-6.

[66]R. W. Emerson, *Journals* (1846), (Cambridge, Mass., 1909-14), VII, 322-3.

[67]R. W. Emerson, "New England Reformers" (1844), *Complete Writings* (New York, 1929), I, 317-8.   [68]"Wealth" (1860), *ibid.*, 551.

18 STEVEN LUKES

velopment was the result of INDIVIDUALISM; operating in an unbounded theatre of action. Everyone was seeking to do all that he could for himself.[69]

And for Walt Whitman, likewise celebrating the democratic system of the North, it incarnated the progressive force of modern history— "the singleness of man, individualism,"[70] reconciling liberty and social justice.

In the hands of the Social Darwinists, such as William Graham Sumner, "individualism" acquired a harsher and altogether less idealistic significance. Sumner, who maintained that "liberty, inequality, survival of the fittest . . . carries society forward and favors all its best members,"[71] offered a purportedly scientific rationale for a ruthlessly competitive society where the individual "has all his chances left open that he make out of himself all there is in him. This is individualism and atomism."[72] In this context, the influence of Herbert Spencer's doctrines as a justification for unrestrained rivalry in business and unscrupulous dealings in politics was immense; he was widely seen as "the shining light of evolution and individualism."[73] These ideas entered into an evolving ideology of private enterprise and *laissez-faire*, postulating absolute equality of opportunity and the equivalence of public welfare and private accumulation. The word was used in this sense by Andrew Carnegie, and by Henry Clews, author of *The Wall Street Point of View* (1900), who spoke of "that system of Individualism which guards, protects and encourages competition," whose spirit was "the American Spirit—the love of freedom,—of free industry,— free and unfettered opportunity. . . ."[74] It was also used favorably by Theodore Roosevelt, Woodrow Wilson, and William J. Bryan. Despite counter trends to the "Gospel of Wealth" and the "Gospel of Success," the term continued to have wide currency until a temporary eclipse during the Depression and the New Deal. It was in 1928 that Herbert Hoover gave his famous campaign speech on the "American system of rugged individualism"; yet the term regained its resonance, as can be seen by the sales of the writings of the contemporary novelist-philosopher, Ayn Rand, in defence of "reason, individualism, and capitalism."

In short, with regard to the American sense of "individualism," James Bryce was right when he observed that, throughout their history, "individualism, the love of enterprise, and pride in personal

[69]J. W. Draper, *History of the American Civil War*, 3 vols. (New York, 1868–70), I, 207–8.

[70]W. Whitman, *Democratic Vistas* (1871), *Complete Prose Works* (Philadelphia, 1891), II, 67.

[71]Quoted in R. Hofstadter, *Social Darwinism in American Thought* (New York, 1959), 51, *q. v. passim., esp.* ch. 3.

[72]W. G. Sumner, *Earth Hunger and Other Essays* (New Haven, 1913), 127–8.

[73]J. R. Commons quoted in Hofstadter, *op. cit.*, 34.

[74]H. Clews, *Individualism versus Socialism* (New York) 1907, 1–3.

THE MEANINGS OF "INDIVIDUALISM" 19

freedom, have been deemed by Americans not only their choicest, but their peculiar and exclusive possession."[75]

(v) *England*. In England, the term has played a smaller role, as an epithet for nonconformity in religion, for the sterling qualities of self-reliant Englishmen, especially among the nineteenth-century middle-classes, and for features common to the various shades of English liberalism. French and German influences can, of course, also be found. Its first use was in Henry Reeve's translation of Tocqueville's *De la Démocratic en Amérique* in 1840. The word was also used pejoratively in the French sense by a great number of thinkers, but especially socialists, to refer to the evils of capitalist competition. Thus, Robert Owen, in specifying his cooperative socialist ideals, argued that to "effect these changes there must be . . . a new organisation of society, on the principle of *attractive union*, instead of *repulsive individualism* . . . ,"[76] while John Stuart Mill (who was much influenced by the Saint-Simonians) asserted that "the moral objection to competition, as arming one human being against another, making the good of each depend upon evil to others, making all who have anything to gain or lose, live in the midst of enemies, by no means deserves the disdain with which it is treated by some of the adversaries of socialism. . . . Socialism, as long as it attacks the existing individualism, is easily triumphant; its weakness hitherto is in what it proposes to substitute."[77] Mill, expounding, not unsympathetically, the ideas of "the present Socialists," wrote that, in their eyes,

the very foundation of human life as at present constituted, the very principle on which the production and repartition of all material products is now carried on, is essentially vicious and anti-social. It is the principle of individualism, competition, each one for himself and against all the rest. It is grounded on opposition of interests, not harmony of interests, and under it every one is required to find his place by a struggle, by pushing others back or being pushed back by them. Socialists consider this system of private war (as it may be termed) between every one and every one, especially fatal in an economical point of view and in a moral.[78]

And the socially-conscious Bishop of Durham, Brooke Foss Westcott argued in 1890 that "individualism regards humanity as made up of disconnected or warring atoms: socialism regards it as an organic whole, a vital unity formed by the combination of contributing members mutually interdependent."[79]

[75]J. Bryce, *The American Commonwealth* (London and New York, 1888), II, 404. For a contemporary statement defending nonconformity and privacy against "groupism," v. D. Riesman, *Individualism Reconsidered* (Glencoe, Ill., 1954).

[76]R. Owen, *Moral World* (1845), quoted in Arieli, *op. cit.*, 406.

[77]J. S. Mill, *Newman's Political Economy* (1851) in *Collected Works* (Toronto, London, 1963--), V, 444.   [78]J. S. Mill, *Chapters on Socialism* (1879), *ibid.*, 715.

[79]*The Guardian* (8 Oct. 1890), quoted in O.E.D.

20 STEVEN LUKES

As to the German sense, this can be seen in the writings of the Unitarian minister William McCall, claimed as a precursor in expounding "the doctrine of Individuality" (along with Humboldt, the German Romantics, Goethe, and Josiah Warren) by John Stuart Mill.[80] McCall, who was influenced by German Romanticism, wrote declamatory books and pamphlets, such as *Elements of Individualism* (1847) and *Outlines of Individualism* (1853), in which he preached the gospel of a new way of life dominated by the "Principle of Individualism," which he hoped England would be the first country to adopt.

Among indigenous uses, the term's reference to nonconformity is evident in the condemnation by Gladstone, who for a time advocated a single state religion, of "our individualism in religion"[81] and in Matthew Arnold's contrast between the Catholics' ecclesiastical conception of the Eucharist and its origin "as Jesus founded it" where "it is the consecration of absolute individualism."[82] The term's reference to the English character can be seen in Samuel Smiles, that ardent moralist on behalf of the Manchester School of political economy. "The spirit of self-help," he wrote, "as exhibited in the energetic action of individuals, has in all times been a marked feature of the English character"; even "the humblest person, who sets before his fellows an example of industry, sobriety, and upright honesty of purpose in life, has a present as well as a future influence upon the well-being of his country." It was this "energetic individualism which produces the most powerful effects upon the life and action of others, and really constitutes the best practical education."[83]

It was as a central term in the vocabulary of English liberalism that "individualism" came to be mainly used in the latter half of the nineteenth century, in contrast with "socialism," "communism," and, especially, "collectivism." Thus the *Pall Mall Gazette* in 1888 spoke of holding "the scales between individualists and Socialists"[84] and the *Times* in 1896 of "the individualists" holding "their own against the encroachments of the State."[85] Though scarcely used by the political economists and the Benthamites, and though, as we have seen, Mill used it in a different and negative sense, "individualism" came to be embraced by the whole spectrum of English liberals, from those advocating the most extreme *laissez-faire* to those supporting quite extensive state intervention.

Among the former was Herbert Spencer, concerned to assist the

[80]Mill's *Autobiography* (1873) (New York, 1960), 179.

[81]W. E. Gladstone, *Church Principles Considered in their Results* (London, 1840), 98, quoted in O.E.D.

[82]M. Arnold, *Literature and Dogma* (1873), (London, 1876), 312, quoted in O.E.D.

[83]S. Smiles, *Self Help* (1859), (London, 1958), 38, 39.

[84]10 Sept. 1888, quoted in O.E.D.   [85]30 Jan. 1896, quoted in O.E.D.

THE MEANINGS OF "INDIVIDUALISM" 21

general course of social evolution by arresting the imminent "drift towards a form of society in which private activities of every kind, guided by individual wills, are to be replaced by public activities guided by governmental will," that "lapse of self-ownership into ownership by the community, which is partially implied by collectivism and completely by communism."[86] Even more extreme than Spencer was Auberon Herbert, author of *The Voluntaryist Creed* (1906) and editor in the 1890's of *The Free Life*, where he described his creed as "thorough-going individualism," advocating among other things voluntary taxation and education, and "the open market and free trade in everything." At the other end of the scale were liberals, such as T. H. Green and L. T. Hobhouse, who favored positive political action for the promotion of a liberal society. For Green, individualism was "the free competitive action of the individual in relation to the production and distribution of wealth," as opposed to "the collective action of society operating through society or the executive"; he believed individualism in this sense to be "a fundamental principle of human nature and an essential factor of the well-being of society."[87] Hobhouse put the matter very clearly: "to maintain individual freedom and equality we have to extend the sphere of social control," and thus "individualism, when it grapples with the facts, is driven no small distance along Socialist lines."[88]

Perhaps the most influential use was that typified by Dicey, who equated individualism with Benthamism and utilitarian Liberalism. For Dicey,

Utilitarian individualism, which for many years under the name of liberalism, determined the trend of English legislation, was nothing but Benthamism modified by the experience, the prudence, or the timidity of practical politicians.

The "individualistic reformers," he wrote, "opposed anything which shook the obligations of contracts, or, what is at bottom the same thing, limited the contractual freedom of individuals" and, in general, they "tacitly assumed that each man if left to himself would in the long run be sure to act for his own true interest, and that the general welfare was sufficiently secured if each man were left free to pursue his happiness in his own way, either alone or in combination with his fellows."[89]

---

[86]H. Spencer, *Principles of Sociology* (London, 1876–96), III, 594. For Spencer's first account of his ideas as the philosophy of individualism *v.* the introduction to the American edition of his *Social Statics* (New York, 1865), x.

[87]Quoted in M. Richter, *The Politics of Conscience: T. H. Green and his Age* (London, 1964), 343.

[88]L. T. Hobhouse, *Liberalism* (1911), (New York, 1964), 54.

[89]A. V. Dicey, *Law and Public Opinion in England* (1905) (London, 1962), 125, 151, 156.

"Individualism" has, in this sense, been widely used to mean the absence or minimum of state intervention in the economic and other spheres, and has usually been associated, both by its adherents and its opponents, with classical, or negative liberalism.

Balliol College, Oxford.

II

Who is the *Übermensch*? Time, Truth, and Woman in Nietzsche

Keith Ansell-Pearson

"Interpretation"

Interpreting myself, I always read
Myself into my writings. I clearly need
Some help. But all who climb on their own way
Carry my image, too, into the breaking day.*

I. Introduction

In this essay I seek to examine the question of the identity of
Nietzsche's *Übermensch* in the light of the intellectual revolution brought
about in our understanding of texts by deconstruction. With its notions
of textuality, interpretation, the metaphoricity of language, and the unde-
cidability of philosophical discourse, deconstruction has radicalized the
way in which we construe questions of authorship. I shall draw freely on

---

* F. Nietzsche, "Joke, Cunning, and Revenge," Prelude in German Rhymes, *The Gay
Science* (1882). I would like to express my gratitude to the Executive Editor, Allan Megill,
and Richard Schacht for their comments on earlier drafts of this essay, which enabled me
to give greater clarity and focus to my argument. I am deeply indebted to two fine readers
of Nietzsche, Daniel Conway and David Owen, for their encouragement of my work and
for sharing their own readings with me. I would also like to acknowledge the generous
assistance of the German Academic Exchange Service (*DAAD*), whose award of a scholarship enabled me to carry out research into Nietzsche's writings at the Kirchliche
Hochschule Berlin under the generous guidance of Professor Dr. Wolfgang Müller-Lauter
in the Summer of 1990. Finally, I should like to thank Mr. R. J. Hollingdale for generously
assisting me in my translation of the unpublished material from the period of the composition of *Thus Spoke Zarathustra*. An earlier version of this essay was first presented,
through the kind invitation of David Wood, at the first annual conference of the Nietzsche
Society of Great Britain held at the University of Warwick in April 1991.

the writings of Jacques Derrida, Luce Irigaray, and Sarah Kofman, to illuminate the puzzling and contradictory status of the *Übermensch* in Nietzsche. I want to show that to raise the question of the identity of the *Übermensch* is also to raise fundamental questions about Nietzsche's authorship and its authority, about the nature of the "we" (his readers) in his writings, and about the figure of woman in his conception of life. It is to explore the issue of how we are to read him, for by exploring the identity of the "over-man" we are exploring our own identity and the possibilities of our own potential post-modern (post-"man") existence.

The notion of the *Übermensch* poses major problems for anyone who wishes to come to grips with the paradoxes and tensions of Nietzsche's thought. Can his promotion of the idea of a humanity "beyond" (*über*) man be taken seriously when much of his thinking is premised on the conviction that all modern ideals which encourage human beings to sacrifice the present for the future are no more than relics of our Christian ascetic past, which have to be discredited by subjecting them to the hammer of the philosopher? As Nietzsche informs his readers in *Ecce Homo*:

The last thing *I* should promise would be to "improve" mankind. No new idols are erected by me: let the old ones learn what feet of clay mean. *Overthrowing idols* (my word for "ideals")—that comes closer to being part of my craft. One has deprived reality of its value, its meaning, its truthfulness, to precisely the extent to which one has mendaciously invented an ideal world.[1]

But in the chapter on the "Genealogy of Morals" in the same book, Nietzsche explains why the ascetic ideal, the ideal of Christianity which teaches human beings to reject earthly life and place all their hopes and dreams in a supraterrestrial beyond, held its grip on the human spirit for so long. The reason was simply because a *"counterideal* was lacking— *until Zarathustra."* Is the "counterideal" offered by Zarathustra (the overman) merely ironic, simply a parody of teachings of redemption found in the major world-religions?[2]

Another problem affecting the coherence of Nietzsche's positing of a notion of the *Übermensch* arises from determining its precise relationship to the doctrine of eternal return. As far back as Georg Simmel, commentators have pointed out that the two principal teachings of Nietzsche's *Thus Spoke Zarathustra* seem to be fundamentally at odds with each other and that this incompatibility is evidence of the incoherence of much of his philosophical project. For example, in his study of 1907 Simmel argues

---

[1] F. Nietzsche, *Ecce Homo*, tr. Walter Kaufmann (New York, 1967), preface, section 2.

[2] An argument of this kind can be found in Daniel Conway's essay, "Overcoming the *Übermensch*: Nietzsche's Revaluation of Values," *Journal of the British Society for Phenomenology*, 20 (1989) 211-24.

that it would appear that "the infinity of the overman's task cannot be reconciled with the finitude of cosmic periods" which is presupposed in the thought of eternal return. As he put it, "within each period, humanity could be vested with only a limited number of forms of evolution, which could be constantly repeated, whereas the ideal of the overman demands a straight line of evolution heading toward the future."[3] Simmel tries to resolve the apparent contradiction between the two teachings by suggesting that the "overman" is best construed in terms of a Kantian as-if which transcends the limitations of our present cognitive awareness. He thus proposes that the overman is to be understood "not as a rigid structure with an absolutely determined content, but as a functional ideal indicating the human form that is superior to the present real one."[4] The view that the two major doctrines of *Zarathustra* are incoherent has recently been most forcefully expressed by Erich Heller, who has argued that they are a "paradigm of logical incompatibility." Whereas the teaching of the overman is designed to inspire us to create "the new, the unique, and the incomparable," the doctrine of eternal return contains the crushing thought that the same will return eternally, and therefore all creation is in vain.[5]

In his instructive reading of *Zarathustra* Laurence Lampert has suggested a way of moving beyond the apparent contradiction between the two main teachings of the book by arguing that it is necessary to read the story of Zarathustra's descent or down-going (*Untergang*) to man as one in which the initial teaching of the *Übermensch* declared in the prologue is progressively and decisively abandoned in the course of the book in favor of the teaching of eternal return. He writes, "It seems to me that one of the greatest single causes of the misinterpretation of Nietzsche's teaching is the failure to see that the clearly provisional teaching on the superman is rendered obsolete by the clearly definitive teaching on eternal return."[6] Lampert is opposed to any interpretation which places the doctrine of the overman at the center of Nietzsche's thought because, he argues, this is to subject the story of Zarathustra's down-going to a

---

[3] G. Simmel, *Schopenhauer and Nietzsche*, tr. H. Loiskandt et. al. (Amherst, 1986), 174.

[4] Simmel, *Schopenhauer and Nietzsche, ibid.*

[5] E. Heller, *The Importance of Nietzsche: Ten Essays* (Chicago, 1988), 12. See Nietzsche, *The Gay Science*, tr. W. Kaufmann (New York, 1974), section 335: "We, however, want to become those who we are—the ones who are new, unique, and incomparable, who give themselves laws, who create themselves." Translation slightly changed from Kaufmann, and in accordance with the original German. Kaufmann has "*human beings* who are new, unique, and incomparable" (my emphasis). But we need to ask who are these "human beings" if not the "ones" who are "*over*human"? I owe this insight to Howard Caygill. See his excellent essay, "Affirmation and Eternal Return in the Free-Spirit," in K. Ansell-Pearson (ed.), *Nietzsche and Modern German Thought* (London, 1991), 216-40, 235.

[6] Laurence Lampert, *Nietzsche's Teaching* (New Haven, 1987), 258.

fundamental misreading which imposes on it the whole notion of the eschatological fulfillment of time that Zarathustra wishes to overcome; it is to abandon the very idea that the problem of humanity lies in the fact that it is in need of redemption. Zarathustra, he argues, overthrows what the Persian prophet Zoroaster has bequeathed to humanity, namely, a prophetic religion that forces earthly, mortal existence to be lived and endured "under the terrible gravity of a future Day of Judgement in which eternal doom or eternal bliss will be decreed."[7]

Despite the illumination these readings shed on the difficulties and tensions of Nietzsche's major notions and teachings, it is my belief that, like a great deal of orthodox Nietzsche scholarship, they rest on an understanding of his philosophy which neglects and ignores the way in which Nietzsche's texts deconstruct their own claims to authority and put into question the identity of author and reader. It is only when we address these sorts of issues that the nature of the contradictions and paradoxes which animate Nietzsche's thought fully come to light. To seek to expose the contradictory nature of his major doctrines, such as the overman and eternal return, is to mistake them for logical truths when they need to be read as powerful fictions or metaphors which refer to experiences and processes. It is a fundamental tenet of Nietzsche's deconstruction of philosophy that "truth" is not something to be "found" or "discovered," but rather that it is to be "created" and is a "process": "introducing truth, as a *processus in infinitum*, an active determining—not a becoming-conscious of something that is in itself firm and determined. It is a word for the 'will to power.' "[8] Nietzsche does not read the truth-claims of philosophy in terms of their supposed accurate reflection of reality as it is in-itself, but as "symptoms" of ascending or descending life. To read Nietzsche we need to learn how to read the tempo of his "signs." According to Nietzsche himself, what is required is an art which lies "beyond" the powers of "modern man" (*moderner Mensch*), namely, what he calls in the preface to the *Genealogy of Morals* an "art of interpretation" (*Auslegung*).[9] In other words, to be able to read him we need to be not *moderner Mensch* but *Übermensch*—or at least on the bridge to it.

II. Nietzsche's "Multifarious Art of Style"

Jacques Derrida has placed the question of style at the center of an understanding of Nietzsche's authorship.[10] His claim is that texts are not

[7] Lampert, *Nietzsche's Teaching, ibid.*

[8] Nietzsche, *The Will To Power*, tr. R. J. Hollingdale and W. Kaufmann (New York, 1969), section 552.

[9] Nietzsche, *On the Genealogy of Morals*, tr. Hollingdale and Kaufmann (New York, 1967), preface, section 8. It could be argued that in positing "life" as "will to power" Nietzsche is being not merely metaphorical but is claiming knowledge about "reality" as it is in itself. The view that a theory of truth is indispensable to Nietzsche's concerns has recently been put forward in a highly instructive manner by Maudemarie Clark, *Nietzsche on Truth and Philosophy* (Cambridge, 1990).

[10] J. Derrida, *Spurs: Nietzsche Styles*, tr. Barbara Harlow (Chicago 1979).

bounded by authorial intent, which means that their meaning lies beyond them and is to be constituted by an active reading. Nietzsche is important to Derrida's task of deconstructing the logocentric and phallocentric bias of the tradition of Western metaphysics because, in the words of one commentator, he "provides . . . a *style* of philosophic writing which remains intensely sceptical of all claims to truth—its own included—and which thus opens up the possibility of liberating thought from its age-old conceptual limits."[11] On Nietzsche's reading of the tradition, philosophers have consistently duped their audiences with claims to *the* "Truth" by effacing the metaphors which constitute their writing. Philosophy is thus based on a suppression of its own roots in figurative language. What this means is that philosophy is based, amongst other things, on an unconscious libidinal economy, a repression of its own desires, and a disregard for the question of style. The task of deconstruction is to undermine the hierarchical oppositions on which Western metaphysics has been built (man/woman, reason/passion, logos/pathos, intelligible/sensible, etc.) and open up the discourse of philosophy to a free play of signs in which new, more complex, hybrid identities can be created. It is not, however, a question of "all style and no substance." A reading of *Thus Spoke Zarathustra* demonstrates this point.

The significance of *Zarathustra*, in which the teaching of the overman is developed at length, is that it is in this work that Nietzsche explicitly addresses the whole problem of the authority of (his) authorship. What the book attempts to dramatize is, in brief, the impossibility of legislating autonomy. This explains why the book is subtitled "for all and none." On one occasion Nietzsche has Zarathustra declare that when he is asked about "the way" to truth and enlightenment, his only honest reply is that it is impossible to speak of such a way, for "*the* way" does not exist.[12] Similarly, the teachings of Zarathustra do not ask for "believers," for as Nietzsche has his hero ask, of what good or use is "belief"? Belief has little to do with truth. Thus, Nietzsche has Zarathustra declare to his disciples that only when they have rejected him and found their own unique and incomparable selves will he "return" to them.[13] At several key places in the unfolding of the story of Zarathustra's descent to humanity, Nietzsche has Zarathustra problematize the status of his identity by asking a whole series of questions: is he a ploughshare? or maybe a fool? is he a poet? is he a good man? an evil man? is he a deceiver, a fulfiller, a promiser, a redeemer? What or who exactly is he?[14] In this way Nietzsche keeps open the meaning of the story and implicates the reader in the book's truth-claims. The reader cannot remain neutral but must respond emo-

---

[11] C. Norris, *Deconstruction, Theory and Practice* (London, 1982), 57.

[12] Nietzsche, *Thus Spoke Zarathustra*, tr. Hollingdale (Middlesex, 1979), "Of the Spirit of Gravity," section 2.

[13] *Ibid.*, "Of the Bestowing Virtue," section 3.

[14] *Ibid.*, "Of Redemption."

tionally, viscerally, and reflexively to the experiences that Zarathustra undergoes. To this end the reader must learn the "art of interpretation" in order to read its "signs" and their rhythms and to engage with the inward experience it seeks to communicate. The question of style in Nietzsche is inseparable from that of the substance of his saying. On his "art of style" Nietzsche writes in *Ecce Homo*:

> To communicate a state, an inward tension of pathos, by means of signs, including the tempo of these signs—that is the meaning of every style; and considering that the multiplicity of inward states is exceptionally large in my case, I have many stylistic possibilities—the most multifarious art of style that has ever been at the disposal of one man.[15]

Nietzsche offers his readers a dazzling array of styles—essays, aphorisms, polemics, parables, and poems—which offer not one "Truth" but many experiences and many truths.

Unlike the embittered and vengeful Rousseau, who in his *Reveries of a Solitary Walker* can only esteem his own sense of selfhood by condemning humanity at large, Nietzsche does not take his revenge upon humanity for neglecting him but instead speaks of his art of style in terms of a "squandering."[16] All his writings, he tells us, are designed as "fish-hooks," but is it his fault if there are no fish?[17] Nietzsche's gift of writing, of communication, springs from an overflowing, abundant fecundity and strength. What is made of them, what interpretations they provoke, and what kind of readers they solicit are beyond Nietzsche's control. And so he tells his life to himself—not out of resentment but out of thanksgiving, as the "Yes of Amen" to life as the eternally self-creating and self-destroying wheel, to life as will to power, and to the ring of recurrence which is "eternity," which, in turn, is "woman." Nietzsche does not have Zarathustra enunciate this last "truth" but *sing* it:

> Never yet did I find the woman by whom I wanted children, unless it be this woman, whom I love: for I love thee, O Eternity!
> For I love thee, O Eternity![18]

---

[15] Nietzsche, *Ecce Homo*, "Why I Write Such Good Books," section 4.

[16] See, for example, J. J. Rousseau, *Reveries of a Solitary Walker*, tr. Peter France (Middlesex, 1979), 27 and 30: "So now I am alone in the world, with no brother, neighbour, or friend. . . . The most sociable and loving of men with one accord been cast out by all the rest. . . . But I, detached as I am from them and the rest of the world, what am I? . . . My fellow-men might return to me, but I should no longer be there to meet them." It should be noted, however, that Nietzsche does recognize that the "greatest danger" he faces is the same one which seduced Rousseau: *disgust* at "man." See *Ecce Homo*, "Why I am So Wise," section 5.

[17] Nietzsche, *Ecce Homo*, "Beyond Good and Evil," 310.

[18] Nietzsche, *Zarathustra*, "The Seven Seals (or: The Song of Yes and Amen")," section 2.

III. The Return of the Overman and the Time of Return

In the prologue to the work Zarathustra descends to humanity after ten years of solitude and announces that man is something to be overcome (*überwunden*). Zarathustra teaches the *Übermensch*, which is to be the meaning of the earth after the event of the death of God. With the force of a categorical imperative, Zarathustra speaks thus:

> . . .The overman *shall be* the meaning of the earth!
> I entreat you, my brethren, *remain true to the earth*, and do not believe those who speak to you of supra-terrestrial hopes! . . .
>
> I want to teach human beings the meaning of their being: which is the overman, the lightning from the dark cloud of man[19]

But in order to go over or across (*übergehen*) it is necessary that we first learn how to go under or perish (*untergehen*). There has never yet been an *Übermensch*, Zarathustra says, for man has yet to learn *how* to go under. When we do go under we experience "the hour of the great contempt," the hour in which our present happiness, reason, pity, justice, and virtue grow loathsome to us.[20] In the discourse entitled "Of the Way of the Creator" in book one, Zarathustra declares that he loves the person who "wants to create beyond (*über*) himself, and thus perishes." As I shall argue, it is through the teaching of eternal return that Zarathustra shows how one can learn to go under. It is the doctrine of return, therefore, that provides the bridge (the way) across (*über*) to the overman. At the same time the vision of the *Übermensch* is designed to inspire in human beings a desire for the experience of down-going and beyond (*über*) man. However, the bridge to the overman does not lead to *the* "way" but to many ways. In section 335 of *The Gay Science* Nietzsche speaks of a "we" who must "become those that they are: the ones who are new, unique, and incomparable, who give themselves laws and create themselves." The significance of the doctrine of eternal return is that it represents a radicalization of Kant's categorical imperative in so far as it establishes the conditions for a truly individual act of willing (self-legislation as self-creation). The eternal return provides the form of universality associated with the categorical imperative only in the act of returning, while what returns (the content) cannot be universal, as each individual's experience of life is unique. Although Kant's formulation of the categorical imperative is often accused of formalism, it does presuppose that the

[19] *Ibid.*, Prologue, sections 3 and 7.
[20] *Ibid.*, section 3.

contents of one's act of willing, whatever they might prove to be, are capable of being universalized so as to apply to all rational beings. The willing contained in the thought-experiment and test of eternal return, however, is one "beyond good and evil." The prologue ends, for example, with Zarathustra declaring that what he seeks is not disciples but companions, whom he calls "fellow-creators and rejoicers." He shall not be herdsman to the herd but instead shall teach by way of example: "I will show them the rainbow and the stairway to the *Übermensch*."[21]

For decades now, generations of English-speaking commentators on Nietzsche have wrestled with the problem of how best to translate the word *Übermensch*. The question which any new reader of Nietzsche wants to ask is: what is meant by the term *Übermensch*? Is it, for example, the type of being in possession of superhuman powers, the superman of legend, or is it the symbol of the humanity of the future which has overcome the nihilism of the modern epoch and the world-weariness of modern humanity? In *Ecce Homo* Nietzsche states that the notion of *Übermensch* is not in any way to be conceived along Darwinian lines or as representing a transcendental ideal of man.[22] The *Übermensch* is thus not an ideal that is posited in terms of an infinite future beyond the reach of mere mortals; it is not "super" or "above" (*über*) in this sense. "I love him," Zarathustra says, "who justifies the humanity of the future and redeems the humanity of the past, for he wants to perish by the humanity of the present."[23] To the last men who are gathered in the market-place, bemused by the madman who announces the death of God, the person who strives for something higher and nobler will always appear as "superhuman." What I think this shows is that Nietzsche, as Walter Kaufmann pointed out a long time ago in his classic study of 1950, is playing with the connotations

---

[21] *Ibid.*, section 9. I examine the connection between the categorical imperative and eternal return in more detail in chapter five of my book, *Nietzsche contra Rousseau* (Cambridge, 1991), especially 194-200.

[22] Nietzsche, *Ecce Homo*, "Why I Write Such Good Books," section 1. I am not persuaded by Bernd Magnus's reasons for not translating the *Übermensch* as "overman" given in his essay, "Overman: An Attitude or an Ideal?" in D. Goicoechea, *The Great Year of Zarathustra (1881-1981)* (New York, 1983), 142-65. Moreover, his claim, made on page 144, that the German word *Übermensch* should be retained in English-speaking discussions because it is non-sexist simply presupposes and assumes what needs to be demonstrated. As I hope this essay shows, a great deal can be learned about the notion by translating it as "overman" and playing with the connotations of the word "*über*." Fully to appreciate the idea it has to be understood in the much wider context of Nietzsche's writings and their attempt to locate the possibilities for a new, artistic post-modern *Mensch*. The key passage here is that on "*moderner Mensch*" in section 8 to the preface of the *Genealogy of Morals*. For further insight see Michael Newman, "Reading the future of genealogy: Kant, Nietzsche, Plato," in K. Ansell-Pearson (ed.), *Nietzsche and Modern German Thought* (London, 1991), 257-82.

[23] Nietzsche, *Zarathustra*, Prologue, section 4.

of the word "*über*" (across, over, beyond).[24] He is trying to show that the desire for change within the self involves both a process of the old perishing (an *Untergang* of the present) and of the new striving to be brought into existence (an *Übergang* to the future). It is a question of giving birth, of child-bearing. The important question concerns how this moment of self-transformation and sacrifice of the self is to be constituted and how one can experience time in a way that is free of resentment.

With the notion of the *Übermensch*, therefore, Nietzsche does not intend Zarathustra to teach something utterly fantastical. In the discourse of *Zarathustra* entitled "Of the Afterworldsmen," for example, Zarathustra says that he teaches a "new will" which is designed to teach human beings to desire not a new path but the one that they have hitherto followed but blindly and to "call it good." It is thus a question of learning how to *become* what we *are*, of undergoing a process of transfiguration. In the discourse entitled "On the Blissful Islands" which appears at the beginning of part two of the work, Zarathustra says that we should reach no further than our "creating will": "Could you *create* a god?—So be silent about all gods! But you could surely create the overman."

It is in the discourse on "Redemption" (*Erlösung*) towards the end of the second part or act that Zarathustra intimates the doctrine of eternal return. In this discourse we witness Zarathustra searching for a doctrine which will teach the human will that it is a will to power (*Macht* as in *machen*—to make or create), that is, a creative and legislative will. The great problem of the will is that it is overwhelmed by the burden and weight of the past which casts a dark shadow over the future. The human will feels impotent in the face of what has been, for it recognizes that one cannot change what is past. It thus sees itself as a victim of the past and in a fit of rage it takes revenge on life. The will's most lonely affliction is that it cannot will backwards and break time's law of change, becoming, and movement. "The spirit of revenge," Zarathustra announces in this key discourse, "that up to now has been mankind's chief concern; and where there was suffering, there was always supposed to be punishment." Zarathustra thus seeks a doctrine which will liberate the will from its fixation on the past which enslaves it to a moral world-order of guilt, punishment, and revenge. What he requires is a doctrine which will restore for humanity the "innocence of becoming," that is, the view of existence which is able to recognize that ultimately life is without meaning and beyond justification; or rather, that life itself contains within it, within its eternal movement of creation and destruction, of change and development,

---

[24] See W. Kaufmann, *Nietzsche. Philosopher, Psychologist, and Anti-Christ* (4th ed., Princeton, 1974), 308.

of pleasure and pain, of joy and suffering, its own justification.[25] The meaning of life is to be found nowhere but within life itself as we live it and shall live it. But instead of such an insight crippling us, we should be inspired by it—to the extent that we are able to affirm unconditionally the eternal return of all the moments of our existence because we recognize that every one of those moments is necessary to who we are.

The central teaching of part three, and arguably of Nietzsche's Dionysian philosophy, is that of eternal return. It is out of the experience of return that the overman will emerge as the one who embodies the creative and innocent will to power and who gaily plays with the wheel of existence conceived as the eternally self-creating and self-destroying. The overman has to be understood as the vision which emerges out of the riddle of eternal return. In *Ecce Homo* the thought (*Gedanke*) of return is said to be the most fundamental conception of *Zarathustra*, for it represents the highest formula of affirmation attainable.[26] The significance of the doctrine is twofold: it is both a teaching on the nature of time and an experience which affirms the creative unity of all things, including that of good and evil.

Clearly, if taken literally as a cosmological hypothesis, the thought of return is absurd.[27] However, if viewed in terms of an imaginative response to the problem of time and time's "it was" (the problem of the past), we see that it proposes an affirmation of the nature of time, of time's passing away, of its becoming and perishing. The peculiar challenge that the thought presents lies in the question that confronts the person who undergoes its experience. Can I accept the destiny of my being in such a way that I can also accept the necessity of my past because, as a creator of the future, I willed it? The test of return teaches a new will by teaching the

[25] For Nietzsche on "the innocence of becoming" see *Twilight of the Idols*, tr. Hollingdale (Middlesex, 1968), "The Four Great Errors," section 8: "What alone can our teaching be? That no one *gives* a human being their qualities: not God, not society, not parents or ancestors. . . . *No one* is accountable for existing at all, for being constituted as they are, or for living in the circumstances and surroundings in which they find themselves. The fatality of their nature cannot be disentangled from the fatality of all that which has been and will be. . . . One is necessary, one is a piece of fate, one belongs to the whole, one *is* in the whole . . . *this alone is the great liberation*—thus alone is the *innocence* [*Unschuld*] of becoming restored."

[26] Nietzsche, *Ecce Homo*, "Thus Spoke Zarathustra," section 1.

[27] Bernd Magnus has pointed out that it is only in the *Nachlass* material that Nietzsche experiments with the idea of eternal return in terms of a scientific hypothesis which states what reality really is like, while the normative import of the idea is emphasized in every work he wrote for publication after 1881. See his essay, "Nietzsche's Eternalistic Counter-Myth," *Review of Metaphysics*, 26 (1973), 604-16. Alexander Nehamas has argued that the presentation of the doctrine in existential terms does not presuppose the validity of the cosmological hypothesis. See his essay, "The Eternal Recurrence," *Philosophical Review*, 99 (1980), 331-56. My reading of the eternal return is one which very much concurs with the arguments made by Magnus and Nehamas regarding its fictional or regulative status.

individual creatively to will the existence which they have so far led only blindly and unknowingly. How well-disposed towards life would we have to be to desire nothing more fervently than its eternal confirmation and seal? Do we have the strength and courage to affirm the eternal return of the "moment" or are we full of pity for life and desire only its self-preservation? These are the kinds of questions we find in section 341 of the *Gay Science*, where the doctrine of return is first presented in Nietzsche's published work in terms of "the greatest weight." The doctrine of return is presented as the greatest weight because it is a doctrine which endows our personal existence with meaning and significance. It teaches us to love life and not to seek redemption from its tragic character. In order to affirm life it is necessary to affirm all of life without selection, subtraction, or addition. Only in this way is it possible to free life from prejudice (pre-judgment) and let it be in all its terrible fecundity and rich variety. This is why the doctrine teaches that in undergoing the experience of the moment—what I would like to call "the time of return"—what the will must will is the return of one's life with every pain and every joy, every thought and every sigh, and everything unutterably small and great all in the same succession and sequence. Why? Because everything we have done, and the manner in which we have done it, is necessary to who we "are." The question is: do we wish to *become* those who we are? What is transformed in the willing contained in the experience of return is not the past itself, which would be impossible, but our attitude towards it.[28] The past is never simply past as we are always reinterpreting and revaluing it in the light of our present needs and our conception of the future. The way that the past can become present is through the experience of the "moment."

The affirmation of the "moment" as the "innocence of becoming" represents the highest affirmation of the temporal and transient character of life, for it reflects an attitude towards life that is above (*über*) moral judgment (beyond any theological or metaphysical opposition of good and evil). Morality for Nietzsche, taken in an absolutist or universalist sense,

---

[28] On this point see Nehamas, "Eternal Recurrence," 34-39. One of the most challenging readings of Nietzsche's doctrine of eternal return as a teaching on how one becomes *what* one is, and which is offered as a critique of Nehamas's "humanist" reading of it, is that evinced by Gary Shapiro in his *Nietzschean Narratives* (Bloomington, 1989), 88-92. Against Nehamas, he argues that the doctrine does not posit an ideal of the integrated, harmonious self (even if that self is created rather than simply given) but rather it affirms the dissolution and dispersion of the self—instead of harmony, there is dissonance, instead of control, there is abandonment, instead of coherence, there is contradiction, instead of identity, there is difference, instead of clarity, there is ambiguity, and so on. I myself find it difficult to understand how eternal return can operate as a self-reflective principle without a notion of integration. Unless "willing" the eternal return leads to an "enhancement" of one's feeling of power and well-being the result, as Nietzsche says, is likely to be a crushing of the will, perhaps even self-annihilation in its literal sense. In this respect, my reading differs from a classic deconstructionist reading of the kind favored by Shapiro.

serves to condemn life for it is unable to affirm "the grand economy of life," which consists in recognizing the creative unity of all things. Morality, by contrast, cannot affirm the whole; the moral person selects what they require for their own self-preservation and fails to see that in the general economy of the whole pain is as necessary as pleasure, that suffering is a precondition of self-overcoming, and that courage can only emerge out of cruelty towards oneself. In order to have the experience of the "moment" it is necessary that one liberate oneself from one's ordinary conception of time in which time is experienced as a series, that is, time in terms of a seriality of past, present, and future. The "moment" provides an insight into the very timeliness of time; that is, it reveals that time is change, decay, ceaseless movement and becoming. In affirming the "moment" we are thus affirming time itself for we realize that it is of the essence of life to die, perish, decay, and degenerate. In willing the eternal return of the moment we are willing the law of life—decay, degeneration, waste, excess—and recognizing that life is the unity of pleasure and pain, of joy and suffering, of good and evil: "Good and evil, and rich and poor, and noble and base, and all the names of the virtues: they should be weapons and ringing symbols that life must overcome itself again and again!"[29]

After Nietzsche thought that the drama was complete in three acts, he added a fourth part to *Zarathustra* in 1885, which he at first published privately. Once again the vision of the *Übermensch* becomes prominent, after having been somewhat cast aside in part three. Thus instead of Nietzsche's abandoning the teaching of the overman in favor of that of eternal return, as argued by Lampert, what we find is that it is in part four that the vision of the overman returns. In the discourse included in part three entitled "Of Old and New Law-Tables," Zarathustra declared that it was out of the recognition of the unity and necessity of all things that he "picked up the word *Übermensch*." Zarathustra reveals further in part four that the overman is the person who has emerged from the experience of the riddle of return and affirmed the import of its teaching. We thus find that in the final part of the book Zarathustra once again— just as he did in the prologue—heralds the vision of the overman in terms of a prefiguration of a future, transfigured humanity.

A vision of the *Übermensch* serves on one level as a consolation for Nietzsche in that the prospect of a new humanity consoles him in the face of the world-weariness of modern *Mensch*. This explains why, in spite of what many commentators may regard as a lack of coherence in his work, Nietzsche stubbornly clings to such an idea. In section two of the discourse in part four entitled "Of the Higher Man" Zarathustra summons up once again a vision of the overman: "Very well! Come on, you Higher Men! Only now does the mountain of mankind's future labour. God has died:

[29] Nietzsche, *Zarathustra*, "Of the Tarantulas."

now *we* desire that the overman shall live!" In section three of this discourse, moreover, he speaks of the overman as his "paramount and sole concern." These are hardly the words of a teacher who has abandoned his original immaculate conception.

On another level the *Übermensch* represents Nietzsche's conception of a humanity which has learned the "art of interpretation" and is able to read the "signs" of philosophy for what they are: symptoms of abundant or degenerating life. In 1885 he begins to write his philosophy of "beyond good and evil" as a "prelude to a philosophy of the future," while in the prefaces written in 1886 to new editions of his earlier books he begins to "name" his future readers and to give them various guises. What becomes clear is that the vision of the *Übermensch* has the status of an artist's creation; it is the product of the imagination of the poet. The question of whether the notion of the *Übermensch* is true or false is, on these terms, frankly irrelevant. Rather the question is to what extent is it a life-enabling, life-enhancing, and life-affirming notion? And life-enhancing for whom?

IV. The Fundamental Entanglement of the Doctrines of Eternal Return and the Overman in the Zarathustra-*Nachlass*

An analysis of the *Zarathustra-Nachlass* reveals that Nietzsche put a great deal of careful thought into how he should present the book's fundamental teachings and conceptions. It is clear that he was led to abandon any thoughts of beginning the book with the doctrine of return when he recognized that Zarathustra and his audience had first to be prepared for its experience, and this preparation takes place through the call to create the *Übermensch*, in which we accept the necessity of sacrificing our present selves in order to go under and over to something greater and nobler. Thus, on one level the conception of the overman represents Nietzsche's concern with the further discipline and cultivation of the human animal once the Christian-moral interpretation of the world has lost its power and ascendancy. This is the specific historical context—the death of God and the devaluation of Western humanity's highest values—in which the vision is promulgated by Nietzsche.

On innumerable occasions in the *Nachlass* Nietzsche portrays Zarathustra as a teacher and lawgiver, ranking him alongside such figures as Moses, Buddha, Jesus, and Mohammed.[30] Zarathustra's task is to descend to human beings in order to show them how they can learn how to overcome themselves. It is his destiny to become what *he* is—the teacher

---

[30] See Nietzsche, *Sämtliche Werke: Kritische Studienausgabe* (henceforth abbreviated to *KSA*), eds. G. Colli and M. Montinari (Munich, 1967-77 and 1988), IX (*Nachlass* 1880-82), 15 [17].

of eternal return. The teachings of the overman and eternal return presuppose and reinforce one another. In a note from June/July of 1883 Nietzsche has Zarathustra forget himself, and "out of the overman he teaches the doctrine of return: the overman *endures it* and *employs it as a means of discipline and training.*"[31] In a note from the Summer/Autumn of the same year, Nietzsche writes:

Principal teaching: achieve completeness and pleasurable feeling at every stage—don't leap!

First the lawgiving. After the prospect of the overman the theory of return is now in an awesome way bearable.[32]

What these notes show is that Nietzsche is led to the overman because he is in need of a vision of a type of humanity which is able to endure *and* affirm the abysmal thought of eternal return. What we discover about the relationship between the book's two fundamental teachings from examining the *Nachlass* material is that for the most part it is the doctrine of return which descends upon Nietzsche first and that he is led to the vision of the *Übermensch* in order to conceive of a human type which can make the thought of return endurable. In several places in the *Nachlass* we see that the overman represents Nietzsche's consolation as the only way in which he can still believe in the possibility of such a thought as the eternal return. The notion of the *Übermensch* thus stipulates the conditions under which an endurance and an affirmation of the eternal return are possible. Similarly, the doctrine of eternal return establishes the conditions for the creation of the overman. A note from the Autumn of 1883 makes this point clear:

Zarathustra is the herald who calls up many lawgivers.

First the lawgiving. Then after this has presented the prospect of producing the overman—great awesome moment (*grosser schauerlicher Augenblick*)! Zarathustra proclaims the theory of return—which is now only endurable to himself *for the first time!*[33]

How is the thought of return to be endured and affirmed? By modern *Mensch* perhaps? But the answer is under our nose, for the overman does not exist in some distant, unknowable future. The new is born out of the old as the child is born out of the parent. Remember, for Nietzsche the law of life is one of "self-overcoming": the question is whether "we"

---

[31] Nietzsche, *KSA*, X (*Nachlass* 1882-84), 10 [47]. I owe a significant debt in my reading of the *Zarathustra-Nachlass* to Marie-Luise Haase and her essay, "Der Übermensch im *Also sprach Zarathustra* und im *Zarathustra-Nachlass* 1882-85," *Nietzsche Studien*, 13 (1984), 228-45.

[32] Nietzsche, *KSA*, X, 15 [10].

[33] *Ibid.*, 16 [86].

(Mensch) desire through an act of creative willing to become those that "we are" *(Übermensch)*. The overman is within us, it is not "out there." Rather, it is a question of giving birth to it by freely undergoing the experience of self-overcoming (from *Mensch* to *Übermensch*). The reason why there has not been an overman so far is because human beings have yet to learn *how* to go under and over or across to that which lies "beyond" themselves. To "men" the *Übermensch* thus has the appearance of a "super" man. After undergoing the experience of return himself in part three of the book, Zarathustra emerges from its riddle with a modified and reformulated vision of the overman which he delivers in part four. The overman is not to be conceived along fantastical lines but simply denotes the transfiguration we undergo when we experience the "moment." A clue is found in the prologue to *Zarathustra* when it is said that the overman is the "lightening" which emerges out of the "dark cloud" of man.

The specific problem which faces Zarathustra—and Nietzsche—is how to teach human beings a doctrine which requires them to overcome themselves but which, when taught, has all the appearances of a new religion and of something impossible to attain except by anyone but a "superman." It is perhaps the great paradox of Zarathustra's vision of the overman that we seek within it something fantastical and monumental, when its true meaning and significance lie before us if only we knew how to become those that we are. As Nietzsche says in a note from the *Nachlass*; "All signs of the overhuman appear as signs of illness or madness to men."[34] Zarathustra is a teacher who deconstructs the ground of his own authority and must do so if he is to teach autonomy. Strictly speaking, the overman cannot be taught but only *undergone*.

V. The Question of the "We" in Nietzsche

It is often noted that the notion of the overman disappears in Nietzsche's work (both published and unpublished) after *Thus Spoke Zarathustra*, making one brief, insignificant re-appearance in section 4 of *The Anti-Christ*. However, what this observation ignores is the extent to which the *Übermensch* also refers to the question of the "we" in Nietzsche, how author and reader are constituted and transformed in the act of reading. It is not, I would contend, until the prefaces 1886 and 1887 that Nietzsche begins to reveal clues as to the real identity of the *Übermensch*. The overman is "we," that is, the readers of his texts, who must decipher their meaning by learning the "art of interpretation," gaining from it the insight that, just as there is no "way," so there is no truth— for truth,

---

[34] *Ibid.*, 5 [1] 250.

38   KEITH ANSELL-PEARSON

like woman, does not exist. There is only truth, woman, and overman in the plural.

In the preface to the second edition of the first volume of *Human, All Too Human* Nietzsche speaks of his work as an exercise in the overturning of habitual evaluations and valued habits, indeed of everything "human, all too human." He describes his writings as a schooling in suspicion, contempt, courage, and audacity. He even goes so far as to admit—in a way that Rousseau, that other great confessor, never could—that all his thinking may be not only a consolation but also a deception. However, to speak like this is to speak "unmorally, extra-morally, 'beyond good and evil.'" He confesses that the "free spirits" are creatures of his own invention which he has created so as not to feel alone and isolated in his task. He looks forward to a day of "great liberation" when individuals will have learned that it is possible to overturn the past and to revalue previous values. "We" shall have become masters of our virtues, of our "for" and "against." Moreover, "we" will have grasped the "*necessary* injustice in every For and Against."[35] Section 7 of this preface provides a real clue to unravelling the identity of the overman, of the "we" in Nietzsche. It is here that Nietzsche posits the free spirit as someone whose existence in the present is governed by a conception of a possible new future which lies pregnant within them:

"What has happened to me," he says to himself, "must happen to everyone in whom a *task* wants to become incarnate and 'come into the world.'" The secret force and necessity of this task will rule among and in the individual facets of his destiny like an unconscious pregnancy—long before he has caught sight of this task or knows its name. Our vocation commands and disposes of us even when we do not yet know it: it is the future which regulates our today.

In the preface to the new edition of the second volume of this work, Nietzsche speaks revealingly of his writings as containing "precepts of health" which may be recommended to those who will read him in terms of a *disciplina voluntatis*.[36] His writings are certainly those of a pessimist, he tells us, but of a pessimist of strength who has overcome all romanticism. In section 6 he raises the decisive question of his work when he asks whether his experience—"the history of an illness and a recovery"—shall have been his personal experience alone or does it possess a truth that is something more? He responds by saying that it is his hope that his "travel books," as he likes to call them (they do speak of journeys and voyages!) have not been written solely for himself and that he now may venture them off again. His writings are thus to be understood as a gift offered to

---

[35] Nietzsche, *Human, All Too Human*, tr. Hollingdale (Cambridge, 1986), I, preface, section 6.

[36] *Ibid.*, II, section 2.

a humanity which, in the act of reading them with the aid of an "art of interpretation," will constitute itself as an over-humanity.

The relationship between health and philosophy is taken up again in the preface Nietzsche wrote to the second edition of the *Gay Science* in the autumn of 1886. He speaks to his readers, significantly, as a "convalescent." The task of life is to transform sickness into health. Nietzsche has discovered that he is a sick animal (he is a "man") and has learned to ask whether a religious or aesthetic craving for some "Apart, Beyond, Outside, Above" (*Oberhalb*)—which must include his own desire for the *Übermensch*—does not suggest that it is sickness which inspires every philosopher. Nietzsche's ultimate test is whether he can affirm this painful truth about himself—namely, that he too, like the ascetics, Christians, and moralists such as Rousseau he castigates throughout his writings, *suffers* from life. What he must do is to affirm this suffering as necessary to his own self-redemption and self-overcoming. He contends that philosophy has not simply been an interpretation of the body, but a misunderstanding of it. What philosophers have done from Plato onwards is to castrate their reflections on life from the body of experience which underlies them. For Nietzsche philosophy is maternal in that it rests on the unity of body and soul. The true philosopher is one who recognizes that her thoughts are born out of the pain of experience which, like the experience of childbirth, should by endowed with "blood, heart, fire, pleasure, passion, agony, conscience, fate, and catastrophe." "Life—that means constantly transforming all that we are into light and flame—also everything that wounds us; we simply can do no other. And as for sickness: are we not tempted to ask whether we could get along without it? Only great pain is the ultimate liberator of the spirit. . . ."[37] It is only the experience of great pain that affords us the deepest insights into the human condition. Nietzsche makes the point that the experience of such pain does not necessarily make us "better" human beings but only more "profound" ones. The result of such "dangerous exercises of self-mastery" should not be "self-forgetting" and "self-extinction"; rather, the task is to emerge a "changed" and "different person." In a passage full of wisdom and love of life (of woman), Nietzsche writes: "The trust in life is gone: life itself has become a *problem*. Yet one should not jump to the conclusion that this necessarily makes one gloomy. Even love of life is still possible, only one lives differently. It is the love for a woman that causes doubts in us."[38] The transformation involved in undergoing this process of self-mastery rests on learning the "art of transfiguration" (philosophy). From our "abysses," and from our "sicknesses" we are to "return newborn": "with a second dangerous innocence in joy, more childlike and yet a hundred times subtler than one has ever been before."

[37] Nietzsche, *The Gay Science*, preface, section 3.
[38] *Ibid.*

40 KEITH ANSELL-PEARSON

What Nietzsche is describing here is the experience of down-going or perishing by which one transfigures everything that one is and emerges beyond (*über*) oneself. The task is to transfigure pain and suffering into joy and a celebration of life, to turn the sickness into good health, and to overcome one's resentment by recognizing the necessity and unity of all things (especially the unity of good and evil); one must "return" as "newborn." What Nietzsche is demanding of his readers is nothing less than that they give birth to themselves—the most difficult of all tasks! In section 343 of book five of the *Gay Science* (also added in 1886/87) Nietzsche stipulates one condition of this task of "self-overcoming," namely, that it be performed free of resentment. He argues that if we want to reach a position "outside morality . . . beyond good and evil" then we must overcome the time we live in "within ourselves" *and* our prior aversion and contradiction against our time; in short, we need to overcome our "romanticism."

What is evident in these prefaces to new editions of his writings is that Nietzsche recognizes that it will be his fate to be born posthumously, and so he invents an audience for himself. He speaks of the coming "free spirits" and describes them variously as "the good Europeans," the "tragic pessimists," and the "self-overcomers of morality." In section 377 of the fifth part of the *Gay Science* (1887) he speaks of the ones who strive to be over-man as the "children of the future," who "feel disfavour with all ideals that might lead one to feel at home in this fragile, broken time of transition." These "children of the future" are the ones who refuse to be "reconciled," "compromised," or "castrated" by the present age. Nietzsche's authorship therefore, lies "beyond" (*über*) himself in this "future" of the *Übermensch*. Nietzsche's future readers will be those who have undergone the test of eternal return and emerged changed and "over" man. Only when "we," Nietzsche's readers, have become what *we* are, is his task complete and can *he* become what he is (the legislator who cannot legislate). Moreover, only once we have rejected Nietzsche will he return to us. Why? Because at that point we will have become those who *we* are: we will have constituted ourselves as the ones who are "new, unique, and incomparable."

VI. Truth and Woman in Nietzsche: The Eternal Return of the Overman as the Return of Woman

On the level of overt pronouncements, Nietzsche's views on woman are straightforwardly those of an aristocrat who sees male-female relationships and the social roles of each sex in strictly functional and unsentimen-

NIETZSCHE'S ÜBERMENSCH 41

tal terms.[39] However, on the level of a textual politics in which the question of style is paramount, there can be found in Nietzsche's writings a celebration of the "feminine" and of woman conceived as sensuality, the multifaceted body, and passion, an affirmation which stands in marked contrast to the masculinist tradition of Western philosophy which has erected the phallus of Reason in a position of superiority over emotion, desire, and passion. It cannot be without significance that Zarathustra's quest for meaning and truth culminates in the recognition of "eternity" understood as a woman. Nietzsche uses the idea of "woman" as a metaphor for life understood as eternal pregnancy and fecundity. It is woman who thus *embodies*, who bears and carries, the overman as life's perpetual desire for self-overcoming.

At the beginning of his preface to *Beyond Good and Evil* Nietzsche poses the question: "Supposing that truth is a woman?" If so, is it not the case, he suggests, that up to now all philosophers have been dogmatists in their assumptions about truth and novices about women, to the extent that they have failed to recognize that truth as such—truth in and for itself, truth as divine, as the Good, as God—does not exist? Woman escapes all attempts to fix her position, to give her a stable identity or an essence.[40] However, woman—like truth—is plural, polysemous, a dissimulating veil behind which lies not *the* truth but another veil, another mask. Derrida writes on this plurality of meaning:

There is no such thing as a woman, as truth in itself of a woman in itself.... For just this reason, there is no such thing either as the truth of Nietzsche, or of Nietzsche's text. In fact, in *Jenseits*, it is in a paragraph on woman that one reads "these are only *my* truths".... The very fact that "meine Wahrheiten" is so underlined, that they are multiple, variegated, contradictory even, can only imply that these are not *truths*.... Even if it should be for me, about me, truth is plural.[41]

Nietzsche's objections to feminism contain the "post-feminist" message that women's attempts to define woman as such commit the same essentialist fallacies as the masculinist tradition of Western philosophy. Derrida writes, "Feminism is nothing but the operation of a woman who aspires

---

[39] A representative sample of Nietzsche's aristocratic views can be found in *Beyond Good and Evil*, sections 231-39. See also the section entitled "Woman and Child" in volume one of *Human, All Too Human*, 150-60.

[40] Derrida, *Spurs*, 55. For a useful introduction to Derrida's reading see Kelly Oliver, "Woman as Truth in Nietzsche's Writing," *Social Theory and Practice*, 10, (1984), 185-99. See also her essay, "Nietzsche's Woman. The Poststructuralist Attempt to do away with Women," *Radical Philosophy*, 48 (1988), 25-29. I treat Derrida's position vis-à-vis feminism much more critically than I do here, in my essay, "Nietzsche, Woman, and Political Theory," in P. Patton (ed.), *Nietzsche, Feminism, and Political Theory* (London, 1992, forthcoming).

[41] Derrida, *Spurs*, 102-3.

42 KEITH ANSELL-PEARSON

to be like a man. . . . It wants a castrated woman. Gone the style."[42] Thus, Nietzsche's "postmodern" (in the sense that it is written as a philosophy of a future *Übermensch*) multifarious art of style, which affirms the pathos of distance, and celebrates a plurality of guises and a multiplicity of meanings, contains positive possibilities for articulating a celebration of identity in difference.

Sarah Kofman has warned against rushing headlong into pronouncing Nietzsche to be an unambiguous misogynist. In a highly instructive essay she has shown the significance of Nietzsche's use of the Greek goddess of Baubô to define the mystery of "truth."[43] What is necessary, Nietzsche says in the 1886 preface to the *Gay Science* where he speaks of Baubô, is to "stop courageously at the surface, at the fold, the skin, to adore appearance," to be superficial "out of profundity." The true philosopher, Kofman astutely notes, is the tragic philosopher for she wills illusion *as* illusion, knowing that woman has reason to hide her truths. "Mastery means to know how to keep oneself at a distance, to know how to close doors and windows and keep the shutters closed."[44] By identifying life and "truth" about life with Baubô, Nietzsche is identifying life not simply with woman but in particular with her reproductive organs which symbolize procreation and fecundity. As Kofman notes, in "the Eleusian mysteries the female sexual organ is exalted as the symbol of fertility and a guarantee of regeneration and eternal return of all things."[45] To this extent, as Kofman points out, Baubô can be taken to signify a female double of Dionysus. Taken together, each as the double of the other, the two—Baubô and Dionysus—prefigure a future mode of reflection beyond the metaphysical distinction of "male" and "female" conceived in terms of a natural hierarchy in which all that is male and masculine is affirmed while all that is female and feminine is negated and denigrated.

Among contemporary French thinkers it is Luce Irigaray who, however problematic and paradoxical such a task may be, has arguably done most to articulate the "feminine" in philosophy.[46] Although it is often accused of postulating a biological essentialism, Irigaray's much misunderstood work attempts to articulate a complex, non-hierarchical experience of the world in which the feminine voice which has been excluded

---

[42] *Ibid.*, 65.

[43] See S. Kofman, "Baubô: Theological Perversion and Fetishism," tr. T. B. Strong, in M. A. Gillespie and T. B. Strong (eds.), *Nietzsche's New Seas* (Chicago, 1988), 175-203.

[44] *Ibid.*, 196.

[45] *Ibid.*, 197.

[46] See L. Irigaray, *Speculum of the Other Woman*, tr. Gillian C. Gill (New York, 1985). Her reading of Nietzsche, *Amante Marine: De Friedrich Nietzsche* (Paris, 1980), has recently been published in English by Columbia University Press. For a good introduction to her work see M. Whitford, *Luce Irigaray: Philosophy in the Feminine* (London, 1991).

from the discourse of philosophy is uttered and heard.[47] Thus, as one commentator has commented, her work seeks to explore "a radically deferred, indeterminate style of writing in order to avoid all essentialisms and stable categories."[48] Thus Irigaray's attempt to "write the body" by evoking the female genitals to describe a libidinal economy centered on touch, feeling, flow, and perpetual play challenges the phallocentric logic of male reason and rationality which has governed the discourse of Western philosophic thinking from Plato to Freud. Nietzsche's attempt at a style of philosophy which seeks to articulate an inward experience, to communicate the passion of the body and the pathos of will to power as eternal life, can thus be seen as a powerful ally in the cause of creating a feminine style of writing.

The overman is a figure that is pregnant with plurality and diversity of meaning and styles. The overman can today be understood as the symbol of a Dionysian post-modern future in which the hierarchical distinctions of Western metaphysics, of phallic Truth, have been overcome. When the overman returns, the "truth" of woman will have arrived. This "moment" of the constitution of woman—and of man—as plurality, diversity, and distance will inaugurate the eternal return of the new, the unique, and the incomparable experience which is beyond any hierarchical opposition of "masculine" and "feminine."[49]

Conclusion

The use and abuse of Nietzsche's writings is clearly something which lies beyond his own control. All Nietzsche can do is to stand testimony to himself in an attempt to inform his readers who and what he is. However, his ideas and doctrines can be interpreted and taken up as much by the impotent and the indolent as they can by the curious and the courageous. As attentive readers of his work, "we" must be cautious in

---

[47] Hélène Cixous, responding to the same charge of essentialism, has argued that "There will not be *one* feminine discourse, there will be thousands of different kinds of feminine words... Until now women were not speaking out loud, were not writing, not creating their tongues—plural, but they will create them, which doesn't mean that others (either men or tongues) are going to die off." See H. Cixous and C. Clément, *The Newly Born Woman*, tr. Betsy Wing (Minneapolis, 1986), 137.

[48] See J. A. Winders, *Gender, Theory, and the Canon* (Madison, 1991), 121.

[49] I realize that this final gesture is a utopian one, "without justification." What I am trying to evoke is another law, another justice. Cixous expresses the predicament of this sort of gesture superbly when she writes: "There is 'destiny' no more than there is 'nature' or 'essence' as such. Rather, there are living structures that are caught and sometimes rigidly set within historicocultural limits so mixed up with the scene of History that for a long time it has been impossible (and it is still very difficult) to think or even imagine an 'elsewhere.'" See Cixous and Clément, *The Newly Born Woman*, 83.

ascribing fixed meanings and stable identities to his principal conceptions and teachings. In drawing attention to the question of style in Nietzsche (which, as I have argued, is also a question about woman and man) it is not my intention to deprive his thinking of its substantiality or to eviscerate its challenge in any way. Instead, it becomes necessary to appreciate that for Nietzsche the styles in which he communicates his thought are crucial to its import and its reception. Nietzsche seeks to write in styles that will facilitate an active reading of his texts and to encourage the existential "art of interpretation" (existential in the sense that his teachings speak to "all and none"). His texts are notable for the way in which they provide the reader with the space to interpret their pretensions, and to do so in a way that challenges notions of coherence, intelligibility, fixed meaning, and identity, and also with the space to deconstruct the authority with which they speak. On one important level, therefore, the notion of the *Übermensch* serves to denote the "future" readers of Nietzsche who have acquired the art of interpretation and who affirm "who" they are by affirming "what" they are: complex, multiple, in tension, paradoxical, playful, contradictory, and different. *Now we must become these that we are* by undergoing the experience of the "moment" and out of it returning "newborn."

In this essay I have tried to show that Nietzsche's preoccupation with style has a substantive basis to it. As an educator Nietzsche's overriding ambition is to promote autonomy in the reader, and to do so by way of example, one that does not seek to encourage straightforward imitation but fellow-creation. As Nietzsche has Zarathustra say in the opening discourse of book four ("The Honey Offering") once he has become who *he* is:

> For I am *he*, from the heart and from the beginning, drawing, drawing towards me, drawing up to me, raising up, trainer, and taskmaster who once bade himself, and not in vain: "Become what you are!"

I would like to suggest, as a final point, that Nietzsche's notion of the *Übermensch* partakes of a similar paradox to the one which animates the tensions of Rousseau's ethical and political thought. Rousseau expresses the paradox of legislation—does the self exist prior to the law or through the act of its (self-) creation?—in the well-known chapter on the legislator in book two of the *Social Contract:* namely, in order to *become* those who wish to become (creatures of virtue), would we not already have to *be* those (the virtuous ones)? Nietzsche's vision of the overman and riddle of eternal return, coupled with his teaching on how one becomes what one is through affirming the entanglement of this vision and riddle, can be understood as an attempt at a resolution of this paradox—a paradox which lies at the heart of an ethics and politics of transfiguration. Whether or not Nietzsche is successful in this attempt to overcome the paradox, is a question which must be left for another occasion. For the *moment*: shall we dance?

University of London.

III

AUTONOMY AND PERSONALITY IN DURKHEIM: AN ESSAY ON CONTENT AND METHOD

BY JERROLD SEIGEL

Emile Durkheim's position as a founder and classic practitioner of modern sociology rests on his pioneering efforts to analyze social solidarity, define the nature of modern societies, give rules for sociological method, and provide examples of empirically based theory on such diverse subjects as suicide and religion. But his writings and his career fascinate those of us who are not professional sociologists for yet more general reasons. Few thinkers have placed the tension between society and individuality—found throughout modern social thought—more squarely at the center of their work. Durkheim insisted that society and the life it created had to be comprehended in its own terms, not in those of individual human nature; yet he often defended individualism as a moral principle, and throughout his life he sought to understand the central importance of individuality in modern life and deal with its consequences. Although students have long understood that Durkheim's attitudes toward individualism were complex, it seems to me that the depths of his ambivalence have not yet been plumbed, leaving both its personal sources and its effects on his development unclarified. Why was the tension between society and individuality so pronounced in Durkheim, and what effect did it have on his thinking?[1]

The question emerges first from the contrast between the two great books by which Durkheim's career is bounded: his first, *The Division of Labor in Society*, dating from 1893, and his last, *The Elementary Forms of Religious Life*, which appeared in 1912. The former sought to specify what was modern about modern social relations and about the morality they engendered and required. The movement from primitive social forms to modern ones was a process of growing differentiation; as societies at once expanded to cover more territory and produced denser concentrations of population, they presented individuals with the need to specialize their activities and to develop their separate personalities. Society changed from an agglomeration of interchangeable segments whose solidarity Durkheim dubbed "mechanical" to a body of highly differentiated but cooperating units whose integration could be called "organic" because its interdependent elements interacted like organs in the higher forms of

---

[1] One study devoted specifically to this issue is Anthony Giddens, "The Individual in the Writings of Emile Durkheim," *Archives Européenes de sociologie* (1971), 210-28. Although sensible and acute, Giddens's attempt to frame the question in terms of the opposition between moral and methodological individualism seems to me too abstract to give access to Durkheim's deeper tensions.

animal life. What held this form of society together was the division of labor itself, and its members actually contributed to social coherence when they furthered that division through individual self-development. Modern citizens were therefore at the opposite pole from primitive people, who would have been acting anti-socially if they had tried to work out individual styles of life or questioned shared ways of thinking.[2]

The Elementary Forms, by contrast, focused on the totemistic practices of various primitive peoples in order to show how religions grew out of group attempts to give symbolic representation to their common life. The sacred was the transfiguration of the social. Sacred symbols were associated with moments of special significance in the lives of social groups, moments when the power of common experience bubbled forth in what Durkheim called "collective effervescence." Although the book concentrated on undeveloped societies, Durkheim made it clear that its subject remained relevant in the twentieth century. All societies depended on such collective representations to make the whole a vital presence within individuals, and Durkheim looked to future moments of quasi-religious effervescence to cure the ills of egotism and anomie that modern individualism brought forth.[3]

Discussions of Durkheim's works have usually focused on their differing notions of how societies cohere; thus it has not often been noticed that the two books have quite opposite things to say about the nature of individuality, especially under modern conditions. One of the central assertions of *The Division of Labor* was that individual freedom expanded as social development progressed. Human history was a story of advancing liberty. "To be a person," Durkheim wrote, "is to be an autonomous source of action. Man acquires this quality only in so far as there is something in him which is his alone and which individualizes him, as he is something more than a simple incarnation of the generic type of his race and his group." The more specialized and complex persons who made up modern societies were "in part freed from collective action and hereditary influences which can only enforce themselves upon simple, general things."[4] The freedom to act independently was the freedom to be different from others.

These formulations contrasted sharply with those Durkheim would put forward in 1912. In *The Elementary Forms of Religious Life* his conception of personal autonomy no longer equated it with individuality. The human personality, Durkheim now explained, was a composite notion made up of an impersonal element and an individual one. The

[2] Emile Durkheim, *The Division of Labor in Society*, tr. George Simpson (New York and London, 1933). See esp. 396ff. for the argument about division of labor as itself the moral basis of modern social integration.

[3] Emile Durkheim, *The Elementary Forms of the Religious Life*, tr. Joseph Ward Swain (London, 1915).

[4] *The Division of Labor*, 403-4; see also 129-30.

individualizing factor was simply the body, which separated each person from every other. But the body was merely material and could not be the source of autonomy, rooted instead in the spiritual factor which religions had identified with the soul, and philosophers with the rational will. Durkheim believed he could specify the real source of this higher part of human nature: it was the part of individuals in which society established its presence. "There really is a part of ourselves which is not placed in immediate dependence upon the organic factor: this is all that which represents society in us." From society came the ideas, sentiments, and beliefs that were the basis of moral life and which had the power to dominate the individual. It followed that this higher part of the personality did not derive from what separated each individual from all the others, but from what all had in common. Identifying this moral and rational part of human beings with the presence society established within them provided a real understanding of the human potential for freedom, because "In a word, the only way we have of freeing ourselves from physical forces is to oppose them with collective forces."[5]

The Durkheim who earlier had identified the individual autonomy that developed through the division of labor with independence from both physical heredity and collective pressures, now reversed himself to make communal forces the source of liberation from the physicality with which he identified individuation. Thus he could conclude that "it is not at all true that we are more personal as we are more individualized." Personal autonomy was not a matter of individual differences but was "superimposed" on individuals from outside.[6]

When the later Durkheim justified individual liberties, it was in terms that conformed to these notions. The sacred character of modern morality in no way gave it immunity from criticism or the right to pursue heretics. Modern faith invited rational questioning, which could only strengthen it. But what justified such liberties was not any property of individuals as such, it was their ability to be bearers of what transcended them. "In the moral realm as in all other realms of nature, the reason of the *individual* is not privileged because it is the reason of the *individual*. . . . [It] is impersonal, human reason which is truly realized only in science. . . . What I oppose to the collectivity is the collectivity itself, but

---

[5] *The Elementary Forms*, 305-7. It should be noted that Durkheim had recognized an organic, bodily foundation to individuality even in *The Division of Labor*, rooted in "representations . . . sentiments and tendencies which relate to the organism and the state of the organism" (198). Here, however, this original individualism was conjoined with another kind, deriving from social differentiation, and which made individuals autonomous to the degree that they were able to develop their differences from others.

[6] *Elementary Forms*, 307. Elsewhere in his later writings he identified freedom with the acceptance of necessity: "To be autonomous means, for the human being, to understand the necessities he has to bow to and accept them with full knowledge of the facts." *Professional Ethics and Civic Morals*, tr. Cornelia Brookfield (London, 1957), 90-91.

AUTONOMY AND PERSONALITY IN DURKHEIM

more and better conscious of itself."[7] Such a view simply inverted Durkheim's earlier assertion that "We no longer think that the exclusive duty of man is to realize in himself the qualities of man in general."[8]

How did Durkheim move from the views about individuality and autonomy expressed in his early book to those we find at the end of his career? The change was part of the development that made him place

[7] Durkheim, *Sociology and Philosophy*, 95-96; quote in Dominick LaCapra, *Emile Durkheim, Sociologist and Philosopher* (Ithaca, 1972), 236.

[8] *The Division of Labor*, 43. In attempting to understand these changes, I shall be arguing against the current orthodoxy, according to which Durkheim's evolution is supposed to take place along a continuum that runs from greater determination to greater freedom. This view is shared by Talcott Parsons, *The Structure of Social Action* (1937; 2nd ed., Glencoe, Illinois, 1949), Chaps. 8-11; Steven Lukes, *Emile Durkheim, His Life and Work* (New York and London, 1972); Dominick LaCapra, *Emile Durkheim, Sociologist and Philosopher* (Ithaca, 1972); and Jeffrey Alexander, *Theoretical Logic in Sociology, II: The Antinomies of Classical Thought, Marx and Durkheim* (Berkeley and Los Angeles, 1982). Alexander argues that Durkheim was drawn, against his will but by the logic of his fundamental assumptions, to take a mechanistic and materialist position in *The Division of Labor*, which contrasted with the more voluntaristic conception of social order he had tried to work out in some earlier essays. Emphasizing the religious basis of social solidarity was his way of recognizing the deeper logical requirements of the more subjective and cooperative vision he was seeking. It may be correct that, in regard to a society conceived at a given historical moment, "if action is assumed . . . to be instrumentalizing and rational, collective structure will be described as external and material, for if motives are always calculating and efficient, action will be completely predictable on the basis of external pressure alone" (*Theoretical Logic in Sociology*, II, xx). But this leaves out the crucial point that *The Division of Labor* is based on the contrast of two historically separate forms of social life, and that the mechanical framework of causation necessary for change to occur in the first is itself broken up in the passage to the second. It may be illogical on some level to claim that the "mechanical" causation Durkheim identifies as the original source of social differentiation can give birth to the forms of individual autonomy he describes under conditions of organic solidarity, but this is what Durkheim does claim in his book.

Anthony Giddens is certainly right ("Durkheim's Political Sociology," *Sociological Review*, n.s. 19 [1971], 477-519) that many of Durkheim's later works continued to characterize modern society in terms of its sharp differentiation of roles and enhanced valuation of individual personality, and he is correct to insist that Durkheim remained in search of ways to resolve the moral crisis he believed modern society was experiencing. But those continuities must not be allowed to veil the point that the two books give very different answers to the central question about the character of individual autonomy.

Parsons seems to me closer to the mark when he argues (*The Structure of Social Action*, 321) that "In a sense, reversion to mechanical solidarity represents the authentic line of Durkheim's development." But because Parsons wants to present Durkheim as pushed by some kind of internal necessity toward Parsons's own understanding of how social action can be grasped, he insists that only the move away from the early "positivist" formulations allows Durkheim to envision society (correctly) as a body of internalized social norms. In fact, such a view of society was already Durkheim's in *The Division of Labor* (as Giddens points out, "The Individual," 223). It is through understanding the nature of Durkheim's inner tensions, rather than his relationship to "correct" social theory (Parsons and Alexander) or his relationship to an adequate comprehension of modern politics (Giddens) that the necessity for his changes can be grasped.

50   JERROLD SEIGEL

religious experience at the center of all social life, primitive and modern, and we can best follow it by looking at the chronology of his ideas about the role of religion in society. Most commentators have shared the view Talcott Parsons advanced in 1937, that Durkheim began to revise his original theoretical formulations toward the end of the 1890s; but more recent writers believe they can point to a fundamental break in his thinking earlier. On the specific question of religion Bernard Lacroix argues that the nearly simultaneous reading of Robertson Smith's studies of primitive religion and the death of Durkheim's father effected a sudden shift in his views during 1895.[9] There is no doubt that Robertson Smith's work was important in making Durkheim see that totemism—rather than animism or magic—was the original and "elementary" religious form. But the evolution of Durkheim's thinking on religion and its implications for his views about individuality can be understood only if we see that his ideas developed more gradually and that they did not achieve their full later form for several years after 1895. This is especially clear if we distinguish, as others have not, between his understanding of religion in general and his ideas about its particular role in modern life.

There seems never to have been a time when Durkheim did not appreciate the social importance of religion. In a review of 1887 he denied that religion was likely to give way to complete unbelief in the future, since it provided an essential link between individuals and the social whole; in *The Division of Labor* he insisted that punishment of crimes was not originally a matter between individuals, as the theorists of the vendetta claimed, but that it was "essentially religious in its origin." This in turn was a sign that penal law was rooted in social consciousness, because "religion is an essentially social phenomenon. Far from pursuing only personal ends, it exercises, at all times, a constraint upon the individual. . . . Offenses against the gods are offenses against society."[10] By 1897, in *Suicide*, Durkheim was able to go further, arguing that the power through which individuals came to conceive forces greater than themselves "is society, of which the gods were only the hypostatic form. Religion is in a word the system of symbols by means of which society becomes conscious of itself; it is the characteristic way of thinking of collective existence."[11]

---

[9] Lacroix, *Durkheim et le politique* (Montreal, 1981).

[10] *The Division of Labor*, 92-93.

[11] *Suicide, A Study in Sociology*, tr. John A. Spaulding and George Simpson, ed. G. Simpson (New York, 1951), 312. The often-cited letter to a Catholic philosophical journal Durkheim wrote in 1907 has been adduced in support of the notion that his views of religion changed suddenly in 1895, but although it refers to this moment (when he read Robertson Smith) as marking "a dividing line in the development of my thought," it does not suggest that a sudden reorientation took place. On the contrary, Durkheim's statement that "all my previous researches had to be taken up afresh in order to be made to harmonize with these new insights" suggests a much more gradual process. See the

What separated all these images of religion from Durkheim's later conceptions was his rejection of any attempt to make religion the basis of *modern* social solidarity. It could not be the remedy for rising suicide rates because it no longer subjected thought and conduct to "a powerful and scrupulous discipline. When religion is merely a symbolic idealism, a traditional philosophy, subject to discussion and more or less a stranger to our daily occupations, it can hardly have much influence upon us. . . . In a word, we are only preserved from egoistic suicide insofar as we are socialized; but religions can socialize us only in so far as they refuse us the right of free examination."[12] The socializing instruments that did not require this sacrifice and that were not foreign to everyday activities were the occupational groups whose organization and development Durkheim was then promoting.[13]

The moment at which Durkheim reversed himself, giving a religious form to the consciousness and practice that attached modern individuals to the social whole, came in 1898, only a year after the publication of *Suicide*. The occasion was Durkheim's entry into the lists as a defender of Alfred Dreyfus and the Third Republic against the clerical and conservative forces arrayed on the other side. Durkheim became one of the chief intellectual partisans of the Dreyfusards as well as an active organizer of meetings and petitions. This activity flowed naturally out of his earlier support for republican values and institutions, but in the course of it he had to answer the anti-Dreyfusard charge that the liberal intellectuals stood for a self-serving, egoistic, and potentially anarchic individualism. Replying in an essay called "Individualism and the Intellectuals," Durkheim gave a new coloration to the individualism he placed at the base of modern society. Agreeing that the utilitarian and critical individualism of eighteenth-century thinkers could have antisocial consequences, he insisted that the individualism he and his party represented was of a wholly different sort. As professed by Kant and Rousseau, it valued human beings not for what made them different from others but for their common participation in humanity. This form of individualism accepted as moral only those actions which "depend not on the particular circumstances in which I find myself, but on humanity in the abstract." From this point of view "duty consists in disregarding all that concerns us personally, all that derives from our empirical individuality, in order to seek out only that which our humanity requires and which we share with all our fellowmen." Such individualism had

---

passage translated in Lukes, 237. The point about the gradual development of Durkheim's religious views has also been made by Jean-Claude Filloux, *Durkheim et le socialisme* (Geneva, 1977), 90-92.

[12] *Ibid.*, 376.

[13] *Ibid.*, 378ff. Durkheim expressed similar views in his 1895-96 lectures on socialism. See *Le socialisme*, 263-65, 290-96. On Durkheim's changing views of occupational groups in creating modern solidarity, see below, note 17.

about it a religious aura, a sense of the sacred majesty "that churches of all times lend to their gods. . . . It is a religion in which man is at once the worshipper and the God." This religion of individualism was the rallying point for modern society and a source of unity, for "the only thing necessary for society to be coherent is that its members have their eyes fixed on the same goal, concur in the same faith."[14]

To be sure, Durkheim had never advocated a form of individualism he thought vulnerable to the charge of fomenting selfishness. But until now he had regarded the individualism fostered by modern society as too close to egotism to serve this unifying function. Just the previous year, in *Suicide*, he expressed his fear that modern individualism contributed to the high suicide rate by detaching individuals from social purposes. "Where the dignity of the person is the supreme end of conduct, where man is a God to mankind . . ., when morality consists primarily in giving one a very high idea of one's self, certain combinations of circumstances readily suffice to make man unable to perceive anything above himself. Individualism is of course not necessarily egoism, but it comes close to it; the one cannot be stimulated without the other being enlarged."[15]

As these words suggest, Durkheim had recognized that individualism was a kind of modern religion before 1898. In *The Division of Labor* he observed that "as all the other beliefs and all the other practices take on a character less and less religious, the individual becomes the object of a sort of religion. We erect a cult in behalf of personal dignity which, as every strong cult, already has its own superstitions." But because it rested on the ruins of so many earlier beliefs the cult of individualism could not provide the same unity earlier religions had. "It is still from society that it takes all its force, but it is not to society that it attaches us; it is to ourselves. Hence, it does not constitute a true social link." Here Durkheim denied that any form of religious consciousness could provide social integration in modern conditions because all religion tried to join individuals on the basis of "likeness" and was therefore fated to recede in importance along with the mechanical solidarity it represented. The argument was part of his insistence that the division of labor itself, rather than any earlier form of solidarity, provided integration for modern societies.[16]

---

[14] Durkheim, "Individualism and the Intellectuals," tr. Mark Traugott, in Durkheim, *On Morality and Society*, ed. with an intro. by Robert N. Bellah (Chicago and London, 1973), 45, 48. That Durkheim's thinking about religion was developing during this period is also shown by the article "De la définition des phenomènes religieux," published in the *Année sociologique* II (1898), 1-28. Here, however, Durkheim was concerned with the obligatory nature of religious phenomena in general, not with the special question of their place in contemporary life.

[15] *Suicide*, 363-64.

[16] *The Division of Labor*, 172-73.

In "Individualism and the Intellectuals," by contrast, a redefined individualism had become "the only system of beliefs which can ensure the moral unity of the country." What made this the case was the very progress of social differentiation which Durkheim had analyzed in his first book, and which sent people off to do their separate jobs and think their separate thoughts. The result now, however, was not that a non-religious form of solidarity was required but that "we make our way, little by little, toward a state, nearly achieved as of now, where the members of a single social group will have nothing in common among themselves except their humanity, except the constitutive attributes of the human person in general." The "communion of spirits" that culti-vating this idea made possible was one that allowed individual differ-entiation to proceed, but at the same time the religion of humanity took on features earlier limited to "mechanical" societies. "The religion of the individual cannot let itself be scoffed at without resistance, under penalty of undermining its authority. And since it is the only tie which binds us all to each other, such a weakness cannot exist without a beginning of social dissolution." The individualist, humanitarian faith was "the last reserve of collective ideas and feelings which is the very soul of the nation."[17]

[17] "Individualism and the Intellectuals," 53-54. Durkheim's changing views about religion in modern society have a parallel in an unrecognized shift in his attitude toward corporate groups, modernized versions of the medieval guilds, which he sponsored as responses to the moral needs of modern life. Durkheim argued for establishing such organizations in his lectures on socialism, in *Suicide*, and in the preface to the second edition of *The Division of Labor* in 1902. It has not been noticed, however, that the function Durkheim attributed to these groupings shifted radically after 1898. In the socialism lectures and in *Suicide*, they were to provide a basic moral integration for the whole of society, performing the crucial work of uniting individuals with people and values outside their own selves which religion could no longer accomplish. That they were not religious in nature was one quality that fitted them for this task under modern conditions (cf. *Suicide*, 383). After 1898, however, Durkheim no longer looked to the corporations for this basic work of social integration. This is clear in the lectures on *Professional Ethics and Civic Morals*, the published text of which contains, according to Marcel Mauss, the version of the course which Durkheim wrote between November, 1898, and June 1900 (see the Preface by H. N. Kubali to *Professional Ethics and Civic Morals*, tr. Cornelia Brookfield, [London, 1957], x). Here Durkheim recommends the professional associations, but not as a way to provide moral integration for society as a whole. Society's overall "civic morals" are assumed to be effective in regard to general questions of conduct, and rooted somewhere else. The problem to which the corporate groups are an answer is only the lack of an effective code of ethics for the world of business and commerce: "Such organization would do no more than introduce into the economic order the reforms already made in all other spheres of national life" (37). The same thing is true in the 1902 Preface to *The Division of Labor*, where the problem is not the lack of a code regulating society as a whole or the state, but that economic life, growing ever more specialized, "escapes their competence and their action" (5). In these later discussions Durkheim made a special point of emphasizing the religious status that corporations had possessed in Roman society, a point absent from his earlier discussions

The Dreyfus agitation was thus—in ways that have not quite been understood—a crucial moment in the evolution that led from *The Division of Labor* to *The Elementary Forms of Religious Life*. Yet the Durkheim of 1898 had not quite arrived at the redefinition of individualism, personality and autonomy we noted at the start. In particular, he was not yet ready to posit the fundamental dualism in human nature that would later come to be central in his thinking. In his lectures on *Moral Education* (given in 1902-3 and apparently delivered without alteration in 1906-7) Durkheim denied that the problem of how moral actions could be both obligatory and free could be solved by a Kantian-type dualism that separated people into a rational part that spontaneously embraced moral duty and a sensual part that resisted it. Morality had to exercise its domination over human nature as a whole, "our total and entire nature needs to be limited, contained, given boundaries, our reason just as well as our feelings." People had to become conscious of moral necessities and accept them with their whole being in order to be simultaneously ruled by morality and free moral agents. No part of human nature could escape "the world and its laws. We are an integral part of the world; it acts on us and penetrates us in all our parts."[18]

Such arguments would be cast aside by 1912, as Durkheim came to envision human beings as divided into warring segments: those purely individual states of consciousness, rooted in organic being, which "connect us only with ourselves," and those collective mental contents, the sources of rationality and freedom, which "transfer society into us."[19] Reserving moral value entirely to that part of human beings which was fully identified with social experience, he left the recalcitrant remainder in precisely the position Kant had assigned it. Doing so resolved a tension that was hard to miss in Durkheim's thinking during the years just following the Dreyfus agitation. In *Professional Ethics and Civic Morals*, for instance, Durkheim depicted human nature as cooperating with social discipline, seeking in it the fulfillment of deeply rooted "social sentiments" and "collective aspirations," even "the epitome and the governing condition of a whole life in common which individuals have no less at heart than their own lives."[20] Yet the same set of lectures contained the observation that "Since the precise function of this discipline is to confront the individual with aims that are not his own, that are beyond his grasp and exterior to him, the discipline seems to him—and in some ways is so in reality—as something exterior to himself and also domi-

---

of them, and that (*Professional Ethics*, 1898-1900) the "cult of the human person . . . has all that is required to take the place of the religious cults of former times" (69).

[18] Emile Durkheim, *L'éducation morale* (Paris, 1925), 126, 135-36.

[19] "The Dualism of Human Nature and its Social Conditions," in *On Morality and Society*, ed. Bellah, 162-63.

[20] *Professional Ethics*, 28-29.

nating him."[21] It is hard to see how Durkheim could have synthesized these two potentially contradictory images of human nature except by accepting a Kantian-type dualism of the sort he resisted in the years around 1900 but accepted in his religious sociology. Accepting it made the volte-face from the views expounded in *The Division of Labor* complete, eliminating the image of moderns as gaining both autonomy and socialization through differentiation in favor of a formula that set personal autonomy and individual differences against each other, and placed individuals in a state of perpetual inner warfare.

How can we understand this movement of Durkheim's thought? In what follows I will try to show that Durkheim's changing views about the relations between society and the individual reflected dilemmas he faced in his own life, and that our understanding of his thinking will lack an important dimension as long as we do not grasp its personal roots. Such a biographical analysis of Durkheim has never been carried out; a recent study of his politics approaches him through the strictly orthodox Freudian categories of oedipal conflict and castration anxiety, but Freudian orthodoxy can sometimes become a substitute for the kind of attention to a particular personality and its texture I will try to offer here. The materials for such a study are, to be sure, limited. Recently the number of personal letters available to scholars has grown, through the efforts of a group at the Maison des Sciences de l'Homme, but even these documents fail to tell us much about Durkheim's early experience and seem to offer only a restricted basis for careful examination of his personality. Nonetheless, the evidence can yield more than has so far been found in it, especially if some long-available public pronouncements are read more carefully.

The basic lines of Durkheim's biography are well-known. From a Jewish family in Lorraine, he was the descendent of a line of rabbis and was at first expected to enter the rabbinate himself. A crisis of faith in his teens helped orient him toward a secular vocation, making him the first member of his family to pursue a career outside the community of Jews. His path resembled that of many other Frenchmen in the nineteenth century, passing through the centralized educational system that had long drawn provincials to Paris and that was becoming a crucial instrument of centralization and secularization for the Third Republic. He attended a Parisian lycée in preparation for the Ecole Normale Supérieure, where his fellow-students included Henri Bergson and Jean Jaurès. After passing his *aggrégation* and teaching in lycées for two years, Durkheim received a fellowship to study contemporary social thought in Germany before accepting an appointment to teach at the University of Bordeaux, beginning in 1887. Both the trip to Germany and the post at Bordeaux owed

[21] *Ibid.*, 14-15.

much to the patronage of Louis Liard, the Republic's Director of Higher Education, who looked to Durkheim to develop the secular civic education a modern democratic regime needed to form its citizens.[22]

Two events at the end of the 1890s helped to define and to enhance Durkheim's position. One was the founding of the *Année Sociologique* in 1897; the periodical became the flagship of sociology as Durkheim and his associates conceived it. The second was the activity on behalf of Dreyfus and his defenders we have already noted. When in 1902 Durkheim moved to Paris to teach at the Sorbonne, he was already one of the Third Republic's chief intellectual figures, and he remained one until his death in 1917.

Such a career put considerable distance between Durkheim and his origins, but neither in his own eyes nor in his family's does he ever appear to have been a rebel against them. Nothing Durkheim or others said about his childhood suggests that his parents ever contested his career plans, or even reacted strongly against his abandonment of Jewish practice. Although too poor to provide much support for his studies in Paris, his family appears to have placed no barriers in his way; more likely they encouraged him. A good many sons of Jewish families from Alsace and Lorraine made careers in the French army or civil service during the late nineteenth century, so that aiming Durkheim at social ascension through education looks like his family's way of participating in a widespread communal strategy.[23] Bernard Lacroix's attempt to cast Durkheim in the orthodox mold of oedipus complex and castration anxiety fails to suggest the shape of his mental evolution.[24] He may have been subject to these Freudian ailments on some level, but the thread that joins his family experience to the larger issues of his career seems to follow a different pattern. His task was somehow to represent and fulfill the close-

---

[22] The best source of biographical information is still Lukes, but interesting additions have been made by Lacroix and Filloux. See Bernard Lacroix, "La Vocation originelle d'Emile Durkheim," *Revue française de sociologie*, 17 (1976) 213-45, and Jean-Claude Filloux, "Il ne faut pas oublier que je suis fils de rabbin," *ibid.*, 259-66, as well as the books of each, cited above. A particularly important source is in the letters published by Victor Kerady in Emile Durkheim, *Textes* (Paris, 1975), II. Durkheim's relations with his associates on the *Année sociologique* have been cast in quite a new light by Philippe Besnard, "La Formation de l'équipe de l'*Année sociologique*," *Revue française de sociologie*, 20 (1979), 7-31.

[23] On the careers of Jews from Alsace and Lorraine, see the literature cited by Lukes, 39n., although he does not draw quite this conclusion from it.

[24] Lacroix, *Durkheim et le politique*. We have dealt with Lacroix's claim that Durkheim's views on religion experienced a sudden reorientation at the time of his father's death early in 1896 above. It should be pointed out that the elder Durkheim had been ill for some time (a circumstance which limited but did not entirely eliminate, the family's aid to Emile in Paris); if subconscious fear and guilt about his own rebellion were at work to bring Durkheim back toward his own religious origins, they were probably operative before—as well as after—1896. In any case it was only in 1898 that Durkheim presented religion as able to create social solidarity under modern conditions.

AUTONOMY AND PERSONALITY IN DURKHEIM

knit vision of communal life, cemented by common belief, that his family embodied, by abandoning it to pursue the career his talents opened up to him.

Georges Davy, a friend who knew Durkheim's family, thought that the sociologist's personality always displayed traits absorbed from his parental milieu: respect for work and effort, together with a refusal to conceal it; a strong loyalty to group values and the moral codes that embodied them; and an austere and demanding sense of duty.[25] Davy commented that Durkheim's character made him a secularized version of the rabbi he did not become: he expounded his doctrine in an impassioned, prophetic, almost mystical tone; his voice was "animated by an ardent faith that, in this heir of the prophets, burned with the desire to forge and temper the conviction of his listeners." Official reports on his lectures at Bordeaux commented on the "ardent" and "militant" proselytism of his lectures, adding that "he understands his teaching as a kind of apostolate." He himself warned his audience not to forget that he was the son of a rabbi; and once, outside the cathedral of Notre Dame, he suggested to a friend that his lectures might better have been given from a bishop's chair than a professor's.[26]

Despite these links to his own milieu, Durkheim's move from provincial obscurity to the heights of the establishment made his life fit a pattern often decried by the Third Republic's enemies: he was, in Maurice Barrès's term, a *déraciné*, one of the uprooted. In his novel of 1897, *Les Déracinés*, Barrès described the experiences of provincials—his exemplars were also from Lorraine—torn out of their native soil by the pull of advancement in Paris and tempted by the example of those who were able to turn the Republic's humanitarian and moralistic slogans into veils for their own ambition. Durkheim seems nowhere to have mentioned Barrès, but the latter's ideas were widely known at the time, and we have seen how important it became for Durkheim, from 1898, to insist that the individualism he represented was not the egotism the republic's critics believed it to be.[27] Certainly he knew the effects of *déracinement*. The sometimes superficial literary culture that dominated the Ecole Normale made him feel isolated, and he seems to have longed to return to what

---

[25] For these continuities, see Georges Davy, "Allocution," in the centenary commemoration of Durkheim's birth, *Annales de l'Université de Paris*, XXX (1960), 16-22, esp. 17; also cited by Lukes, 40.

[26] Filloux, "Il ne faut pas oublier que je suis fils de rabbin," *art. cit.*, and LaCapra, 28-29. The official reports on Durkheim's teaching at Bordeaux are cited from Durkheim's dossier in the Archives Nationales by Terry Nichols Clark, *Prophets and Patrons: The French University and the Emergence of the Social Sciences* (Cambridge, Mass., 1975), 183n.

[27] "Individualism and the Intellectuals." Later, in 1902, Durkheim also made a point of insisting that the *Année Sociologique* was not an expression of his personal views but a collective, "impersonal" enterprise.

58   JERROLD SEIGEL

he called "the good simple people" of his province. One of his close friends, Victor Hommay, committed suicide soon after both left the Ecole Normale. Durkheim wrote an obituary notice for Hommay, noting that he had grown up "accustomed to the warmth of family life" and found the "feeling of emptiness and isolation familiar to all those who come to complete their studies in Paris" difficult to bear.[28] Later he echoed that description in regard to those who freed themselves from the religious faith that bound their communities together and who might become subject to what he called "egoistic suicide": "the more the family and community become foreign to the individual, so much the more does he become a mystery to himself, unable to escape the exasperating and agonizing question: to what purpose?"[29]

Signs that he felt both driven and anxious in regard to the career he pursued so intently are difficult to miss. A fellow-student at the Ecole Normale described him as becoming more eloquent when he was "more strained, more nervous."[30] In his last year there Durkheim experienced an illness which Davy thought might have been the result of worry and overwork and which seems to have impaired his performance on the *aggrégation*.[31] Anxiety that he was not profiting sufficiently from his German sojourn nearly made him cut the trip short; at Bordeaux the rector of the university reported that Durkheim endangered his health by overwork, and his nephew, who lived with him there, remembered that he would have conversation only at mealtimes.[32] Durkheim experienced states of "moral fatigue" or "malaise mentale" throughout his life, according to his letters; mentioned in 1898, in 1900 the condition was continuous for at least two years after his move to Paris. At that time he attributed his state above all to abandoning the "rigorous life" (*vie sévère*) he had led at Bordeaux, and which "bucked me up" (*me tenait*). He added later that "I have to fight more and more against my taste for soft dreaminess and absolute relaxation," a penchant he kept so well hidden that we are surprised to find him talking about it.[33] Davy

---

[28] Both these quotes are cited by Lukes, 42 and 48. For the text of the obituary notice Durkheim wrote for his friend Hommay, see *Textes*, II, esp. 422-24, where Durkheim makes clear that he and Hommay had shared the burden of cheering each other up in their dark moods, each recommending work to the other as a specific.

[29] *Suicide*, 212.

[30] Lukes, 47, citing G. Davy, "Emile Durkheim: l'homme," *Revue de metaphysique et de morale*, 26 (1919), 188-89; cf. also Davy, "L'oeuvre sociologique d'Emile Durkheim, quelques souvenirs," in *L'Europe*, 22 (1930), 281, where Davy described "the principal characteristic" of Durkheim's eloquence of "une véhémence contenue, une trépidation inhibée."

[31] Georges Davy, *L'Homme, le fait social et le fait politique* (Paris, 1973), 20.

[32] Lukes, 99-100.

[33] Durkheim, "Lettres à Celestin Bouglé," réunis par Philippe Besnard, *Revue française de sociologie*, 17 (1976), 177; *Textes*, II, 423, 455-56, 459-60.

described his personality as a "curious alliance between a mind so assured, so much master of its ways, and a sensibility so quivering."[34]

Readers of Durkheim's famous study of *Suicide* have not usually noticed the hints that some of its descriptions of individuals at sea in a world that offered them no firm natural attachments were meant on some level to apply to himself. He attributed the rise in modern suicide rates to the rapidity with which modern society was moving from mechanical to organic solidarity; such a fevered pace of change produced a "morbid . . . state of crisis and perturbation." That he himself would have been particularly subject to the effects of this quick change is clearly implied in his description of Jewish milieux like the one out of which he had come. Faced with hostility from outside, "each community became a small, compact and coherent society with a strong feeling of self-consciousness and unity. Everyone thought and lived alike; individual divergences were made almost impossible by the community of existence and the close and constant surveillance of all over each." Being suddenly cut lose from such tight communal values seemed to Durkheim the quintessential circumstance behind the modern propensity for self-annihilation; the relevance of such a diagnosis to himself seems clear in his description of "the scholar who dies from excessive devotion to study" as an "embryonic suicide."[35]

We can see the dominant themes of Durkheim's social theory arising out of these elements of personal experience by looking with some care at the earliest of his public pronouncements that has come down to us. In 1883 he gave a talk to the graduates of the *lycée* at Sens where he had been teaching. Its subject was the existence of "two quite different sorts of men: the great and the little." Were the deepest purposes of nature fulfilled only in the elite few who were able to penetrate to her secrets, as Ernst Renan believed, or ought the special abilities of the elite be sacrificed to the general well-being of all, as a more democratic view seemed to require? Durkheim rejected both these alternatives. The two groups were necessary to each other, the first providing the second with examples of a higher form of life and an impetus for improvement and the second offering the first the sympathy, admiration, and escape from isolation its members required. He therefore recommended that his listeners "maintain a vivid sense of your own dignity," while rejecting the temptation to "glory in being self-sufficient." Recognizing what they owed to others and to society, they would learn that "there is a certain way of being guided that takes nothing away from your independence."[36]

Helping individuals to arrive at just this understanding—that they

[34] Davy, *L'Homme, le fait social*, 20.

[35] For these passages see *Suicide*, 369, 160, 145-46.

[36] The "Discours au lycéens de Sens" was first published in *Cahiers internationaux de sociologie*, 43 (1967), 28-32; in English (tr. Mark Traugott) in Bellah, *op. cit.*, 25-33.

owed their autonomy to the guidance of society and the social differentiation it fostered—would be a central purpose of *The Division of Labor*. In the Sens talk Durkheim referred to the opposition between the great and the little as a division of labor: to place the few capable of understanding in contact with a truth that might be unpleasant to contemplate, leaving the great mass happy in their lesser awareness, would be "pushing the division of labor to its final limits." Here, in his earliest known mention of the theme he would make central to his first formal theory, social division took a form especially relevant to Durkheim's experience.

To mold a man of intelligence, it is necessary to "drain, distill, condense" millions of lesser intellects. Should a nation wish to enrich itself in great men, it gathers and concentrates all its vital forces in a single point of territory. Then, on the territory thus prepared, it soon sees divine intellects blossom. But the life which it has accumulated in a single spot and which a few individuals have absorbed has been withdrawn from the rest of the nation. This is why the body of the society languishes and soon dies of inanition.

This, we remember, was the Durkheim who had felt isolated and empty in Paris, objected to the superficial polish of the mostly literary culture in fashion there, and longed to go home to the "good simple people" of his province. Expressing a similar unease, the 1883 talk envisioned that homecoming in a different way, describing the thinker who would find sympathy and admiration in others by returning "to the masses which have remained behind him. . . . He therefore repays, a hundred times over, all that has been loaned him."[37]

Durkheim's graduation speech was thus about a division of labor which he had experienced himself, and toward which he felt deeply ambivalent. Such an observation might seem a mere play on words if the Sens talk had not also pointed to the basic distinction between two forms of society that would be developed in his first book. Contacts between the elite and the common people were important to society's well-being, Durkheim explained, because a people with no contrast between genius and the masses would be immobile, almost dead. "All the individuals which compose it resemble each other: they would therefore not even conceive of changing." This was Durkheim's first evocation of the social condition he would later label "mechanical solidarity"; here, however, it was not yet a historical stage but a situation that would follow on the absence of individual greatness. Only the appearance of a great man could reveal the possibility of a superior form of existence to stand as a goal for other people's efforts. "Humanity perceives that it has not arrived at the end of its course. Here is a superior form of existence which was unknown until now and which it will now work to realize." That France was not such a moribund society could be attributed to the existence of

[37] "Address to the *Lycéens* of Sens," 27, 30, 31.

AUTONOMY AND PERSONALITY IN DURKHEIM

people formed in its centralized educational institutions, and to the long history of government action that—even if for selfish aims—made this form of national development possible.[38]

It is surprising to find Durkheim attributing a society's escape from the immobility of individual sameness to the example provided by great men, since his later teaching would be founded precisely on the denial that individual differences could effect social change. That denial took shape in his mind gradually after 1883. In an essay of 1885 Durkheim still argued, against the sociologist Gumplowicz, that social change did not have to take its start from external causes, attributing it instead to the differences between individuals, just as he had in the Sens talk.

Doubtless if everything were absolutely homogeneous, all would remain immobile and at the same level. But as similar as the members of a society may be, there exist differences between them that provoke changes. This differentiation of individuals is even tending to increase more and more today, as Doctor Le Bon has demonstrated [in his researches on comparative brain sizes], and this it is that makes social transformations become more and more rapid.

If the individual was an effect of his social milieu and not a cause, "what is this milieu made of, if not of individuals?" Individuals were agents in the sense that every change in social relations had to pass through them and be effected by them.[39]

It is not possible to say exactly when Durkheim abandoned this view, but the reorientation appears to have been complete by the time he returned from Germany to begin teaching at Bordeaux. What seems clear is that the reasons for the change were neither empirical nor theoretical, but moral. Returning from Germany in 1887, he wrote in his official report that French students had to be taught the reality and advantages of sympathy and sociability by making them see that "our personality is made up in great part of loans, and that, separated from the physical and social milieu that contains him, man is only an abstraction."[40] These words echoed Durkheim's image of 1883, which depicted the beneficiaries of French centralized education repaying their debts to society by inspiring and fertilizing it. But Durkheim had now determined to make this lesson the central message of his teaching, creating a perspective from which attributing so much importance to individual differences created a moral danger not clearly visible before. In his preface to *The Division of Labor* Durkheim insisted that change was moral only when its purpose was to perfect an existing state of being: otherwise alterations

---

[38] *Ibid.*, 31-32.

[39] The passages are reprinted in *Textes*, I, 364 and 351-52.

[40] Quoted by Bernard Lacroix, "La Vocation originelle d'Emile Durkheim," *Revue française de sociologie*, 17 (1976), 299n. This notion of loan and repayment was a central theme of the social theory of solidarism to which Durkheim's views have often been linked.

might be proposed in the name of some merely imagined, hence potentially limitless ideal. Moral action had to recognize that the "highest perfection can be determined only in the function of the normal state, for that is the only model from which corrections can be made." Attempting to act otherwise—for instance in imitating individuals who diverged from the normal average for a given society—

would be to admit an ideal, coming from some unknown source, imposing itself from outside, a perfection whose value has not been brought forth from the nature of things and under the conditions they depend upon, but which brings forth the desire from I know not what transcendental and mystical virtue; a sentimental theory which has no part in scientific discussion. The only ideal that the human mind can propose is to improve what is. It is in reality alone that one can learn the improvements it demands.[41]

We shall return to Durkheim's fear that individuality unrestrained by the discipline of an existing social state contained an impetus toward the abolition of all limitations in a moment. Its presence here did not lead him to deny totally the importance of superior individuals; he noted in *The Rules Sociological Method* two years later that the great men whom societies persecuted as criminals often pointed the way to new forms of thought and action, giving the example of Socrates and arguing that modern intellectual freedom was prepared by those who violated the restrictions earlier societies placed on it. But he insisted in the next chapter that the different ways individuals found to react to their environments could not lead to social change unless wider, more powerful causes independent of individual will were also at work. (These were the sorts of factors—such as population growth and the pressure to create new forms of activity it brought—he labelled "mechanical" in *The Division of Labor*.) "In this way each individual has his own history, although the bases of physical and social organization remain the same for all." Individual differences would never again seem to Durkheim great enough to be the causes for a society moving to new ground or taking another direction.[42]

Before we can try to say what this series of developments tells us about the underlying impetus for Durkheim's overall evolution, we need to note that the labor division he analyzed in his first book still bore important features of the one he had described in the Sens talk, and that it was precisely these features that allowed him to point to its moral function in society. Affirming that it had such a function was crucially important to Durkheim, but it seemed questionable at first because the

[41] The original preface to *The Division of Labor* is printed as an appendix to the translation cited, 435.

[42] *Rules*, 102, 121-23. Here I cannot enter into the question of how Durkheim's changing views about the power of individual differences bore on his relations with his great rival Gabriel Tarde, whose sociology was based on the notion of imitation.

civilized forms of life labor division made possible were devoid of real moral value. Economic activities met needs, but not moral ones, since industry and commerce were often pursued for selfish reasons and had iniquitous results. The same was true of art, which was the sphere of absolute liberty and therefore "absolutely refractory to all that resembles an obligation." Science was moral sometimes, but only for the few who could pursue it to the end; for society as a whole science was a thing of indifference and "outside the moral sphere." Only if conceived differently—in terms of needs it created rather than ones it met—could the division of labor show its moral function. "Certain kinds of differences attract each other. They are those which, instead of opposing and excluding, complement each other." Such attractions led individuals to realize their own insufficiency and to seek what they lacked in other people. Seen from this point of view, the economic services rendered by dividing labor were "picayune compared to the moral effect it produces," namely creating a feeling of solidarity between persons.[43]

Durkheim gave only a few examples of these differences. Apart from the distinction of genders, which he mentioned a bit later on as the basis of conjugal society in the family, he specified only that "a theorist, a subtle and reasoning individual, often has a very special sympathy for practical men, with their quick sense and rapid intuitions; the timid for the firm and resolute, the weak for the strong and conversely." This contrast now suggested how societies could be established on a basis other than individual similarity; it allowed Durkheim to consider the division of labor not in the light of the "superficial" and "temporary" phenomenon of economic exchange but as the moral basis of the solidarity he called "organic." In this light the division of labor might "serve not only to raise societies to luxury, desirable perhaps, but superfluous; it would be a condition of their existence."[44]

Seeing that Durkheim's way of claiming a moral significance for the division of labor in his book brought him back to the form of division he had described in the Sens talk, suggests what had happened to his thinking between 1883 and 1893. As the idea of a general social division of labor absorbed the earlier contrast between an intellectual elite and ordinary people, the phenomenon of individual differences lost its ability to be a source of change; but by losing its causal significance it acquired a new, moral one, revealing the phenomenon of interdependence and mutual need that underlay modern organic solidarity. This pattern of reorientation in Durkheim's thinking had much in common with the one revealed by his later changes after the middle of the 1890s. Both times the efficacity of individual differences was reduced, as they lost first their ability to effect historical change and later their contribution to person-

[43] *The Division of Labor*, 56.
[44] *Ibid.*, 55, 63.

ality and autonomy. ("It is not at all true that we are more personal as we are more individualized.") And both times the moral importance of the division of labor was heightened, becoming first the basis for the organic and functional solidarity of *The Division of Labor*, and later the condition for the modernized religion, founded on the abstract humanity which was all that modern individuals had in common, propounded in "Individualism and the Intellectuals." Each one of Durkheim's successive positions tried to affirm the value of individual differences on one level while denying it on another, granting them new moral significance while successively reducing their causative power.

Behind this development lay the recurring discovery that each limited recognition Durkheim gave to individual independence and difference turned out to license an egotism he believed to be tamed before. He sought to attach individuals to society at every stage, but he kept finding that the ties he fashioned were not strong enough, and had to be re-made. In the Sens talk Durkheim tried to integrate the special individuals who formed the elite by showing that they could find fulfillment only through contributing to the lives of ordinary people; but by the time of *The Division of Labor* this attempt to further social well-being by encouraging deviations from the "normal average" failed to anchor individual imaginations sufficiently in reality and had to be replaced by a "mechanical" perspective that located change outside of individual control. Later, when the definition of personal autonomy in terms of individual differences advanced in that first book turned out to locate individualism too close to egotism, the tie was cut by separating autonomy from individualization and grounding it instead on disregard for "all that derives from our empirical individuality, in order to seek out only that which our humanity requires and which we share with all our fellowmen."

Durkheim's continuing need to respond to the discovery that forms of individualism he once took to be morally positive contained dangers he had not recognized calls to mind a theme he often sounded explicitly in his writings. (We have already seen it at work declaring immoral all attempts to deviate from "the normal average" in the Preface to *The Division of Labor*.) Human individuals needed to be restrained by some external force because their cravings and appetites were otherwise insatiable. Both in his lectures on socialism and in *Suicide* Durkheim contrasted human beings with animals, on the grounds that the latter ceased to desire things when their instinctual appetites were satisfied, whereas human reflection, ever alert, kept discovering new reasons for desiring more and more. The limitless quality of human desires in the absence of an outside force to regulate them was one reason men did away with themselves: "our capacity for feeling is an insatiable and bottomless abyss." There was nothing either in the human organism or human psychology that marked a limit to such needs. Without any external force to set limits, human appetites became "insatiable, that is, morbid."[45]

Durkheim made the point more colorfully in his lectures on *Moral Education*:

The ensemble of moral rules truly forms a sort of ideal barrier around every man, at the feet of which the flood of human passions comes to die, unable to go further. And by the fact that they are contained, it becomes possible to satisfy them. As soon as that barrier is weakened at any point, the human forces hitherto contained fall tumultuously through the open breach; but once unleashed they can no longer find any stopping point, they can only strain themselves unhappily in the pursuit of an end that always escapes them.[46]

In 1906 he argued against divorce by mutual consent on the ground that marriage gave people a moral strength they could not find within themselves. "By assigning a definite, determinate, and in principle invariable object to his desires, it prevents them from wearing themselves out in the pursuit of ends which are always new and always changing, which grow boring as soon as they are achieved and which leave only exhaustion and disenchantment in their wake." But marriage could perform this function only to the degree that the bonds it created were established by society and remained outside individual control. If conjugal ties could be broken at will, marriage would cease to have the same virtue.[47]

---

[45] Emile Durkheim, *Suicide*, 247. Durkheim, *Le socialisme. Sa définition—ses débuts*, ed. Marcel Mauss (Paris, 1928), 289.

[46] Emile Durkheim, *L'Éducation morale* (Paris, 1925) 47-48. Only by setting this pervasive and central theme aside is Jeffrey Alexander able to give his account of the later Durkheim as elaborating a conception of order that is voluntary and spontaneous because "adherence to order can become part of individual desire itself" (*op. cit.*, 227). Durkheim certainly claimed that society inserted itself into the interior of individuals, but the process was one that did violence to individual nature, however morally beneficial it might claim to be, and it led not to a harmonious unification of individual desires and social rules but to the conflicted dualism of human nature about which Durkheim often spoke. I think Alexander is in general right to assert that "individual volition will be eliminated if moral order is denied, for only if the individual is differentiated from his external environment—only if he can control internal resources—can he achieve a more volontary status" (145). But it does not follow from this that every social theory which gives a moral status to order creates harmony between social rules and individual wills, and Durkheim's later thinking is precisely an example of the opposite case. To claim that "for the implication—no matter how unintended—of coercion and power he substituted the notions of volontary adherence and sacred authority" seems to me at best one-sided.

[47] "Divorce by Mutual Consent," originally in *Revue Bleue*, 5 (1906), now in *Emile Durkheim on Institutional Analysis*, ed. and tr. Mark Traugott (Chicago and London, 1978), 240-52; quoted passage 247-48. Durkheim's worries about the boundlessness of individual subjective existence are best documented from the late 1890s to the end of his life (they are relatively absent in *The Division of Labor*), but he seems to have felt them much earlier. In the *lycée* at Sens his students were struck by his interest in the philosophy of Arthur Schopenhauer, giving him the nickname "Chopin" (originally "Schopen") in

JERROLD SEIGEL

Durkheim's anxious insistence that individuality was the source of a constant impulse to escape from discipline and that moral rules had therefore to be independent of individual wills, gave conscious expression to the pattern that underlay his theoretical history: each successive mode of limiting individuals turned out to provide an insufficient barrier to the breakthrough of egotism. The worry and its effects appeared again in the development that moved Durkheim from the position he took up while defending Dreyfus to the final formulations of the years around World War I. The faith he advocated in 1898 was a universal humanitarian one; to deify the human person expressed cosmopolitan values that transcended any particular nation.[48] Durkheim had often identified himself with cosmopolitanism before. But his enthusiasm for supra-national values cooled when it appeared that they might be invoked against the moral discipline provided by national life. This he found to be the case in socialist internationalism. Durkheim was always an opponent of revolution, and—unlike some of his younger followers—his sympathy for socialism as a program to extend social justice and put an end to economic immorality never brought him to accept party membership. In a public debate during 1907 he admitted that some of the criticisms socialists directed against existing states as creatures of wealth and privilege were well-founded, "collective personalities being no more perfect than individual personalities." Nonetheless there existed a "normal, indispensable *milieu* of human life," which was "la patrie *in abstracto*," the abstract or ideal nation, without which no human aspirations could be realized, and which had to be defended against all attacks.[49] The reasons for this position Durkheim spelled out more fully in his lectures on *Professional Ethics and Civic Morals*. Insisting as he often did that individuals required moral rules to restrain their otherwise dangerous longings and that such rules had to be embodied in social organizations beyond the reach of individual wills, Durkheim saw internationalism as a threat to this necessary discipline and restraint. "Some forms of belief in a world state, or world patriotism, do themselves get pretty close to an egotistic indi-

---

response to it. Schopenhauer was the thinker who warned individuals against the promptings of their personal desires; human wishes could never be satisfied because they were the expressions of a cosmic will that used individuals for its purposes, filling them with ever-renewed and insatiable longings, behind which the real goals of the cosmic force always remained hidden. For Durkheim and Schopenhauer, see André Lalande, "Allocution," in the centenary commemoration of Durkheim's birth, *Annales de l'Université de Paris*, XXX (1960), 25. Lalande's comments have been somewhat exaggerated by Jean-Claude Filloux, 14n. and 50. Filloux presents Schopenhauer only as the source of Durkheim's views about the infinity of desire, not about the need for individual renunciation.

[48] "Individualism and the Intellectuals," 51ff. See also *The Division of Labor*, 405, and for a later example, *The Elementary Forms*, 493.

[49] See the transcript of the session in Emile Durkheim, *La Science sociale et l'action*, ed. Jean-Claude Filloux (Paris, 1970), 292-300.

vidualism. Their effect is to disparage the existing moral law, rather than to create others of higher merit. It is for this reason that so many minds resist these tendencies, although realizing that they have something logical and inevitable."[50]

Durkheim's stance may have owed something to the sense that socialism was a threat to his own class position, but it seems to have been shaped at least as much by the deeper fear that political struggle would release something of that boundlessness of individual appetites—including his own—which he so anxiously invoked throughout his writing.[51] In any case his retreat from internationalism helped to shape his religious sociology. The religion Durkheim thought appropriate to modern society in 1898 took universal human individuality as its object of worship, but the elementary and universal religion he identified as necessary to all social forms by 1912 deified not universal humanity but the particular society out of which it arose. In "Individualism and the Intellectuals" the religion of individuality was required because the continuing progress of labor division, and the differentiations it brought left modern men with nothing in common save their humanity; the cult that recognized this promoted "the rights of the collectivity," but it did not begin with them. The religion of *The Elementary Forms*, by contrast, gave expression to society as a being which stood apart from individuals; the object of religious devotion no longer had anything to do with how far the division of labor had progressed. The distinction was one Durkheim could veil as long as he identified modern society's religious consciousness with the celebration of humanity itself; when the possibility arose that the idea of humanitarian universality could be used to question society's moral discipline, then even the rational individualism of Kant had to be restrained, lest its universalism weaken the real community of the nation. It was religion's task to strengthen this community, not undermine it.

In this way the last phase in Durkheim's evolution gave expression to the dynamism that had driven all the others. As each of his attempts to reconstitute community through individuality revealed a weakness that allowed the dreaded power of egotism to break through, Durkheim was led to discover new forms of social integration, more able to restrain individual desiring. The persisting power of these tensions suggests that

---

[50] *Professional Ethics and Civic Morals*, 74.

[51] One sign of this is Durkheim's repeated use of the metaphor of the "mold" (*moule*) that was to shape and limit subjective forces. In *The Division of Labor* (420) moral rules are "so many molds in which activities must run"; in *Rules* (70) social facts were "like molds into which we are forced to cast our actions"; in *Moral Education* too (23), moral rules were "molds, of fixed shape, into which we must cast our actions"; and in *The Elementary Forms* (488) the socially-derived categories of logic were "permanent molds for the mental life." It was on himself, at least as much as others, that Durkheim felt the need to impose these limits.

the community Durkheim sought to reconstitute on modern, "organic" lines always remained—somewhere in his unconscious mind—the premodern, "mechanical" one he had left behind in his family. His intellectual evolution followed the recurring pattern outlined above because theory was his mode of responding to the contradictory project that shaped his life: to affirm and exemplify the ancient communal values he associated with his family by abandoning it for the life of *déracinement* that made him representative of the different world and time outside. The perpetual inner struggle between individual self-affirmation and social obligation to which his sociology of religion finally testified was his own.

Comparable contradictions, expressed in comparable patterns of recurrence, can be found in the careers of other thinkers. The attempt to discover such patterns, linking thought to the personal and social experience out of which it arises, is—I would argue—the purpose of psychologically oriented biographical studies in intellectual history.[52] Nor do these patterns constitute merely the "background" of a theoretical system; the real import of a thinker's propositions often remains hidden without them. Recent debates about interpretation and method in the history of thought have made use of J. L. Austin's distinction between the locutionary and illocutionary characters of statements, between what a thinker says ("It's going to rain") and what his utterance is meant to do (make me take my umbrella). And, as John Dunn points out, "There are occasions on which one cannot know what a man means unless one knows what he is doing."[53] But it is too seldom recognized that "what a thinker is doing" is rooted just as commonly and powerfully in his own inner universe of needs and meanings as in his relations with the world outside.

I think the failure to acknowledge this has led to a long established misreading of Durkheim's evolution. Students and critics with diverse points of view all agree that Durkheim gave progressively greater autonomy to individuals as he passed from the "mechanical" and functionalist analysis of *The Division of Labor*, to the view of society as organized around a shared, internalized religious consciousness set out in *The Elementary Forms*. The reading of Durkheim offered here suggests that—within the limits he always sought to impose on individuals— precisely the opposite is the case. The "mechanical" explanations for

---

[52] Elsewhere I have tried to use a similar method to comprehend Marx's development: overcoming idealism in order to know the world in its real, material form was not the achievement of a single moment in Marx's history but the continuing—and never completed—project of his whole life. See Jerrold Seigel, *Marx's Fate: The Shape of a Life* (Princeton, 1978).

[53] John Dunn, "The Identify of the History of Ideas," in *Philosophy, Politics and Society*, 4th series, ed. Peter Laslett, W. G. Runciman, and Quentin Skinner (Oxford, 1972), 166.

social development and differentiation offered in *The Division of Labor* were necessary to Durkheim in order to maintain his claim for the moral status of the division of labor, first advanced in very different terms in 1883; his reason for giving up the notion that individual differences caused social change, advanced in the Sens talk, was to establish the moral coherence of modern social forms, so that he could discover a space for autonomous individual moral action within them. Those who find that the early Durkheim's functionalist view of historical development gave less room to such autonomy than his later, "idealist" writings have ignored the changes introduced in the latter, which made personal autonomy depend on the very internalization of a single communal consciousness that *The Division of Labor* reserved to "mechanical" solidarity. [54]

Durkheim is well known for his attempt to eliminate psychological explanations from sociology, a project he pursued so intently that even some of those who worked with him on the *Année Sociologique* found his views obsessive and extreme. [55] He wrote to Celestin Bouglé in 1897:

[54] See above, note 8. One further issue needs to be addressed in this regard: Durkheim's developing views about the social causation of ideas. It is true, as Steven Lukes has pointed out, that what Durkheim wrote in 1898 seemed to limit the dependence of thought on social structure he had posited earlier. Writing of "Individual Representations and Collective Representations," he said that ideas, most notably religious ones, grew up out of previously formulated representations, rejecting the attempt to trace every religious notion to "this or that character of the social structure." But for Durkheim this was not an argument in favor of the autonomy of ideas. On the contrary, the problem with the attempt to trace particular ideas to particular features of social life was that its failure to make a convincing case in regard to the smaller details of myths and religious practices cast doubt even on the connections that could be well and clearly established between the general shape of a given society's religion and the main features of its social life. "And this is what has often led people to deny the social character of religion: they have believed that it is formed in large part under the influence of extra-sociological causes because they have not seen an immediate tie between the majority of religious beliefs and the organization of societies." Just because religious ideas were sociologically determined at a remove did not mean they were less socially-based. This would be shown, Durkheim hoped, once progress had been made in determining "the laws of collective ideation." The whole essay was an argument for the need to conceive society as a being different from the individuals who made it up, and as therefore able to produce different sorts of ideas. See "Représentations individuelles et représentations collectives," *Revue de metaphysique et morale*, 6 (1898), 273-302 (quotes 299-301 and n.); cf. Lukes, 234. It seems likely that Durkheim at this point may have been moved by a desire to distinguish his kind of social determination from the materialism of the Marxists, as Jeffrey Alexander has observed (see his summary of his views in "Rethinking Durkheim's Intellectual Development I: On 'Marxism' and the Anxiety of Being Misunderstood," *International Sociology*, 1 [1986], 91-107; and, for a contemporary comment, Celestin Bouglé's note on Durkheim's article, in *Année Sociologique*, 2 [1898], 154-55); but distancing himself from Marxism did not lessen Durkheim's attachment to his own form of social determinism.

[55] See the very interesting article of Philippe Besnard, "La Formation de l'équipe de l'*Année sociologique*."

JERROLD SEIGEL

"It is necessary, don't you agree, to reject present critical practices, which consist too much in seeing the author beneath the work and to classify talents instead of taking note of the results and their importance. Where science is concerned, shouldn't the classification of men be a simple response to the classification of the things—views or documents—we owe to them?"[56] Yet he recognized the importance of personal, subjective factors in regard to others, noting the tendency of social theories to express "the preconceptions of the author," and the "numerous vestiges of that anthropocentric postulate which, here as elsewhere, blocks the path to research." Those words must apply to him too (as few would deny today), likewise the caution expressed in *The Division of Labor*, that "even the moralist who thinks he can, through thought, overcome the influence of transient ideas, cannot do so, for he is impregnated with them, and no matter what he does, he finds these precepts in the body of his deductions."[57] The personal and objective standards to which Durkheim aspired were ones that—on some level or other—no form of scholarship can reject. Yet we feel required to reply, failing to see the author beneath the work may make it difficult to recognize what joins that work together as a whole, thereby losing sight of meanings that the individual parts reveal only when the links between them are restored. Some may be uncomfortable with the idea that social theories are so deeply intertwined with the biography of their creators. But our knowledge of the human world must be able to survive the recognition of its personal sources, or it cannot survive at all.

Princeton University.

[56] Durkheim to Bouglé, June 20, 1897; in *Textes*, II, 398.
[57] *Rules*, 38, 46. *The Division of Labor*, 397.

IV

Durkheim's Individual in Society: A Sacred Marriage?

Mark S. Cladis

The characteristic *sacredness* with which the human being is now invested . . . is not inherent. Analyze man as he appears to empirical analysis and nothing will be found that suggests this *sanctity*; man is a temporal being. But . . . the human being is becoming the pivot of social consciousness among European peoples and has acquired an incomparable value. It is society that has *consecrated* him. Man has no innate right to this aura that surrounds and protects him against *sacrilegious trespass*. It is merely the way in which society thinks of him, the high esteem that it has of him at the moment, projected and objectified. Thus very far from there being the *antagonism* between the individual and society which is often claimed, moral individualism, the *cult* of the individual, is in fact the product of society itself. It is society that instituted it and made of man the *god* whose servant it is.[1]

This passage, from an essay written by Durkheim in 1906, is replete with religious rhetoric. Is it not odd for an atheist to employ such language? Another curiosity: Durkheim claims that there is no antagonism between the individual and society. Yet anyone familiar with Durkheim's thought knows that he often talks of conflict between the individual and society. Concerning our individual and social natures, for example, Durkheim writes that "there is a true antagonism between them. They mutually contradict and deny each other. We cannot pursue moral ends without causing a split within ourselves, without offending the instincts and the penchants that are the most deeply rooted in our bodies."[2]

What, then, in Durkheim's view, is the relation between the individual and society, and how are we to account for the pervasive religious vocabu-

---

[1] Durkheim, "The Determination of Moral Facts," tr. D. F. Pocock, *Sociology and Philosophy* (New York, 1974), 59 (my emphasis).

[2] Durkheim, "The Dualism of Human Nature," tr. Charles Blend, ed. Robert Bellah, *Emile Durkheim: On Morality and Society* (Chicago, 1973), 152.

lary marking Durkheim's later work? These two questions, I argue, are closely related, and by addressing the first I hope to shed light on the second. I show that for Durkheim religion underscores the fundamentally social nature of knowledge and, therefore, of human existence.

"Religion," writes Durkheim, "is *the way of thinking characteristic of collective existence.*" This remarkable claim needs to be understood in the context of Durkheim's social epistemology. Having read the available ethnographic material of his day, Durkheim was struck by the multiplicity of ways of organizing and categorizing the world. It was as if distinct societies and cultures lived each in their own world. Even the most seemingly simple human ability, such as seeing resemblances, could be manifested variously. In his and Mauss's neglected essay, "Primitive Classifications," they write that "what is conceived in one [society] as perfectly homogeneous is represented elsewhere as essentially heterogeneous."[3] And in the introduction to *The Elementary Forms of Religious Life* Durkheim writes, "the categories of human thought are never fixed in any one definite form; they are made, unmade and remade incessantly; they change with places and times."[4]

The two leading epistemological doctrines of his day, empiricism and a priorism, could not account for the variety of worlds Durkheim had encountered in ethnographies and historical studies. The empiricists, according to Durkheim, satisfy our sense that the individual's perception of the world is direct and unmediated; yet they deprive reason of its "universality," "necessity," and "authority." The upshot of this criticism is that the implicit individualism of empiricism cannot account for the *coherence* found within a given cultural world view. Tlingit Indians, for example, do not *choose* to see the similarity between a dog salmon and a dog (a similarity I have never been able to see). They just see it. Such vision carries a sense of necessity, authority, and—from a Tlingit's perspective—universality. If one doubts this, try protesting the similarity to a Tlingit.

The a priorists, on the other hand, recognize the universality, necessity and authority of human thought. The mind, transcending experience, imposes on it the universal and binding categories of reason. But of this the a priorists cannot give a satisfactory account. For as Durkheim writes, "it is no explanation to say that [the powers of reason] are inherent in the nature of the human intellect."[5] Kantians have shown why experience alone cannot produce human cognition. They are to be applauded for this. But "the real question," Durkheim claims, "is to know how it comes that

---

[3] Durkheim and Marcel Mauss, *Primitive Classifications*, tr. Rodney Nedham (Chicago, 1963), 86.

[4] *The Elementary Forms of the Religious Life*, tr. Joseph Ward Swain (New York, 1965), 28. From now on, *The Elementary Forms*.

[5] *Ibid.*, 27.

experience is not sufficient unto itself, but presupposes certain conditions which are exterior and prior to it." Moreover, a priorism cannot account for the *variety* of worlds. If the powers of the mind are innate, why can I not detect the similarity between a dog salmon and a dog?

Durkheim maintains that progress toward a solution is possible by studying religion, for we are thereby "given a means of renewing the problems which, up to the present, have only been discussed among philosophers."[6] Some might ask, What solution to an epistemological problem could possibly arise out of studying that messy cultural stuff, religion? Durkheim's response is that reason itself is shaped by unkempt socio-historical institutions, and religion has been an especially formative one. What might seem to be basic, universal categories of human thought such as time, space, class, number, cause, substance, and personality are in fact culturally specific categories, whose medium is language. Even the distinction between right and left or the law of non-contradiction, according to Durkheim, is a social-linguistic artifact and is "far from being inherent in the nature of man in general."[7]

How does Durkheim account for a variety of coherent worlds? What is his solution? In good pragmatist style, he holds on to what is valuable in both the empiricist and the Kantian positions. He notes that "if this debate seems to be eternal, it is because the arguments given are really about equivalent."[8] He manages to salvage the intuitions on both sides and to minimize their opposition by bringing to this epistemological debate insight from his religious investigations. The chief insight is this: if "the social origin of the categories is admitted, a new attitude becomes possible, which will enable us to escape both of the opposed difficulties."[9] His solution, then, is to socialize the idealists and the empiricists. Yes, human reason operates with categories, but these categories are not inherent in humans but are created in the particular activities of various peoples. And yes, the individual does "directly" perceive the world, but that world is and always has been a social world, or as Durkheim puts it, "the world is inside of society."[10]

Now, lest Durkheim sound like a radical relativist, which he is not, I need to add that even while Durkheim unabashedly fleshes out the social nature of knowledge, he insists that we, as individuals, do not *make* our world: "We speak a language that we did not make; we use instruments that we did not invent; we invoke rights that we did not found; a treasury of knowledge is transmitted to each generation that it did not gather itself, etc. It is to society that we owe these varied benefits, and if we do not

[6] *Ibid.*, 21.
[7] *Ibid.*, 25.
[8] *Ibid.*, 28.
[9] *Ibid.*
[10] *Ibid.*, 490.

ordinarily see the source from which we get them, we at least know that they are not our own work."[11] Investigating distant times and places, Durkheim tells us of diverse worlds, wrestles with the epistemological problems posed by them, and declares that the world is not a result of "our own work" but of evolving traditions, categories, and institutions.

When Durkheim claims that the world is not a result of our making, the "our" refers to you and to me and to any other individual or group today. This is not to say that Durkheim denies human creativity or that he thinks novelty impossible. Durkheim the historian is quite aware of the vital role played by imagination and ingenuity. He rejects fatalism (the idea that individuals are "radically situated") as an inaccurate description of and normative prescription for modern individuals. Durkheim does, however, recognize and feature the fact that people work with inherited materials. This social inheritance is all-important for him, because it signifies an intimate relation between individuals and their sociolinguistic communities. Having said this, consider how Durkheim accounts for the objectivity we sense in the world.

Durkheim begins his lectures on pragmatism by citing "the pragmatists' " (primarily James's and Dewey's) criticism of rationalism and empiricism. According to these two philosophical theories, "reason is thought of as existing outside of us . . . and truth is a given, either in the sensory world (empiricism) or in an intelligible world, in absolute thought or Reason (rationalism)."[12] Yet the pragmatists, according to Durkheim, insist that "*we* make reality": "1) truth is human; 2) it is varied and variable; and 3) it cannot be a copy of a given reality."[13] Durkheim shares the pragmatists' sentiment that "truth is not a ready-made system: it is formed, de-formed and re-formed in a thousand ways; it varies and evolves like all things human."[14] And he sees an affinity between the pragmatists' project and sociologists':

Herein lies the interest of the pragmatist enterprise: we can see it as an effort to understand truth and reason themselves, to restore to them their human interest, to make of them human things that derive from temporal causes and give rise to temporal consequences. . . . It is here that we can establish a parallel between pragmatism and sociology. By applying the *historical* point of view to the order of things human, sociology is led to set itself the same problem. Man is a product of history: there is nothing in him that is either given or defined in advance. . . . Consequently, if truth is human, it too is a human product. Sociology applies the same conception to reason. All that constitutes reason, its principles and categories, has been made in the course of history.[15]

[11] *Ibid.*, 242-43.
[12] Durkheim, *Pragmatism and Sociology*, tr. J. C. Whitehouse, ed. John B. Allcock (Cambridge, 1983), 12.
[13] *Ibid.*, 85 and 37.
[14] *Ibid.*, 24.
[15] *Ibid.*, 67.

Durkheim's reference to history at this point is revealing, and it becomes the basis of his criticism of pragmatism. The pragmatists, Durkheim claims, say that we make reality, and for them "the 'we' means the individual." This individualism Durkheim finds disturbing, for it fails to address his problem of how coherent, shared worlds are established: "individuals are different beings who cannot all make the world in the same way; and the pragmatists have had great difficulty in solving the problem of knowing how several different minds can know the same world at once."[16] We do not have to accept Durkheim's assessment of the pragmatists in order to appreciate his solution to the problem of how to reconcile a social epistemology to some philosophical and every day intuitions about coherence, truth, and objectivity: "If one admits that representation is a *collective* achievement, it recovers a unity which pragmatism denies to it. This is what explains the impression of resistance, the sense of something greater than the individual, which we experience in the presence of truth, and which provides the indispensable basis of objectivity."[17]

Collective representations—patterned ways of viewing, describing, and explaining the world—guarantee a significant amount of social agreement that furnishes coherence and constitutes objectivity. What has Durkheim done? He has accounted for—and thereby attempted to safeguard—the *impersonal* character of reason, objectivity, and truth by disclosing their settled, socio-historical grounding. In notable ways, then, we do *find* a world already set up by language, institutions, and beliefs. These are not made or chosen by the individual, these are "the given," that is, the stuff of history—institutions, language, and beliefs—into which individuals are "thrown" (to use Heidegger's metaphor). The given is not a set of determinate facts to be interpreted in one absolute way. Our interpretations of the world (whether they concern *A Tale of Two Cities* or the Thirty Years War or T-cell lymphoma) are indeed guided by objectivity. But that objectivity (whether it pertains to literary theory or history or science) is itself constituted by the stuff of history, whose nature could be—and has been—described as interpretations of interpretations.

Durkheim, if in one of his positivistic moods, will talk as if institutions, language, and beliefs are determinate—even if social—facts. But at his best he recognizes degrees of indeterminacy *and* steadiness of a variety of social facts. The constraints of history (and history includes our thinking and speaking equipment) carry with them the weight of objectivity, the guiding force of reason, and the sacrosanct character of truth. If these qualities or virtues are esteemed, one reason is we know that they are found in the world and not arbitrarily made.

Durkheim is quite concerned with the notion of truth and with saving

[16] *Ibid.*, 85.
[17] *Ibid.*, 85.

its reputation. Why? Truth plays an important social role. It pertains to what I am calling inescapable aspects of human existence—our socio-historical inheritance. Durkheim notes that "it is one thing to cast doubt on the correspondence between symbols and reality; but it is quite another to reject the thing symbolized along with the symbol. This pressure that truth is seen as exercising on minds is itself a symbol that must be interpreted, even if we refuse to make of truth something absolute and extra-human."[18] It is the social, historical aspects of truth—of those things called true—that account for its "pressure" on us.

In an age marked by increased individualism and the eclipse of many traditional communities and social practices, Durkheim fears that the benefits of liberalism could be outweighed by its deleterious byproducts. He reminds us that when we inhabit the modern world (or worlds) we still receive many shared truths and goals. We live in a public world, a world not simply of our own, private making. Durkheim attempts to expose and strengthen those ties that join us to each other and to a common past and shared future. The rights and dignity of the individual are perhaps the most salient features of our solidarity in modern demo-cratic nations. Yet these are accompanied by various social commitments and obligations, and they need to be situated in a shared, moral context (call it democratic republicanism), lest they promote egoism instead of what Durkheim calls moral individualism, a common set of liberal disposi-tions and virtues. Pointing to socially shared representations and histori-cally situated institutions is, for Durkheim, a step toward a happier liberal society.

Durkheim's epistemology, then, underscores the social nature of all knowledge: aesthetic, moral, and scientific. He articulates the social nature of knowledge in the idiom of collective representations, concepts, and ideals. I want to focus on his use of the term "ideal."

Think of ideals as sacred collective representations that promote moral unity and well-being. They are cherished social values and beliefs and goals—the soul of a society—and as such they combat egoism, "forcing the individual to rise above himself."[19] Modern, industrial society could not flourish with a sophisticated division of labor but without public ideals. More is required than bureaucratic efficiency and experts in public policy. Moreover, societies cannot be understood adequately without ref-erence to their ideals: "To see a society only as an organized body of vital functions is to diminish it, for this body has a soul which is the composition of collective ideals."[20] In short "the principle social phenomena, religion,

[18] *Ibid.*, 68.

[19] Durkheim, "Value Judgments and Judgments of Reality," *Sociology and Philosophy*, 92.

[20] *Ibid.*, 93.

morality, law, economics and aesthetics, are nothing more than systems of values and hence of ideals."[21] Sociology, then, studies not only morphological facts but also social ideals.[22]

Ideals, on Durkheim's account, are not static, universal principles discovered in scholars' studies. On the contrary, ideals are "essentially dynamic, for behind them are the powerful forces of the collective."[23] Nor, for that matter, are ideals idealistic goals or utopian scenarios. They are not, as Durkheim says, "cloud cuckoo land."[24] When Martin Luther King, Jr., said "I have a dream," he was appealing to concrete, operative ideals embedded in portions of North American society. When Durkheim said "to love one's society is to love this ideal [moral individualism]," he too was appealing to palpable ideals.[25]

Has Durkheim gone from a materialist to an idealist? I think not. First, the question implies that at some point Durkheim *was* a materialist. Durkheim, however, never attempted systematically to render a culture's values, beliefs, and goals as an expression of its material substratum. Second, idealism is not an apt description of his mature position. It is true that he disassociates himself from materialism. In the *Elementary Forms*, for example, he notes that he wants to avoid "a simple restatement of historical materialism. . . . In showing that religion is something essentially social, [I] do not mean to say that it confines itself to translating into another language the material forms of society and its immediate vital necessities."[26] Yet on the same page he writes, "we take it as self-evident that social life depends upon its material foundation and bears its mark."

We would do better not to tag Durkheim as an idealist. When he writes "the ideal is not 'cloud cuckoo land'; it is *of* and *in* nature," he is distinguishing ideals from both noumenal principles and academic conjecture. Ideals are not the result of private speculation. More likely, such speculation springs from historically situated ideals. Think of ideals not as innate features of the Mind or of Nature, for they are, as Durkheim puts it, subject to time and space. They are *natural* but only in so far as they are produced by social, historical forces, and these forces, according to Durkheim, are basic to human existence. Here then, in good pragmatist form, Durkheim challenges not only the materialist-idealist dualism but also the nature-culture dualism. Social and cultural things—language, texts, customs, beliefs, means of production, in a phrase, any and all social institutions—are in principle no more or less mysterious than gravity or

---

[21] *Ibid.*, 96.
[22] See *ibid.*, 96.
[23] *Ibid.*, 93.
[24] *Ibid.*, 94.
[25] Durkheim, "The Determination of Moral Facts, " 59.
[26] Durkheim, *The Elementary Forms*, 471.

gravy. Social ideals, Durkheim writes, are "subject to examination like the rest of the . . . physical universe." They are real. They are tangible.

Durkheim's social epistemology, which sought to do away with the empiricism/a priorism dichotomy, is a middle way, or put better, a different way. It portrays an inextricable, transactional relation between the material world and the conceptual world. To speak of two worlds, in fact, is misleading. Durkheim materializes ideals and idealizes matter—and historicizes both. In the process, he attempts to overcome a set of tyrannous dualisms—empiricism and a priorism, materialism and idealism, nature and culture. The resulting position, I believe, appropriately describes the materiality of beliefs, values, and customs, as well as the sociality of knowledge, facts, and logic.

Showing how Durkheim's social epistemology springs from his religious investigations will put us in a good position to appreciate his thought on individuals in society. From the start Durkheim was interested in religion, but he claims that he did not recognize its singular importance, especially for modern societies, until the mid 1890s. Contrary to many of his commentators, I believe Durkheim's new position on religion developed not so much out of a new conception of religion, but from a fresh understanding of the nature of modern societies.

Durkheim's earliest essay on religion defines it as a set of collective representations providing a socially indispensable common faith.[27] In *The Division of Labor* he dismisses the accepted definition of religion as beliefs about "a being or beings whose nature [man] regards as superior to his own."[28] The definition, he claims, is inadequate, for religion pertains not only to relationships with the supernatural but to a variety of "legal, moral and economic relationships." Religion's characteristic feature is not a unique set of beliefs, in this case beliefs about the supernatural. Religion's peculiarity, rather, pertains to how its beliefs and practices are held, and how they operate. Collective convictions pertaining to any number of beliefs and practices when "shared by a single community of people inevitably assume a religious character."[29] Religion, then, is the central or guiding set of beliefs and practices of a community. This early account of religion basically corresponds to Durkheim's later thought. However, according to the Durkheim of *The Division of Labor*, religion's days are numbered:

If there is one truth that history has incontrovertibly settled, it is that religion extends over an ever diminishing area of social life. Originally, it extended to everything; everything social was religious—the two words were synonymous.

[27] See Durkheim, "Les Etudes de science sociale," *Revue philosophique*, 22 (1886), 68-69.
[28] *The Division of Labor*, tr. W. D. Halls (New York, 1984), 118.
[29] *Ibid.*, 119.

EMILE DURKHEIM

Then gradually political, economic and scientific functions broke free from the religious functions.... In short ... the sphere of religion ... is continually diminishing. This regression ... is bound up with the basic conditions for the development of societies and thus demonstrates that there is a constantly decreasing number of beliefs and collective sentiments that are both sufficiently collective and strong enough to assume a religious character.[30]

Within a few years of writing this, however, Durkheim reverses his position. He now claims that religion permeates modern societies. Although its beliefs and practices have changed, at least in Europe, its basic form has not: robust, collective beliefs and practices are still prevalent. The political, economic, and even scientific realms are infused with the religious. Individual rights, notions of economic fair play, and the spirit of free inquiry, for example, are fraught with the sacred.

Durkheim's reversal springs not from a radically new understanding of religion per se but from a new understanding of modern society. This novel approach is exhibited, for instance, in 1899, when he notes that "between science and religious faith there are intermediate beliefs; these are common beliefs of all kinds, which are relevant to objects that are secular in appearance, such as the flag, one's country, some form of political organization, some hero, or some historical event, etc."[31] Many secular beliefs, he claims, are "indistinguishable from religious beliefs proper." Indistinguishable because modern France, like traditional societies, has a common (even if "secular") faith: "The mother country, the French Revolution, Joan of Arc, etc., are for us sacred things which we do not permit to be touched. Public opinion does not willingly permit one to contest the moral superiority of democracy, the reality of progress, and the ideal of equality...."[32]

I am not suggesting that Durkheim's thinking on religion remains entirely unchanged from 1899 until his death in 1917. In the 1899 article on religion, for example, Durkheim attempts to distinguish religion-as-traditionally-understood from other social phenomena by placing practices—rituals—within the special domain of religion. As he later broadens his notion of ritual to include more and more "secular" activities, he abandons this attempt. But I am suggesting that, above all, Durkheim's notion of modern society, rather than his notion of religion, undergoes radical revision. He begins to perceive continuity between modern and traditional societies. A common faith is no longer a unique attribute of traditional societies. Modern societies, too, are in need of, and are developing, their own common faiths. The relevant distinction between the two types of society now rests on the different contents of their faiths.

[30] *Ibid.*, 119-20.
[31] Durkheim, "De la Définition des phénomènes religieux," *L'Année sociologique*, 2 (1899), 20.
[32] *Ibid.*

80   MARK S. CLADIS

Democracy as opposed to collectivism, for example, or free inquiry as opposed to blind faith, distinguish the two. Here we can applaud Durkheim's description of the continuity between traditional and modern societies, without having to accept his description of the discontinuities. (Technological differences, I believe, are the only contrasts that can be stated in general.)

Durkheim's new position is not perhaps surprising, given all we know about his earlier work. What is surprising is that in *The Division of Labor* he seems uncertain and unconcerned about whether modern societies have a common faith, and he asserts that "the sphere of religion . . . is continually diminishing." Be that as it may, Durkheim's involvement in the Dreyfus Affair in the late 1890s surely inspires him to pursue a course different from that found in *The Division of Labor*. During the Dreyfus Affair, Durkheim believed that he was witnessing a modern society stirred and social ideals renewed as moral community was forged. He discerned a common (liberal) faith that was reaffirmed and extended by the Dreyfus Affair. This faith—call it moral individualism—supported the rights and dignity of the individual *and* the idea that one does not live for oneself alone but for one's fellows. Durkheim thus found a powerful vocabulary for articulating the social dimensions of modern democratic society. It was the vocabulary of religion.

We are now in a position to grasp the connection between his mature understanding of religion and his social epistemology. In the *Elementary Forms* Durkheim defines religion as "a unified system of beliefs and practices relative to sacred things, that is to say, things set apart and forbidden— beliefs and practices which unite into one single moral community."[33]

Durkheim maintains that in traditional societies many collective representations were religious, because they pertained to the entire society. For example, imagine that the East side of a river is sacred, the home of a Dog Salmon totem, while the West side is profane. On the West side lies the village where profane activities such as hunting, eating, defecating, and sex take place. On the East side occur the sacred feasts and rituals. Now, representations beget representations—sacred representations producing more sacred ones, and profane ones as well. From the religious distinction between the sacred and profane, for instance, is derived the scientific notion of the law of non-contradiction. Together, sacred and mundane collective representations constitute the socio-linguistic world. Knowledge, then, is a set of varied public institutions and representations—some sacred, some not.

Durkheim's genealogy of sacred and profane representations strikes one as mythical. His work is more interesting and helpful when it investigates the character, not the origin, of religion. He is at his best when he

[33] *Elementary Forms*, 62.

explores the ways religion can be described as collective representations that inform a community's moral vision. What is religion? What is the sacred? It is those authoritative (that is, socially entrenched) concepts and ideals that shape a common perception of, and therefore life in, the moral universe.

On this account, religion is pervasive in modern, secular society. We find it wherever public, normative concepts are employed. The upshot of this—morally and epistemologically—is that human life is, in a significant sense, life together. There can be no *radically* private human existence. To exist in a world is to understand that world, and understanding is comprised of public representations. "I think, therefore I am" is satisfactory if we take the "I think" as a social involvement. "I partake, and therefore I am" is probably more descriptive of human existence than is Descartes's formula. It is more descriptive, and, in Durkheim's view, it is also a normative position insofar as it challenges some atomistic assumptions found in classical liberalism.

This depiction of religion—as sacred, social institutions fashioning our lives—enables Durkheim to articulate the public, fixed nature of moral knowledge and practices. Fixed, but not beyond alteration. Religion, as Durkheim understands it, emerges variously out of the play of countless factors, some material, some not. The both fluid and fixed nature of religious representations is, of course, true of all representations, including scientific and prudential ones. What is distinctive of collective religious representations? Theirs is the domain of guiding ideals and values that promote moral unity. Every society, then, to the extent that it exhibits moral unity, can be said to possess a common faith, that is, to be religious.

This common faith does not require fatalistic uniformity. It can permit conflict. It can permit pluralism. These considerations depend on the content of the faith. In liberal democratic societies, a salient feature of a common faith could be a set of dispositions and procedures for resolving or living with a variety of conflicts. And a pluralistic society could be said to have a common faith that obtains in some social spheres, and a variety of faiths in others. A common faith, then, on Durkheim's account, is not incompatible with pluralism.

I see no reason to complain that, given Durkheim's new position, any set of shared ideals and practices promoting moral unity could be labeled "religious." Many in the field of religious studies, having grown wary of essentialistic definitions of religion, are willing to adopt pragmatically a variety of definitions for a variety of occasions. I find Durkheim's definition useful for articulating the social nature of ideals and practices that sustain and extend democratic institutions.

I now want to return to the question posed at the beginning of this essay: what can be said about the connection between Durkheim's religious investigations and his account of individuals in society?

82 MARK S. CLADIS

To begin with, Durkheim describes the rights and dignity of the individual as sacred ideals. Elsewhere I have outlined in detail Durkheim's notion of moral individualism—the cult of the individual.[34] Here it is enough to indicate that moral individualism pervades his later work. In "The Determination of Moral Facts" (1906), for example, Durkheim writes, "Moral life begins with membership of a group. . . . In so far as [an individual] is a member of the collectivity . . . he tends to take on some of its dignity and he becomes an object of our affection and interest. To be a member of the society is . . . to be bound to the social ideal. . . . It is then natural that each individual participates to some extent in the religious aspect which this ideal inspires."[35]

Léon Brunschvicg, the French neo-Kantian philospher, objects to Durkheim's insistence that individual liberties are *social* institutions. He suggests that the progress of civilization be seen as allowing "individual freedom more and more the exercise of its right of resumption against the material structure of society." Durkheim replies,

It is not a matter of resumption but of an accession made by the grace of society. These rights and liberties are not things inherent in man as such. If you analyze man's constitution you will find no trace of this sacredness with which he is invested and which confers upon him these rights. This character has been added to him by society. Society has consecrated the individual and made him pre-eminently worthy of respect. His progressive emancipation does not imply a weakening but a transformation of the social bonds.[36]

This is not to say that any transformation of the social bonds be construed as emancipating. What does count as emancipation, by Durkheim's lights? A whole host of things, but in the context of his conversation with Brunschvicg, Durkheim says, "[F]reedom consists in deliverance from blind, unthinking physical forces; this [the individual] achieves by opposing against them the great and intelligent force which is society. By putting himself under the wing of society, he makes himself also, to a certain extent, dependent upon it. But this is a liberating dependence. There is no paradox here." Storms and plagues, no doubt, count as "blind, unthinking physical forces." Yet so do racism, economic injustice, and child abuse. Durkheim's account requires a bit of unpacking. Freedom is frequently taken to refer to the absence of constraints. Durkheim, however, never accepts this. As a social theorist Durkheim knows that to be humanly alive is to move felicitously within the many contours of social constraints, that is, social beliefs, practices, and institutions. "Kant," Durkheim writes, "declares that the human person should be autonomous. But an absolute

[34] See chapter 1 of my *A Communitarian Defense of Liberalism: Emile Durkheim and Contemporary Social Theory* (Stanford, 1992).

[35] "The Determination of Moral Facts," 52-53.

[36] Durkheim, "Replies to Objections," *Sociology and Philosophy*, 72.

autonomy is impossible. The person forms part of the physical and social milieu; the person is bound up with it and can be only relatively autonomous."[37]

Durkheim's concept of situated freedom has, unfortunately, been interpreted by many as a type of social coercion hostile to any form of individualism and free will. This I say is unfortunate because of the central roles freedom and "individualism" play in Durkheim's work. For Durkheim freedom is not the absence of social constraints but living among just constraints (which involves scrutinizing them) and desiring them. On the other hand coercion in the context of modern democratic societies has to do with immoral threats to an individual's dignity, liberty and rights. Such threats fall under the category of "blind, unthinking physical forces," for they are, by Durkheim's logic, as material as any hurricane or disease. Social injustices, then—including intentional ones—are blind, unthinking forces.

Durkheim's understanding of freedom as a moral positioning in society—not outside it—is but another way of affirming that there is no *fundamental* antinomy between democratic societies and the individual. His religious investigations assist him here. The moral authority that "religious" ideals possess and the moral unity that "religious" practices secure enable Durkheim to give a radically social description of the individual's existence. Sacred ideals draw the individual into the collective, facilitating a moral existence. Far from there being an essential cleft between society and the individual, Durkheim claims in *The Elementary Forms* that "the individual gets from society the best part of himself, all that gives him a distinct character and a special place among other beings, his intellectual and moral culture."[38] Again, this is not to say that the individual's social nature precludes all conflict between the individual and various social spheres. The point is that there is no basic, natural antagonism between society and the individual (as, for example, Rousseau or Freud might have us believe), and that in fact the very notion of "the individual" is a social convention. Modern democracies, then, which champion individual rights, incur no unique or unusual problem relating the individual to society. Difficulties exist. But these have to do with specific, concrete situations and not with a fundamental friction.

I have shown how sacred collective representations associate the individual with society. Mediation occurs on still another level. Profane concepts, like sacred ones, constitute a common ground on which diverse members of a society stand. Profane, here, means pedestrian and ordinary, not blasphemous or impious. To speak of a door as hard or a berry as sweet involves shared, profane concepts. Ordinary events and activities, then, indicate social affinity. Durkheim underscores the depth of public

---

[37] *Leçons de sociologie: physique des m urs et du droit*, (1950), 82.
[38] *The Elementary Forms*, 388.

84 MARK S. CLADIS

connectedness to counter the individualistic bent of many Cartesian, Spencerian, and even some Kantian models of human nature.

Yet Durkheim never suggests that the social nature of knowledge, in and of itself, can bring about a flourishing society. He does not hold—contrary to the claims of some of his commentators—that every collective representation is sacred, that is, promotes moral community. Agreement on the hardness of a door or the sweetness of a berry does not *morally* connect individuals. Such "profane" agreement, morally speaking, often guarantees little more than success in finding our way to a battlefield.

This is one reason Durkheim's discovery of the sacred in modern existence is of some importance. Profane agreement is not enough. An elemental, social (communitarian) description of human activity can counter baneful atomistic epistemologies. But if personal and public virtue are to be established or sustained, it will be largely by way of the promising forces of normative sacred ideals and practices. And modern democratic traditions, according to Durkheim, if we sufficiently attend to them, carry such promise.

The connection is clear, then, between Durkheim's frequent use of religious language and his claim that "very far from there being the *antagonism* between the individual and society which is often claimed, moral individualism, the *cult* of the individual, is in fact the product of society itself."[39] The presence of the sacred signals the absence of radical conflict between individuals and society. In democratic societies moral individualism represents a set of sacred ideals and practices uniquely centered on the individual. Yet there is room for doubt: doubt as to whether Durkheim's claim (that there is no antagonism between the individual and society) is true; and, consequently, doubt as to whether Durkheim actually meant that there is no conflict whatsoever.

To some extent I have already addressed the second doubt. There are a thousand and one ways to talk about the individual's relation to society. Durkheim knows this. He also knows there is a multitude of *contingent* conflicts that occur between individuals and various social spheres, such as the domestic or civic. When he claims there is no antagonism between the individual and society, he is in conversation with historical figures such as Hobbes and Rousseau on the one hand and with contemporaries such as Brunetière and Bergson on the other. All four hold that there is a fundamental antagonism, even if each understands the consequences of that antagonism differently. Durkheim, however, rejects the very idea of a basic antagonism. In a phrase, Durkheim's position is that "the characteristic attributes of human *nature* come from *society*."[40] Human beings are naturally social; culture is a natural phenomenon.

[39] "The Determination of Moral Facts," 59.
[40] *The Elementary Forms*, 388 (my emphasis).

The first doubt is settled. Insofar as I have suitably limited the scope of Durkheim's claim, the claim is true. In light of that, the second doubt is also settled, though it requires more discussion. To say Durkheim's claim does not refer to all antagonism is not to say enough. I need to make sense of Durkheim's comments that suggest there is antagonism, as when he says, "society has its own nature, and consequently, its requirements are quite different from those of our nature as individuals; the interests of the whole are not necessarily those of the part."[41] This example comes from an essay in which Durkheim describes the human as *homo duplex*. Humans possess two qualities, traditionally known as body and soul. The former is profane, and refers to private sensations and egoistic propensities; the latter is sacred, and refers to public concepts and morality. Insofar as these two qualities are at war with each other, "our joy can never be pure; there is always some pain mixed with them; for we cannot simultaneously satisfy the two beings that are within us."[42]

Before I give my interpretation of Durkheim's *homo duplex* I will provide what I take to be the standard reading of it. This reading, I believe, is forcefully and articulately advanced by Sheldon Wolin and Jerrold Seigel.[43] The reading takes Durkheim to be pursuing an "uncompromising campaign against the subject," displaying a marked "hostility against the individual."[44] For the sake of social order, in this view, Durkheim places the highest premium on public agreement. Even mundane concepts are seen as significant means to engender profound agreement, and not as mere tools to capture reality. The individual's nature is twofold: on the one hand it is a receptacle to be filled by society; on the other it is a rebellious self, fighting against the mandates imposed by society. The result is a picture of "human nature sharply divided against itself . . . the opposition between what came from inside the individual and what came from society."[45] The war Durkheim wages, then, is against "the individual"—a formidable menace to social cohesion.

To this interpretation I have three objections. First, it ignores an outstanding feature of Durkheim's mature work: his emphasis on the *desirability* of pursuing social goals. Durkheim complains that "Kant's hypothesis, according to which the sentiment of obligation was due to the heterogeneity of reason and sensibility, is not easy to reconcile with the fact that moral ends are in one aspect objects of desire."[46] If Durkheim objects to positing an absolute antagonism between individual desire and

---

[41] Durkheim, "The Dualism of Human Nature," 163.

[42] *Ibid.*, 154.

[43] I am thinking primarily of Sheldon Wolin's *Politics and Vision* and Jerrold Seigel's excellent yet unpublished essay, "Objectivity and the Subject in Durkheim." Their arguments for what I am calling the standard reading are among the best.

[44] Seigel, *ibid.*, 27; Wolin, *ibid.*, 387.

[45] Seigel, *ibid.*, 13 and 14.

[46] "The Determination of Moral Facts," 45-46.

86   MARK S. CLADIS

social (or universal) obligation, it is because he does not conceive of human nature as fatally divided against itself. From *Suicide* until his death, Durkheim increasingly uses the voluntaristic vocabulary of love, respect, and desire—as opposed to fear, obligation, and coercion—to describe the individual's relation to society. In his renewed interest in religion we see Durkheim disputing the supposed dichotomy between private inclination and public obligation. Doubting that "the imperative was, in fact, the religious element in morality," Durkheim argues that "the more sacred a moral rule becomes, the more the element of obligation tends to recede."[47]

My second objection closely follows the first and can be stated briefly. The standard reading ignores Durkheim's commitment to that social ethic, moral individualism. Moral individualism suggests, if nothing else, that far from displaying "hostility against the individual" Durkheim champions the worth, dignity, and rights of the individual. Moreover, Durkheim claims that moral individualism is a salient feature of modern democratic traditions and societies. Moral individualism, then, does not place the individual in opposition to democratic society.

My third objection is that the standard reading overstates Durkheim's concern for social order. I have dealt with the theme of Durkheim and social order elsewhere.[48] Here I will limit my response to Seigel's contention that

The possibility of objective knowledge diminished in the later Durkheim, not because he came to assign individual subjects a positive role in acquiring it, but because the distinction between subjective and objective mental contents was dissolved by the necessity to declare *whatever* arose from society to be objective. What loosened Durkheim's grip on the objectivity he desired so strongly was precisely his *uncompromising campaign against the subject* . . . the smallest chink in the armor of discipline and objectivity threatens to give entry to a whole host of destructive demons and enemies. Here the fear of social collapse and of scientific breakdown are one fear.[49]

It is curious that Durkheim's sophisticated epistemology is construed as a design against "destructive demons and enemies," that is, against subjects or individuals. Curious because Durkheim's mature epistemology develops concomitantly with his moral individualism; curious because near the end of his life Durkheim calls the principle of free examination (holding suspect a piece of the "objective") the sacred of the sacred. Seigel describes Durkheim's epistemological position negatively: "the impulse to define as objective whatever can be set against the subject."[50] Durkheim, however, has no need to set objective knowledge over and against the

---

[47] Durkheim, "Replies to Objections," 70.
[48] See my *A Communitarian Defense of Liberalism*, Chapters 8 and 9.
[49] Seigel, "Objectivity and the Subject in Durkheim," 27 and 28 (my emphasis).
[50] *Ibid.*, 29.

subject. In fact this is the virtue of Durkheim's epistemology: it provides a way between objectivism and subjectivism. Objectivity, in Durkheim's view, is made possible by variously established social beliefs. But this no more means that *anything* set against the subject is objective than it means that society can hold *anything* to be objective. As if he were addressing Seigel on this very issue Durkheim, in *The Elementary Forms*, asserts that the concept's "unique rôle is not the assuring of a harmony among minds, but also, and to a greater extent, their harmony with the nature of things. . . . The concept which was first held as true because it was collective tends to be no longer collective except on the condition of being held as true: we demand its credentials of it before according it our confidence."[51] It is hard to know how to take this passage, especially the phrase "harmony with the nature of things." Perhaps Durkheim is saying nothing more than: what's really important about concepts is not that they are shared but that they are true; sharing concepts—social agreement—is a condition of knowledge, but not the object of knowledge. Or perhaps Durkheim is attempting to sneak in a correspondence theory of truth. In either case, the passage casts doubt on the claim that Durkheim has an "impulse to define as objective whatever can be set against the subject."

Some might claim that I have described Durkheim's view on objectivity in the same way as Seigel: objectivity as socially produced, collective representations. There are, however, two important differences. First, I do not claim that Durkheim's social epistemology is the result of his opposition to the subject. I claim, in fact, that his epistemology respects subjects by locating knowledge within the social world—the world of subjects. This, as I have said, does not mean that subjects or societies arbitrarily fabricate knowledge and objectivity, such that anything could be held as true. Rather this is to state a condition of knowledge: it is always socially construed, historically situated. At his worst Durkheim maintains the traditional subject/object dichotomy and gives the subject an engaging and dynamic role in the pursuit of objective knowledge. At his best, Durkheim challenges the dichotomy itself, and the subject becomes a part of the world as much as the world becomes a part of the subject. In either case Durkheim is not opposing the subject.

The second difference is that I take Durkheim's epistemology to be a normative description of the interconnectedness of human existence, and not a means—or an ideology—for securing social order. To say that knowledge is constituted by public representations and that therefore there can be no radically private human existence, is not the same as to say that objectivity (public agreement) insures social stability or that subjectivity (for example, public dissent) threatens it. Durkheim the Dreyfusard is a case in point. His conscientious dissent from an anti-Semitic consensus is articulated in the shared moral languages of his day. Initiation

[51] *The Elementary Forms*, 485-86.

88   MARK S. CLADIS

and participation in public representations are prerequisites of rationality and therefore of moral dissent. They in no way block social criticism.

The standard interpretation of Durkheim's *homo duplex*, I believe, places it in great tension with much of his thought. I hope to make clear the continuities between *homo duplex* and Durkheim's life work. This requires removing *homo duplex* from the anti-individualist framework constructed by the standard reading, and placing it in the anti-Spencerian (anti-egoistic utilitarian) framework of Durkheim's own thought. Durkheim does not oppose the individual for the sake of order, yet he does oppose the egoist for the sake of the individual and society.

The text often cited in support of the standard reading is Durkheim's essay, "The Dualism of Human Nature and its Social Conditions." Hence I too will concentrate on that essay. Durkheim begins this work, as well as many others, with a reference to history: "It is only by historical analysis that we can discover what makes up man, since it is only in the course of history that he is formed."[52] Next he states that his historical studies have revealed a duality in human nature. Actually, it would have been more apt to say "dualities," since Durkheim goes on to mention more than one, and suggests that some are more prominent than others, depending on whose history is being discussed. A generic dichotomy is described in the vernacular "the body and the soul." The body-soul dichotomy symbolically represents a host of dualities. Durkheim mentions three. There is dualism number one: private sensations (like seeing red) versus public concepts (like *homo duplex*). There is dualism number two: private activity (quenching my thirst) versus moral activity (providing for the homeless). Later in the essay Durkheim introduces another generic dichotomy—the profane and the sacred—and with it dualism number three: mundane personal preoccupations (washing the dishes) versus extraordinary public occasions (the assassination of Martin Luther King, Jr.).

Not one of these dualisms is absolute. The first one Durkheim often qualifies. In *The Elementary Forms*, for example, arguing that the difference between collective and private representations is not categorical, Durkheim writes, "We do not wish to say that there is nothing in the empirical representations which shows rational ones. . . . A complete analysis of the categories should seek these germs of rationality even in the individual consciousness."[53] Experience involves collective representations, even as collective representations entail experience. The second dualism Durkheim qualifies in "The Dualism of Human Nature." He states, "It is an error to believe that it is easy to live as egoists. Absolute egoism, like absolute altruism, is an ideal limit which can never be attained

---

[52] "The Dualism of Human Nature," 150.
[53] *The Elementary Forms*, 28-29, n. 18.

in reality."[54] And in the same essay he tempers the third dualism by noting that between daily routines and singular public incidents there are a host of periodic "public festivals, ceremonies, and rites of all kinds."[55]

I take the three dualisms as ideal types (to use a Weberian term). In "The Dualism of Human Nature" and elsewhere Durkheim crafts conceptually precise polarities in order to highlight historical events and trends. When he applies these polarities, however, to concrete, empirical realities, he softens the contrasts. To fail to note this, to fix one's attention on the ideal types alone, is to miss Durkheim's nuanced interpretations of history and modern society. It is also to consider dualisms literal that were intended to be ideal (in the Weberian sense).

The three dualisms, then, are "ideal," but they are not illusory. Durkheim dismisses those theories, such as empirical and idealistic monism, that attempt to remove what these dualisms represent by simply denying them. Durkheim sides, rather, with "the great religions of modern man" that insist on "the existence of the contradictions in the midst of which we struggle."[56] And yet amid his talk of the human struggle springing from *homo duplex* Durkheim does not oppose the individual pole and champion the social pole of the dualisms.

Again, I do not mean to deny that Durkheim articulates a variety of dualisms. I do, however, question any interpretation that takes the dualisms as a sign of hostility against the individual. What, after all, does the antagonism represented by each dualism amount to? The discord between sensations and concepts amounts to this: "our concepts never succeed in mastering our sensations and in translating them completely into intelligible terms"; and therefore "a science that would adequately express all of reality" is but "an ideal that we can only approach ceaselessly, not one that is possible for us to attain."[57] Dualism number one, then, appears in no way to be hostile toward the individual. It is simply one example of Durkheim's residual empiricism. Dualism number three (mundane personal preoccupations versus extraordinary public occasions) does not carry any significant conflict. In fact, when noting how social ideals arising from extraordinary public occasions are "themselves individualized," Durkheim writes that "because they [the ideals] are in close relation with our other representations, they *harmonize* with them, with our temperaments, characters, habits, and so on."[58] This dualism, then, suggests the promise of harmony at least as much as the possibility of conflict.

If hostility toward the individual exists in any of the three dualisms, it must be in dualism number two (private activity versus moral activity).

[54] "The Dualism of Human Nature," 153.

[55] *Ibid.*, 161.

[56] *Ibid.*, 156.

[57] *Ibid.*, 153.

[58] *Ibid.*, 153 (my emphasis).

90   MARK S. CLADIS

In fact there is in some cases much hostility on Durkheim's part toward the private side of this dualism. This animosity, however, is not aimed at the private side per se, but rather at forms of life characterized by it. Egoists (whose loves are centered excessively about themselves, and who are often captivated by external goods such as wealth, power, and status) lead lives that conflict with the obligations and loves we associate with moral activity. These persons, in Durkheim's view, are unhappy and are alienated from self and society. Of course the tension borne by dualism number two is not reserved for egoists alone. We all experience it. I love the expensive whiskey Wild Turkey, and I desire to make monthly payments to sponsor an impoverished child. If I forgo the Wild Turkey so I can afford to help a child, I am, as Durkheim says, making a sacrifice, even if I desire it: "We can accept this sacrifice without resistance and even with enthusiasm, but even when it is accomplished in a surge of joy, the sacrifice is no less real."[59] No doubt Durkheim is correct. In placing one love above the other, I have lost my whiskey. But I have not lost myself. In fact Durkheim would want to argue that I have made a small step toward finding (or making) myself. The point is this: insofar as there is tension between private activity and moral activity, and insofar as Durkheim shows "hostility" toward the private side, it should be understood as a censure against self-seeking egoistic or Spencerian dispositions. This, however, fails to qualify as "hostility against the individual."

I have no desire to erase the lines of tension that Durkheim intended *homo duplex* to convey. My aim is to locate *homo duplex* in the context of Durkheim's life work. In that context the interesting antagonism of *homo duplex* becomes clear: it expresses, in the words of Santayana, in what ways "we identify ourselves not with ourselves." Durkheim does not fear or loathe "the individual." His campaign, rather, is against atomistic individualism and egoism and the sorrow that accompanies these. When he employs a religious vocabulary to describe the deep commitments that modern individuals share, he is battling against those epistemological and political theories that support weak or strong versions of methodological individualism. But this line of his thought, I have argued, needs to be understood in light of his eloquent defense of the dignity and rights of the individual. It is in this spirit that we are to read him, as when he writes, "The human personality is a sacred thing; one dare not violate it nor infringe its bounds, while at the same time the greatest good is in communion with others."[60]

Vassar College.

---

[59] *Ibid.*, 152.
[60] "The Determination of Moral Facts," 37.

V

J. A. HOBSON AS A NEW LIBERAL THEORIST:
Some Aspects of his Social Thought Until 1914

By Michael Freeden

It is rather surprising that John Atkinson Hobson (1858–1940) who never received the full recognition he merited during his lifetime, should suffer the same fate after his death. He is, of course, well-known as a forerunner of modern economic thought—and was lauded as such by Keynes—and as the author of a searching and critical study of imperialism, much quoted by Lenin. But an oft neglected fact is that this prolific writer and remarkable analyst was probably the most penetrating theorist and formulator of the new brand of social-liberalism that emerged in pre-First World War Britain and, moreover, a visionary prophet of social welfare thought as we know it today. True, Hobson saw himself primarily as an economist or rather an economic heretic,[1] but he was never a purely economic thinker. He eventually found it impossible to devote himself to "an arid economic science" which took money as its final criterion of value.[2] Even Hobson's anti-imperialism was not entirely detached from internal social problems, as questions of empire were seen by him to push workingclass demands unjustly aside.[3] In concentrating, then, on what was broadly termed at the time "The Social Problem" Hobson demonstrated his ability both as scientific methodologist and as social theorist, and in a wide range of books and articles constructed a body of thought which, although somewhat repetitive, displayed a high degree of consistency.

Hobson's main concern was to create a comprehensive science of human welfare. He did not subscribe to the narrow, insulated, viewpoint which detaches science from humanism.[4] Rather, he saw the weakness of economic and political studies in their over-independence and in a methodological inability to generalize. These defects were the result of a false belief that inductive science could work alone, unaided by *a priori* deductive processes of reasoning.[5] The essential inclusion of values in any significant study of society was a clear reflection of Ruskin's great hold on Hobson's way of thinking. It was Ruskin who had intentionally reintroduced values into political economy by defining it as a science of human welfare which included all human efforts and satis-

---

[1] Thus the title of his autobiography *Confessions of an Economic Heretic* (London, 1938).

[2] *Ibid.*, 55.   [3] Hobson, *A Modern Outlook* (London, 1910), 304.

[4] Hobson, *Work and Wealth* (London, 1914), viii.

[5] Hobson, *The Social Problem* (London, 1902), 262.

factions. He had insisted on reform being subjected to conscious, ethical standards, and had envisaged the end of economic activity as the production of "life" or "souls of a good quality." This approach Hobson saw as furnishing the goal required to give meaning to sociology as a science and to social progress as an art.[6] Hobson's conception of sociology was therefore neither *wertfrei* nor reductionist. He pointed out that even "inductive science" began with the *a priori* step of collecting and ordering facts on the basis of external principles embodying the objects and ends of the process of investigation.[7] In the same way, one could not exclude human principles, which are part of human thought, from the study of humanity. The recognition of the centrality of principles and ideas in human life dominated Hobson's thought simply because—and here he agreed with Ruskin—man was not a human mechanism but a conscious, rational, and emotional being.[8]

Indeed, Hobson's insistence on the place of ideas in the study of society puts him outside the period's mainstream of political interpretation, though not of philosophical thought. Already in 1891 he warned against the common deception that abstract theories were not operative forces. Underneath local or temporal expediencies and chance happenings there was always a large principle which provided the key to the logic of events.[9] In a way, Hobson, by including ideas in the subject-matter of empirical scientific analysis, is a precursor of modern sociological thought. On the level of social action, too, he repeatedly criticized contemporary social reformers who saw "theory" and "principle" as awkward encumbrances to progress, which in their view could only be achieved by compromise and experiment: ". . . our practical reformer . . . sees how very apt principles are to get in the way and to clog the wheels of progress."[10]

As against these pragmatic, piecemeal reform attempts Hobson opposed the necessity of conscious, coherent ideas as guidelines and urged this upon the Liberal party. A policy of social reconstruction depended on an intelligible formulation of principles.[11]

In creating a relatively coherent body of ideas drawing upon various ideological sources and systems, Hobson epitomizes the eclectic intellectual searching of a liberalism trying to confront an increasingly inexplicable and unruly reality with an adequate theory. The result, though not flawless, turned out to be quite viable and has received the accolade of public consensus in Western democracies. To those who

[6] Hobson, *John Ruskin Social Reformer* (London, 1898), 74, 79, 87.
[7] *The Social Problem*, 65.   [8] *John Ruskin*, 75, 86.
[9] Hobson, *Problems of Poverty* (London, 1891), 196.
[10] Hobson, *The Crisis of Liberalism: New Issues of Democracy* (London, 1909), 114–15; written in 1896 and published in *The Progressive Review.*
[11] *Ibid.*, 137.

would see Hobson's eclecticism as an example of liberal intellectual compromise between borrowed systems of thought, one could only reply that it is that compromise itself which constitutes an essential part of the liberal intellectual contribution.

The two themes Hobson tried to combine with liberalism were an idealism showing affinities to Hegelian analysis, on the one hand, and a socio-biological approach to the study of human groups, on the other. The key idealist concepts of wholeness (i.e., universalism), consciousness (the centrality of thought, knowledge, and self-awareness), and rationality recur again and again. These are related to the notion of the state as a social organism.

In his critique of existing approaches to social reform Hobson singled out for attack their concrete and discrete viewpoints: "Everywhere the pressure of special concrete interests, nowhere the conscious play of organised human intelligence!"[12] At first the rising humanitarianism of the nineteenth century, as exhibited in literature, merely reacted to individual cases of suffering and failed to understand the economic causes of "the condition of the people." Then arose movements which sensed some moral defects in the functioning of the industrial system and highlighted social questions concerning factories and mines, the workings of the Poor Law, sanitation, etc. But even they could only suggest limited concrete reforms and remained distinctively sentimental in their origins. The evident failures of personal kindness and charity, and piecemeal individual treatment ". . . illustrate the final inefficacy of these forces, when unguided by larger principles of social justice."[13]

What an adequate treatment of social problems demands is, then, the over-all, total, perspective. This universalism means not only the need for a general guiding principle but a perception of the unity of the social question. Man's mental processes make this imperative, for a concomitant of his rationality is a demand for order and wholeness in thought and conduct.[14] The movement towards rationalism, which a universalistic viewpoint dictates, is, as with Hegel, coupled with an ethical transformation from egoism to altruism. The identification of individual and social aims and the strengthening of social sympathy which characterize this process are seen by Hobson as "the spirit of social reform, as distinguished from the concrete measures of reform."[15]

Actually, it is surprising to what extent Hobson, wittingly or not, echoed Hegel. Hobson's theory of the evolving rational consciousness is

[12] *Ibid.*, 115.

[13] Hobson, "The Ethics of Industrialism," *Ethical Democracy: Essays in Social Dynamics*, ed. S. Coit (London, 1900), 84, 85, 88.

[14] *The Social Problem*, 2, 3.

[15] *Work and Wealth*, 309.

almost dialectic, despite his expressed dislike of the method,[16] and he clearly endorses the idealist transcending of individualism. Thus, Hobson forsees the individual becoming aware of the interconnectedness of society, a perception that will cause him consciously to realize his personal freedom in actions that are a willing contribution to the common good.[17] Consciousness of social units is a necessary precondition for the rational adaptation and ordering of their resources and forces: "the supreme condition of social progress is for a society to 'know itself'."[18] This final stage is attained by a process not dissimilar to Hegel's threefold movement from immediate ("instinctive") altruism and universality, through mediate (differentiated) egoism and particularism, to united self-conscious rationality and universality.[19] Thus Hobson sees as the first stage of socio-economic development "a purely instinctive organic economy," based on natural functions, which "allows little scope for individuality of life." It implies a procreative unit in which the individuals are subservient to the group and achieve fullest expression by promoting the ends of the species, i.e., by successful parenthood. Then comes an actual piece of dialectic reasoning:

It might almost be said that the dawn of reason is the dawn of selfishness. For rational economy involves a conscious realisation of the individual self, with ends of his own to be secured and with opportunities for securing them. The earliest conception of this separate self and its ends will naturally tend to be in terms of merely or mainly physical satisfaction. Thus the displacement of the instinctive by the rational economy is evidently a critical era, attended with grave risks due to the tendency towards an over-assertion of the individual self and a consequent weakening of the forces making for specific life.[20]

This is a more than adequate description of Hegel's civil society, with rationality creating and being created out of egoism, operating at first on a lower level but to be re-harnessed in full upon the emergence of the state. Finally, "Only as this animal self becomes spiritualised and socialised, does the social race-life reassert its sway upon the higher plane of human consciousness."[21]

On the subject of property, however, Hobson goes one step further than Hegel. Insofar as civil society is an economic system based on ownership of private property, property is one of the mainstays of the Hegelian social system. Indeed, property as the externalization and ob-

---

[16]This dislike was also attested to by a friend, who recollected that Hobson had "dismissed the dialectical method as a frivolous pedantry." H. N. Brailsford, *The Life-Work of J. A. Hobson* (Hobhouse Memorial Trust Lecture, London, 1948), 6.

[17]*Work and Wealth*, 304.   [18]*The Social Problem*, 261.

[19]These are objectivized in the three stages of family, civil society, and state. Cf. Hegel, *Philosophy of Right*, paras. 157, 158, 181–85, 257–58.

[20]*Work and Wealth*, 22.   [21]*Ibid.*, 23.

jectivization of self is essential for the development of a rational person.[22] Similarly, Hobson sees private property as necessary to the realization of the moral and rational ends of the individual. Yet he differs crucially from Hegel in that he would also see public property as essential to the self-realization of the community.[23] For Hobson public property is the private property of the community—regarded as an individual with moral ends set apart from those of its members. Furthermore, Hobson sensed the emergence of a rational humanitarianism which would find the egoism and competition of the existing industrial system morally reprehensive.[24] But then Hegel considered the ethical life of the state rooted in human behavior as exemplified in primary social structures, and conceived of the identity of the individual with the state, and in the state, in different terms (i.e., as a unity of opposites) than did Hobson in his model, which we shall presently deal with.

Elsewhere, when discussing the self-governing workshop, Hobson reflects Hegel's analysis of the growing universality of the economic organization of civil society.[25] The solidarity of such a group is a moral improvement on individual self-interest. On the other hand, even a federation of trade unions is a "class" solution to the demands of labor and thus still in the region of an individualism which contravenes the social good.[26] Hobson is quite clear about economic development being meaningless without attending moral and spiritual progress though, unlike Hegel, this is a matter of human choice and will being trained and exercised at every stage, and not an inevitable deterministic process. Such development depends on a "conscious and, therefore, moral" effort to marshall economic resources so as to achieve qualitative as well as quantitative improvement. It also depends on the ability of each social group to assimilate moral and intellectual opportunities created by spiritual and educational reformers.[27]

There arose, though, a more basic difference between Hobson and the school of Idealism which caused him subsequently to modify the idealist notion of spiritual progress towards an ethical state. Before the advent of the new century, during Hobson's activities in the Ethical Movement and his association with *The Progressive Review,* the influence of Oxford Idealism had made itself felt. The leaders of the Ethical Movement, a few of whom even were Oxford philosophers, preached the need for an applied social and personal ethics based on a

---

[22]Hegel, *Philosophy of Right,* paras. 41–51.
[23]Hobson, "The Ethics of Industrialism," 104.
[24]"Selfishness is inherent in competition; force is inherent in bargaining."   *Ibid., 92.*
[25]Hegel, *Philosophy of Right,* paras. 183, 250–51.
[26]Hobson, "Of Labour," *Good Citizenship,* ed. J. E. Hand (London, 1899), 102–04.
[27]*The Crisis of Liberalism,* 190–91.

rational, not theological, conception of moral welfare. *The Progressive Review,* too, although political-economic in its outlook, was guided by a belief that progress was "cultural" in the widest human sense of the term.[28] However, in 1914 Hobson wrote:

[Society] must be treated as a vital structure capable of working well or working ill. I say vital structure, not spiritual structure, for I hold the tendency to interpret social organisation exclusively in terms of ethical ends, and as existing simply for "the realisation of an ethical order," to be unwarranted. The men who form or constitute a Society, or who enter any sort of social organisation, enter body and soul, they carry into it the inseparable character of the organic life, with all the physical and spiritual activities and purposes it contains.[29]

This aptly summarizes the perspective that had emerged in Hobson's mind during the twenty years before the war. Economics and politics had to be harmonized by a social ethics and then brought under a broader concept of the art of human welfare.[30] Unlike the implications of idealist theory, the ethical order was not immanent in social behavior, nor was social behavior reducible to ethical life. This is central to Hobson's understanding of society. In terms of the intellectual origins of his thought this means that his idealism was tempered by an emphasis on biological processes, especially by the "organism" model and by evolutionary theory.[31] And Hobson, though differing essentially from Spencer on questions of political theory, credited him with revolutionizing modern thought in this field. Spencer had impressed on the educated world that Man was part of nature, thus refuting the traditional dualist approach. The idealists now had biological proof of the progress of Reason in the concrete world.[32]

The physical aspects of social life were never lost upon Hobson. Already in his study of Ruskin, Hobson had credited the former with perceiving that every great social question had its roots in physiology.[33] Moreover, one of Hobson's arguments against current philanthropy had been its continuous tendency to endeavor to supply higher wants before the lower wants were satisfied; to insist on moral elevation of the masses prior to environmental reforms. Even worse, this was often not only the policy of private charity but of the state. Hobson saw this refusal to regard life as an organic whole as an instance of the "mo-

---

[28] *Confessions of an Economic Heretic,* 54–56.

[29] *Work and Wealth,* 14.   [30] *Confessions of an Economic Heretic,* 55.

[31] *The Social Problem,* 3: "The organic conception of society and the historic conception of continuity are two chief products of modern thinking which have modified profoundly—if they have not, indeed, transformed—the conception of social progress."

[32] Hobson, "Herbert Spencer," *South Place Magazine,* 9 (Jan. 1904), 49–55.

[33] *John Ruskin,* 155.

nadist fallacy." For the practical reformer, he claimed, the satisfaction of the lower material need preceded in importance that of the higher. The latter could not exist if it had no soil out of which to grow.[34]

The term "organism" was best fitted to describe the nature of the physical and spiritual structure of society. It alone made the evolution of industry intelligible.[35] Although Hobson admitted that the organism analogy was a matter of convenience of language and conceded that the difference between society as an organism and animal organisms might make it more profitable not to use the same word, he observed that recent biological research had strengthened the tendency to regard society as an organism even on its physical side.[36] True, sometimes Hobson seems to have perceived the organic model as being more analogous to the non-physical aspects of society, because he accepted the notion that society is a moral, rational organism with a psychic life of its own.[37] But he tended more towards the view that the impulses to form societies originate in organic gregarious instincts and feelings which, although spiritualized and rationalized, carry a biological import.[38]

It appears, then, that the "organism" is a general concept adumbrating the close interdependence and connectedness of all facets of social life and is inevitably left rather loose. Indeed, Hobson adopts it in the accepted way that models are used nowadays—"it is more appropriate than any other concept, and some concept must be applied."[39] He decided against using a psychological instead of a biological term on grounds of intellectual expediency. The organic concept was simply clearer and more forceful, and could be spiritualized to cover all aspects of human life,[40] although for the time being, due to inadequacies of scientific methodology, the frontiers of physiology and psychology should be respected.[41]

Just as we saw before that Hobson tempered his idealism with the awareness of the physical roots of social life, he was now prevented from totally accepting the socio-biological theories of the period by his belief in the power of ideas, of the human spirit. He thus occupies the middle ground between these two systems of thought, and it is his concept of organism that bridges the gap. Hobson's reservations to the latter type of theory, reservations which uphold the moral and spiritual spheres of human existence (and we shall try to show below that this uncertainty manifests itself in his examination of the relation between

---

[34] *The Social Problem*, 82; *The Crisis of Liberalism*, 207.

[35] *Work and Wealth*, vi.

[36] *The Crisis of Liberalism*, 71.

[37] *Ibid.*, 73. Cf. *Work and Wealth*, 12.

[38] *Work and Wealth*, 14.

[39] *Ibid.*, 15.

[40] *Ibid.*, 18.

[41] *The Social Problem*, 257–58.

the individual and the social spheres), extend not only to the "organism," but to current ideas on social evolution. Hobson rejected, of course, the attempt to endow the struggle for survival with positive ethical content. But he even questioned Huxley's endeavor "to contrast social with cosmic development." Huxley, says Hobson, had wrongly urged that social progress meant replacing the cosmic process by an ethical process, the end of which was not the survival of the fittest in all aspects, but of those who were ethically fittest.[42] Hobson would appear to be more of an evolutionary than Huxley in maintaining the existence of universal processes of organic development to which human society, too, conforms. Whereas Huxley negates continuity of development by "suddenly" superimposing ethical motives on humanity, Hobson sees social and spiritual forces (although not existing from the start) as evolving during the struggle for life. Ethical fitness is itself one of the conditions that determine survival and it triumphs over other non-ethical conditions as part of the cosmic process, not in defiance of it.[43]

All this is not to deny the validity of current evolutionary and biological theory *in toto*. It is only that biology has exaggerated the physical implications of the term "organism" and distorted the true conception of social evolution by enforcing narrow interpretations of selection and survival.[44] Social evolution in general is more akin to intellectual and moral progress. It is not mechanically deterministic but a matter of exercising human intellect. Hobson even tried to fit evolution into the general mainstream of classical liberalism and of the "progress" theories. He observes that eccentric conduct, although possibly wasteful and socially injurious, is from the standpoint of race progress an experiment in life. All new steps in social progress start as individual aberrations. "Modern biology and its companion science psychology enforce most powerfully the plea of J. S. Mill."[45]

With this theoretical framework Hobson tackles the social question. This, stated in its widest form, is:

Given a number of human beings, with a certain development of physical and mental faculties and of social institutions, in command of given natural resources, how can they best utilize these powers for the attainment of the most complete satisfaction?[46]

[42]*John Ruskin*, 104; quoted from T. H. Huxley, *Evolution and Ethics*, The Romanes Lecture (Oxford, 1893), 33.

[43]*John Ruskin*, 104–05. However, Hobson overlooked Huxley's partial retraction in a footnote(19) to his Romanes lecture, where he stated that "strictly speaking, social life and the ethical process . . . are part and parcel of the general process of evolution." Huxley, *op. cit.*, 56.   [44]*Work and Wealth*, 17, 118–20.

[45]Hobson, "Character and Society," *Character and Life*, ed. P. L. Parker (London, 1912), 94–95.

[46]*The Social Problem*, 7. This derives from Ruskin's query: "How can society consciously order the lives of its members so as to maintain the largest number of noble and happy human beings?" Quoted by Hobson, *John Ruskin*, 155.

This is ostensibly couched in utilitarian terms, though Hobson understands the concept of utility as being more qualitative than quantitative, more Mill than Bentham.[47] The use of the term "social utility" is, again, a matter of expediency. It is meant to avoid fleeting estimates of efforts and satisfactions and to substitute for them an objective standard of reference.[48] Operatively, this entails organizing a social machine which can minimize social waste, minimize costs, and maximize social satisfaction, or social welfare.[49] The human, as distinguished from the money and the "real" dividend, is the amount of vital or organic welfare conveyed in the producing and consuming processes.[50] Hobson suggests detailed "steps needed to convert 'costs' and 'utilities' from terms of cash into terms of human life,"[51] but of course such steps can only be based on subjective impressions of individuals, nor are they measurable. This is why his science of welfare is really a "super-science," or rather a science combined with an art.

Hobson is himself aware that his cardinal concept of organism is a "metaphysical" assumption. It is the expression of forces conscious and unconscious, individual and social, which compose the social personality.[52] Society is an organism in a broad, qualitative, sense of the term. Society creates values, desires, and needs, and a proper science of human welfare must be directed to upholding and satisfying them. Social reform implies redesigning society in such a way as to conform to these values; implies—and this is the original sense of the word—a return to a form of society that is considered the true and primal one.

Hobson's notion of welfare, in conjunction with his concept of organism, encompasses all human needs, "lower" and "higher," physical and spiritual, provided, of course, they comply with the demands of social utility. He rejects the idea that certain types of food and physical supports are necessary to life and work while others are superfluous: ". . . physical, moral, intellectual, are not watertight compartments of humanity," and welfare would include not only the physical necessities of life, but "Good air, large sanitary houses, plenty of wholesome, well-cooked food, adequate changes of clothing for our climate, ample opportunities of recreation . . . ," and further, ". . . art, music, travel, education, social intercourse. . . ."[53] Moreover, "routine satisfaction of the common needs of life" is not enough. Beyond a high uniform level of welfare throughout society, part of the general income

[47] *The Social Problem*, 4–5. As to the nature of Hobson's utilitarianism, see below.

[48] Either in relation to the social needs of a given populace or based on human experience and "enlightened common sense." See *The Social Problem*, 48; *Work and Wealth*, 320–22.

[49] *The Social Problem*, 64, 43–45.

[50] *Work and Wealth*, 33.

[51] *The Social Problem*, 45.

[52] *Work and Wealth*, 350.

[53] *The Social Problem*, 78–80.

must be used to stimulate the free development of individuals which is essential to social progress.[54] We shall examine below the implications of "the art of social welfare, humanism,"[55] as the means to guarantee social progress. At present it is worth mentioning a "natural" reason Hobson gives for advocating the art of social reform: the physiological demands of human nature are constant and therefore conservative, whereas only the non-physical aspects (which cannot be catered for by current scientific methods) put forward new wants and press for a fuller life.[56]

To summarize, the "super-science" of human welfare consists, on the one hand, of a quantitative science—limited, standard, and uniform—tending common human needs, to the furtherance of which machinery can be harnessed. On the other hand, it is the artistic side of human life—differentiated, value-impregnated, and creative.[57] Social progress is a collective art which does not owe its creativity to the social sciences. They must serve social progress, rather than direct it.[58] But the artistic side too must be made the subject of systematic research in order to achieve what Hobson ultimately wants—a total, action-oriented study of human well-being.

However, one must also ask: Why is *social* utility the absolute standard of reference? Here one has to turn to the causes and types of social problems Hobson sees as being at the bottom of the immediate need for social reform. Basically it is a question of production and consumption which, in the broadest sense, includes all forms of human activity.[59] The essential point is to avoid waste in both these processes. One major aspect of waste in the production process is unemployment (and added to this misemployment and underemployment). The unemployment question refers in a broad sense to unemployed productive power in labor (including the "idle" upper class),[60] land, and capital.[61] The fact that this is a source of individual suffering was not stressed by Hobson at all; after all, that facet had been highlighted enough in his time. What struck him was the lack of a comprehensive system for educating and utilizing the productive powers of members of society for social purposes.[62]

A second source of waste is that involved by the energy put into competition.[63] This is part of Hobson's complete rejection of the *laissez faire* ideology on all fronts, in the name of political, economic, and evolutionary theory. Historical fact proves there never existed real

[54] *Work and Wealth,* 137–38.
[55] *Ibid.,* 225.
[56] *The Social Problem,* 105.
[57] *Work and Wealth,* 168, 76, 330.
[58] *Ibid.,* 359.
[59] *Ibid.,* 159.
[60] "The Ethics of Industrialism," 99.
[61] *The Social Problem,* 249.
[62] *Ibid.,* 9.
[63] *The Social Problem,* 10.

HOBSON AS A NEW LIBERAL THEORIST 101

freedom to work as one liked, nor does the history of factory legislation corroborate the existence of freedom of contract.[64] As economic theory, *laissez faire* never ensured the justest and the most efficient distribution of national income—i.e., the most conducive to fullest and best productive work.[65] Thirdly, Hobson denies the contention of those evolutionists who see competition as an essential and exclusive vitalizing factor in human development.[66]

Then there is the question of waste in consumption: a large part of the goods have no human or social value.[67] The largest proportion of waste is in the non-material expenditure of the well-to-do classes on recreation, education, and charity. The reason for this is, again, the "experimental" nature of social evolution. When the requirements of physical survival are no longer predominant and human life contains an increasing number of elements which have no "survival value," the possibilities of error and disutility also multiply.[68] This calls for reeducation in the arts of consumption.[69] But the other aspect of waste in consumption is that people frequently cannot make use of what is offered them because of social disutility in the distribution.

This entire discussion links up neatly with Hobson's economics and his well-known theory that "under-consumption" was responsible for the crises of the capitalist system. As it was caused by an unequal social distribution of the "power to consume," the solution was to increase that power among the underprivileged working classes. At the same time Hobson cast a grave doubt upon the scientific rationale of that great Victorian moral imperative—thrift.[70] The application of correctives to defects of the economic system would provide simultaneously a solution to the problems of mal-distribution, unemployment, and the material comfort of the working classes. But this would have to be accompanied by profound political and moral changes.

The manifestation of these social mal-functions is poverty. It perpetuates a sense of antagonism between classes and masses and could pose a threat to social stability.[71] But Hobson, in suggesting solutions, is far from recommending a socialist revolution. In fact, he would aspire to the basic ethos of a nonrevolutionary situation—a sense of justice psychological and subjective by nature and not involving "objective" class consciousness:

This sense of getting and giving his due must be regarded as the subjective basis of modern social morality, involving a recognition of substantial justice

---

[64] *Problems of Poverty,* 187–88. [65] *Work and Wealth,* 176.

[66] Hobson, *The Evolution of Modern Capitalism* (London, 1926; 1894¹), 418–20.

[67] *Work and Wealth,* 37. This obviously derives from Ruskin's "illth."

[68] *Ibid.,* 145, 117. [69] *The Evolution of Modern Capitalism,* 406.

[70] *Ibid.,* 288, 375–76, *passim.* [71] *The Social Problem,* 15.

embodied in the existing political and economic order . . . just in proportion as a man recognises that in his case this ideal is approximately reached does he respect himself, and, what is no less important, his fellows.[72]

Although it is plain that the thought of a social-liberal must necessarily relate to socialism, Hobson's attitude to it was not unequivocal—something not very surprising in view of the hold-all qualities of the term. Throughout his writings, Hobson exemplifies the vagueness confronting young radicals of his period. A great deal of intellectual wrestling was needed in order to decide exactly what elements of which socialism were to be assimilated into the body of rejuvenated liberal thought. What Hobson later recalled in his autobiography is most revealing. Writing of the 1890's he said:

The time for an effective general challenge of Capitalism was not yet ripe. Revelations of poverty, together with the extension of trade unionism to the unskilled workers (dramatized in the Dock Strike of 1889), were the direct stimuli of the "social reforms" of the nineties, and brought into being the Labour Party, which was soon to assume the name, if not the substance, of Socialism. But though my opinions and my feelings were beginning to move in the direction of Socialism, I was not a Socialist, Marxian, Fabian, or Christian.[73]

Although Hobson did not accept a specific socialist doctrine, he read into socialism all elements that corresponded to his composite view of society. Thus, admitting "the different grades of loose meaning attached to the term Socialism," he related it as a philosophical term to organic theory and saw it implying an organic view of social life and imposing a unifying common end on the members of a society.[74] At first, Hobson came out strongly in favor of factory legislation and the like, which he saw as the yet unconscious manifestation of the spirit of socialism. This was what Harcourt had meant when declaring "we are all socialists now."[75] In later writings Hobson explicitly rejected the doctrines of theoretic socialism and offered instead his version of "practicable Socialism": ". . . equal opportunity of self-development and social aid, so as to live a good and happy life." This meant supplying all workers at cost price with economic conditions necessary to educate and employ their personal powers.[76] Still, he increasingly relied on socialist principles when working out such radical demands for equality. Thus, his singling out of mal-distribution as the root of all social evil was reflected in his repeated echoing of the old socialist slogan: "From each according to his powers, to each according to his needs."[77]

[72]"Character and Society," 66.   [73]*Confessions of an Economic Heretic*, 29.
[74]*John Ruskin*, 176.   [75]*Problems of Poverty*, 191, 199.
[76]*The Crisis of Liberalism*, 172–73.
[77]Hobson, "The Re-Statement of Democracy," *Contemporary Review*, **81** (1902), 262–72. This too is immediately assimilated in Hobson's outlook as the motto is nothing else than "the full organic formula" (268).

The condemnation of mal-distribution did not merely emanate from economic considerations. To understand this one must refer to the theory of social value which Hobson shared with many radicals of the period. On this matter Hobson had originally adopted an outlook that was in his opinion a socialist one. The conscious socialist (to be distinguished from Harcourt's "socialists") demands that the community refuse to sanction absolute private property because much of the value of each individual's work is due to the cooperation of society. This gives the community the right to secure for itself a share in the social value it has helped to create. Even the non-material creator uses intellectual forms which are embodiments of thoughts and feelings moulded by his nation, if not humanity at large.[78] However, Hobson took exception to the socialist viewpoint that *all* value is social. He concentrated on the "bête noire" of his time—unearned increments. The dissipation and reapportionment of this surplus was to be the primary object of all social-economic reforms.[79]

Here is the key to the financial policy of social reformers. Taxation of the surplus[80] combined with high wages for the workers (secured by agreement with the employers or by state regulation) are the methods to counter mal-distribution and establish a more equal and stable society. No wonder that Hobson delightedly hailed the radical budget of 1909 as an audacious, even revolutionary, approach to the financing of social reform.[81] The 1909 budget followed almost exactly Hobson's theory of taxation which he had spelled out in 1906.[82] It had substituted the canon of "ability to pay" for the false view of taxation as an attack on property rights of individuals. It was the first national attempt to secure for the state large portions of the unearned increment. It was directed against the monopolies of land and liquor, whose beneficiaries owed their wealth primarily to legal protection by the state. But its main importance was in its concentration on the enlargement and graduation of income tax and estate duties. These applied to the growing sources of modern wealth and would, therefore, secure the need to provide a constantly increasing revenue for social reform, a need which characterized the new Liberal finance, as opposed to the traditional Liberal concern with retrenchment.

The increased role the state was to play in social affairs leads us to state socialism, a limited form of which Hobson seemed more and more inclined to accept.[83] Such a tendency was a consequence of his theory of society, which deemed public progress impossible unless the state took

[78]*Problems of Poverty*, 198; *The Social Problem*, 148.

[79]*The Social Problem*, 152; *Work and Wealth*, 188.

[80]Hobson, "Is Socialism Plunder?" *The Nation*, 19/10/1907.

[81]Hobson, "The Significance of the Budget," *The English Review*, 2 (1909), 794–805.

[82]Hobson, "The Taxation of Monopolies," *Independent Review*, 9 (1906), 20–33.

[83]Hobson, *The Science of Wealth* (London, 1911), 254ff.

over the property it made and needed. If a state could show the social origins of the values of land, tramways, gas-works, and the like, it had a right and a duty to administer them. This was "progressive socialism." But Hobson tried to establish a general framework for state socialism, to which end he applied three criteria for public action through the state, namely: the public should undertake works which it is best capable of administering, which supply common necessities, and which are prone to abuse by private enterprise.[84]

The ultimate argument for socialization was the release of the individual will from costly and repellent routine work, so that the social will could find in that work its self-realization.[85] Socialization should be complemented by state enactment of industrial regulations to protect wage earners and consumers.[86] But the direct social control which replaced the private profit-seeking motive was not to be total. Hobson repeatedly warned against the imperialism and the socialism which brought in their wake an absolute ascendancy of the state. He also emphasized that beyond the above limitations he was talking about a competitive society which still left a wide open field for individual liberty in private enterprise.[87]

As to qualitative production, the creative, artistic element in human life, essential to social progress, does not lend itself to routinization. The domain of socialism is that of machinery, not art.[88] And here again—an echo of original Marxism, so far removed from, indeed dialectically opposed to, comprehensive state socialism:

An artist must produce the whole of a product—a product with a unity; it must be the direct expression of his personal skill, directed to the individual work in hand. The first of these conditions negates division of labour; the second, machinery.[89]

Here is Marx's aesthetic vision, his abhorrence of specialization and of the capitalist industrial system.[90] But, of course, Hobson retains this only for the "higher" aspects of social life and welcomes competition in the qualitative artistic sphere of production.

The place of socialism in Hobson's thought brings us to the central issue of social-liberalism—the reformulation of the relation between the individual and society and the reorientation of the old liberalism to changing conceptions of social life and social responsibility. The com-

[84] *The Social Problem*, 152–54, 175.   [85] *Work and Wealth*, 305.

[86] Hobson, "The Four-Fold Path of Socialism," *The Nation*, 30/11/1907.

[87] "The Taxation of Monopolies," 25.

[88] *The Social Problem*, 180, 244.   [89] *Ibid.*, 181.

[90] There is more than a hint of Marxist "alienation" in such a sentence: "For the work only calls for a fragment of that 'self' and always the same fragment. So it is true that not only is labour divided but the labourer. And it is manifest that, so far as his organic human nature is concerned, its unused portions are destined to idleness, atrophy, and decay." *Work and Wealth*, 87.

HOBSON AS A NEW LIBERAL THEORIST

bination of industry and art in the field of human activity is an indicator to that relationship. The harmony based on the differentiation between routine industries and arts is at the same time intended to resolve the antagonism between individualism and socialism.[91] The fact that the harmony is one of differentiation makes one sense again the dialectical tension in Hobson's theories, though it is one which lays the stress on the final difference: insistence on "particular" wants makes a man an artist and exempts him from the tendency towards mechanized capitalist production and socialism. There, in Hobson's opinion, lies the gist of the problem of social progress.[92] We return here to a sort of particularism in which creative people (perhaps this is somewhat akin to Mill's "eccentrics") are accorded special conditions under which to flourish. Of course, ideally all are to be accorded such conditions; this is really a basic liberal principle.[93] After all, "man is not only one with his fellows, but also one by himself," and a qualitative conception of social progress implies an increase in work that is individual in character and an increase in the enjoyment of such work.[94]

But Mill's qualitative Utilitarianism cannot wholly be said to correspond to Hobson's mode of thought. In one main sense Hobson is not a Utilitarian, despite his attempt at a qualitative (and non-operative) delineation of a cost-utility calculus. He is no Utilitarian in that he does not believe in the harnessing of self-interest to achieve common benefit. Interestingly enough, in an article published in 1900, Hobson still could state:

... every interference with or dictation to the individual regarding the use of land, capital, labour, or any other economic power, must justify itself by showing that by interference with an abuse of power, it is increasing the aggregate of human liberty,[95]

thus remaining firmly anchored to a nineteenth-century liberal viewpoint. But a year later he wrote:

The added self-interest of each man does not constitute the collective organic interest of society; to suppose it does involves one more return to the false "monadism" which we abandoned in setting up a standard of "social utility."[96]

The above quotation is at the same time a denial of "economic liberalism" and the theory of the natural harmony of interests. The contrary, declares Hobson, often asserts itself— "a genuine antagonism between the apparent interests of individuals and of the whole community."[97] Hobson arrives at the conclusion that the individual as a

[91] *The Social Problem*, 246. [92] *Ibid.*, 183.

[93] Though Hobson believes that most socialists, too, "would be prepared to stake the value of their Socialism upon the single test of its active promotion of individuality in freedom of life, ..." *The Social Problem*, 183.

[94] *Ibid.*, 182, 184. [95] "The Ethics of Industrialism," 97–98.

[96] *The Social Problem*, 254. [97] *The Evolution of Modern Capitalism*, 406.

206 MICHAEL FREEDEN

separate unit and the sole focus of interest is meaningless.[98] It is impossible to explain these shifts in Hobson's views as a chronological development. Throughout his works there is an uncertainty as to the relative weight of the welfare of the social organism, on the one hand, and the liberty of its members, on the other. Thus in 1891, in contrast to the quotation (to note 95) above, he demanded adequate conditions of home life for the young "at whatever cost of interference with so-called private liberty of action."[99] Though interference on behalf of the young was also advocated by Mill, such a categorical statement can hardly be seen as compatible with the liberal tradition.

The point is that even "positive" liberty is extremely difficult to equate with individualism, once it is to be realized within the provisions of organic theory. Take what the best-known English exponent of "positive" freedom had to say:

When we speak of freedom as something to be so highly prized, we mean a positive power or capacity of doing or enjoying something worth doing or enjoying, and that, too, something that we do or enjoy in common with others. We mean by it a power which each man exercises through the help or security given him by his fellow-men, and which he in turn helps to secure for them.[100]

Hobson's understanding of positive freedom, seen from the perspective of the social organism, amounts to something else:

Little trouble is yet taken to discover the special aptitudes of citizens in relation to the special needs of society, the best methods of training these aptitudes, and of furnishing, not negative and empty "freedom" to undertake this work, but the positive freedom of opportunity. A whole cluster of "education" problems, manual and mental, demanding, not a separate empirical solution, but a related organic solution, with direct regard to full economy of social work, appears as part of the Social Question. Every failure to put the right man or woman in the right place, with the best faculty of filling that place, involves social waste.[101]

There is a Platonic ring to this passage. Elsewhere, indeed, Hobson seems willing to efface personal choice and democratic principles by means of a Rousseauist "general will."[102] Liberal-democratic axioms, such as "every man's life is of equal value to society," and "no taxation without representation" are rendered absurd, in his opinion, by the concept of a moral organism generating a "general will." Even Mill, says Hobson, "was feeling his way to the true formula of political as of economic justice"[103] when he denied the validity of the "one man one vote"

[98] *Work and Wealth,* 308.   [99] *Problems of Poverty,* 169.

[100] T. H. Green, *Liberal Legislation and Freedom of Contract* (Oxford, 1881), 9–10.

[101] *The Social Problem,* 10.

[102] In the explanation of this term we come across one of the rare occasions when Hobson recognizes his intellectual debt to Rousseau, Hegel, and Bosanquet. "The Re-Statement of Democracy," 265.   [103] *Ibid.,* 268.

principle. Yet Hobson retains these axioms because, pragmatically, the power of the purse makes for social responsibility, and because all known forms of political inequality cannot be recommended as they derive from qualities irrelevant to the public interest.

It is significant that the compliance with a "general will" appears together with the use of that basically illiberal word "efficiency," so popular at the turn of the century and so misappropriately exploited. Hobson understood social efficiency as the desire of individuals to merge their separate ends of individuality and to conform to the "general will" seeking by rational, conscious progress the welfare of society as a whole. This contained the idealist formula of subordinating "passing caprices and desires" to a sense of social service which implied, on the part of the individual, knowledge and rational self-control. Inevitably, Hobson saw the next step as a supreme and direct social control over the choice of work of individuals, at least as far as routine services were concerned.[104]

However, even those opinions do not deny Hobson the right to speak for liberalism. After all, a potentially "illiberal" element has always been part and parcel of a body of thought based on a belief in the ultimate rationality of man. It is, rather, when Hobson questions human rationality and the right to exercise free choice as such that he temporarily divorces himself from the liberal mainstream. Such a case is his discussion on the selection of the fittest. Here the non-liberal core of his intellectual influences seems finally to have broken through. One finds a mixture of Ruskin, the principle of efficiency, and Social Darwinism in Hobson's definition of the prohibition of anti-social marriages as a plain demand of social welfare, the purpose of which is to prevent any increase in the number of epileptics, criminals, and sufferers from hereditary diseases.[105] True, Hobson admits that in the interests of limitation of state action there should be no direct selection by society. But social vetoes upon "anti-social propagation" involving "public medical certificates of marriage" and "heavy penalties" virtually amount to the same and have an unpleasant association. Then questions arise such as what constitutes sound stock, is it physical and/or mental; who decides; is heredity the only cause of human deficiency and, if not, why must morally defective people be relegated to the ranks of second class citizens? It would appear that in justifying "breeding" as essential to social welfare Hobson forgets that individual free choice is itself intrinsic to social welfare. A liberal society must tolerate experimentation as one of the costs in the social utility equation. But by the time eugenics had established itself in the scientific world and was exciting public debate, Hobson was adopting a slightly more cautious

[104] *The Social Problem,* 263, 254–55.
[105] *John Ruskin,* 156; *The Social Problem,* 214–17.

108 MICHAEL FREEDEN

attitude. Environment, education, and economic opportunities, rather than direct control, could be manipulated to encourage the best type of parents to reproduce. He now admitted that there was a limit to individual sacrifice for the good of the kind, a limit to the duty due to posterity. Each generation had to live its own life.[106]

The issue of controlled selection seems, then, to have been an aberration more than a pillar of Hobson's thought. The dualism of individualism and society is not satisfactorily resolved either way. But Hobson makes an interesting attempt to substitute a more complex formula for Mill's simple abstraction. Mill had, of course, drawn the somewhat arbitrary division between self-regarding and other-regarding acts—the first being the absolute domain of the individual, the second calling for social intervention if harmful to society.[107] This is denied by Hobson on two points. First, because there are no absolute rights of individual liberty and secondly, because some injury to the social order must be the perpetual price of progress.[108] While breaking with the acknowledged oracle of liberalism on the question of *a priori* delimination of fields of action, Hobson does not refuse to grant individualism a sanctuary. As noted above, he often insisted that handing over functions to the state should be motivated by the desire to transfer individual energy and initiative from lower to higher work. Or else he reminds Liberals that they should require each new interference on the part of the state to justify itself by creating more liberty than it takes away.[109]

The crux of the matter, however, incorporating the novelty Hobson aims at injecting into liberalism, is the following:

The unity of . . . social-industrial life is . . . a federal unity in which the rights and interests of the individual shall be conserved for him by the federation. The federal government, however, conserves these individual rights, not, as the individualist maintains, because it exists for no other purpose than to do so. It conserves them because it also recognises that an area of individual liberty is conducive to the health of the collective life. Its federal nature rests on a recognition alike of individual and social ends, or, speaking more accurately, of social ends that are directly attained by social action and of those that are realised in individuals.[110]

In short, Hobson seems to be offering a feedback solution: concerted social action releases individual energies the fostering of which is conducive to society as a whole. This, and only this, is the *raison d'être* of

[106] Hobson, "Eugenics as an Art of Social Progress," *South Place Magazine*, 14 (Aug. 1909), 168–70.

[107] J. S. Mill, *On Liberty* (London, 1910), 72–73.

[108] "Character and Society," 94, 96. Cf. *Problems of Poverty*, 187.

[109] *The Social Problem*, 246; "The Four-Fold Path of Socialism," *The Nation*, 30/11/1907.

[110] *Work and Wealth*, 304.

individualism. It also explains what ostensibly appears to be Hobson's "middle class" moralizing about the need for strengthening individual character: social reform is ultimately dependent upon developing socially useful psychical traits.[111]

Let us conclude by following this thread of Hobson's critique of various reform initiatives and see how some of his practical reform suggestions combined with his attempt to rejuvenate liberal theory. Although at first Hobson had regarded factory and public health Acts, employers' liability Acts, and other protective industrial measures as indicating "the spirit of socialism," his reservations as to this socialism were that it was inspired by the intention of protecting certain sections of the working classes. This is a projection of that particularism already mentioned to which Hobson objected—"a chief and special benefit is conferred upon some particular persons or class."[112] As the social question must be approached from a universalistic viewpoint which assimilates private valuations in an over-all conception of human welfare, reform measures can only be applied to the benefit of certain groups as long as "these services are directed and intended less to fill the deficiencies of a class than to protect and improve the social organism as a whole."[113] It also explains why some contemporary issues, such as education, temperance, and disestablishment, seemed to Hobson to distract from the central questions of social reform—because of their typical middle class, and therefore particularistic, origins.[114]

Another related aspect of middle-class reform attempts is the outlook represented by the Charity Organisation Society, a frequent target of Hobsonian diatribes. Not only is their lauding of thrift futile because the average worker is unable even to support his family,[115] but they commit the basic error of regarding the isolated human will as the *primum mobile,* although no man is capable of self-support.[116] Charity thus ". . . substitutes the idea and the desire of individual reform for those of social reform, and so weakens the capacity for collective self-help in society."[117] Furthermore, reform should be social not only in application but in origin. "Social evils require social remedies."[118] A properly constituted society can supply all its legitimate needs out of its own resources.[119]

Ultimately, even established measures of dealing with social ills,

---

[111]"The Ethics of Industrialism," 98; *The Social Problem,* 286.

[112] *The Social Problem,* 196–97.

[113] *The Social Problem,* 287; *The Science of Wealth,* 220; *Work and Wealth,* 197.

[114]*A Modern Outlook,* 304–05.   [115] *The Social Problem,* 202–03.

[116]*The Crisis of Liberalism,* 206–07; this chapter was first published in the *Contemporary Review,* **70** (1896); "Of Labour," 197.

[117] *Work and Wealth,* 296.   [118]*John Ruskin,* 199; *Problems of Poverty,* 138.

[119] *Work and Wealth,* 297, 254.

110   MICHAEL FREEDEN

such as public relief and legislation, including national insurance, are classed by Hobson as palliatives. The one is a kind of charity while the other only substitutes a compulsory legal responsibility for a natural moral one.[120] But it is important to realize that Hobson, sensibly enough, understood the necessity, even desirability, of such "palliatives" when offered by the state. Not only were they beneficial to the whole social body—as the organic analogy taught—but they were an acknowledgement of society's obligations towards its members.[121] In the long run the pressing social questions of the time could only be solved by such a growing sense of duty.[122] The wrongs they occasioned had to be dealt with in the light of moral and political theory.

With this in mind and to this purpose Hobson tries to adapt some of the basic tenets of liberalism. This is especially salient in his treatment of "natural rights." As we have already observed when examining Hobson's departure from Mill, there exist for Hobson no absolute rights of the individual. Taking the natural right of property, Hobson gives its meaning a twist. "Natural" does not denote the innate and self-evident *ratio* but rather corresponds to certain physical and psychological traits, or needs, of the individual. And "right" becomes a relative term, a matter of social expediency. Thus, whatever is required to maintain the productive power of workers is their natural property, secured by considerations of social utility as a right in accordance with natural laws.[123] These laws are "natural" in the sense that, unless the "right" of property is recognized, human nature will refuse the effort asked of it. But such a refusal would be a concomitant of need, not a result of the "egoistic" nature of a man who has to be motivated in order to perform.

This links up with a rather confusing use of the term "property." Hobson uses it both for the product and for the process which, in the latter sense, includes "the scope of [the producer's] private activity and satisfaction"—in other words, the psychological fuel needed to continue producing. Now this satisfaction is obviously greater in nonroutine artistic and intellectual work. Therefore, such satisfaction being in Hobson's opinion adequate compensation for the effort of producing, the creative producer "has not the same natural right to the full market value of his poem as the weaver or the shoemaker to the value of his product." The only essential concrete property is that "necessary to maintain, from the material physical standpoint, the energy required for work."[124] Once a society has evolved which can infuse an element of art and human interest into all work and which will actualize the al-

---

[120] *Problems of Poverty*, 101, 119, 144.
[121] E.g., "The Four-Fold Path of Socialism," *The Nation*, 30/11/1907.
[122] "Of Labour," 106.
[123] *The Social Problem*, 102–03, 105.   [124] *Ibid.*, 108, 109, 173.

truistic, social nature of the individual, there will be no more private motivation to acquire property and the individual will forego any external inducement to work in the form of extra remuneration.[125] The final significance of this theory is again rather reminiscent of original Marxism.

Hobson connects the theory of property logically and substantially to a scrutiny of the primary natural right—that to life. Operationally defined, the right to live implies a state guarantee of a minimum standard of life and the provision of public work when necessary.[126] But again, the ultimate validity of the "right to labour," ". . . resides not in the claims of the individual, but in the duty of society to furnish, as far as it is able, the necessary conditions of a sound physical and moral life to its members."[127] Even then such relief ought not to be more than a public expediency and should never be construed as a mode of organic reconstruction.[128] As to a minimum standard of living, a sufficient and regular weekly income is imperative to the health of a family and to a sense of security which is the foundation of a moral and reasonable life.[129] But of course the minimal wage is only marginal to Hobson's concept of welfare. In the last resort, social welfare is qualitative and based on altruism. Thus, contrary to current views on the subject, the minimum wage could very well be the maximum wage. Wages—i.e., "to secure an ampler right of property to the individual worker than is represented by his bare wage of subsistence or of working efficiency"[130]—are a matter of social utility, catering to the profit motive and, hopefully, ephemeral. This is in sharp contrast to the down to earth mood Hobson displays when dealing with the actualities of contemporary industrial society. Here he again differentiates the principles he adheres to from socialist ones, in that he recognizes the importance of incentives and of adjusting individual payment to individual services.[131] This vacillation between realities and desiderata is rather too common a feature in Hobson's writings.

Occasionally one has the impression that Hobson is pushing the organism analogy too far. Thus one comes across the notion of a

---

[125] *Ibid.*, 173. But compare this to n.131 where Hobson seems to be taking a more realistic line.

[126] *Ibid.*, 201.   [127] "Of Labour," 109.

[128] *The Social Problem*, 200; Hobson, "The Right to Labour," *The Nation*, 8/2/1908.

[129] *Work and Wealth*, 192.

[130] *The Social Problem*, 103.

[131] "Social reform, whether applied through politics or not, consists in a thoughtful endeavour to discover and apply the minimum incentive for maximum personal efficiency. In so far as this is consistent with an equalisation of incomes, it is a double levelling process, levelling up and down; but when the nature of any personal effort involves a higher scale of payment, adequate provision for such discrimination must be made." "Are Riches the Wages of Efficiency?" *The Nation*, 9/11/1907; cf. "The Taxation of Monopolies," 25-26.

112   MICHAEL FREEDEN

government of experts—the nerve centre—acting as pivot to a system of feedback in which the individuals—the cells—have the vital, yet marginal "right continuously to convey information and advice." When the policy directives return from the centre "it is advantageous to the organism that . . . rights of suggestion, protest, veto and revolt should be accorded to its members."[132] But such a literal and elitist interpretation of the organism model is the exception rather than the rule, though even that could be integrated into liberal theory. Besides, one must remember that not the least justification of the "feedback" formula when adapted to liberalism is the indispensability of each member of the body politic. Government becomes diseased if any part is left to atrophy through lack of participation. The functioning of society is dependent on the thoughts, feelings, and interests of men and groups finding expression in acts of public government.[133] This is why Hobson advocated proportional representation and the use of the referendum[134] and, in view of the inevitable extension of state interference, displayed an increasing keenness to push home the need for a civic spirit. Its function would be to check and contain the state, to prevent corruption and enhance solidarity. The general will was now presented in its democratic aspect as a manifestation of public-spiritedness playing freely through the institutions of the state and controlling the policy of the government.[135] Moreover, the liberal emphasis on the importance of voluntary associations was preserved.[136]

It seems safe to say that Hobson is trying to reform liberalism from *within*. His main criticism of Ruskin—the admiration for whom is so manifest in Hobson's works—is that Ruskin was "illiberal" and displayed a disbelief in the efficacy of representative institutions and in the ability of the people to advance their true interests. And yet, what redeems Ruskin in Hobson's eyes is that on matters of social reform "Mr. Ruskin is much nearer to the more enlightened Liberals of his day and ours than he is willing to admit,"[137] and that a convergence of views between Ruskin and Mill was noticeable.

Hobson's recurring ambiguity is that of a liberal grappling and trying to come to terms with a new understanding of society resulting in

[132]"The Re-Statement of Democracy," 269–70.

[133]Hobson, "The New Aristocracy of Mr. Wells," *Contemporary Review*, **89** (1906), 487–97.

[134]Hobson, "Is Socialism a Spoils System?" *The Nation*, 2/11/1907, and *The Crisis of Liberalism*, Pt. I, chaps. 2, 3.

[135]Hobson, "Political Ethics of Socialism," *South Place Magazine*, **13** (April 1908), 128–31; "State Interference," *op. cit.*, **13**, (Jan. 1908), 78–79; and "Charity as an Instrument of Social Reform," *op.cit.*, **14** (Aug. 1909), 161–63.

[136]"The Ethics of Industrialism," 102; *John Ruskin*, 203–04.

[137]*John Ruskin*, 185, 189. Cf. a similar view expressed by E. T. Cook, "Ruskin and the New Liberalism," *The New Liberal Review*, **1** (1901), 18–25.

a complex statement of social aims and of the relationship between the individual and the state. Indeed, his criticism of the Liberal party often was that they were not resolute in developing what he believed, and what they were slowly coming to see, was a new social conscience and consciousness. But by 1914, looking back on the achievements of a Liberal government, Hobson could note with satisfaction that the party of progress had shed its Whiggish element and was rapidly replacing Victorian liberalism with social radicalism.[138] A revived social philosophy seemed at last to be in the process of realization along the lines Hobson had already adumbrated some time before:

Liberalism is now formally committed to a task which certainly involves a new conception of the State in its relation to the individual life and to private enterprise. That conception is not Socialism, in any accredited meaning of that term, though implying a considerable amount of increased public ownership and control of industry. From the standpoint which best presents its continuity with earlier Liberalism, it appears as a fuller appreciation and realisation of individual liberty contained in the provision of equal opportunities for self-development. But to this individual standpoint must be joined a just apprehension of the social, viz., the insistence that these claims or rights of self-development be adjusted to the sovereignty of social welfare.[139]

St. Antony's College, Oxford.

[138] Hobson, *Traffic in Treason* (London, 1914), 10, 14.
[139] *The Crisis of Liberalism*, xii.

VI

Sociability and Social Conflict in George Herbert Mead's Interactionism, 1900 - 1919

Andrew Feffer

During the 1970s and 80s philosophers, psychologists, and intellectual historians revived the Pragmatist tradition in American philosophy. They devoted the greater share of study to the work of Charles S. Peirce and John Dewey. A number of scholars, however, also participated in a minor but persistent revival of interest in the work of George Herbert Mead, Dewey's partner and collaborator at the University of Chicago and one of the founders of social psychology in the United States.

One generally welcomes renewed attention to a thinker and writer of such unappreciated brilliance as Mead. This renaissance would be no different were it not for the fact that it yielded relatively little in the way of historical study. While many scholars have established Mead's intellectual credentials, only a few have spent much time investigating the genesis of Mead's ideas or determining what his writing meant in the context of American intellectual, social, and political history. A thorough intellectual biography (not to mention *any* sort of biography) of Mead still waits to be written.[1]

I would like to use this essay to begin deepening our historical knowledge of Mead's work, and to do so in a particular manner. Historian

---

[1] Two published biographical studies known to me as of this writing have contributed greatly to our understanding of Mead but focus primarily on the explication of his published works. David Miller, *George Herbert Mead: Self, Language and the World* (Austin, 1973); Hans Joas, *G. H. Mead: A Contemporary Reexamination of his Thought* (Cambridge, 1985), has done the most to place Meadian theory in social context; and see his introduction for a survey of the literature. For a very different interpretation from the one presented in this essay, see Stephen Diner, *A City and its Universities* (Chapel Hill, 1980), 5, 36-43, 86-129, 149-50; and "George Herbert Mead and Reform in Chicago" (unpublished 1973 manuscript at Chicago Historical Society).

Daniel Rodgers argues that one of the limits to our understanding of political concepts is our reluctance to view them as rhetorical tools used in contentious political environments. Political language at various times has become the object of dispute between identifiable political factions and contending social groups. Those fighting over territory and power also fought over the meaning of words, over their use, over their reference, even over their rightful ownership. And because control of words and the discourses of political power were so important in determining the outcome of more tangible conflicts, political language played a key role in mapping out the political terrain of American history.[2]

The problems Rodgers identifies in the general history of American political ideas can be found in our more particular history of Mead's intellectual development. Even as a philosopher Mead addressed politically freighted issues. For Mead both theoretical and applied psychology functioned as social practice, guiding and inspiring social and political activism, in which he was personally involved. The activist nature of Mead's writing presents us (as readers in the present) with a problem of clearly identifying both the intended and unintended meanings of his key terminology, which, like the political language of any era, is subject (if viewed in context) to just those contentions Rodgers describes. Did Mead's frequently used term "social control," for example, refer to greater state power or to more just forms of social organization? There is ample room for both interpretations in the context of social and political dispute during Mead's lifetime. What did Mead and his contemporaries mean by "democracy"? Did Mead genuinely embrace a radically participatory democracy? Or shall we accept the more established condemnation that Mead's generation simply used democratic rhetoric in the pursuit of middle-class professional power?[3]

To answer these questions we need to place Mead's philosophy in a clear historical context, viewing it against the Chicago reform culture of the turn of the century, which Mead and his colleagues helped create. While I do not want to argue that Mead's psychology is entirely bound to that political and cultural context, it is essential to study his words and ideas against the terrain of significant events, institutions, and people. Like Rodgers, I would like to focus on several "keywords," used by Mead, his colleagues and his generation, and begin to uncover their political and historical nuances. Most of these terms cluster about the notion of a "social self" that formed the core of Mead's interactive social psychology: "sociability," "sociality," "social consciousness," and "the social self" are a few. Other terms linked Mead's concept of the social

---

[2] Daniel Rodgers, *Contested Truths* (New York, 1987), Prologue.

[3] Joas, 10; Diner, *A City and its Universities*, 25, 59, 89; Dmitri Shalin, "G. H. Mead, Socialism and the Progressive Agenda," *American Journal of Sociology*, 93 (1988), 913-51.

116   ANDREW FEFFER

self to broader political issues; for example, the physiological and psychological notion of "coordination" and its political equivalent "cooperation." Mead referred these terms to each other and intended them to share common meanings, as did John Dewey and the lesser-known members of the University of Chicago faculty, on which Mead spent most of his career.

Mead generalized from these interrelated terms with a reformist political intent. He tried to form a critical vocabulary and a set of theories that would emphasize human qualities incompatible with free-market capitalism. To achieve "cooperation" in the new century, he tried to demonstrate that social reciprocity (a more fundamental form of cooperation) is a natural part of human character. This goal motivated much of the philosophical and psychological studies in Mead's department. Resulting theories in turn laid the groundwork for moderate social reform that emerged in Chicago between 1890 and 1910, a reformism preferred by Mead and his circle. The political significance of Mead's philosophy, however, was not as clear as the above statement implies. As I hope to show, Mead and his colleagues did not always control the significance of their words and theories. Their contentious political environment also shaped their philosophy. The theory thus followed the contours of actual social change and political dispute in Chicago between 1894 and 1919.

Dewey and Mead. Mead began writing about the social self around 1900. By that time John Dewey already had been exploring the philosophical implications of cooperation for over fifteen years.[4] In the 1890s Dewey refined earlier arguments about the evolution of human action into his mature theory of the reflex circuit or "coordination," which was presented in his famous 1896 article criticizing reductionist stimulus-response models of human behavior (or, as Dewey called them, "reflex-arc" psychologies). By this time Dewey had abandoned much of his early theological language for the terminology of scientific psychology, but he did not change substantially his overall argument. In his reflex-arc critique Dewey characterized action as a form of "reconstruction," in which the agent constantly constitutes an object world (as well as a subjective identity) out of his problematic encounter with his biological and social environment.

Dewey addressed this argument to fellow philosophers, psychologists, and theologians, but ethical and political concerns also strongly motivated him. He wrote the reflex-arc critique just two years after wandering into the midst of the Pullman strike, Chicago's worst social conflagration of the century. In this unfolding historical context Dewey wanted, in de-

---

[4] For a fuller account see my "Between Head and Hand: Chicago Pragmatism and social reform, 1886-1919" (Ph.D. diss., University of Pennsylvania, 1987), chapters 4 and 6.

veloping his theoretical alternatives to reductionist psychology, to demonstrate two things.

First, like the German idealists and liberal theologians who inspired him, Dewey hoped to show that the rational was immanent in experience. Rational consciousness and spirituality emerged out of the struggle for survival, transforming it into "intelligent" and ethical "action," that is, behavior with a rational goal. As a fully integrated circuit of "coordination," human action remained habitual and automatic until the individual encountered a problem in its environment, interfering with habitual fulfillment of needs. Ideas, beginning with the most primitive impulsive intention and ending with the most abstract philosophical theory, served in the circuit as plans for the adjustment of behavior to new problematic situations. A successful adjustment would lead to a new, provisionally successful habit, and the circuit would begin again. Rational consciousness evolved in a continuous fashion from fundamental psychological and biological functions, such as neural reaction responses to stimuli, or impulses. "Reflex-arc" responses, then, contained a kernel of human rationality and constructive intelligence. An organic continuity existed between the elements of human action: the rational was immanent in the impulse.[5]

Second, Dewey, influenced by the Social Gospel of the 1880s, hoped to show that a cooperative rather than prudential rationality emerged from human impulse, based on socially constructive reciprocity rather than individual pecuniary gain. The inclination of many Darwinists (including physiological psychologists) to align evolutionary theory with some kind of utilitarianism threatened to strengthen philosophical justifications of a market-oriented and individualistic capitalism. Dewey tried to escape the utilitarian implications of the most mechanistic and reductionist psychologies then emerging out of the post-Darwinian controversy.[6] That which is most lofty in human nature, he argued, *does* emerge from the material struggle. "Reconstruction" (meaning reform), cooperation, and reciprocity are, argued Dewey, psychologically and therefore biologically natural to humans. Thus, the reflex-arc critique made an important political as well as philosophical point, which many

[5] Dewey, "The Reflex-Arc Concept in Psychology," *Psychological Review*, 3 (1896), repr. in Jo Ann Boydston et al. (eds.), *John Dewey, The Early Works* (5 vols.; Carbondale, 1973), (hereafter referred to as *EW* with volume number), V, 96-109; Dewey, *Psychology* (New York, 1891), reprinted as *EW* II, *passim*; Dewey, "Soul and Body," *Bibliotheca Sacra*, 43 (1886), reprinted in *EW* I, 96-98.

[6] Dewey argued this case in many essays. A few are: John Dewey,"Evolution and Ethics," *Monist*, 8 (1898), repr. in *EW* IV, 3-11; Dewey, *The Ethics of Democracy* (Ann Arbor, 1888), repr. in *EW* I, 227-52; Dewey, *Outlines of a Critical Theory of Ethics* (Ann Arbor, 1891), repr. in *EW* III, 239-338. For a full discussion of Dewey's interest in liberal theology and the Social Gospel see Daniel Day Williams, *The Andover Liberals* (New York, 1941), passim; Bruce Kuklick, *Churchmen and Philosophers* (New Haven, 1985), 191-98; Feffer, chapters 2-4.

118   ANDREW FEFFER

hoped would lead to a stronger concept of reciprocity or cooperation specially applicable to the social problems of the late nineteenth century. If purpose and spirituality could be shown to emerge naturally in human evolution, then a major hurdle could be overcome in justifying a more humane social ethic, one which stressed Christian harmony in historical development rather than the tooth-and-nail struggle for survival.[7]

Dewey, however, encountered serious philosophical obstacles to his effort to reconstruct psychology and society. An evolutionist like most of his contemporaries, Dewey argued that an individual achieved social and ethical "conduct" because in the broadest sense one *had* to for the purposes of survival. It was not particularly convincing, however, to argue that social consciousness developed as an adaptation to individual need. This obviously was not Dewey's intent. Yet he could not adequately distinguish his understanding of sociality and its origins from a Utilitarian calculus or Darwinian prudence. Dewey did not demonstrate that the prudent "intelligence" by which an individual discovered the means to achieve the goals of ongoing action necessarily (and psychologically) involved recognizing the significance and autonomy of others.[8]

Mead and the problem of sociability. George H. Mead joined Dewey at the University of Michigan in 1891 and followed the older philosopher to Chicago in 1894. During the 1890s Mead, picking up where Dewey left off, tried to establish the natural origins of social cooperation in human evolution without relying on Darwinian or Utilitarian notions of individual prudence. By 1909, as the result of this effort, Mead had laid the foundation of his interactionist social psychology.[9] He refined his theory in a series of articles on the social nature of the self and of consciousness between 1909 and 1913. By 1914 a fairly complete outline of Mead's mature social psychology, such as is usually taken from his later lectures, *Mind, Self and Society*, could be found in lectures given that year at the University.

Around 1900 Mead began exploring how and why humans evolved into social beings, trying, like Dewey, to demonstrate the social nature

---

[7] Dewey, "The Reflex-Arc Concept in Psychology," 109.

[8] Thus Dewey opened his philosophy to the long prevailing interpretation of it as a form of utilitarian Darwinism. See, e.g., Gail Kennedy, "The Pragmatic Naturalism of Chauncey Wright," *Studies in the History of Ideas*, III (3 vols.; New York, 1935), 486, 503; also Philip Wiener, "Chauncey Wright's Defense of Darwin and the Neutrality of Science," *JHI*, 6 (1945), 27; Dewey, *The Study of Ethics: a Syllabus* (Ann Arbor, 1894), repr. in *EW* IV, 338-39.

[9] For some reason Joas does not trace Mead's interest in sociability to Dewey, Joas, Chapter 3. Mead's personal odyssey from devout but troubled son of a Congregationalist minister reveals much about the roots of his social theory in late-nineteenth century religious conflict. See Robert Crunden, *Ministers of Reform* (New York, 1982), chapter 1; Feffer, 55-75.

MEAD'S INTERACTIONISM

of ethical conduct, using the terms of experimental psychology. It was with the later work of Wilhelm Wundt that Mead began a psychological argument for the social nature of man. Wundt appealed to Mead for two reasons. First, Wundt argued that language begins with the gesture, initially an impulsive act, or near act, which becomes, in a social context, a sign of emotion and intention. Because language is an act rather than a reflection of ideas or transcendent meanings, its content, rather than being the subject matter of logic and philology, instead should be the subject matter of a functionalist psychology that studies voluntary acts. Mead found Wundt's study particularly appealing because the German philosopher interpreted communication and sociality in psychological terms. The community "mind" or *Volkseele* inhered in the common language which emerged from the psychological processes of social interaction.[10]

Second, Wundt's language theory seemed to confirm Dewey's belief in the continuity between reason and impulse. Wundt's notion that the primitive "gesture" led to fully developed language linked the individual's irrational, biological nature with the socially ordered world of communication, suggesting the continuity between impulsive, unreflective behavior and rational socialized conduct. Unlike traditional philologists, wrote Mead, Wundt "is able to refer the beginning of language to the primitive impulse to expression. The sound is at first but a gesture" (*Lautgeberde*). Wundt, according to Mead, could move fluidly from the physical gestures to sound gestures to articulate language, demonstrating the origins of language in the primitive act (that is, in human and animal biology) "instead of being forced to build it up out of intellectual elements."[11]

Building on a critical interpretation of Wundt's theory, Mead speculated that social consciousness emerged as an interaction between individuals (or "forms," as Mead called them) through the interplay of gestures. The key to social organization and to the origin of social attitudes would then be in communication, the way in which "the conduct of one form is a stimulus to another." This "stimulus" is for the other to perform a certain act, which in turn becomes "a stimulus to [the] first to a certain reaction, and so on in ceaseless interaction." It was not the similarity of acts that constituted or encouraged social interaction but the meaning each act had, in terms of the act's consequences, for the other "form." Thus, "[t]he probable beginning of human communication was in cooperation . . . where conduct differed and yet where the act of the one answered to and called out the act of the other." This seemed the solution to Dewey's dilemma. Communication did not begin in prudence or com-

---

[10] Wilhelm Wundt, *Völkerpsychologie* (2 vols.; Leipzig, 1900), I, Einleitung; Mead, "The Relations of Psychology and Philology," *Psychological Bulletin*, 1 (1904), 377.

[11] *Ibid*, 380, 382.

petition nor in imitation but in constructive cooperation. This suggested that sociability likewise did not emerge as a prudent strategy for individual adaptation, but was present with the appearance of language.[12]

Mead, however, needed to extend Wundt's theory to address fully the problems raised by Dewey. Mead believed that Wundt's theory of language still did not adequately explain the emergence of sociability or communication from individual gestures and impulses. Wundt, like most of his contemporaries in laboratory psychology, began with the individual as a unit of analysis, explaining sociability as something added on to that individual identity.[13] Mead wanted to explain that individual identity, in fact all aspects of individual psychology, with sociability as a starting point. "Until the social sciences are able to state the social individual in terms of social processes, as the physical sciences define their objects in terms of physical change, they will not have risen to the point at which they can force their object upon an introspective psychology."[14] He wanted not just a theory of communication but a scientifically convincing genetic psychology of human cooperation. In other words Mead hoped to convince his readers that people could not be human, in any sense of the term, *unless* they were social (that is, cooperative).

Mead particularly found fault with Wundt's explanation of the meaning of gestures. Gestures are acts that signal something to another individual. What they signal, however, was a matter of some dispute. Wundt argued that gestures signalled emotional states and that those emotions constituted the meaning of the gestures. In the broadest sense Mead agreed. But according to the prevailing psychologies, emotions were reactions to stimuli. Wundt accepted this prevailing view, and it was on this count that Mead considered Wundt's explanation mechanistic, based upon individualistic reflex psychology. Mead preferred Dewey's theory, which paralleled his critique of the reflex-arc, that the emotions are "truncated acts," acts which do not achieve their purpose because they are inhibited either by circumstances or by the actor. Emotions signify the inhibition of the act, and spur the actor to find a solution to the problem.[15] A gesture, by expressing an emotional state, then, expresses an intended or an inhibited act. An animal gnashes its teeth when it wants to tear at the throat of another animal but has not yet done so, expressing the emotional state which reflects the unsatisfied desire, the uncompleted response to the combative "situation."

[12] Mead, "Social Psychology as Counterpart to Physiological Psychology," *Psychological Bulletin*, 6 (1909), 406.

[13] Mead, "1914 Class Lectures in Social Psychology," *The Individual and the Social Self* (Chicago, 1982), 37.

[14] Mead, "What Social Objects Must Psychology Presuppose?," *Journal of Philosophy*, 7 (1910), 176.

[15] Mead, "1914 Class Lectures in Social Psychology," 40; Dewey, "A Theory of Emotion," *Psychological Review*, 1 (1894), 2 (1895), reprinted in *EW* IV, 152-88.

The gesture, thus, does not express simply an emotional state but also signifies to the other the possible consequences of the emotional state, of the truncated act which constitutes the emotion—the "value of the act for the other individual." As the other responded "in terms of another syncopated act" a "field of social signification" was born, within which communication and social interaction would take place. Gestures had meanings "when they reflected possible acts," i.e., possible consequences for another individual who could see in that gesture a repressed yet still latent act.[16]

Upon Wundt's theory of the gesture Mead grafted a conception of meaning adopted from Dewey and Josiah Royce—that for a sentient being the meaning of an object is the purpose that object will serve in some foreseeable future or the role it will play in some action that culminates desire or need. Like Dewey and Royce, Mead argued that meaning involved the reference, through signs (that is, ideas, emotions, and "attitudes"), to future acts and experiences. But that meaning, continued Mead, could only be constituted as an intention conveyed to some "other" through gestures and language. According to Mead, therefore, meaning was actional (as Dewey argued), but it was also fundamentally social. In this way the play of gestures represented "the birth of the symbol, and the possibility of thought," a form of "sublimated conversation." Thus, Mead argued, "reflective consciousness implies a social situation which has been its precondition."[17]

Mead believed he had added two things to Wundt's theory of the gesture. First, by referring the meaning of gestures entirely to social acts, Mead believed he had eliminated a main vestige of individualistic psychology that referred psychological events in the other direction to internal states of mind (in this case internal emotions). Second, by externalizing and socializing emotional states, Mead laid the groundwork for socializing even more fundamental psychological concepts. In 1910 Mead expanded this second line of argument. In two articles Mead tried to demonstrate that consciousness of the self and of objects also had cooperative social origins.

Arguing from the principle that "meaning is consciousness of attitude," Mead concluded that one cannot be *self*-conscious without a consciousness of others because the self is no more than an awareness of one's own attitude. It is only through the responses of others to one's actions, especially to one's gestures, that one becomes conscious of one's own attitudes, including one's self-identity. Thus, "[o]ther selves in a social environment logically antedate the consciousness of self which

---

[16] Mead, "Social Psychology as a Counterpart to Physiological Psychology," 407.

[17] Mead, "Social Consciousness and the Consciousness of Meaning," *Psychological Bulletin*, 7 (1910), 399; Mead, "Social Psychology as Counterpart to Physiological Psychology," 407.

introspection analyzes. They must be admitted as there, as given, in the same sense in which psychology accepts the given reality of physical organisms as a condition of individual consciousness." The self is not "an attitude which we assume . . . toward our inner feelings," (i.e., private introspection), but one directed "toward other individuals whose reality was implied even in the inhibitions and reorganizations which characterize this inner consciousness."[18]

Two years later Mead described two kinds of self that evolved from the primary interpersonal interaction. There is no true self in the philosophical meaning of the term, argued Mead. We do not identify ourselves first as "knowers" that precede the experience, physical or social, of the world. We are primarily object rather than subject, "me" rather than "I." Our self identity follows rather than precedes conversation whether it is the actual conversation of language or the "inner conversation" that Mead argued constituted thought. The self is a constant product of an imagination striving to see itself as others see it. The absolute subject, the "I," the self of Descartes, of idealism, of Kant's transcendental apperception, is never accessible to us. It is forever immanent in our conversations with others and ourselves, the sum total of our social experience.[19]

Sociality, however, penetrates consciousness and perception even more deeply. Not only can we not know ourselves without first being enmeshed in some form of symbolic social interaction, but our consciousness of things, of physical objects, post-dates our entrance into the conversation of gestures. For us an object can only be an object if it retains some meaning in the course of our practical activity. Since Mead argued that consciousness of meaning emerges from the play of gestures, then it would follow that consciousness of objects themselves depends upon social interaction. So Mead contended that "[w]hatever our theory may be as to the history of things, social consciousness must antedate physical consciousness" and that "experience in its original form became reflective in the recognition of selves, and only gradually was there differentiated a reflective experience of things which were purely physical."[20]

Thus, by 1910 Mead had demonstrated (to his *own* satisfaction) that consciousness is social and that the objects of our consciousness (including the self) are socially constructed. Sociability, concluded Mead, is not just grafted onto the experience of fully conscious, rational individuals already capable of prudent decisions (including the decision to recognize other

---

[18] Mead, "What Social Objects Must Psychology Presuppose?," 179. "We are conscious of our attitudes because they are responsible for the changes in the conduct of other individuals," wrote Mead: "Social Consciousness and the Consciousness of Meaning," 403; see also "1914 Lectures on Social Psychology," 46.

[19] Mead, "The Mechanism of Social Consciousness," *Journal of Philosophy*, 9 (1912), 405-6.

[20] Mead, "What Social Objects Must Psychology Presuppose?," 180.

people). Sociability developmentally precedes conscious rationality, individual self-identity, and even the objects between which individuals rationally or prudentially choose.

The Cloud of Witnesses. When providing an account of Mead's philosophical development, one should not willingly stop here. My purpose is not to defend or dress up Mead's theory but to show its contextual significance. As Dewey proclaimed in 1896, "the point of this story is in its application." It was no coincidence that Mead developed these theories while he was occupied with mediating conflicts between Chicago industrialists and their workers. Mead's discourse on social psychology was inaccessible to most participants in Chicago's class struggle, but Mead addressed his writing to the problems raised in that conflict as much as to the inadequacy of earlier social psychologies.[21]

Virtually all of the department's members participated in the social reform movements that flourished in Chicago after the 1890s. Dewey came to Chicago not only to head the department but also to establish his University Laboratory School from which to "reconstruct" society by fostering "democratic" education. Mead continued the struggle for democratic schools after Dewey's departure from Chicago in 1904. Mead's primary involvement in educational reform came through his membership in the City Club, a fraternal organization of Chicago professionals and small businessmen interested in progressive reform. Mead sat on and eventually chaired the club's educational committee, for which Mead directed an influential study on vocational and industrial education. Mead's involvement in social and labor reform, however, went far beyond school politics. Through the City Club Mead, together with his colleague James H. Tufts, also directly mediated labor-management conflicts in the city's industries. Mead helped negotiate a settlement to the garment strike of 1910; and although the agreement fell through, its principles became the basis for the model arbitration agreement of 1915 between the clothing workers and Hart, Schaffner, and Marx, the city's largest clothing manufacturer. Several years later Tufts sat on the arbitration board that supervised that agreement, which soon was extended to cover most of the major clothing firms in the city. As part of their crusade for the peaceful mediation of labor disputes, both Tufts and Mead earned reputations as consistent advocates for union recognition.[22]

As he struggled in the pages of learned journals to demonstrate the cooperative origins of all consciousness, Mead preached to Chicagoans the need for industrial cooperation and reciprocity between capital and labor. The key common term in Mead's psychology and his reform was "cooperation," or reciprocity. Mead called for cooperation between

[21] Dewey, "The Reflex-arc Concept in Psychology," 109.
[22] Feffer, chapter 8; Shalin, 924.

classes and opposing social groups, which would be based upon the reciprocity natural to human interaction and communication: "[T]he recognition of the given character of other selves" (i.e., the recognition of others as significant) comes "from psychology itself, and arises out of the psychological theory of the origin of language and its relation to meaning."[23]

Such a synthesis of psychology and social analysis became the hallmark of Chicago's activist social psychology and a linchpin of later liberal political discourse. For Dewey the organic continuity of human action had suggested that the social conflict tearing Chicago apart, caused by the inadequate social organization of modern industrial society in general, reflected a break in the coherence of human psychology. The factory system and the market place had divided the psychological functions between different classes, thereby creating opponents in the political arena as well. Mead agreed. Industrial leaders controlled the "intellectual" functions of production, such as planning and evaluation. Their employees participated only as the hands, the final executors of social action.

Dewey and Mead depicted the social conflicts of their day in the psychological terms of the reflex-arc critique. Labor and capital acted out on a social and political scale the circuit of psychological coordination that Dewey had proposed as an alternative to reflexology. Owners and managers pursued a conservative politics of a class unaffected by social ills, expressing a psychology of "rational" managerial planning. The responsibilities of management inclined them habitually to perpetuate hitherto successful forms of social conduct and organization, even when it was to the detriment of the city's manual workers.[24] Social problems, however, emerged from the habitual practice of a society run by an intellectual and economic elite. The working class responded to these problems as a class that experienced the injustices and hardships of industrialism directly. Having been denied intellectual training and control, workers (especially the unskilled) tended toward politics that expressed the essentially impulsive nature of manual activity, to the exclusion of political foresight. They haphazardly experimented with and projected, in radically utopian and revolutionary form, new social practices. This, according to both philosophers, was the nature of the "radicalism" that flourished in the working class districts of "red" Chicago, and that periodically enflamed (as the middle class saw it) social conflagrations such as the Haymarket incident or the Pullman strike. Yet this could be a functional relationship. Industrial management and po-

[23] Mead, "What Social Objects Must Psychology Presuppose?," 177.

[24] Mead, "Industrial Education, the Working Man and the School," *Elementary-School Teacher*, 9 (1908-9), 369-83; Mead, "1914 Class Lectures in Social Psychology," 86-93; James H. Tufts and John Dewey, *Ethics* (New York, 1908), ch. 12 (written by Tufts).

litical leadership conservatively protected social habits but conceded new, provisional practices under the demand of impulsive "radicalism." New practices that dealt with a problem successfully would be implemented as new habits. As Dewey argued in 1897, the two sides psychologically and socially needed each other and needed to resolve social conflict through reconciliation because it was only through the interpenetration of impulse and habit that psychological and social development could occur.[25]

Mead considered it especially urgent "to establish a theory of social reform among inductive science" that would mediate between "conservatism" and "utopian" revolution.[26] Without changing Dewey's political or philosophical assumptions, Mead deepened the elder philosopher's psychological explanation of social conflict. Not only is social reciprocity psychologically necessary to social order, but without it even human consciousness would be impossible. The thought which makes us human, what Mead called the "inner conversation," depends upon social cooperation and reciprocity even if it is only implicit in the evolution of human capacities.

In applying this psychology to politics, Mead and Dewey tried to balance impulse against reason, radical vision against conservative habit. The central feature of their social psychology was cooperation between social classes, each of which articulated a partially developed facet of human psychology. The goal for Mead and Dewey was "social control," but by that they meant a form of cooperative self-control through reciprocal agreements, such as the arbitration agreement that governed Chicago's garment industry in the teens. Such agreements required that opposing classes take the roles of their opponents, recognizing the other's perspective in order to be able to find a new social practice acceptable to all and beneficial to a reconstructed social order. They should not, just as all social interactions should not, involve the imposition of authority or the imitation by subordinates of prescribed habits. "The important character of social organization of conduct or behavior through instincts is not that one form [i.e., one individual] in a social group does what the others do, but that the conduct of one form is a stimulus to another to a certain act, and that this act again becomes a stimulus to [the] first to a certain reaction, and so on in ceaseless interaction."[27] Social control, argued Mead, is the process of "constantly carrying about with us this self which is seen through the eyes of others" and subjecting that self-image to criticism.[28] As Mead's colleague, Edward S. Ames,

[25] Dewey, *The Significance of the Problem of Knowledge* (Chicago, 1897), repr. in *EW* V, 4-24.

[26] Mead, "The Working Hypothesis in Social Reform," *American Journal of Sociology*, 5 (1899), 367.

[27] Mead, "Social Psychology as Counterpart to Physiological Psychology," 406.

[28] Mead, "1914 Class Lectures on Social Psychology," 72.

126   ANDREW FEFFER

declared, we live in a "cloud of witnesses." Our self-identities are determined by our interaction with people of different social stations, different ethical and political viewpoints, different personal needs, and, through literature, different eras.[29]

The world according to Mead was a Greek drama of roles and choruses, interacting, readjusting, and responding. Social life and language, maintained Mead, involve the "continued readjustment of one individual to another." So do social reconstruction and individual growth, the "play back and forth between the selves," between impulsive tendencies embodied in real individuals or in the imaginary voices of one's inner conversation, the real or imaginary cloud of witnesses.[30] Individual intellectual and moral development, in fact, is a form of social reconstruction; for while "the organization of this inner social consciousness is a reflex of the organization of the outer world," the individual nonetheless strains to "reconstruct" the conflicting chorus of his consciousness. As the individual comes to terms with his conflicting social roles, he proposes a new order to the society as well.[31]

Mead's social conception of the "self" and his commitment to social reconstruction have led historians to link Mead's theory with European social democracy. Like the European socialists, Mead insisted that the labor movement and its social democratic leaders most effectively contributed to "reconstructing" society. Social democratic labor, guided by theorists such as Ferdinand Lasalle, created a situation "in which people *had* to put themselves in the place of others." Labor *demanded* reciprocity, a voice in the chorus, and therefore, through the constructive expression of worker demands, "forced communities to think in social terms" and individuals to "put themselves into other people's places."[32]

Labor's demands encouraged constructive social reform in yet another manner peculiar to the role workers played in industrial society. A capitalist economy, Mead argued, distorted human social psychology by forcing everyone to enter practical, industrial relations through the exchange of money, as wages and profits, on the marketplace. Consequently, the industrialist who does not actually work in the factory he owns can no longer understand the actual social relations involved in manufacturing, nor can he grasp the "human products of the process," the hardships and injustices of industrialism. Rather than put himself in the place of others, the industrialist calculates the bottom line of his ledger book.

The industrialist's pecuniary narrowmindedness, his inability to understand the factory system in social rather than merely economic terms,

---

[29] Edward S. Ames, *The Higher Individualism* (Boston, 1915), 67-71.

[30] Mead, "1914 Class Lectures on Social Psychology," 43, 75.

[31] *Ibid.*, 74; Mead, "The Social Self," *Journal of Philosophy*, 10 (1913), 377.

[32] Mead, "1914 Class Lectures on Social Psychology," 98.

leads him to adopt a narrow and abstract philosophy of life, hedonism, the calculation of one's own pleasure and pain without regard to others and without a real understanding of the objects he finds pleasurable.[33] While the industrialist may have a practical understanding of the economy and of money, he has little understanding of the practicalities of life in the concrete. This side of experience is reserved in limited form for the industrialist's workers, who produce society's goods. In such a situation a barrier is erected between people, deep within the social psychology of industrial life. Mead had argued that the natural form of practical activity involves the coordination of present experience and future possibility. In perception this coordination occurs, Mead continued, between the "contact stimuli" of touch and ingestion and the "distance stimuli" of seeing and hearing. For animals this coordination is fairly primitive and immediate, involving little inhibition of impulse or delay of gratification. For humans the coordination of distance and contact stimuli occurs within the matrix of social communication by means of linguistic signs. Objects originally took form in the consciousness of primitive men (and children) because of this social "situation."[34]

Mead did not present this last facet of his theory directly as a social psychological critique of industrialism, but one can piece together some of its political implications without too much conjecture. Through history the experience of contact and distance stimuli became divided between classes or castes or, in the best of times, between people occupying different functional roles. Workers handled the concrete objects of social existence, while elite castes and intellectuals understood the world in abstract terms. To the latter the calculation of the future came easy. But the exigencies of the present, the direct contact with industrial life, lay beyond their experience. So in order to become perceptually and psychologically whole, the rationality of the businessman had to be united through communication and reciprocal cooperation with the manual practicality of the industrial worker.[35]

While championing the labor movement, however, Mead rejected European socialist theories of revolutionary class conflict. If the occupation of separate roles amounted to a significant or enduring conflict, something would be socially and psychologically wrong. If we should perceive ourselves as members of a class or caste, then our efforts (to pursue radical social change or promote a limited social interest) would defy the natural development of social relations. For Mead and his colleagues class conflict was a vestige of primitive societies governed by

---

[33] *Ibid.*, 96-97, 100.
[34] Mead, "Concerning Animal Perception," *Psychological Review*, 14 (1907), 383-90.
[35] Mead, "1914 Class Lectures on Social Psychology," 100.

128 ANDREW FEFFER

military practices in which people identified themselves exclusively as members of a clan, caste, or nation.[36]

Going even further than this historical condemnation, Mead held class consciousness disrupted our natural social and psychological growth. When an individual belongs to a caste, he is unable to take the role of someone from another caste, for that is precluded by the rules of caste membership: "Where there is a fixed, stratified society, a person does not present himself in the form of another. . . ." This inability to assume another's role prevents the caste member from reconciling conflicts in the caste system. One can no longer reform the social order because "there is no social problem" to reform (that is, it is not recognized) and because one is not able to reconcile unassumed roles. Nor does one hear an inner conversation between opposing selves because that ability requires assuming the roles of socially significant "others." Thus, personal development is also limited. Someone who is unable to "enter into the place of the other" is, Mead insisted, "intellectually deficient." "Inability to put yourself in the place of another puts up a barrier, prevents grasping of the social situation at all. The process of clear and adequate thinking is the process of putting one's self completely in the place of the other. The process of thought is simply the abstraction of this social procedure."[37] The object of constructive social conflict is "such a reconstruction of the situation that different and enlarged and more adequate personalities may emerge." The new social situation is truly reconstructed only if "all the personal interests are adequately recognized" and if one has a "new world harmonizing the conflicting interests into which enters the new self." It is only under the conditions in which individuals assume roles integrated in a harmonious social whole that truly "democratic consciousness" occurs.[38]

In a normally developing social "situation," opposing social roles simply represented conflicting but reconcilable social functions. This ability to achieve consensus in any conflict, Mead believed, existed on the most fundamental psychological and linguistic level. Humans form their conceptions of the world through the reconciliation of conflicting stimuli. An example from Dewey's 1896 essay illustrated Mead's point. A child confronted with a flame, Dewey had argued, "reconstructs" his understanding of the flame by playing with it. At first the child is attracted by the flame, as if it were a toy. The child fits the flame into a set of perceptions that do not distinguish flames from toys. More importantly, habitually *behaving* as though the flame were a toy, the child grabs the

[36] Tufts and Dewey, *Ethics*, 500; Mead, "1914 Class Lectures on Social Psychology," 87.

[37] *Ibid*., 68, 95.

[38] Mead, "The Social Self," 379; Mead, "1914 Class Lectures on Social Psychology," 95.

flame and is burned. Now at this point (or after a few more attempts) the child has learned that the flame is a flame, that is to say, a bright, shiny, but dangerous and painful object. But, Dewey asked, what *exactly* has the child learned? Dewey analyzed the problem as a process of adjusting habitual behavior to new, problematic stimuli. The child can treat the flame as a toy until interacting with it as if it were a toy, and this makes painfully problematic the *habit* of playing with all bright objects. The child deals with that problem by coming up with a new set of ideas and habits that distinguish *behaviorally* between toys and flames.[39]

Mead looked at the problem from a slightly different angle, as a situation in which the child is trying to reconcile two opposing perceptions or conceptions (of the object as plaything and of the object as dangerous) and therefore two different *roles*. After initially being burned the child now has two objects in the field of consciousness, the flame as bright shiny toy-like object and the flame as dangerous. When the child comes up with a new habit of dealing with flames and similar objects, he or she is learning to perceive the object in a more complete way by finding an object that combines the earlier two: the flame looks like a toy but burns like a flame. In this way the child reconciles contradictions faced in his or her experience. Up to here Mead did not significantly expand Dewey's theory. But Mead, dissatisfied, asked, how does this happen? How can the child do this but not, say, a dog? Animals could not perceive objects as men do. "[T]here is a conscious construction which men carry out that we do not find in the lower animals," contended Mead. "There is an ability to hold in consciousness the conflicting stimulations and tendencies to respond in a conflicting fashion."

We can perceive objects clearly because we are able to see ourselves from more perspectives than one. Our conflicting versions of the object before us, our conflicting sets of raw data, our hypotheses, really represent conflicting responses we might make to given stimuli. Our ability to see those responses comes from our ability to view ourselves in different roles, the role, for example, of the child avoiding flames or, alternatively, the role of the child burning his fingers. Our process of reflection, of forming hypotheses (and habits), argued Mead, amounts to "our own responses to our own replies to these conflicting stimuli." Thought is a "field of discourse, a social field." But it is a process in which we reconcile all opposing tendencies, all roles. It is a process of achieving agreement between the conflicting voices.[40] Our ability to reason and act rationally, then, depends upon our natural ability to reconcile opposing voices within the cloud of witnesses that constitutes our consciousness. This "self" construction, the creation of new roles out of old conflicting ones, is

[39] Dewey, "The Reflex-arc Concept in Philosophy," 97-99.
[40] Mead, "1914 Class Lectures on Social Psychology," 52-53, 77.

130   ANDREW FEFFER

fundamentally human. It is also naturally "cooperative," conciliatory, and social, in the manner Mead prescribed for opposing social groups.

The Twilight of Cooperation. Mead's manner of naturalizing social reconciliation, of course, presented serious problems. First, the changing context of Chicago's political and social conflicts clouded the notions of cooperation and reciprocity employed by Mead and his colleagues. Early in the reform movement the demand for reciprocity implied a radical change in the relationship between the city's economic elite and the laboring poor. "Cooperation," as Mead saw it, in fact all normal human interaction, required giving a voice (in the social chorus and the inner conversation) to the as yet voiceless victims of the factory system. In the context of the 1890s giving workers a voice would have been liberating. More substantially, industrial mediation and workplace cooperation entailed, at the very least, union recognition and suggested that employees should participate in the management of their workplaces. However conservative many unions actually were, calling for open recognition of their right to bargain collectively for industrial workers was still a fairly radical proposal.[41]

But times changed, and as the business leaders of Chicago realized that new forms of industrial organization would be necessary to maintain social order and economic stability, the meaning of "cooperation" shifted in a conservative direction. Gradually, reformers succeeded in making the political system more responsive to the demands of the city's poor. Such was the case in the arbitration of labor disputes and in the regulation of housing and public utilities. These improvements, however, were limited in scope and on terms set by the city's business leaders. To the extent that "cooperation" began to govern industrial and urban relations, it confined working class aspirations as much as it gave voice to their demands for a true industrial and urban democracy.

This result, however, should not have surprised anyone. The ambiguous legacy of cooperative social reform was latent in reform ideology and rhetoric as expressed in the general political discourse and in the more specific writings of intellectuals like Mead. From the start Chicago's social groups contested the notions of industrial democracy and social cooperation employed by Mead and others. The working class used "cooperation" to promote workers' power in various workplaces. The city's industrial leaders, on the other hand, used "cooperation" and similar words to demand greater responsibility from Chicago's working class.

Nowhere was this clearer than in the city school system, where the militant Chicago Teachers Federation (CTF) demanded teachers' councils that would control curriculum and administration of the schools.

[41] Edwin Witte, *Historical Survey of Labor Arbitration* (Philadelphia, 1952), 3-4.

The initial dispute arose over the dispensation of tax money and the level of teachers' salaries, issues raised by the fledgling CTF led by union activist and political radical Margaret Haley. Haley and the union, however, soon broadened their movement. Haley considered the Chicago school board's perennial campaigns for teaching efficiency and centralization of authority part of a broader attack by a corporate elite on democratic institutions. The school, Haley argued, is the training ground of future citizens. Unless they are taught by autonomous teachers, those students will simply be groomed for roles as factory operatives and servants. A truly democratic school system should remain under the control of teachers and the lower level district superintendents, who, unlike the central administrators, were usually former teachers. Workplace and educational reciprocity, from Haley's point of view, involved genuinely participatory and democratic control of work and schooling.[42]

More conservative reformers, however, often allied with commercial and business organizations, spoke differently of educational democracy and cooperation. The city's civic and business leaders had to contend with an educational system unsuited to the needs of a city rapidly growing in population and territory. Their solution, centralization, suited the ideological predilections of the business elite. A powerful school superintendent during the first decade of the century, Edwin Cooley, promoted the centralization program. Like the teachers, Cooley used the rhetoric of reciprocity and cooperation. But for Cooley cooperation meant responsibility and the submission to the larger and more centralized plans of the community, represented by Chicago's Commercial Club. Teachers had to cooperate with the school board, cease irresponsible demands (such as teachers' councils), and recognize the rational forms of social and educational administration which civic leaders thought right and just. Not surprisingly, an essential part of Cooley's, the Commercial Club's and the school board's program was removing the teachers' union, and this was successfully achieved with the passage in 1916 of the notorious "Loeb rule" outlawing teachers' organizations.[43]

By no means did Dewey and his colleagues attack corporate leaders with Haley's vehemence or invective, but they made common cause with Haley, the CTF, and the local labor movement in several important educational disputes. In 1908 Chicago's business leaders began, as part of their effort to centralize decisions over public school curriculum, to

[42] Margaret Haley to Jane Addams, May 4, 1906, Anita McCormick Blaine Papers, Wisconsin Historical Society; *Bulletin* of the Chicago Teachers' Federation, number 35, September 25, 1903, 4.

[43] Marjorie Murphy, "From Artisan to Semi-professional: White Collar Unionism Among Chicago Public School Teachers, 1870-1930," (Ph.D. diss., University of California, Davis, 1981), passim; Edwin G. Cooley, *Vocational Education in Europe* (Chicago, 1912); Minutes for November 23, 1908 of City Club Committee on Education (City Club Papers, Chicago Historical Society).

132   ANDREW FEFFER

promote public vocational education. Ironically, vocationalism built upon
an already existing movement led by Dewey and Mead calling for education relevant to the needs and interests of the laboring poor. Industrial
education and manual training, Mead and Dewey believed, would foster
reciprocity between classes by engaging the interests of working-class
children more effectively and by mediating in a common school system
between the children of conflicting classes. Business vocationalism, however, strove to construct a school system divided into intellectual and
industrial tracks, an unacceptable arrangement for the Chicago philosophers, teachers, and the city's labor movement. From 1908 until 1917,
when federal statutes made the issue moot, Mead and his colleagues
lobbied against the vocational education promoted by Chicago's industrial
elite.[44] They also frequently argued for teachers' autonomy from administration and from commercial interests (including textbook publishers).
The only educators sensitive enough to devise a truly child-centered
common school curriculum, argued Dewey, were those in close daily
contact with the students.[45] Mead supported the right of the teachers'
union to bargain collectively for its members as well as for the principle
of teachers' control and even advocated (provisionally) the creation of
teachers' councils. But like Cooley, Mead expected a level of responsibility
from the teachers that they were not willing or able to give, particularly
in the political context of the 'teens, when the school board's assault on
teachers' autonomy was most intense. In 1907 Margaret Haley did not
cooperate fully with a temporarily liberal (but still centralizing) school
board, and this indicated to Mead that the Chicago Teachers' Federation
was not holding up its end of the bargain. The teachers, of course, saw
it differently.[46]

Similarly, both Mead and colleague James Tufts expected of labor
leaders and their union members an unreasonable level of social and
economic responsibility. Even though in 1908 Mead advocated moderate
forms of workers' self-management, it was contingent upon proper education to the responsibilities of "social control" and rational self-control.
Later, Mead bitterly criticized labor's unwillingness to cooperatively forgo
wage increases while their employers profited heavily from war produc-

[44] Mead, "Introduction," *A Report on Vocational Training in Chicago* (Chicago, 1912);
Feffer, 294-316; Sol Cohen, "The Industrial Education Movement, 1906-17," *American
Quarterly*, 20 (1968), 95-110.

[45] Dewey, "The Educational Situation," *School Journal* (1901), repr. in *John Dewey,
The Middle Works* (Carbondale, 1977), 272; see also Ella Flagg Young, *Isolation in the
Schools* (Chicago, 1901), 75 and passim, for a classic and often cited statement of the
Deweyan position; also Young, untitled article in the *Bulletin* of the Chicago Teachers'
Federation, vol. II, no. 32, May 22, 1903.

[46] Mead, "The Educational Situation in the Chicago Public Schools," City Club
Bulletin, 1 (1907), 132-35; George H. Mead to Helen Castle Mead, July, 1906 (Mead
Papers, Regenstein Library, University of Chicago).

tion. He was equally unhappy with labor's heightened demands after the war, when it was clear that corporations had enriched themselves in the previous two years, while wages and benefits had stagnated. Mead could only complain that American labor had not reached the level of responsibility or political awareness of their British counterparts.[47]

Oddly, Mead left little room in his social psychology for the persistent and irreconcilable conflicts that characterized the Chicago context. As a result, his expectations for cooperative reforms were unrealistic, psychologically as well as politically. As critics have pointed out, while Mead tried to explain the emergence of rationality, he presumed an already rational individual subject as a starting point. Why was it necessarily the case that individuals would be able to reconcile opposing voices in their inner conversation or in the outer cloud of witnesses, in their consciousnesses or in the social environment? Why not the persistence of psychological conflict or psychosis? The persistent social disorder of modern America might be better explained by a theory that assumed a fundamentally irrational and coercive self rather than a rational conciliatory one.[48]

Mead's social psychology only explained a limited set of social relations, those in which parties agree beforehand that rational and amicable resolutions of conflict shall be reached. Knowledge of the other's role is no guarantee of ethical reciprocity, which insures that the knower will act for that other's benefit. The knower may, if he is a confidence man or a thief who is skilled at sizing up his mark, use that knowledge to gain a selfish advantage. The same principle applied to advertising (emerging at the time Mead wrote), especially that which used knowledge of consumer desires and needs to manipulate buying.

A more pertinent case for Mead involved the managers of Chicago industry with whom he negotiated on behalf of the city's working class. By the 1920s many industrialists, repudiating the hedonism of classical economics, tried more sophisticated, "corporate" personnel policies, enlisting the expertise of men and women educated or influenced by professors at the University of Chicago (for example, Earl Dean Howard, one of Tufts' former students and Hart, Schaffner, and Marx's spokesman in the clothing arbitration agreement of 1915). By the 1920s, a form of capitalist relations within the corporation developed that applied some of the notions (though not necessarily self-consciously) of reciprocity and cooperation championed by Mead and his colleagues. The rise of welfare capitalism, which incorporated social psychology into workplace

---

[47] Mead, "Industrial Education, the Working-man and the School," 380-83. "Labor is being difficult," Mead wrote to his daughter-in-law, Irene Tufts Mead, about labor demands for higher wages, George H. Mead to Irene Tufts Mead, July 18, 1919; see also Mead's correspondence to Irene T. Mead for August 26, 27, and 29 and for September 6, 1919 (Mead Papers, Regenstein Library, University of Chicago).

[48] Julian Henriques, et al, *Changing the Subject* (London, 1984), 17-19, 23.

134   ANDREW FEFFER

management, did not truly involve the kind of "expanded self" Mead
had in mind but rather allowed factory managers to control workplace
relations in the pursuit of higher profits.[49]

The relevance of Mead's psychology to the political context was its
strong suit, but paradoxically it was at that intersection of politics and
psychology that we find its greatest weakness. We can find part of its
failure in the fact that by 1917 the Chicago philosophers had been beguiled
by the success of progressive reform institutions. That success, in the
case of labor arbitration for example, was limited only to opening dialogue
between the leaders of opposing social groups and classes. Dialogue gave
a voice to the previously voiceless, but it was not enough. Unfortunately,
the outcome of social conflict was usually decided not reciprocally but
by the unbalance of power in favor of dominant classes and groups. The
laboring poor and others could only exert limited influence over their
own future.

In the specific political context of Chicago at the end of the Gilded
Age, Mead and his colleagues found themselves in a dilemma. Their
political universe rapidly polarized between conflicting social forces, each
interpreting America's political heritage and political lexicon differently.
While the Chicago philosophers preached some form of liberation for
those suffering the worst excesses and restrictions of the industrial system,
they also preached restraint and tried, whenever possible, to mediate class
differences rather than take "sides" in industrial conflicts. So although
they criticized unrestricted capitalism, Mead and his colleagues cautiously
avoided the radical socialism and anarchism of the urban working class.
Their centrist position in the political sphere worked its way into the
Chicago philosophy as a broader political and philosophical ambivalence.
This ambivalence shaped their theory.

We can find another source of Mead's failure, however, in the philosophy itself. Mead and his colleagues believed that a rational social
order based on cooperation and reciprocity lay immanent in the present,
in the actual social and political relations of late nineteenth-century
America. Since the days when Dewey wrote apologetics for the liberal
churches, the Chicago philosophers had argued that values are immanent
in what exists. This meant that scientific study could elucidate values,
goals latent in a factual present—more specifically, that Mead could
indeed find, through the exploration of biologically based psychology,
the seeds of social cooperation in the necessary conditions for human
consciousness.

[49] Richard Edwards, *Contested Terrain* (New York, 1979), passim; Dewey was indirectly involved in an early experiment in such welfare capitalism, one which management
approached with little sincerity and which degenerated into a means of breaking a later
strike. Robert Ozanne, *A Century of Labor-Management Relations at McCormick and
International Harvester* (Madison, 1967), 41-43; also James Weinstein, *The Corporate
Ideal in the Liberal State* (Boston, 1968), ch. 1.

The philosophical immanence of values also meant, however, that the ethical goals of social reform could only be found by determining what ideals were realistic. Thus, Mead and his colleagues demanded that no utopia guide the politics of the present, that radically "impulsive" visions of the future should not dictate terms to the habits of the past. And yet their own belief in cooperation and reciprocity hardly conformed to the reality of social relations. The gradual improvement of society through cooperation and reciprocity did not lie within the grasp of the present. It needed some kind of vision as a guide to dialogue, a greater witness above the cloud of witnesses, a conversationalist outside the inner and outer conversation.

Paradoxically this dilemma led Mead simultaneously to embrace and deny utopian advocacy. Almost in desperation Mead and his colleagues continually sought guidance from institutions and political leadership that stood above the fray, whether from labor leaders sufficiently "responsible" or political "visionaries" like Woodrow Wilson, who preached something resembling Christian reciprocity but meant something quite different. In 1917, showing remarkable naiveté about the behavior of the politically powerful, the entire department supported the war effort. They actively contributed to a propaganda machine that squelched criticism and rationalized the widespread suspension of civil liberties.[50] Consistently, Mead and his colleagues turned to the state as the source of "cooperative" authority despite the fact that the state and its subsidiary institutions usually lay in the control of one party to a dispute and, as the behavior of Wilson's Justice Department in 1919 demonstrated, were far from sensitive to the needs and desires of its critics.

When viewed in the context of turn-of-the-century political and social conflict, then, one sees in Mead's writing two "souls" created by the contradictions of the theory and of the moment. On the one hand Mead demanded a dialogue, democratically freeing the voices immanent in industrial Chicago. On the other hand he advocated stifling those voices that tried to rise above the dialogue when it became fruitless to continue discussion. The fact that the dialogue could not continue fit neither with Mead's original intention nor with the theory he constructed to solve the problems of social conflict and injustice.

Union College.

---

[50] See, for example, Mead, *The Conscientious Objector* (New York, 1918); Tufts recounted his war activities in a letter to Ralph Ricker, October 31, 1937 (Tufts Papers, Frost Library, Amherst College).

VII

HENRY ADAMS, THE SECOND LAW OF THERMODYNAMICS, AND THE COURSE OF HISTORY

By Keith R. Burich

In 1910 Henry Adams penned *A Letter to American Teachers of History* in which he outlined a theory of history based on the Second Law of Thermodynamics. In short, the Second Law predicts the constant and irreversible dissipation of energy culminating in the "Heat Death" of the universe. Adams argued that man could not escape the fate of the universe and offered the decay and disorder of modern civilization as evidence that the process was already well underway. Coming from the "doyen" of American historians whose brilliance had been so recently displayed in *The Education* and *Mont Saint-Michel and Chartres*, Adams's amateur scientific dalliances proved most disturbing. Neither his contemporaries nor subsequent generations of historians have been able to decipher Adams's cryptic message, although most are certain that anything emanating from Henry Adams must be profound, even if wrong-headed. The confusion can partially be attributed to Adams's passion for protecting the privacy of his innermost feelings and thoughts. Nowhere was this passion more evident than in his love of the paradox, which he often employed but never as effectively as in his application of the Second Law of Thermodynamics to history. It has been the failure of "American teachers of history," both past and present, to unravel the riddle of the Second Law that has led to the misinterpretation of Adams's mixing of science and history.

Although every other aspect of Adams's life has been the subject of numerous revisionist interpretations, his scientific thought received its definitive treatment in William Jordy's thorough and authoritative study, *Henry Adams: Scientific Historian*, published in 1952.[1] Jordy was highly critical of Adams's attempt to apply the laws of science to history, particularly the Second Law. Jordy mustered as much scientific evidence as possible to demonstrate that Adams's application of the Second Law to history was based upon distortion, simplification, and just plain ignorance of science and the scientific method. He argued that the Second Law did not necessarily predict the inexorable dissipation of heat and attributed Adams's attraction to the law to his "irrational" obsession with finding an "inclusive, determinate, absolutist and simple scheme for history. . . ."[2]

Adams himself lent credence to Jordy's charges when he admitted

[1] William Jordy, *Henry Adams: Scientific Historian* (New Haven, 1952).
[2] *Ibid.*, 218.

that his failure to "fix for a familiar moment, a necessary sequence of human movement"[3] in history led him to seek in science a unifying formula or principle, like Newton's laws of motion, that would enable him to plot the course of history as one would the path of a comet, an anology of which Adams was particularly fond. After all, historians naively "arrange sequences—called stories or histories—assuming in silence a relation of cause and effect."[4] His own *History of the United States* contained numerous allusions to the mechanical nature of historical processes and inferences that history was determined by the laws governing the motions of material bodies. If he had hoped to cloak those inferences with science's authority, as historians have assumed, he soon learned that scientists no longer claimed either certainty or universality for their laws. As Adams phrased it, "Suddenly, in 1900, science raised its head and denied."[5]

Adams's disappointment was clearly visible in *The Education*, which was a long lamentation over the failure of a lifetime of "education" spent in search of unity and order, whether through history or science. Jordy contrasted Adams's despair over his failure to achieve the "larger synthesis" he so passionately sought with the patience of contemporary scientists who were similarly frustrated by their failure to detect the luminiferous ether and reduce light to the laws of Newtonian mechanics. Although they eventually failed to do so, they did not, Jordy contends, succumb to the crippling despair that paralyzed Adams in the face of the increasing complexity of the modern world.[6]

That Adams should turn to science was not in itself irrational. The intellectual history of the nineteenth century is replete with examples of historians, philosophers, theologians, and just plain cranks attempting to deduce the laws governing human behavior from the laws of nature. Nor was Adams's fascination with Newton's laws of motion necessarily unreasonable. Ever since Newton had shown the way by explaining the "System of the World" in mechanical terms, scientists had successfully reduced almost all natural phenomena to matter in motion. To be sure, light remained a vexing problem, but the fact that mechanical models had been extended to other non-observable phenomena such as electromagnetism afforded scientists the comfortable assurance that finding a mechanical description of light was only a matter of time.[7]

[3] *The Education of Henry Adams* (Washington, D.C., 1907), 334. All references in this paper are to the original, privately printed edition, with the author's manuscript annotations, in the Henry Adams Papers, Massachusetts Historical Society, Boston, Massachusetts.

[4] *Ibid.*

[5] *Ibid.*, 396.

[6] Jordy, *Henry Adams*, 239-40.

[7] Lawrence Badash, "The Completeness of Nineteenth Science," *Isis*, 63 (1972), 48-

That the fruitfulness of mechanical explanations had a profound impact on other disciplines was shown by the prevailing materialism in biology, the social sciences, religion, and history.[8] Thus, the connection Adams made between mechanics and history was not unusual, especially since scientists referred to mechanical explanations as the "historical method" for the obvious reason that it permitted the physicist to trace effects back to their causes.[9] While Newton would have rejected the determinism implicit in such reasoning, mechanics had been associated with determinism ever since the eighteenth century, when the French mathematician La Place observed that a scientist armed with the laws of mechanics and a knowledge of the position of all the material bodies in the universe could recreate the past and predict the future.[10] Little wonder that Adams might have been attracted by such a simple yet powerful tool that would enable him to bring both man and nature under one comprehensive theory.

Unfortunately, Adams's faith in science was not requited. As he explained in *The Education,*

he insisted on a relation of sequence, and if he could not reach it by one method, he would try as many methods as science knew. Satisfied that the sequence of men led to nothing . . ., while the mere sequence of time was artificial, and the sequence of thought was chaos, he turned at last to the sequence of force; and thus it happened that, after ten years pursuit, he found himself lying in the Gallery of Machines in the Great Exposition of 1900, his historical neck broken by the irruption of force totally new.[11]

The forces to which he was referring were the rays emitted by radium recently discovered by the Curies. The fact that the radium atoms seemed to explode spontaneously without apparent cause suggested that randomness was operative at a fundamental level in nature. His search for a single, simple law governing the forces of history was dashed by the realization that the chaos that lay repressed just beneath the surface of society, waiting to erupt, was the stuff of which nature itself was made.

Adams labeled the rays "wicked," "anarchical," "parricidal," and "chaotic" for their willful disobedience of the laws of mechanics. Equally

---

58; Martin J. Klein, "Mechanical Explanation at the End of the Nineteenth Century," *Centaurus*, 17 (1972-3), 58-82.

[8] For two excellent studies of the nineteenth century's fascination with the Second Law see Stephen G. Brush, "Thermodynamics and History," *The Graduate Journal*, 7 (1967), 477-565; and Erwin Hiebert, "The Uses and Abuses of Thermodynamics in Religion," *Daedalus*, 95 (1966), 1046-80.

[9] P. M. Heimann, "Molecular Forces, Statistical Representation, and Maxwell's Demon," *Studies in the History and Philosophy of Science*, 1 (1970), 200.

[10] Stephen G. Brush, "The Development of the Kinetic Theory of Gases. VIII. Randomness and Irreversibility," *Archive for the History of the Exact Sciences*, 12 (1974), 33.

[11] *Education*, 334.

HENRY ADAMS AND HISTORY

disturbing was the fact that the rays "played no part in man's consciousness."[12] There were no corresponding observable phenomena to which they could be compared in formulating a mechanical model of their behavior. Instead of a universe composed of sensible masses moving in paths determined by known laws, Adams had entered a world of infinitesimally small particles travelling at fantastically high speeds and encountering one another in chance collisions which could only be described in statistical or probabilistic terms. "In plain words, Chaos was the law of nature; Order was the dream of man."[13]

According to Jordy, it was at this point that Adams turned to the Second Law of Thermodynamics to explain the chaos he encountered in both nature and society.[14] Entropy, or the irreversible dissipation of energy predicted by the Second Law, seemed to offer the only explanation of the decay and disorder so painfully visible in the modern world. While he had attempted to measure that decline from the twelfth to the nineteenth centuries with the two volumes *Mont-Saint-Michel and Chartres* and *The Education*, he portrayed it most poignantly in his *Letter* to his fellow historians.[15]

In that essay Adams cited mounting evidence of man's decline in the form of increasing rates of suicide, insanity, alcohol and drug abuse, and other aberrations that belied the prevailing faith in the infinite and uniform upward evolution of mankind. Even more disturbing was the continuing "enfeeblement" of man's mental powers as reflected in the deterioration of his noblest instincts—religion, law, manners, morality, and art. Man had succeeded in stemming temporarily the tide by capturing and putting nature's forces to work, but those forces, like his mental powers, were also subject to the dissipative tendencies of the Second Law. As more and more energy was expended in a furious attempt to avoid the inevitable, the dissipation of energies, both mental and physical, would accelerate until a deadening, faceless equilibrium was reached among men and molecules alike.

The shrillness of Adams's warnings certainly support Jordy's contention that Adams's attraction to the Second Law was "irrational." Although a few historians have suggested that Adams was only attempting to stand modern science on its head by carrying its mechanical determinism to its logical, if absurd, extreme, most have accepted Jordy's premise.[16] For example, George Hochfield treated the *Letter* as the cul-

---

[12] *Ibid.*, 333.

[13] *Ibid.*, 395.

[14] Jordy, *Henry Adams*, 137.

[15] Henry Adams, *A Letter to American Teachers of History* (Baltimore, 1910).

[16] See especially Howard M. Munford, "Henry Adams and the Tendency of History," *New England Quarterly*, 26 (1959), 79-90. Nevertheless, Adams's major biographers have uncritically accepted Jordy's contention that Adams seriously intended to apply physical laws to history, even though they all recognize the paradoxes inherent in Adams's scientific

mination of the quest for unity that Adams had initiated twenty years earlier with his presidential address to the American Historical Association in 1894 entitled "The Tendency of History." As Hochfield concluded, "Having failed to establish unity within the limits of his own experience or within the range of his practical ideas, Adams turned to science as a way of fixing a meaning for all of history and hence, by indirection, for his own apparently pointless life."[17] If Hochfield and the others are right, then Adams had selected the wrong vehicle to convey his message, for the Second Law was neither mechanical nor deterministic. In fact its paradoxical nature had proven so baffling to scientists that it had become the center of controversy among physicists at the very time Adams began his flirtation with science. On the other hand it just may have been the Second Law's paradoxical nature that appealed to Adams as the perfect riddle with which to confound his colleagues. Before that possibility can be explored, a reassessment of the Second Law and its relationship to developments in modern physics is necessary.

The Second Law was given its first, albeit incomplete, expression, by the French engineer Sadi Carnot in 1827. Carnot was concerned with improving the efficiency of steam engines, but he laid the foundation for the formulation of the Second Law by establishing that heat always flowed spontaneously and irreversibly from hotter to colder bodies, resulting in the irretrievable loss of heat available for work.[18] The fact that, once lost, the heat was not recoverable, was a matter of great concern to nineteenth century engineers, who plumed themselves on the increasing efficiency and power of their machines. It is easy to see how they could label this natural tendency of heat "dissipation" or "degradation," and associate it with "disorder." Not only did the irreversibility of heat flow limit the efficiency of their machines, it was essentially uncontrollable and, more importantly, defied the laws of Newtonian mechanics.[19]

Newton's laws of motion are reversible; that is, any sequence of actions is the same whether it is run forward or in reverse, much like reversing a film of the collision between two billiard balls. However, if heat flows from a hotter to a colder body until state of equilibrium is reached, nothing can return the heat to its original form. Thus, the loss of heat or "mechanical effect" through such processes as conduction posed a challenge not only to technology but to the very foundation of classical physics.

---

approach to history. See, for example, Ernest Samuels, *Henry Adams: The Major Phase* (Cambridge, Mass., 1964), 474-96; Elizabeth Stevenson, *Henry Adams, A Biography* (New York, 1955), 356-60; R. P. Blackmur, *Henry Adams* (New York, 1980), 263-77.

[17] George Hochfield, *Henry Adams: An Introduction and Interpretation* (New York, 1962), 131-32.

[18] Martin J. Klein, "Carnot's Contribution to Thermodynamics," *Physics Today*, 27 (1974), 22-28.

[19] Brush, "Randomness and Irreversibility," 6.

This was particularly vexing to nineteenth-century physicists who hoped to find a mechanical explanation of heat. The difficulty could be partially overcome by assuming that heat was a form of energy which was transferred through the motions of a body's constituent parts, that is, its molecules. Although the molecular nature of matter was not yet established, that heat was a measure of a substance's molecular motions raised the possibility of a mechanical explanation of heat.[20] The only stumbling block was the irreversibility of heat flow, a problem that led to the introduction of one of the most imaginative analogies in modern physics by the British physicist James Clerk Maxwell in the form of his nimble fingered "demon."

Maxwell was brought to thermodynamics by his work on the kinetic theory of gases. In 1860 Maxwell advanced his theory that the molecular velocities of a gas were not uniform but were randomly distributed along a normal or bell shaped curve. Maxwell was influenced by probability theory, which had become quite popular in the nineteenth century in the analysis of birth, death, suicide, and crime and divorce rates.[21] Indeed, the analogy between social statistics and Maxwell's distribution theorem is illuminating. Although individual murders or deaths were random phenomena, the average number of such events displayed a remarkable stability over time. Similarly, the average molecular velocity of a gas conceals the fact that there are molecules with velocities significantly faster or slower than the average. In other words the behavior of individual molecules cannot be extrapolated from the behavior of gases treated in mass.[22]

Maxwell guessed that the random distribution of molecular velocities might explain the irreversibility of the Second Law. To demonstrate his point, Maxwell conjured his famous "demon" and stationed it at an aperture between two gases with different kinetic energies or temperatures. The demon is instructed to allow to pass from the hotter to the colder gas only those molecules that have a lower velocity than the average velocity of the molecules in the colder gas. Conversely, he will allow only those molecules to pass from the colder to the hotter gas which have velocities higher than the average velocity of the molecules in the hotter gas. In this way the average molecular velocity or temperature of the hotter gas will increase at the expense of the colder gas. More precisely, heat will have flowed from a colder to a hotter body in violation of the Second Law.[23]

[20] Crosbie Smith, "A New Chart for British Natural Philosophy: The Development of Energy Physics in the Nineteenth Century," *History of Science*, 16 (1978), 234-41.

[21] Ian Hacking, "Nineteenth Century Cracks in the Concept of Determinism," *Journal of the History of Ideas*, 45 (1983), 455-75.

[22] Heimann, "Molecular Forces," 201.

[23] Martin J. Klein, "Maxwell, His Demon, and the Second Law of Thermodynamics," *American Scientist*, 58 (1970), 84-97.

142   KEITH R. BURICH

Maxwell's purpose was to demonstrate that on a molecular level, violations of the Second Law could take place. Although such violations were statistically unlikely, they were possible since there was nothing to prevent the process he described even without the assistance of a demon. Thus the Second Law had only a statistical rather than an absolute certainty. The significance of this conclusion becomes more apparent if the analogy is carried one step further and, once the demon has completed his task, the partition is removed. The result would be the reestablishment of an equilibrium with a kinetic energy or temperature equal to the average kinetic energies of the two gases before the mixing. The establishment of a new equilibrium through the mixing of the two gases is the fundamental irreversible process described by the Second Law. The process cannot be reversed except in highly improbable situations such as the appearance of a "demon" with the ability to determine the paths and velocities of an enormous number of molecules.[24]

In the absence of such assistance, the molecules would spontaneously move from a more ordered state, with most fast molecules in one area and most slow ones in another, to a more disordered state with a normal distribution of molecular velocities. More importantly, the inability of mere mortals to determine the direction and velocity of molecules makes it impossible to apply the laws of mechanics on a molecular level except in a statistical or probabilistic sense, since those values are necessary for any mechanical description. Thus, it appeared not only that molecules possessed some natural tendency toward disorder but that tendency suggested that there was something essentially non-mechanical (read "indeterminate") about their behavior.[25]

It should be noted that Maxwell did not intend to suggest that molecular motions were random. He did not believe that chance was involved at a microscopic level despite the usefulness of statistical methods in kinetic theory and now thermodynamics. Rather, statistical methods were made necessary by our ignorance of molecular behavior. Indeed, some form of determinism was necessary if his demon was able to "determine" the directions and velocities of molecules in order to sort them.[26] Nevertheless, the very fact that he had to conjure a "demon" to reverse the irreversible suggested that the laws of "rational" mechanics which governed the motions of visible bodies did not apply at a microscopic level. The laws of mechanics permitted the reversal of molecular motions, but they could not explain the low probability of such an event. The motions of molecules could not be reversed as simply as one might reverse the collision of two billiard balls. Molecules, both before and after such

---

[24] Heimann, "Molecular Forces," 204; Brush, "Irreversibility and Indeterminism," 614; and "Randomness and Irreversibility," 41.

[25] Brush, "Randomness and Irreversibility," 57-67.

[26] Brush, "Irreversibility and Indeterminism," 614.

collisions, appeared to act capriciously, making it difficult for Maxwell and others to avoid applying such adjectives as "irregular" to molecular motions.[27]

Indeed, by the 1890's the German physicist Ludwig von Boltzmann, then the chief and nearly sole defender of a mechanical description of the Second Law, conceded that irreversibility could only be explained by positing a state of molecular "disorder" or "chaos." In mass, molecules tended irreversibly toward a state of disorder, but that macroscopic tendency was a function of the "unwillingness" of molecules to return to their initial states except in extremely rare cases. The possibility of molecules moving from a disordered to an ordered state, or heat being transferred from a colder to a hotter body, was subtly transformed from an anomalous fluctuation in an otherwise determined system to merely another chance occurrence amidst an infinite number of random or indeterminate events. In other words irreversibility raised the paradoxical possibility that processes such as entropy that appeared to be mechanically determined were, at bottom, functions of random events.[28]

Thus, at the very time that Adams supposedly turned to the Second Law for its mechanical determinism, the paradoxical nature of irreversibility was forcing scientists to introduce, however grudgingly, hitherto unacceptable concepts such as randomness and indeterminacy. Although Adams's scientific knowledge has been considered amateurish at best, his readings were extensive and quite sophisticated, especially in the area of physical chemistry and energy physics, the two areas in which irreversibility posed the greatest challenge to extending the mechanical world view. Consequently, he could not have been unaware of the controversies swirling about the Second Law.

It is well known that Adams was introduced to these issues through the writings of the American physical chemist Willard Gibbs. It was Gibbs's "phase rule" that Adams first attempted to apply to history in his "The Rule of Phase Applied to History" written in 1909.[29] However, it has escaped the notice of Adams's biographers that Gibbs played a pivotal role in the application of statistical methods to thermodynamics.[30] Moreover, Adams was perceptively aware that the adoption of statistical

[27] James Clerk Maxwell, "On the Dynamical Evidence of the Molecular Constitution of Bodies," *The Scientific Papers of James Clerk Maxwell*, ed. W. D. Niven (New York, 1965), 41.

[28] Brush, "Irreversibility and Indeterminism," 615-18; "Randomness and Irreversibility," 57-71.

[29] Adams, "The Rule of Phase Applied to History," in *The Degradation of the Democratic Dogma* (New York, 1920), 267-311.

[30] Martin J. Klein, "Josiah Willard Gibbs," in *Dictionary of Scientific Biography*, ed. Charles C. Gillispie (New York, 1972), 5: 386-93; Elizabeth W. Gardner, "James Clerk Maxwell," *American Journal of Physics*, 37 (1969), 146-55.

144   KEITH R. BURICH

methods undermined the certainty of any theory of history or science.[31] Adams also read *L'Energie* by the German physical chemist Wilhelm Ostwald, the leader of the "energeticists" whose attacks on classical mechanics for its failure to accommodate irreversibility virtually ostracized Boltzmann from the German scientific community.[32] So vituperative were the attacks that they alledgedly led to Boltzmann's suicide in 1906, a clear measure of the seriousness of the debates raging over thermodynamics at the time of Adams's interest in the theory. Adams's library also contained well annotated copies of the British physicist Alexander Findlay's *The Phase Rule and Its Applications* and the Scottish physicist Balfour Stewart's *La Conservation de L'Energie*, both of which discussed the problems of describing energy in mechanical terms.[33] But in truth all of Adams's scientific readings at that time contained discussions of the obstacles to extending the mechanical world view to a variety of phenomena, including entropy.[34]

Of particular importance in this regard was Henri Poincaré's *La Science et l'hypothèse* and Lucien Poincaré's *La Physique moderne*. Both volumes contain discussions of the problems posed by irreversible phenomena. Indeed, irreversible phenomena were of such concern that Henri Poincaré considered them "beaucoup plus rebelles" than light, a passage which Adams underlined.[35] Poincaré himself was embroiled in the controversy over the Second Law and attempted to demonstrate that entropy could be reversed.[36] Adams also highlighted a passage from Lucien Poincaré's volume which noted that irreversibility was a function of the laws of probability and so was distinguished from the absolute certainty accorded the laws of classical mechanics.[37] Both books contained discussions of other examples of the "mouvements irreguliers" of "materière subtile," such as the kinetic theory of gases, Brownian motion, and the discontinuous nature of radioactivity that required statistical rather than

[31] *Education*, 351-52, 447, 451, 501.

[32] Adams's library in the Massachusetts Historical Society contains only Ostwald's *Vorlesungen über Naturphilosophie gehalten im Sommer 1901 an der Universität Leipzig* (Leipzig, 1902). However, he made frequent reference to Ostwald's *L'Enérgie* in the *Letter*.

[33] Findlay, *The Phase Rule and Its Applications: An Introduction to the Study of Physical Chemistry* (London, 1906); Stewart, *La Conservation de l'énergie* (Paris, 1899).

[34] Of greatest significance was Ernst Mach's *Science of Mechanics*, with its criticism of classical mechanics, which had a profound effect on an entire generation of physicists, including the young Einstein. Although his library does not contain a copy, Adams's notes from it are contained in an undated notebook in the Henry Adams Papers in the Massachusetts Historical Society. To this should also be added John B. Stallo's *La Matière et la physique moderne* (Paris, 1899), an annotated copy of which is contained in Adams's personal library in the Massachusetts Historical Society.

[35] H. Poincaré, *La Science et l'hypothèse* (Paris, 1902), 207.

[36] Brush, "Randomness and Irreversibility," 67-77.

[37] L. Poincaré, *La Physique moderne* (Paris, 1906), 84.

purely mechanical explanations.[38] And both authors vainly struggled to explain how such apparently random phenomena were actually mechanically determined.

As we have seen, the kinetic theory was directly related to the controversy over irreversibility, as was Brownian motion, while Max Planck's quantum theory of radiation grew out of concern over the failure to find a mechanical explanation for irreversibility.[39] All three suggested a fundamental randomness to nature. Adams made frequent reference in his correspondence and writings to the kinetic theory, to Brownian motion, and to radiation as examples of the failure of classical mechanics. He even referred to Maxwell's demon and recommended it for the presidency, presumably for its ability to sort order out of chaos.[40] Clearly, Adams was aware of the problems that irreversible phenomena and the indeterminate behavior of molecules created for classical mechanics when he challenged his fellow historians to escape the dire predictions of the Second Law.

Indeed, Adams began his *Letter* with the observation that the three-hundred-year ascendancy of the "mechanical theory of the universe" had ended with Kelvin's and Clausius's announcement that the universe was running down.[41] Adams was also careful to inform his readers that the dissipation of energy was not a simple linear process, for "Energy had a way of coming and going in phases of intensity much more mysterious than the energy itself."[42] According to Adams, these "phases" consisted of "contractions" or concentrations of energy against its natural tendency toward equilibrium or disorder, followed by explosions or "catastrophes" that returned the system to a state of equilibrium.[43]

Adams clearly was describing the process effected by Maxwell's demon. In reality, however, the whole process was dependent upon the random behavior of individual molecules, which meant that the stability of any equilibrium was always tenuous and subject to those explosions, leaps, or catastrophes that fascinated Adams. The random behavior of individual molecules could be attributed to "hidden variables" or disguised by treating them in the average. But Adams, like many scientists of that time, including Planck and Einstein, chose not to dismiss them so easily. Instead, he focused on the "catastrophes" of nature and history to challenge the naive faith of his fellow historians in the uniform, upward progression of mankind.

[38] H. Poincaré, *Science et l'hypothèse*, 176.

[39] Brush, "Irreversibility and Indeterminism," 618-30; Martin J. Klein, "Thermodynamics and Quanta in Planck's Work," *Physics Today*, 19 (1966), 23-32.

[40] Adams to Brooks Adams, 2 May 1903, *Henry Adams and His Friends*, ed. Harold Dean Cater (Boston, 1947), 545.

[41] *Letter*, 1-2.

[42] *Ibid.*, 14-5.

[43] *Ibid.*, 127.

146   KEITH R. BURICH

In the *Letter*, he offered numerous examples of deviate behavior—suicides, insanity, murders, idiocy—all purely random events which could not be explained by any mechanical social theory, pessimistic or optimistic, without taking into account the underlying "heterogeneity" of history. He cited other discontinuities—geological catastrophes, evolutionary mutations, the extinction of species and stars—to counter uniformitarian theories that ignored the discontinuities which produced historical changes. Aside from their irreversibility, these examples had no apparent relationship to the Second Law. That is, they were discontinuous events which produced radically altered states and could not be reversed. To do so would require the exact reversal of the whole train of preceding causes, a situation as improbable as the intervention of Maxwell's demon.

Adams's most telling example was Dollo's law, which amounted to an application of probability theory to evolution. The French biologist Louis Dollo postulated that evolution was irreversible since evolutionary development was a function of discontinuous mutations which were not likely to recur in an order precisely inverse to that in which they originally appeared.[44] Dollo's Law was the biological analogue of the Second Law, for both evolution and entropy were functions of discontinuities with extremely low probabilities of recurrence. History could also be viewed as a function of singular, discontinuous, non-recurring events which could not be subsumed into any deterministic mechanical theories. Just as the apparent determinism of the Second Law dissolved, under closer scrutiny, into the randomness of individual molecules, so the "necessary sequences" that historians tried to establish were like Zeno's arrow, "continuous from the beginning, of time, but discontinuous at each successive point."[45]

These discontinuities were certainly perplexing to scientists and historians alike, but they helped Adams explain

. . . much that had been most obscure, especially the persistently fiendish treatment of man by man; the perpetual effort of society to establish law, and the perpetual revolt of society against the law it had established; the perpetual building up of authority by force, and the perpetual appeal to force to overthrow it; the perpetual symbolism of a higher law, and the perpetual relapse to a lower one; the perpetual victory of the principles of freedom and their perpetual conversion into the principles of power. . . . The physicists had a phrase for it, unintelligible to the vulgar: "All that we win is a battle,—lost in advance,—with the irreversible phenomena in the background of nature."[46]

In sum, irreversible phenomena based on random events, whether the

---

[44] Stephen Jay Gould, "Dollo on Dollo's Law: Irreversibility and the Status of Evolutionary Laws," *Journal of the History of Biology*, 3 (1970), 189-212.

[45] *Education*, 400.

[46] *Ibid.*, 401.

"anarchist's bomb" or the "metaphysical bomb of radium," were the forces that determined the course of time which history eventually chronicled. Without them the universe would settle into a stable equilibrium. But, as Adams warned, "if one physical law exists more absolute than another, it is the law that stable equilibrium is death. A society in stable equilibrium is . . . one that has no history and wants no historians."[47]

History was not a record of civilization's unbroken upward progression but a series of futile attempts to concentrate "mankind into a single dense mass like the sun" in order to increase the energy or force at society's disposal.[48] They were futile since irreversibility required that any attempt to concentrate energy against its will would at best be only a temporary reversal, much like that effected by Maxwell's demon, and would not prevent the ultimate reversion of energy to its natural state of disorder. As Adams warned, "order was an accidental relation obnoxious to nature; artificial compulsion imposed on motion; against which every free energy of the universe revolted. . . ."[49] Hence, the "explosions" and "contractions" of history were the inevitable and irreversible result of the rebellion of "individual forces" against the centralizing forces of society.[50]

The irony of this predicament Adams had originally discussed in *The Education*. Increasing a society's forces required the expenditure of an enormous amount of energy that quickly became unavailable for work according to the requirements of the Second Law. Thus progress, if it was to be achieved and measured by the amount of energy at a society's disposal, was an illusion, and history was the unfortunate tale of man's pursuit of that illusion. From the very beginning, man had sought to impose order on his environment by expanding the arsenal of forces at his disposal, whether it was a bow, gunpowder, steam, electricity, or the Cross. The first victim had been the Roman Empire:

The economic needs of a violently centralising society forced the empire to enlarge the slave system to enlarge its slave system until the slave system consumed itself and the empire too, leaving society no resource but further enlargement of its religious system to compensate for the losses and horrors of the failure.[51]

The pursuit of force inevitably resulted in the irrecoverable waste of human "energy," whether in the form of Roman slaves or defenders of the Cross or the millions more that Adams feared would soon be sacrificed

[47] *Letter*, 186.
[48] *Ibid.*, 127.
[49] *Education*, 401.
[50] *Letter*, 127.
[51] *Education*, 419.

148   KEITH R. BURICH

in Europe to secure a supply of coal for the dynamos, like the sacrifices offered to the gods by pagan priests.

Nevertheless, man blindly continued the pursuit, perhaps in the name of a higher law, larger synthesis, or simply progress, but always under the vain mechanical illusion that the motions of masses, molecular or human, could be determined much as Maxwell's demon reversed the molecular tendency toward disorder.

What was far more serious, he had seen the number of minds, engaged in pursuing force.—the true measure of its attraction,—increase from a few scores or hundreds, in 1838, to many thousands in 1905, while they chased nature into hiding-places where nature had never known it to be, making analyses that contradicted being, and syntheses that endangered the elements. No one could say that the social mind now failed to respond to new force, even when the new force annoyed it horribly. Everyday nature violently revolted, causing so-called accidents with enormous destruction of property and life, while plainly laughing at man who helplessly groaned and shrieked and shuddered, but never for a single instance could stop.[52]

Man had sacrificed his freedom to science as he became increasingly dependent upon forces beyond his control. The tragedy had been compounded with the appearance of an "avalanche" of new forces in 1900, before which "the man of science stood . . . as bewildered and helpless, as in the fourth century, a priest of Isis before the Cross of Christ."[53] Regardless of how much force man amassed, he could no more determine the course of history than he could the direction of molecules.

In seizing upon the Second Law, Adams attempted to expose the fallacy of the determinism and materialism which dominated the nineteenth century and which Adams had captured in his powerful image of the Dynamo. The Second Law had proven something of an embarrassment to scientists who prided themselves on their ability to reduce all of nature to matter in motion governed by the laws of rational mechanics. The irrational elements in either nature or history could no longer be ignored or buried under an "ocean of statistics."[54] Indeed, it was the attention that scientists paid to the indeterminate behavior of an increasing number of natural phenomena that led to such major developments in modern physics as quantum mechanics, with its indeterminacy principle. Similarly, Adams looked to singular historical events to demonstrate that there was no necessary or predetermined direction to history. One such episode was the Gothic "explosion" of the twelfth century which produced the cathedrals devoted to the Virgin, the antithesis of the nineteenth century's Dynamo.

To Adams, both the Virgin and the Dynamo symbolized the mys-

[52] *Ibid.*, 431-32.
[53] *Ibid.*, 425.
[54] *Letter*, 188.

terious forces that had "dragged," "wrenched," and "coerced" man throughout history. The ability of the dynamo to create electricity from steam and coal was no less mysterious than the power of reproduction symbolized by the Virgin. However, her fecundity was not only responsible for the underlying continuity between successive generations, it was also the wellspring of mankind's wonderful diversity and consequent resistance to order and uniformity. Thus, she symbolized both unity and multiplicity, order and anarchy, the basic antinomies of history; and there was no doubt in Adams's mind that her sympathies lay with man's constant rebellion against the laws of science, society, or religion. As Adams wrote in *Mont-Saint-Michel and Chartres*:

Man concentrated in herself the whole rebellion of man against fate; the whole protest against divine law; the contempt for human law as its outcome; the whole unutterable fury of human nature beating itself against the walls of its prison house, and suddenly seized by the hope that in the Virgin man had found a door to escape. The convulsive hold which Mary to this day maintains over human imagination was due . . . to her sympathy with people who suffered under law—divine or human. . . . She cared not a straw for conventional morality, and she had no intention of letting her friends be punished . . . for the sins of their ancestors or the peccadilloes of Eve.[55]

In return, man responded with thousands of cathedrals and chapels dedicated to the Virgin. Her compassion had liberated man's imagination, a freedom, expressed in Gothic architecture, which "knew no mathematical formula of precision."[56] This was a far cry from Francis Bacon's pronouncement that "The imagination must be given not wings but weights," which, Adams contended, had led to man's slavish worship of the machine.[57] But, "All the steam in the world could not, like the Virgin, build Chartres."[58]

The Gothic outburst of the twelfth century was one of those spontaneous, irreversible events that, like all irreversible phenomena, defied simple cause and effect, mechanical explanations. More importantly, the fact that this "explosion" created "four-fifths" of man's "noblest art" suggested that creativity itself was an act of rebellion. If so, then the twelfth century's devotion to the Virgin certainly stood in poignant contrast to his own century's worship of the Dynamo.

The capture and control of nature's forces, symbolized by the Dynamo, necessarily required the capture and control of man's own creative energies. According to the Second Law, there could be no uncompensated increase of energy. In other words increasing the force at society's disposal could only be achieved at the "cost of the intensity of individual forces."

[55] Adams, *Mont-Saint-Michel and Chartres* (Cambridge, Mass., 1927), 276-77.
[56] *Ibid.*, 353-54.
[57] *Education*, 423.
[58] *Ibid.*, 339.

150   KEITH R. BURICH

As Adams explained, "The individual, like the crystal of salt, is absorbed in the solution, but the solution does the work which the individual could not do."[59] However, the Second Law also required that any concentration of energy against its will could only be temporary and that, once those individual energies were expended, they could never be recovered.

The choice confronting modern civilization was "the same old dilemma of Saint Augustine and Descartes—the deadlock of free-will."[60] The individual's energies could either be expended freely and creatively as in the twelfth century or sacrificed in society's quixotic and potentially destructive crusades, such as the one he predicted would soon engulf Europe in war. Adams did not intend to sit idly by and watch the wanton waste of human energy. As he explained shortly after writing the *Letter*, "My idea is that the world outside—the so-called modern world—can only pervert and degrade the conceptions of the primitive instinct of art and feeling, and that our only chance is to accept the limited number— the one-in-a-thousand born artists and poets—and to intensify the energy of feeling within that radiant center."[61] In a sense Adams seemed to be trying to reverse the irreversible. And why not? Progress was the result of man's willful disobedience of the laws of nature and society. It was through acts of sheer will that man was able to transform "himself from a hypothetical eocene lemur ... into a man speaking an elaborately inflected language."[62] Free will was the source of those "variations" or leaps upon which both evolution or history depended. On the other hand, " 'Thou shalt not' is the beginning of law."[63]

Unfortunately, Adams's weapons in this battle were limited to his pen. He wrote the *Letter* as an appeal to the "classical historian, with his intuition of free-will and art," in hopes of attracting him into the lists against the "socialist frame of mind which we are already floundering in...."[64] Adams deplored the tendency of modern society, whether socialism or corporate capitalism, toward a suffocating uniformity. He worried aloud in the *Letter* that the "social organism, in the recent views of history, is the cause, creator and end of the Man, who exists only as a passing representative of it, without rights or functions except what it imposes. As an organism, society has always been peculiarly subject to the degradation of energy."[65] The role of the historian in this struggle was to teach that history was not "a force resulting in motion which

[59] *Letter*, 123.

[60] *Ibid.*, 160.

[61] Adams to Albert Stanborough Cook, 6 August 1910, *Letters of Henry Adams (1892-1918)*, ed. Worthington Chauncey Ford (Boston, 1930), 546-47.

[62] *Letter*, 94-95.

[63] *Ibid.*, 123.

[64] Adams to Charles Milnes Gaskill, 14 March 1910, *Letters (1892-1918)*, 537.

[65] *Letter*, 260.

cannot be other than what it is."[66] Any presumption of necessity to the course of history only strengthened the forces of "collectivism" at the expense of those pockets of resistance to society's increasing demands for uniformity.

If there was a certain stridency to Adams's appeal to his colleagues, it was because they seemed ready and even willing to acquiesce in the stifling conformity required by modern society. Indeed, it was only to elicit some response, some sign of "energy" or "motion" among his fellow historians, that he "kicked" them "in the stomach as violently and insultingly" as he could with the Second Law.[67] He explained to James Franklin Jameson, to whom he had forwarded the "Letter" for distribution, that "they would prove me wrong if they were to show any reaction to me."[68] He begged to be "annihilated by a competent hand" but never to be taken seriously.[69] He always referred to his science as "illustrative," a "jigsaw puzzle," or simply a "joke." Even in his 1894 presidential address to the American Historical Association, when he first alerted his colleagues of the dangers of emulating science too closely, he offered his observations "in the paradoxical spirit of casual conversation."[70] Unfortunately, Adams's joke failed; his colleagues never did resolve the paradox of the Second Law, which was also the paradox of history. But to have expected otherwise would have required historians to teach that time, whether measured by entropy or history, was not a "necessary sequence of cause and effect" but a series of indeterminate and irrepressible "explosions."

Canisius College.

---

[66] Adams, "The Tendency of History," in *Degradation*, 129.

[67] Adams, to Charles Milnes Gaskill, 2 August 1910, *Letters (1892-1910)*, 546.

[68] Adams to James Franklin Jameson, 3 April 1910, *Adams and his Friends*, 680.

[69] *Ibid.*, 646-47.

[70] Adams, "Tendency," 133.

VIII

The Transformation of Spengler's Philosophy of World History

John Farrenkopf

That Oswald Spengler, one of the most famous philosophers of history in the twentieth century, profoundly changed his ideas on world history after publishing his major work, *The Decline of the West*,[1] is virtually unknown to scholars contributing to the literature in English on his thought.[2] Yet it is not unheard of for speculative philosophers of history to experience a sea change in how they formulate their bold answers to the riddle of history. Indeed, Spengler's renowned successor, Arnold Toynbee, went so far as to transform his philosophy of world history in the middle of his massive work, *A Study of History*.[3]

1924 had marked a watershed in Spengler's life. As the Weimar Republic entered into a short-term period of stability, he suddenly abandoned his political ambitions and intrigues and reaffirmed the comparatively passive vocation of *Privatgelehrter*. At the same time he commenced what has been appropriately described as "the second phase of Spenglerian thought,"[4] which extended to his death in 1936. *The Decline of the West* had surveyed, in speculative philosophical fashion, the history of the

---

[1] Oswald Spengler, *Der Untergang des Abendlandes: Umrisse einer Morphologie der Weltgeschichte*, I, rev. ed. *Gestalt und Wirklichkeit*, II, *Welthistorische Perspektiven* (Munich, 1923).

[2] However, it is known to leading Spengler experts publishing in German and French. See Anton M. Koktanek, *Oswald Spengler in seiner Zeit* (Munich, 1968), and Gilbert Merlio, *Oswald Spengler: Témoin de son temps* (Stuttgart, 1982).

[3] Arnold J. Toynbee, *A Study of History*, I-XII, (London, 1934-61). An authority on Toynbee has recently suggested that he may have been well advised to have written a second book on world history instead of completing *A Study of History*. "Toynbee's transvaluation of values between the time he planned his great work and the time he completed it was so far-ranging that he might have been wiser to abandon his original outline entirely in 1946, and write a new and different book to explain his revised vision of the pattern and meaning of history." William H. McNeill, *Arnold J. Toynbee: A Life* (New York, 1989), 227.

[4] Koktanek, *Spengler in seiner Zeit*, 363.

152

civilizations, or in Spengler's terminology, cultures (*Kulturen*), which have arisen since around 3500 BC.[5] In 1924, approximately two years after completing the second volume of his *Hauptwerk*, the ambitious thinker, except for brief intervals when his passion for politics reasserted itself, increasingly and ultimately almost exclusively focused his attention on the vast period of civilizational development which preceded that of the rise of cultures.[6] The excitement generated by some of the greatest discoveries hitherto made in the allied fields of archeology, prehistory, and ethnology and his friendship with the unorthodox ethnologist, Leo Frobenius, fueled Spengler's enthusiasm for the study of prehistory.[7]

Spengler pursued two related projects. In the second volume of *The Decline of the West* he had already declared his intention to produce a tome on metaphysical questions relating to the human experience of world history.[8] The second project involved the composition of a major work on prehistory and early civilizational history. In his sedulous study of this immense subject Spengler sought to illumine the origins of the cultures whose cyclical qualities and different cultural styles he had investigated in his *Hauptwerk*. Moreover, despite his continuing awareness of the discontinuities in world history exemplified by the recurrent phenomenon of civilizational growth and decay, he strove, in sharp contrast to the relativistic perspective he had championed in *The Decline of the West*, to ascertain the direction and significance of history for the whole of mankind. Spengler, who had emphatically denied in his *Hauptwerk* that mankind had a collective historical destiny,[9] publicly voiced in 1931 his aspiration to fathom "the great secret of the destiny of man."[10] He entertained the hope that his projected works, in combination with his already published *Hauptwerk*, would constitute a bona fide universal history.

Unfortunately, Spengler was unable to finish either of these parallel projects, not only because of his worsening health but more likely because they were extraordinarily ambitious. Thus, the new vision of world history he conceived in his later years unfortunately never achieved the kind

[5] Spengler places the beginning of the ancient civilizations of Egypt and Babylon at about 3000 BC; contemporary historical knowledge indicates that civilization first emerged in southern Mesopotamia, in Sumer, approximately 3500 BC, Egypt follows around 3100 BC. Spengler, *Der Untergang des Abendlandes*, II, 46; J. M. Roberts, *The Pelican History of the World* (Harmondsworth, England, 1983), 58.

[6] Anton M. Koktanek, introduction to *Frühzeit der Weltgeschichte: Fragmente aus dem Nachlass* by Oswald Spengler, ed. A. M. Koktanek in collaboration with Manfred Schröter (Munich, 1966), vii.

[7] *Ibid.*, xiv.

[8] Spengler, *Der Untergang des Abendlandes*, II, 3.

[9] "But 'mankind' does not have a goal, an idea, a plan, as little as the genus of butterflies or orchids has a goal. 'Mankind' is a zoological concept or an empty word" (Spengler, *Der Untergang des Abendlandes*, I, 27).

[10] Oswald Spengler, *Der Mensch und die Technik: Beitrag zu einer Philosophie des Lebens* (Munich, 1931), v.

154 JOHN FARRENKOPF

of detailed, systematic exposition his original philosophy of history had attained in his chef d'oeuvre. However, the Spengler specialist Anton M. Koktanek diligently collated and edited his extensive notes on prehistory and early civilizational history and his metaphysical speculations about world history, publishing the material in the mid-sixties in two separate volumes, *Urfragen* (*Primary Questions*) and *Frühzeit der Weltgeschichte* (*Early Period of World History*). Both tomes are structured in conformance with provisional outlines found in Spengler's *Nachlass*. Before his death in 1978 Koktanek also produced an authoritative biography of Spengler and a large edited volume of correspondence. These four products of his years of painstaking research in the Spengler Archive[11] are indispensable for scholarly inquiry into Spengler's historical universe.[12]

Scholars writing in English on Spengler, including some who have authored critical works dealing solely with his thought, were unaware that the philosophy of history he had showcased in *The Decline of the West*, underwent a metamorphosis after he simultaneously absorbed the criticism of the work[13] and significantly expanded the scope of his inquiry. These scholars, among them experts in historical philosophy who have written either an article, a chapter or short book section, or an entire book on Spengler, including H. Stuart Hughes in his excellent standard critical work on him,[14] do not argue the important thesis that Spengler profoundly changed his philosophy of world history.[15]

---

[11] The Beck *Verlag*, Spengler's life-long publishing house, transferred possession of all of the archival material to the Bavarian State Library on 12 February 1990. The Spengler Archive houses an extensive collection of material on his life and thought. The wealth of documents; photographs and sketches; miscellaneous papers, interviews, and newspaper articles; accounts by third parties; original letters to and from Spengler; notes intended for an autobiography which was never written; and papers and diaries of his sister, Hilde Kornhardt, were indispensable in Koktanek's research of his authoritative biography of Spengler. The largely biographical material is complemented by the rich collection of scholarly papers. Of particular interest to students of historical philosophy are his numerous aphoristic notes on metaphysics and world history and his unpublished fragments on politics including partial drafts of memoranda to the German Kaiser and the nobility apparently composed during World War I and notes for the projected continuation of *Years of Decision* as well as unpublished poems, unfinished dramatic and epic compositions, and scattered reflections on questions of poetry and the visual arts.

[12] Of the following books, only the collection of letters has been translated into English, and in abridged form at that. Oswald Spengler, *Briefe 1913-1936*, ed. Anton M. Koktanek in collaboration with Manfred Schröter (Munich, 1963); Koktanek, *Spengler in seiner Zeit*; Oswald Spengler, *Urfragen: Fragmente aus dem Nachlass*, ed. Anton M. Koktanek in collaboration with Manfred Schröter (Munich, 1965); Spengler, *Frühzeit der Weltgeschichte*.

[13] "Even though he did not expressly respond to significant objections to his philosophical and historical conception, being proud of his apparent immutability, they nonetheless affected him and induced him, to move from his first philosophy towards a new, more universal conception" (Koktanek, introduction to *Urfragen* by Spengler, xiv).

[14] H. Stuart Hughes, *Oswald Spengler: A Critical Estimate* (New York, 1952).

[15] See in this regard R. G. Collingwood, *The Idea of History* (Oxford, 1961), Bruce

The reader may ask himself why Spengler, with his thirst for universal knowledge, failed to concede the need to significantly remodel his original philosophy of world history. One should not forget that *The Decline of the West* was the source of the fame of a proud man who had previously been an obscure *Gymnasiallehrer*. Moreover, his major work had brought down an avalanche of criticism upon him; an admission of the necessity of significant revision might have precipitated a storm of ridicule from a host of already unsympathetic critics. Furthermore, as a prominent participant in the political controversies of interwar Germany, he earnestly desired to maintain the myth of the infallible prophet and analyst of world history and politics.

The corollary to the question why Spengler never acknowledged the necessity of making major changes in his philosophy of world history is why numerous scholars did not discern the metamorphosis in his thought. Firstly, he failed to present his new vision of world history in a large-scale, systematically organized work. Moreover, Spengler's unwillingness to concede either to the public or to his circle of intimates that his original philosophy of world history required substantial revision compounded the difficulty encountered by scholars in perceiving the remarkable transformation in his ideas. Since the controversial *Hauptwerk* attracted the lion's share of the critical attention devoted to the Spengler corpus, most scholars with an interest in his ideas, who wrote before Koktanek's publication in the mid-sixties of the crucial *Nachlass* material, simply adhered to the erroneous view that the ponderous two volumes of *The Decline of the West* contained virtually everything of importance its author had to say about world history. Thus, they failed to perceive the striking changes in Spengler's historical philosophy we will presently consider. However, it should be emphasized that one can still perceive many of the changes in his historical philosophy without reference to the posthumously published material by attentively perusing the entirety of his published works, particularly the slim treatise *Man and Technics*.[16] Most scholars who have written on Spengler in English since the mid-sixties have either ignored

---

Mazlish, "Spengler," in *The Riddle of History, the Great Speculators from Vico to Freud* (New York, 1966), William Dray, "A Vision of World History: Oswald Spengler and the Life-Cycle of Cultures," in *Perspectives on History* (London, 1980), Hughes, *Oswald Spengler*, John F. Fennelly, *Twilight of the Evening Lands: Oswald Spengler—A Half Century Later* (New York, 1972), and Klaus P. Fischer, *History and Prophecy: Oswald Spengler and the Decline of the West* (Durham, N.C., 1977).

[16] Spengler, *Der Mensch und die Technik*. In this regard, *Man and Technics* should be ideally read in conjunction with the following pertinent selections in Oswald Spengler, *Reden und Aufsätze*, ed. Hildegard Kornhardt (Munich, 1937) including, "Plan eines neuen Atlas Antiquus," "Altasien," "Das Alter der amerikanischen Kulturen," "Der Streitwagen und seine Bedeutung für den Gang der Weltgeschichte," and "Zur Weltgeschichte des zweiten vorchristlichen Jahrtausends," as well as with Oswald Spengler, "Achäerfragen" (Second part of "Zur Weltgeschichte des zweiten vorchristlichen Jahrtausends"), Hildegard Kornhardt (ed.), *Die Welt als Geschichte*, 6 (1940).

156   JOHN FARRENKOPF

the vital material edited by Koktanek for whatever reason, or in cases where they have utilized it, have not appreciated its significance.[17]

In parts of his biography of Spengler, Koktanek treats in much different fashion the same subject as this author does in this paper. Yet Koktanek by no means thought that *Oswald Spengler in seiner Zeit* offered his final word on the ideas of this unusual thinker. In fact, he considered his biography to be more of a highly informative account of Spengler's life than a thorough interpretation of his controversial and complex work. Thus, Koktanek declared his intention, in the introduction to *Oswald Spengler in seiner Zeit*, to produce a comprehensive study, a "methodical-systematic interpretation" (*Auslegung*) of the philosophical, political, and historical dimensions of Spengler's thought entitled, *Das triadische System Oswald Spengler: Philosophie—Politik—Geschichte*, which would supplement his biography.[18] Yet his death in 1978 unfortunately prevented him from fulfilling this important task. Thus, Koktanek certainly did not exhaust the subject of the transformation of Spengler's philosophy of world history, although he has admirably enhanced our understanding of it.

Now let us turn our attention to analyzing the principal elements of what can be arguably called Spengler's second philosophy of world history, as pieced together here both from works published either in his lifetime or posthumously and from unpublished *Nachlass* material. In his major work he had boldly designated his comparative historical morphology as the most advanced approach to historical analysis of his era, tantamount to a "Copernican discovery."[19] Yet in the introduction to one of his final publications Spengler implied that he had recognized the necessity of striving to surpass the historical philosophy showcased in *The Decline of the West*. As he observed, "world-historical vision, only emerging among us during the last hundred years, has not yet attained its possible heights."[20]

No longer does Spengler maintain, from the position of methodical,

---

[17] Fennelly, who devotes very little space to these two works in his book on Spengler, denies their importance. With respect to *Urfragen*, he asserts, "one would like to believe that, had he lived, Spengler would never have permitted this volume to appear in print." *Frühzeit der Weltgeschichte* is dismissed as being "without real significance" (Fennelly, *Twilight*, 23-24). Klaus P. Fischer, who also enjoyed the advantage of having been able to peruse Spengler's posthumous works, fails to see that he developed a catastrophic vision of world history in the twilight years of his life. In the concluding chapter of his book, he declares that "Spengler merely argued that the Faustian culture, whose creative energy has now been spent after one thousand years, must give way to a more youthful, a more creative culture." He concludes the line of argument by erroneously maintaining, "In sum it is a great mistake to assume that to be a Spenglerian implies *ipso facto* to be either a pessimist or a fatalist" (Fischer, *History and Prophecy*, 228-29).

[18] Koktanek, *Spengler in seiner Zeit*, xv.

[19] Spengler, *Der Untergang des Abendlandes*, I, 23.

[20] Spengler, "Zur Weltgeschichte," in *Reden und Aufsätze*, 159.

philosophical relativism set forth in his *Hauptwerk*, that his philosophy of world history is only valid for denizens of Western civilization.[21] Now he asserts in bold Hegelian fashion that the process of world history has finally achieved the necessary stage of maturity, which permits the comprehension of its essence. "The twentieth century has finally become mature enough to penetrate to the ultimate meaning of the facts, out of whose entirety world history actually consists."[22] Spengler, in approaching prehistory and early civilizational history and contemplating their place in the totality of human existence, is deeply interested in ascertaining the overall pattern of world history, the main forces which produce it, and the underlying meaning of world history concealed behind the phenomenal facade of historical events. As in his major work, he continues to sharply reject the utilization of cause and effect analysis. Indeed, the tradition of German historicism, in striking contrast to Western positivism, embraced the methodological position that the study of history necessitated intuitive approaches to understanding rather than causal explanation. Spengler goes further than mainstream German historicism in this regard, arguing that the creative act of immortal poets, like Aeschylus and Shakespeare, in applying the power of poetic insight to the dramatic exploration of the human condition, can be duplicated in historical philosophy. It is the enormous ambition of this thinker, who composed unfinished historical dramas on Christ, Tiberius, and Napoleon, to be the dramaturge of world history itself, to achieve full poetic consciousness of the terror and wonder of the entire range of human historical experience. The task of the philosopher of universal history is to capture the greatness and tragedy at the heart of humanity's historical destiny.[23]

In *The Decline of the West* Spengler drew the distinction between two major periods in world history, that of the high cultures,[24] commencing around 3000 BC, and that of primitive culture or prehistory, which, in his estimation, began with the onset of the last Ice Age.[25] He considered early man as forming the largely undifferentiated foundation upon which the high cultures arose. "Primitive man only possesses history in a biological sense,"[26] he had dogmatically asserted. Originally, with his relative disin-

---

[21] Spengler, *Untergang des Abendlandes*, I, 61-62.

[22] Spengler, *Der Mensch und die Technik*, 4.

[23] Spengler, *Frühzeit der Weltgeschichte*, 4 (#8).

[24] In *The Decline of the West* Spengler normally employs the term *Kultur* to designate what in Anglo-Saxon historiography is typically called a civilization. When he contrasts a *Kultur* with the primitive culture of prehistory, he switches to the term *hohe Kultur* (high culture). In his *Spätwerk* he introduces the term *Hochkultur* (high culture) which is likewise equivalent to the *Kulturen* of his *Hauptwerk* (Spengler, *Der Untergang des Abendlandes*, I, 23ff; Spengler, *Der Untergang des Abendlandes*, II, 38; Spengler, "Plan eines neuen Atlas Antiquus," in *Reden und Aufsätze*, 103).

[25] Spengler, *Der Untergang des Abendlandes*, II, 38.

[26] *Ibid.*, 57.

158   JOHN FARRENKOPF

terest in the cultural significance of prehistory and early civilizational history, Spengler had asserted that humankind, prior to the emergence of each of the successive high cultures, had manifested merely the "primeval spiritual condition of an eternal-childlike humanity."[27] This is, to say the least, an unsatisfactory treatment of this vital phase in civilizational development. Nonetheless, it should be remembered in his defense that he went on to become one of the first historical philosophers to survey not only the realm of recorded history but the vast temporal expanse of prehistory as well.

Spengler, who was obviously not a professionally trained prehistorian, although he was well-read in the scholarly literature in German, English, and French in the field, viewed with disfavor the conventional approach prescribing the classification of periods of prehistory according to materials and objects collected from archeological finds.[28] He contended that instead, prehistory should be studied as a succession of epochs of human spiritual or psychological existence.[29] Spengler now divides world history into four instead of merely two distinct stages of cultural development, which sequentially unfold subsequent to the remote dividing line at which human beings spiritually emancipated themselves from the animal kingdom. The first three periods, which he had simply lumped together in *The Decline of the West* as one lengthy age of primitive culture, are labelled with Spartan economy of expression, "a", "b", and "c," corresponding to the Paleolithic, the Late Paleolithic and Neolithic, and the Late Neolithic and early civilization respectively. Spengler concentrated most of his research energy on the "c" phase of prehistory, which laid the foundation for the early civilizations. The final and fourth stage of world history is that of the high cultures or civilizations, the typology of which remains that unveiled in *The Decline of the West*.

Spengler's daring thesis in his *Hauptwerk* of the autonomous character of civilizations, their relative insulation from external civilizational influences, is a radical extension of the doctrine of individuality (*Individualitätslehre*) in German historicism. His problematic position continues to deservedly receive much criticism.[30] Yet already in 1924, only two years after he finally wound up his work on *The Decline of the West*, in discussing his "Plan eines neuen Atlas Antiquus," Spengler manifested a pronounced interest in going beyond his key thesis of cultural individuality to explore the complex role of cultural interaction in universal history. He visualizes primitive cultures composing a world of dynamic interplay.

---

[27] Spengler, *Der Untergang des Abendlandes*, vol. I., 142.

[28] Spengler, *Frühzeit der Weltgeschichte*, 29 (#67).

[29] *Ibid.*, 1 (#1).

[30] See, for example, the following, Joseph Vogt, *Wege zum historischen Universum: Von Ranke bis Toynbee* (Stuttgart, 1961), 70; Dray, "Oswald Spengler and the Life-Cycle of Cultures," 121ff; and Detlef Felken, *Oswald Spengler: Konservativer Denker zwischen Kaiserreich und Diktatur* (Munich, 1988), 64.

SPENGLER'S PHILOSOPHY OF WORLD HISTORY   159

"The primitive cultures encompass the entire earth, they have used all the seas along the coasts and island chains as go-betweens and form, with their spheres and currents a living whole, without which one is not able to survey the origin and prior history of the great cultures."[31] Civilizations themselves are now conceived to be involved in significant cultural interchange. Thus, the Sassanid Empire is characterized as "a most decisive creation at the crossroads of four high cultures."[32]

Spengler, with his penchant for evocative nomenclature, conceives the symbols of lava, crystal, and amoeba to illustrate the character of the successive, prehistoric cultural periods. According to his chronology, the age of lava spans the years from approximately 100,000 to 20,000 BC, the era of crystal stretches from about 20,000 to 8000 BC, and the period of amoebas extends from roughly 8000 to 3000 BC.[33] The first two periods of primitive culture do not develop organically; consequently the onetime student of mineralogy assigns them names derived from that discipline instead of biology. The epoch of "a" culture or lava is one of first beginnings, when the first representatives of the human race are dramatically expelled upon the surface of the earth like lava during the eruption of a volcano. The age of "b" culture or crystal witnesses human psychological awakening, the birth of instinctual comprehension, the transition from formless into form, when light penetrates into the human soul. In the era of "c" culture this phase of coming-to-consciousness deepens, human beings become aware of themselves as individuals, languages arise, tribes of a couple thousand people take shape and collective human enterprise emerges.[34] The "c" cultures, organic in nature, participate in, as wandering cultures, (*Wanderkulturen*),[35] substantial cross-cultural interaction. Like amoebas they are extremely mobile, expansive, and flowing. Spengler differentiates between three "amoebic" cultures which stand out for their exemplary development in the prehistoric record in comparison with those which remain obscured by the passage of time. He declines to give them geographical names because of their mobility and changing boundaries,[36] instead christening them with colorful names derived from ancient legend and mythology, Atlantis, Kasch, and Turan. They each have a comparatively short life-span of roughly 3,500 years.[37] Just as Spengler emphasized the primacy of cultural pluralism in the history of civilizations, he underscored, in historicist fashion, the cultural variation of prehistory. "But actually, there has never existed a human culture in general, but only

[31] Spengler, "Plan eines neuen Atlas Antiquus," in *Reden und Aufsätze*, 100.

[32] *Ibid.*, 103.

[33] See Koktanek's "Comparative Table of the Four Cultural Stages." Spengler, *Frühzeit der Weltgeschichte*, 492.

[34] Koktanek, introduction to Spengler, *Frühzeit der Weltgeschichte*, xvi-xvii.

[35] Spengler, *Frühzeit der Weltgeschichte*, 217 (#35).

[36] *Ibid.*, 219 (#41).

[37] *Ibid.*, 76 (#72).

160 JOHN FARRENKOPF

independent cultures of individual form, consequently also, at all times, separate developments."[38]

The primitive Western culture of Atlantis, a maritime one which built megaliths,[39] centered around Spain, Morocco, and the northern Sahara,[40] flowing north to Orkney and Denmark, and eastwards to Egypt, Sudan, and Akkad.[41] The early Southern temple-building culture of Kasch, had its center of gravity in the area demarcated by the Persian Gulf, Oman, Baluchistan, and Hyderabad.[42] The primitive Northern culture of Turan, stretching from Scandinavia to Korea, is the heroic, martial culture of the three, the home of the war-chariot.

The high cultures, organisms like their primitive amoebic progenitors and with their diverse styles of magnificent urban culture, are rooted plant-like in a specific, geographical area. Atlantis and Kasch fuse to form the origins of the high cultures of Babylon and Egypt.[43] The invasions of the nomadic warriors of Turan about 1500 BC, who swept down from the north upon the civilized peoples of Egypt, Minoan Crete, Babylon, the Indus valley, and early China, laid the foundations for the "half-Nordic" Graeco-Roman, Aryan Indian, and Chinese high cultures.[44]

Spengler's iconoclastic interpretation of prehistory suffers from three conspicuous deficiencies. Firstly, he denies, as an adherent of de Vries's mutation theory and as an opponent, like Nietzsche before him, of Darwinian thought, the idea that the human species has undergone a gradual process of biological evolution.[45] Secondly, in claiming that the first representatives of the human race appeared approximately 100,000 BC, his "age of lava" dawns much too late. Since Spengler's death the discovery of new paleontological and archeological evidence in combination with breakthroughs in techniques for dating it have enabled scientists to greatly push back the time when early man is envisioned as having emerged in the process of evolution. Thus, the oldest prehistorical artifacts have been recently estimated to be about 2.6 million years old.[46] Thirdly, Spengler rejects the idea that Paleolithic and Mesolithic man engaged in significant social intercourse, contrary to contemporary anthropological theory.[47]

Nonetheless, Spengler does succeed in sketching out a provocative philosophical anthropology, which, integrated in his greatly modified

[38] Ibid., 30 (#69).

[39] Ibid., 204 (#1).

[40] Ibid., 219 (#41).

[41] Ibid., 223 (#52).

[42] Ibid., 219 (#41).

[43] Ibid., 219 (#40).

[44] Spengler, "Der Streitwagen," in Reden und Aufsätze, 150-52.

[45] Spengler, Der Mensch und die Technik, 18ff.

[46] John A. J. Gowlett, Ascent to Civilization: The Archaeology of Early Man (New York, 1984), 39.

[47] Spengler, Der Mensch und die Technik, 23ff.

SPENGLER'S PHILOSOPHY OF WORLD HISTORY   161

philosophy of history, merits attention. Man rises in defiance of the natural world because of a primordial contradiction in his makeup. He is animated with the spirit of a proud beast of prey (*Herrentier*), like that of an "eagle, lion, [or] tiger," yet is distinguished by a degree of physical weakness on a par with that of animals who comprise the prey of carnivores (*Beutetier*). This constitutional incongruity is the source of his tragedy.[48] While Rousseau imagines man in the hypothesized state of nature to be a superlative physical specimen and detects no incipient, irresolvable conflict between man and the natural environment in the process of civilizational development,[49] Spengler conceives of primitive man as finding himself in a condition of relative, corporeal "powerlessness," which contrasts sharply with his high intellectual aptitude. Through the process of civilizational development man strives to resolve this existential dilemma, compensating for his physical weakness and vulnerability through the cultivation and employment of his powerful intellect. "The entire existence of the human race is [directed towards] the overcoming of its powerlessness."[50] Thus, culture is not the harmonious teleological end of history as Kant had speculated,[51] but "the weapon of the weak against nature."[52]

The "later" Spengler became deeply interested in the fundamental issue of the nature and implications of the interchange of humankind with the natural environment. Indeed, his greatly revised philosophy of world history offers an excellent vantage point for contemplating the intensifying global ecological crisis, of which the visionary thinker deserves recognition as a prophet. Spengler, who considered modern Western or Faustian civilization to be distinctively dynamic, expansive, and transformative of its environment, did not completely ignore the question of its impact upon the ecosystem in *The Decline of the West*. In its final pages he argued that modern civilization was exhausting the planet's energy resources and would, after its decline, leave the face of the earth permanently altered.[53]

Yet Spengler, who was socialized during a period of explosive industrial growth in Germany, went on to conceive an alarming vision of the nature of the interchange between humanity and the natural environment throughout the course of history. Man is a Promethean being endowed with the unique ability to create his own technics.[54] He is an inventive

---

[48] Spengler, *Urfragen*, 343, 344 (#21, 22).

[49] Jean Jacques Rousseau, *A Discourse on the Origin of Inequality* in *The Social Contract and Discourses* (1755; London, 1973), 48ff.

[50] Spengler, *Urfragen*, 344 (#22).

[51] Kant, "Idee zu einer allgemeinen Geschichte in weltbürgerlicher Absicht," in *Kleinere Schriften zur Geschichtsphilosophie, Ethik, und Politik*, ed. K. Vorländer (1784; Hamburg, 1973).

[52] Spengler, *Urfragen*, 344 (#21).

[53] Spengler, *Der Untergang des Abendlandes*, II, 623ff.

[54] Spengler does not use the term technics in a restrictive sense. Technics signifies for him not modern technology as it has arisen since the industrial revolution in the middle of the eighteenth century but the techniques, procedures, and methods practiced by

162   JOHN FARRENKOPF

and resourceful upstart locked into a revolutionary struggle with nature from remotest times.[55] "Artificial, contrary to nature is every human work from the lighting of fire to the achievements, that we in high cultures actually designate as artificial ones. The prerogative of creation is torn from nature."[56]

The technics which the intellectual capacity of human beings allows them to develop and refine, should not be understood as enduring triumphs of rationality, but instead as counternatural Promethean means which ineluctably lead to their destruction.[57] While Hegel in his *Lectures on the Philosophy of History* celebrated man's ability to reshape the natural environment as eminently rational,[58] Spengler appreciated its profoundly irrational and negative qualities. World history is the saga of the tragic and hopeless struggle between man, the proud beast of prey (*Raubtier*), and nature which will be waged to its bitter end.[59]

The conflict between man and nature escalates during the industrial revolution into a veritable war.[60] The war waged between humankind and nature achieves its tragic zenith in Western civilization.

The Faustian, West European culture is perhaps not the last, but certainly the mightiest, most passionate, through its inner contrast between comprehensive intellectualization and deepest, spiritual turmoil the most tragic of all. It is possible that a feeble straggler comes along yet, somewhere on the plain between the Vistula and the Amur and in the next millennium. But, here is the struggle between nature and man, who through his historical existence has rebelled against her, practically fought to its end.[61]

Although consciousness of the danger of a global ecological catastrophe has only emerged in the 1960s, already, in 1931, a profound vision of global ecological crisis clearly assumed a prominent place in Spengler's new conception of world history. "Everything organic succumbs to the spreading organization. An artificial world penetrates and poisons the natural one."[62] He grasps the extremely dangerous quality of the extraordinarily sophisticated, yet ultimately brutal mastery of the environment the human race has won.

---

humans in order to accomplish an extraordinary diversity of goals in a world envisioned to be one of self-assertion and struggle (Spengler, *Der Mensch und die Technik*, 5ff, 17, and 22).

[55] *Ibid.*, 22-23 and 39.

[56] *Ibid.*, 24.

[57] Spengler, *Urfragen*, 343 (#21).

[58] Hegel, *Vorlesungen über die Philosophie der Geschichte* (1840; Frankfurt am Main, 1970), 237 and 295.

[59] Spengler, *Der Mensch und die Technik*, 24-25.

[60] *Ibid.*, 6.

[61] *Ibid.*, 44.

[62] *Ibid.*, 55.

The mechanization of the world has entered into a stage of most dangerous, excessive tension. The face of the earth with its plants, animals and people has been altered. In a few decades most of the great forests have disappeared, have been transformed into newspaper and consequently climatic changes have occurred, which threaten the agriculture of entire populations; countless species like the buffalo have been completely or almost completely wiped out, entire races of men like the North American Indians and the Australian aborigines have been brought virtually to a state of extinction.[63]

Opposition to industry and technology had increased in Germany under the growing impact of the industrial revolution. However, prominent German intellectuals who either skeptically regarded or directly opposed the process of industrialization did not generally embrace as extreme a position as Spengler did in his twilight years. Wilhelm Heinrich Riehl, perhaps the most radical among his contemporaries during the years from 1850 and 1890 in his critical stance towards modernization, argued that the harmful consequences of the process of industrialization could be partially offset through intervention by the state to protect wilderness areas.[64] Ernst Rudorff, pioneer of the Movement for the Protection of the Countryside Against the Effects of Industrialism (*Heimatschutzbewegung*), with his aesthetic critique of ecological damage, clung to the hope that the unspoiled beauty of the romantic German countryside could be maintained by consequentially limiting the tourist excursions of supposedly decadent urbanites.[65] The distinguished political economist, Werner Sombart, despite his insights into the "Dämonie der Technik," was persuaded that society could intelligently manage the process of industrialization and keep its negative effects to a minimum.[66]

Assigning centrality to the conflict between humanity and nature in the process of civilizational development is only one of the many major differences between the philosophy of history Spengler expounded in *The Decline of the West* and the greatly altered philosophy in his *Spätwerk*.[67] He reverses himself about the idea of the meaning of history, a fundamental concern of speculative historical philosophy. In attacking the idea of progress like his mentor Nietzsche, Spengler sought to refute the post-Enlightenment notion that humankind was moving towards a supreme goal, whether it be peace, democracy, socialism, greater prosperity or what have you.[68] In *The Decline of the West* he sharply took issue with

---

[63] *Ibid.*, 54-55.

[64] Rolf Peter Sieferle, *Fortschrittsfeinde?: Opposition gegen Technik und Industrie von der Romantik bis zur Gegenwart* (Munich, 1984), 149ff.

[65] *Ibid.*, 161ff.

[66] *Ibid.*, 281.

[67] The term *Spätwerk* refers to the published and unpublished material of a historical-philosophical nature taken as a whole which Spengler produced subsequent to the completion of the composition and revision of *The Decline of the West* in 1923.

[68] Spengler, *Der Untergang des Abendlandes*, I, 26ff.

164   JOHN FARRENKOPF

the proposition that world history possessed any grand or overarching meaning. For the significance of history was fragmented, having its locus in each of the essentially independent cycles of *Kultur* and *Zivilisation*. The meaning of history, in keeping with Nietzsche's thesis of "perspectivism" and the relativity of truth, was held to be relativistic in nature; it varied according to the unique and transitory perspective of each civilization. Although the "late" Spengler still holds world history to be composed of distinctive civilizational traditions, he now is convinced that, nonetheless, they are ultimately subsumed within the comprehensive and meaningful process of world history.

Spengler's concern with the meaning of world history as a totality entailed important consequences for his earlier views on cross-cultural influence. World history retains prominent cyclical qualities for the "late" Spengler, in that its final stage, that of the several cultures examined in his *Hauptwerk*, still manifests phases of cyclically developing culture and civilization. However, he evidences a willingness to drop the thesis that cross-cultural influences are not of major importance in world history, justifiably a target of vocal criticism of *The Decline of the West*. Indeed, in an unpublished note, West European culture is now acknowledged to be a synthesis indebted to the contributions of its predecessors. ". . . During the golden age of classical literature, the Teutons had only hunted and wore animal skins. A culture is actually the synthesis of several cultures."[69]

The Decline of the West delivered a pioneering critique of the idea of progress, which dominated Enlightenment and post-Enlightenment historical thought in the diverse writings of Condorcet, Hegel, Ranke, Macaulay, Comte, Bancroft, and Marx. Although the book unquestionably displayed in a fundamental way a pessimistic orientation, Spengler interestingly rejected with a measure of justification being labelled a pessimist because the term had a pejorative connotation and downplayed his resolute modernism, i.e., his commitment to imperialism, global commerce, and applied science and technology. Spengler, in an essay *Pessimismus?*, composed in 1921 as a response to his numerous critics, emphasized that his deterministic vision of decline was by no means "catastrophic" in nature. The transition from *Kultur* to *Zivilisation* meant that the West was entering into its final, organic stage of development and might magnificently exhaust its possibilities in the emergent epoch of world history. Indeed, one could say "perfection" (*Vollendung*) instead of "decline" (*Untergang*).[70]

Spengler, in the course of his intellectual odyssey, intensifies his pessimism about the character and direction of history. In 1921 he protested,

[69] *Politica*, #84 L1d, Spengler Archive.
[70] Oswald Spengler, "Pessimismus?," in *Reden und Aufsätze*, 63-64.

"No, I am not a pessimist."[71] Twelve years later he proudly called his philosophy "strong pessimism" and "brave pessimism."[72] Moreover, the brooding thinker far more emphatically identifies world history with tragedy than he did in *The Decline of the West*. Although Spengler did describe in his *Hauptwerk* the historical cycle of each of the cultures as being governed by a tragic logic, it nonetheless underwrote his aesthetic vision of the sublime harmony of eternal rise and decline. Now, he contends that human history in its entirety is deeply tragic. "Every high culture is a tragedy; the history of humanity as a whole is tragic."[73]

Fundamental to every philosophy of history, whose distinguishing characteristic is change, is the concept of historical time. Spengler revolutionizes in his *Spätwerk* his concept of historical time. In *The Decline of the West* he argued that each cultural cycle was endowed with its distinctive historical tempo. Thus, while the classical world leisurely moved along in its historical development in andante; the dynamic West pressed onward in allegro con brio.[74] In his attempt to develop a unified vision of world history which integrates within it the various, independent, civilizational traditions, he moves beyond his earlier idea that each high culture possesses its own distinctive tempo. He propounds the new thesis that the process of world history since around 5000 BC flows in an accelerating tempo, which is clearly observable with the emergence of the first high cultures. The quickening pace of world history takes on tragic dimensions as it rushes towards its climatic end.

At the latest, two millennia later, the high cultures in Egypt and Mesopotamia already begin. One sees, the tempo of history assumes tragic dimensions. Earlier, millennia played scarcely a role, now every century becomes important. The rolling stone approaches in tearing leaps the abyss.[75]

Historical philosophers frequently make use of imaginative analogies to give vivid expression to their interpretation of the nature of history. Since the analogy was for Spengler the indispensable tool of the historical philosopher,[76] a brief consideration of the analogies he formulated in order to succinctly illustrate his key historical-philosophical ideas will economically capture the nature of the metamorphosis of his philosophy. The prime analogy in *The Decline of the West* is that drawn between a culture and a plant; they each undergo an organic process of birth, growth, and decay. Moreover, the succession of cultures, like a series of differentiated representatives of the same species of plants which follow each other

---

[71] *Ibid.*, 75.

[72] Oswald Spengler, *Jahre der Entscheidung*, I, *Deutschland und die weltgeschichtliche Entwicklung* (Munich, 1933), 9 and 13.

[73] Spengler, *Der Mensch und die Technik*, 52.

[74] Spengler, *Der Untergang des Abendlandes*, I, 146.

[75] Spengler, *Der Mensch und die Technik*, 27.

[76] Spengler, *Der Untergang des Abendlandes*, I, 4.

166   JOHN FARRENKOPF

in the eternal cycle of nature, do not combine to form an overarching meaning—world history does not possess a significance which transcends the finite life-span of a culture. Furthermore, despite the stubborn resistance of hopeful and optimistically oriented thinkers to the unpalatable notion that such a splendid creation as Western civilization could succumb to a process of decline, the analogy does have positive overtones—nature is fecund, life-giving, eternal.

Spengler deepened in his *Spätwerk* his appreciation of the ultimately self-destructive potentialities of the unparalleled dynamism, expansionism, and transformative energy of Western civilization, which were foreshadowed in his major work. Moreover, as we have seen, he reached the conclusion that world history experienced an acceleration in the tempo at which significant historical development took place. In the latter stages of his intellectual development, Spengler crafts an arresting analogy in characteristic, Nietzschean aphoristic form to describe the nature of the world-historical process, which captures these two important ideas. Now the history of civilization is likened to a thoroughly destructive, irreversible and accelerating process, which is typified by the manifestation of an increasing magnitude of energy and mass and driven towards an identifiable terminus—the natural disaster of an avalanche.

What distinguishes every late and early one [high culture], is the degree of intellectual tension, which leads to catastrophe. The division between element and spirit in life grows. The birth of culture already is accomplished under terrible internal convulsions and everything, which emerges in political, religious, economic forms, is laden with increasing fatality. It drives something, that began around 5000 BC, towards the end like an avalanche.[77]

While Hegel regarded world history as progressively expressing rationality, Spengler viewed world history as superficially manifesting human rationality, but at a deeper and more significant level attesting to the primacy of human irrationality and will. In Hegel's system the process of the advancement of freedom in consciousness is carried out by the nations. According to Spengler's conceptualization, the "heaven-storming" cultures raise humanity to a pinnacle where it experiences the extreme consciousness of tragedy.[78] For Hegel world history is the triumphant march of the *Weltgeist*, for Spengler, a student of Hegel's archrival Schopenhauer, it is the march of the *Weltwille*, the tragic, irrational odyssey of human will towards catastrophe. The world will is the irresistible, daemonic ethos which shapes human history contrary to rational criteria, in opposition to humankind's wishes that it could be otherwise and to its frustrated

[77] Spengler, *Frühzeit der Weltgeschichte*, 485 (#147). The analogy between civilizational development and an avalanche is employed in *Man and Technics*. "The rolling stone approaches in tearing leaps the abyss." Spengler, *Der Mensch und die Technik*, 27.

[78] Spengler, *Urfragen*, 360.

SPENGLER'S PHILOSOPHY OF WORLD HISTORY

ideals. And while the world spirit of Hegel progresses from East to West, the world will of Spengler moves, as we shall see, from South to North.

The human will [of high cultural man], led by his thinking, imagines to be able to form the world according to his ideals—that is optimism. But history realizes itself entirely independently of our wishes and desires. We think in one way, and the world will [*Weltwille*] in us drives otherwise.[79]

Spengler held Schopenhauer, who exerted a formative influence upon his mentor Nietzsche, in great esteem, once referring to him as "the last philosopher."[80] As he remarked in *The Decline of the West*, his epochal significance lay in his penetrating portrait of "the entire world as will, ... motion, force, direction."[81] For Schopenhauer, Nietzsche, and Spengler the will is the protagonist of world history; the intellect is relegated to the position of supporting actor. While Schopenhauer's pessimism about life leads to the strategy of withdrawal, that of Spengler goes with Napoleonic elan on the offensive; his "brave pessimism" yields recurrent affirmations in the spirit of Nietzsche's yea-saying. While history is an infinite temporal process for Schopenhauer and does not achieve an end point in Nietzsche's teaching of the eternal return, according to Spengler, their successor in German cultural pessimism, man's will, his instinctual energy, power world history towards its ineluctable end. "The tragedy of human will [constitutes] the imperative of his entire existence until the end."[82]

The notion that a revolutionary new typus of culture might conceivably emerge in a distant millennium and supersede the high culture as the highest form of collective human existence, which Spengler toyed with in his major work, is abandoned.[83] He now enthrones high culture as the ultimate stage in civilizational development. They are now rather ominously termed final cultures (*Endkulturen*).[84] Furthermore, Spengler implicitly retracts his trailblazing, anti-Eurocentric thesis in *The Decline of the West* that each of the eight cultures is of equal cultural significance.[85]

... The second millennium BC was decisive in the destiny of world-historical man. The old, hot southern cultures, Egypt and Babylon, come to an end. The center of gravity of great happening gravitates towards the colder, more intense and highly spiritually refined, harder struggling North, and this movement has continued. Here, in a colossal sweep from Western Europe up to East Asia, arose inwardly related, new forms of human spirituality, to which the languid world feeling of the South is foreign. Here one begins to experience life as a riddle,

---

[79] *Ibid.*, 349 (#39).

[80] Spengler, *Eis heauton*, #109, Spengler Archive.

[81] Spengler, *Der Untergang des Abendlandes*, I, 433.

[82] Spengler, *Frühzeit der Weltgeschichte*, 480 (#132).

[83] "It is also uncertain, whether a sudden event in the existence of the earth will introduce a totally different form" (Spengler, *Der Untergang des Abendlandes*, II, 42).

[84] Spengler, "Zur Weltgeschichte," in *Reden und Aufsätze*, 158.

[85] Spengler, *Der Untergang des Abendlandes*, I, 23.

because it is no longer easy and is not completely self-evident any more. Thinking, which turns away from proximity and instantaneousness and from directness and immediacy of action, acquires first here a great form. The concerns of life, the deed, becomes more important than mere physical existence. And now the feeling and reflection of the individual is directed towards the deed. Upon this foundation, in struggle against that older world feeling, there arise next to each other the Graeco-Roman, Indian, and Chinese high culture, all three half-Nordic, more individualistic, more domineering, grappling with more profound experiences, proud of these experiences instead of avoiding them, but in the South burning oneself out in the Southern climate.[86]

In this passage Spengler engages in a revaluation of the cultural ethos of the Graeco-Roman historical cycle, the necessity of which, for the consistency of his greatly altered philosophy of world history, he characteristically never conceded. Spengler believed that the glorification of the classical world in which Winckelmann, Herder, Goethe, Hegel, and Nietzsche indulged in diverse fashion, inhibited insight into the psychological novelty of modernity. In *The Decline of the West* Spengler attempted to overcome this celebration of the classical world by drawing a brilliant yet exaggerated portrait of antiquity, undervaluing its individualistic, creative qualities. He emphasized in his introduction to his major work that "the magnificence of the spiritual conception" and "the power of the rise" of Indian, Babylonian, Chinese, Egyptian, Arabian, and Mexican culture "surpassed" by "many times" that of the classical world.[87] Thus, for example, while the passion for recording the past and the monumental architecture of the glorious ancient civilization of the Nile were lauded, classical antiquity was depreciated as the culture "of the small, easy, and simple."[88] As we can clearly see in the excerpt above, Spengler now properly attributes a greater sense of individualism and creative energy to the classical world. Apollonian culture is promoted to the rank of "half-Nordic,"[89] while Egypt and Babylon are demoted to "the languid world-feeling of the South." This reappraisal of the ethos of these high cultures performs the vital function of smoothing the way for his formulation of an upward-spiralling model of civilizational development we will presently elucidate.

In his second philosophy of world history Spengler has enriched his evaluation of the human condition. He considers the deeply tragic history

---

[86] Spengler, "Zur Weltgeschichte," in *Reden und Aufsätze*, 158-59.

[87] Spengler, *Der Untergang des Abendlandes*, I, 23.

[88] *Ibid.*, 262.

[89] The term "Nordic" was introduced into the scientific and popular discussion about the role of race in culture and history in 1900 by the French anthropologist Joseph Deniker, and came into vogue in the 1920's in Germany. In this connection, it should be stressed that Spengler never attributed to race a role in cultural development (Geoffrey G. Field, "Nordic Racism," *JHI*, 38 [1977], 523).

of the human race to constitute merely an episode in the destiny of the world.

World history appears very much different than even our own time permits us to dream. The history of man is, measured by the history of the plant and animal world upon this planet, to say nothing of the life-span of the universe, short, an abrupt rise and fall of a few thousand years, something of no account in the destiny of the earth, but for us, who have been born into it, of tragic greatness and power.[90]

The brief history of the high cultures constitutes no longer a discontinuous series of unrelated scenes, but the final act in the epic tragedy of humankind.

[Man] is an element of all-living nature, which rises in rebellion against nature. He must pay for this defiance with his life. Through this act of defiance man distinguishes himself from all other living things, which as pure nature are blended with the tapestry of the natural universe.
[Mankind] is the hero of this tragedy, [world history] the final act of the tragedy itself.[91]

While Kant optimistically viewed the species of man as being immortal,[92] Spengler ascribes an ephemeral nature to man. The history of humanity is rapidly approaching its ineluctable end. "Man is an episode, a moment in the destiny of the world. The greatest part of the tragedy of culture is already past. The end dawns."[93] Indeed, in the treatise *Man and Technics*, the present era is assigned to the fifth act, which brings to a dramatic conclusion the four stages of world history—"We stand today at the climax, there, where the fifth act begins. The final decisions will be reached. The tragedy comes to a close."[94]

In mankind's final epoch, as the black storm clouds of world history ominously billow upon the brooding horizon, a searing moment of lucidity is granted so that man may comprehend the terribleness of his fate.

What distinguishes culture and high culture altogether, is the greatness of man, the height and depth of souls, which grow in desire and in suffering up to the high noon of world history in the onset of heroism. The great cultures are its battles: the victories until the redness of sunset and then the look over the battlefield into the terrible in vain of it all.[95]

In this tragic and irresolvable struggle between the human species and

---

[90] Spengler, *Der Mensch und die Technik*, 8.
[91] Spengler, *Urfragen*, 337 (#1).
[92] Kant, "Idee zu einer allgemeinen Geschichte," 8.
[93] Spengler, *Urfragen*, 350 (#43).
[94] Spengler, *Der Mensch und die Technik*, 52.
[95] Spengler, *Frühzeit der Weltgeschichte*, 30 (#70).

170 JOHN FARRENKOPF

nature, civilized man brings about an ecological catastrophe, mutilating
the earth from which he sprang.

Higher man is a tragedy. With his graves he leaves the world behind a battlefield
and wasteland. He has drawn plants and animals, the sea and mountains into his
decline. He has painted the face of the world with blood, deformed and mutilated
it. But there was greatness in it. When he is no more, his destiny will have been
great.[96]

Spengler was ambiguous about whether or not the end of modern
civilization would be tantamount to the demise of humankind. At times
he uses language which conveys the image of the approaching end of
world history as a distinct possibility, more often as an inexorable outcome. Spengler, at one point in his contemplation of the end of civilized
man, which (one should not forget) he engaged in before the advent of
the nuclear age, speculates that the world may witness a return to the
very low population levels characteristic of prehistoric times.[97] However,
our Cassandra does unequivocally indicate that he believes that the great
line of accelerated civilizational development, stretching from the southern civilizations of Egypt and Babylonia, to the northern, "harder-
struggling" Graeco-Roman world and the West, will be decisively brought
to a close in the chaos of the decline of Western civilization.[98]

World history now manifests for the "late" Spengler an over-arching
line of development which spans the individual cultures. The high-cultural
plurality surveyed in *The Decline of the West* is emplaced within a larger
framework in which world history forms to a significant degree a unified
process. The very fact of the emergence of the genus of high culture as a
civilizational stage was adjudged to be a mere accident in his main work;[99]
now, it is seen as a necessary act in the awesome spectacle of humanity's
revolt against the natural world. Integrating the two historical-
philosophical paradigms of *The Decline of the West* and his *Spätwerk*, he
emerges with an upward-spiralling model of the world-historical process
which climaxes in apocalypse. World history is characterized by an accelerating tempo of development, an increase in the dimensions of the catastrophe, and a tragic intensification of human consciousness. Thus, the
decline of the West is no longer to be understood as merely an isolated
event, a macro-historical phenomenon without earth-shaking ramifica-
tions for the course of world history, but as its ultimate phase.

---

[96] *Ibid.*, 9 (#20).

[97] "The tiny number of human beings in primeval times, which completely changes
the picture. Germania at the time of Tacitus had 2.3 million inhabitants; that must have
been already immeasurable in comparison with primeval times. Then it was perhaps
10,000. How will it be in the future, when the final culture has faded? Again a reduction
to tiny numbers?" (Spengler, *Frühzeit der Weltgeschichte*, 34 [#80]).

[98] Spengler, *Der Mensch und die Technik*, 44.

[99] Spengler, *Der Untergang des Abendlandes*, I, 188.

Spengler's philosophy of world history in the twilight of his life emerges as a remarkable vision of tragedy. World history soars upward, spiral-like, straining to reach ever higher stages of spiritual and mental refinement (*Durchgeistigung*), until the crescendo disintegrates in an apocalyptic finale. The greatness of the human race resides not in its purported capacity to use its intellectual abilities to form enduring "rational" modalities of civilization, but in its transitory, Nietzschean, heroic experience of extreme vitalism and creativity.

Spengler's *amor fati*, his willing acceptance of the tragedy of world history, does not merely reflect the yea-saying philosophical stance of Nietzsche, but to a degree the German historicist view towards historical reality as well. In the German historicist tradition it was assumed that history constituted a meaningful process, that all that has grown naturally or historically is good. Spengler, like the exponents of the German historicist tradition and Hegel as well, adopts an affirmative attitude towards history. However, the historical pessimist inverts the optimistic German historicist estimation of the nature of history. Leading representatives of historicism, including Humboldt, Ranke, and Droysen, envisioned history as manifesting the transcendent ethical order of a benevolent God, Spengler, as the unjust order of an unloving God or one indifferent to human suffering, one who permits free rein to man's tellurian and daemonic energies. Spengler's position approximates that of Nietzsche, who regarded the *Diesseits*, the world of our sense experience and the arena of our history, as the real world; the *Jenseits*, the realm of the ideal or of Providence is dismissed as a chimera. Moreover, the rejection by the German historicist tradition of human pleasure and utilitarian values, which Spengler echoes, reinforces his own affirmative stance towards the pain and suffering of history. The extreme vitalism of world history, manifested in the terrible conflict of man both against the natural world and his fellow man, must be affirmed in his eyes.

The preceding analysis of the metamorphosis of Spengler's philosophy of world history enables us to see in bold relief the transformation in his overall perspective from one amalgating optimism and pessimism to one of deep, unadulterated pessimism. His original position, as elaborated in *The Decline of the West*, displays both optimistic and pessimistic features. Although his vision of the decline of the West certainly has a pessimistic quality, in that he prophesies the inevitable demise of the modern world, on the other hand, the nonapocalyptic and cyclical qualities of his vision of the decline of the West express a kind of compensatory optimism. A new culture, that of Russia, will arise to replace that of Western civilization, as world history proceeds majestically in cyclical fashion.[100] Moreover, although modern technology will have permanently altered the face of

---

[100] "The next millennium belongs to the Christianity of Dostoyevski" (Spengler, *Der Untergang des Abendlandes*, II, 237).

the earth after the West has disappeared as a civilizational force, it is not initially considered by him as being dangerously injurious to the ecosystem. His original vision of international political transformation is pessimistic in that it foresees the eruption of a terrible struggle for global hegemony and the eventual collapse of the Occident as a result of internal decadence and external pressure. Yet, it is optimistic from a Germanocentric perspective, in that he envisions Germany to be the modern-day Rome—the architect of a monumental *imperium Germanicum*. The philosophy of world history expressed unsystematically in Spengler's *Spätwerk* is uncompromisingly pessimistic; it envisages the apocalyptic end of modern civilization through irresistible historical forces.

Before concluding his inquiry, this author wishes to consider the question whether the historical philosophy found in Spengler's *Spätwerk* is an expression of his politics and fully supportive of his controversial political goals. Although Spengler was afflicted with cultural despair, there is no doubt that originally he was also infected with power-political optimism, and consequently intended *The Decline of the West* to generate enthusiasm among the *Weltpolitik* generation of Wilhelmine Germany for his grandiose vision of German attainment of global primacy. In his late work, Spengler continued to celebrate martial values and placed even more emphasis on conflict and struggle in history than he had in the second volume of *The Decline of the West*, with its conspicuous quasi-Social Darwinistic qualities. However, one should not overlook the fact that his vision of human history became so pessimistic that it ended up being of doubtful usefulness for stirring up support for imperialistic statecraft. Having experienced the shocking military collapse of imperial Germany and the outbreak of socialist revolution in the fall of 1918, hyperinflation in the twenties and social and political turmoil throughout much of the Weimar period, Spengler sank into a state of profound pessimism about the future of Germany and the West as a whole.[101] Thus, in 1931, he painted in the concluding lines of *Man and Technics*, not a triumphant scene of a Roman legionnaire doing his part to conquer a sprawling empire, but a macabre death scene in which a Roman soldier, who duteously remains on sentry duty in Pompeii, is killed as the city around him is obliterated. Spengler could only enjoin his fellow citizens to emulate this ethic of futile but honorable self-sacrifice in the modern world, which he saw ineluctably moving towards destruction.[102] The extreme historical pessimism he came to represent in his *Spätwerk* borders on being incompatible with political activism.

---

[101] In fact, he fears that Germany might emerge from the approaching Second World War a permanently occupied land. "But I am talking here about Germany, which in the storm of facts is more seriously threatened than any other land, whose existence, in the alarming sense of the word, stands in question" (Spengler, *Jahre der Entscheidung*, 2).

[102] Spengler, *Der Mensch und die Technik*, 62.

Spengler's reflections on world history constitute a masterful two-stage critique of the idea of progress. This problematic thesis, delivered in diverse forms by a chorus of intellectual luminaries, has virtually dominated modern Western historical philosophy, having succeeded for the most part in drowning out the occasional dissenting voices of Vollgraff, Lasaulx, Gobineau, Burckhardt, and Brooks and Henry Adams. In *The Decline of the West* Spengler critiqued the idea of progress by advancing an imaginative model of essentially independent civilizations undergoing a cycle of rise and decline. Yet, he overreached himself in his daring effort to thoroughly discredit the widely accepted thesis of historical progress by denying the elements of civilizational continuity and the consciousness, which has become a fundamental part of the Western historical outlook since the Enlightenment, of the profound, onward movement of world history. In his *Spätwerk* Spengler recaptures the idea which he originally negated, that world history, despite its diversity and complexity, may be profitably conceived as a largely interrelated series of events. Yet he simultaneously markedly improves his critique of the idea of progress, not by relying exclusively upon the argument of civilizational decline, but by ingeniously fashioning a vision of world history as a largely integrated, upward-spiraling process climaxing in catastrophe.

By virtue of the transformation of his philosophy of world history, Spengler has arguably succeeded in helping to illuminate what may ultimately prove to be the awful blackness of the demise of modern civilization. In a century compelled to be more conscious of the ofttimes irrational nature of historical forces by the hammer blows of two world wars, genocide, global economic depression, and the specter of nuclear incineration, his vision of world history is a powerful one and of great timeliness despite its relative obscurity. Given that Vollgraff, Lasaulx, Gobineau, Burckhardt, and Brooks and Henry Adams treated the problem of the civilizational crisis of the West in the less drastic categories of decline, decadence, sterility, and exhaustion, Spengler merits recognition as the first historical pessimist of the modern West to conceive of world history in truly apocalyptic terms. The extraordinary, accelerating process of civilizational development spanning the end of the last Ice Age around 9000 BC to the global diffusion of modern Western civilization in the twentieth century may eventually reveal itself to be, not a wonderful tale of human progress, but perversely analogous to an avalanche driven towards a cataclysmic terminus. The intensification of the world-wide ecological crisis; the outbreak of global nuclear Armageddon; or the synergistic interaction of the collapse of international economic order, the population explosion, and the exacerbation of the North-South crisis, could herald the end of history in a profoundly irrational, Spenglerian sense. Undoubtedly, most of Spengler's critics will continue to write him off as a mere prophet, poet, or a proponent of purportedly outmoded speculative historical philosophy discredited by the fashionable approach of analytical and critical historical philosophy. Yet only the future, the father of historical time, will ultimately determine if modern civilization, the product of the genius of the West, has triumphed as historical optimists have argued, or, to converse with Spengler, the master spirit of historical pessimism, whether we will experience the final catastrophic phase of its decline.

University of Virginia.

IX

GRAMSCI'S INTERPRETATION
OF FASCISM

BY WALTER L. ADAMSON*

In the six years before his 1926 arrest by Mussolini's police, Gramsci wrote some 250 pages on the peculiar new political phenomenon of fascism. Prison officials later did their best to prevent the further development of this analysis, but there are nonetheless many passages in the *Prison Notebooks* which deal with it *sub rosa* and reveal subterranean connections between his understanding of fascism and the formulation of his larger theoretical standpoint. Although nearly every serious work on Gramsci makes at least passing allusions to this writing, no one has yet subjected it to a careful analysis. Here I propose to document the emergence and development of Gramsci's attitude towards, and understanding of, fascism within the more general context of his political ideas. I shall then show how much of the conceptual universe of the *Prison Notebooks* was invented to come to grips with the nature of fascist rule, and indeed, with the entire history of Italy's failed revolutions from 1848-1920 to which fascism was the tragic epilogue. It is in this ironic sense that fascism made Gramsci the great twentieth-century *political* theorist of Marxism.

While students of Gramsci have alluded to his understanding of fascism, students of interpretations of fascism rarely allude to Gramsci. This is unfortunate for many reasons, but especially because it tends to reinforce the all-too-prevalent myth that Marxist writers on fascism have recently become theoretically sophisticated, a development, it is often implied, which owes to the now manifest absurdity of what in the 1930s could be plausibly advanced at least by those with myopically proletarian mind sets.[1] For while many of the writings of Palmiro Togliatti and Palme Dutt, as well as the declarations of Comintern Congresses, constitute an official interpretation which caricatures and even disastrously misrepresents the reality of fascism,[2] Gramsci's writings openly violate nearly every stereotype

---

* My thanks to Molly Nolan, Charles Maier, and Herbert A. Deane for their comments on and criticisms of an earlier version of this article.

 [1] For an example of this tendency, see A. James Gregor, *Interpretations of Fascism* (Morristown, N.J., 1974).

 [2] For a summary review of some of this official literature, see John M. Cammett, "Communist Theories of Fascism," *Science and Society*, 31: 2 (Spring 1967), 149-63.

176 WALTER L. ADAMSON

of such Communist interpretations. He did not, for instance, hold to any crude thesis of "fascism as the last stage of capitalism," or to the view that it was the "agent of the big bourgeoisie" or of "finance capital," or even to the view that it was the simple reflection of some exclusive set of class interests. As early as 1921 he saw that it was not merely "reactionary" and that it had complex internal divisions reconciled only in a common fear of, and antipathy towards, the proletariat. Moreover, Gramsci anticipated many of the views now in favor among historians of fascism—that it is best studied as an outgrowth of the war,[3] and that it was essentially a movement within the urban and later rural areas of the economically more developed Italian north[4]—so that his analysis of the "two fascisms" of 1921-22 has been cited as definitive.[5] Finally, in an effort at a theoretical clarification of the tenuous links he saw between the fascists and their bases of support, he undertook an analysis of fascism as an "exceptional state" and of the "relative autonomy of politics" forty years before the French structuralism of Poulantzas led him to the same considerations.[6]

I. To begin retracing the historical trajectory of this interpretation, we must return to the fall of 1920. It is mid-October; the Turin working class has just suffered a devastating defeat over their occupation of the factories. Gramsci and others in the communist faction of the Italian Socialist Party (PSI) have blamed the vacillations of its leaders for the defeat and are preparing for the likely formation of a new Italian communist party. In this perspective, the suddenly noticeable increase in violence by fascist *squadristi* can be explained as due to an anti-proletarian "reaction" and thus assimilated without difficulty to Italy's traditional past.

Such is the tack Gramsci adopted in his first articles on fascism.[7] He had predicted the previous spring that a failed proletarian offensive would bring a "tremendous reaction"; now he assimilated his correct prediction to the view that "reaction has always existed" in

---

[3] Ernst Nolte and Roberto Vivarelli have each stressed this point; see the former's *Three Faces of Fascism* (London, 1965), 3-9 and 167-77, and the latter's "Italian Fascism," *Historical Journal,* **17**: 3 (1974), 644.

[4] On this point, see Federico Chabod, *A History of Italian Fascism* (London, 1963), 48, and Adrian Lyttleton, *The Seizure of Power* (London, 1973), 51-52.

[5] *Ibid.,* 430, n. 66.

[6] Nicos Poulantzas, *Fascism and Dictatorship* (London, 1974).

[7] All citations from Gramsci's work are taken from *Socialismo e fascismo* (Turin, 1966), *La Costruzione del partito comunista* (Turin, 1971), *Quaderni del Carcere,* 4 vols. (Turin, 1975)—cf., *Selections from the Prison Notebooks,* eds. Q. Hoare and P. Nowell Smith (New York, 1971), and cf., *Selections from the Political Writings, 1910-1920,* ed. Q. Hoare (New York, 1977); hereafter abbreviated *S.F., C.P.C., Q.C., S.P.N.,* and *S.P.W.* respectively, the year of composition in parentheses.

Italy as part of a popular impulse towards charismatic leaders in times of stress. This time it was part of an international crisis, the "outgrowth of the failure of the imperialist war," and it offered convincing proof for any who still needed it that the bourgeois state was incapable of "coming to terms with the Italian productive forces."[8] Yet despite this weakness, and despite fascism's fast increasing strength and aspiration to "become a state," Gramsci at this point did not quite take fascism seriously and treated it as though it were merely the pathetic residue of a brutal war.[9] Publicly at least, he remained certain that the proletariat would soon prevail; indeed, prior to the PSI's Livorno Congress in January, Gramsci's writing on fascism was less a response to its intrinsic danger than a dramatization of the need for a new PCI.[10]

Shortly after the new year, a wave of fascist violence of unprecedented intensity swept across Northern Italy. Still convinced of fascism's transitory character, Gramsci pointed to its petty bourgeois base and to the fears of this class that the large-scale structure of the new and dominant industrial forces had eliminated its economic function. In Turin, he argued, a fascist base was confined almost entirely to shopkeepers, a small part even of the petty bourgeoisie, and he concluded that the workers could prevail there even in an armed struggle.[11] Yet by mid-February Gramsci was beginning to develop an analysis of the divisions internal to fascism, and in this way paid some tribute to its rising political prowess. Fascism, he now suggested, had two faces: a radical one represented by unemployed veterans, nationalists, and legionaries who supported D'Annunzio's invasion of Fiume, and a conservative one represented by Mussolini's diverse but more middle class and more organization-minded urban constituency.[12] He would develop this analysis further by late summer, but he already saw its most crucial consequence: that fascism was not a unified bloc and that the proletariat must seek to locate its fissures precisely and to split them open still further.[13]

In the post-1923 period when Gramsci assumed the PCI chairmanship, this insight led him to formulate a new anti-fascist strategy of united front. Now as editor of *L'Ordine Nuovo*, the PCI daily, he was more concerned with building the new party's mass base through an unceasing propaganda barrage against the PSI, Italy's version of "Barnum's circus."[14] Interestingly, however, he did make an effort

---

[8] *S.P.W.*, 191, 352-53, 360 (1920).   [9] *S.P.W.*, 353 (1920), 372 (1921).

[10] A good example is his January 11 article on "Fiume," used to discredit PSI chairman Serrati; cf. *S.F.*, 34-36 (1921).

[11] *S.F.*, 9-10, 55-56 (1921). The accuracy of Gramsci's analysis of the early petty bourgeois character of fascism is now commonly acknowledged; cf. Lyttleton, *op. cit.*, 55 and 106.

[12] *S.F.*, 76-79 (1921).   [13] *S.F.*, 297-99 (1921).   [14] *S.F.*, 172 (1921).

178 WALTER L. ADAMSON

to confer with D'Annunzio in April, and a secret meeting was actually arranged at the lakeside resort of Gardone, though D'Annunzio never appeared.[15] Shortly thereafter, Gramsci penned "Forze elementari," a startling advance in his analysis of fascism which, as Alastair Davidson has suggested, is one of the most provocative single pieces on fascism Gramsci ever wrote.[16] Consider the following:[17]

> It has by now become evident that fascism can only partly be assumed to be a class phenomenon, a movement of political forces conscious of a real goal; it has overflowed, it has broken loose from every organizational framework, it is superior to the will and intention of every regional or central committee, it has become an unleashing of elemental forces within the bourgeois system of economic and political governance which cannot be stopped: fascism is the name for the profound decomposition of Italian society which could not but accompany the profound decomposition of the state and which can today be explained only with reference to the low level of civility [culture] which the Italian nation has reached in sixty years of unitary administration.

Here in one long sentence, written in April 1921, a year and a half before the March on Rome, lie many of the features that would come to distinguish Gramsci's analysis from the Comintern clichés of later years. Fascism is based on a cross-class appeal and cannot be explained merely in class terms; it is bound up with a profound decomposition of civil society and parliamentary government in Italy. Fascism also appeals, as the article's later reference to a "barbaric and anti-social psychology" makes clear, to irrational elements in the human psyche. Yet—and this is a crucial point for grasping Gramsci's entire intellectual outlook—he was unable now or later to explain this irrationalism in anything but the most rationalistic of terms.[18] Here the resort was to a national character argument about the "human immaturity" of the Italian people, an affliction, apparently, to which the working class was entirely immune.[19]

---

[15] See Sergio Caprioglio, "Un Mancato incontro Gramsci-D'Annunzio a Gardone nell'aprile 1921 (con una testimonianza di Palmiro Togliatti)," *Rivista storica del socialismo*, 5, 15-16 (Jan.-Aug. 1962), 263-73.

[16] *S.F.*, 150-51 (1921); Alastair Davidson, *Antonio Gramsci: Towards an Intellectual Biography* (London, 1977), 189.   [17] *S.F.*, 150 (1921).

[18] Davidson's suggestion (*op. cit.*, 190-91) that "Forze elementari" "reminds us of many of the 'mass psychological' or 'cultural' historians of fascism" (he mentions Reich, Neumann, Kohn, Mosse, and Weber) breaks down on this point. The first writer within the Marxist tradition to come to grips with the irrational and mythic elements to which fascism appealed was probably Theodor W. Adorno; cf. Susan Buck-Morss, *The Origin of Negative Dialectics* (New York, 1977), 19. See also Ernst Bloch, "Nonsynchronism and the Obligation to Dialectics," and Anson Rabinbach, "Ernst Bloch's *Heritage of Our Times* and the Theory of Fascism," both in *New German Critique*, 11 (Spring 1977), 5-38.

[19] Cf. also *S.F.*, 168 (1921).

Ultimately, "Forze elementari" is perhaps best understood as an effort to come to grips with the full meaning of Italy's still unresolved national crisis, and from this to fathom the means by which the proletariat might still play the role of a national savior. Gramsci seems hardly to waver in his view that this remains the overwhelmingly likely outcome of the crisis. In June and July his articles did turn repeatedly to an image of a fascist *colpo di stato* (a possibility to which the socialists are blind because of their "pseudo-Marxism").[20] Yet this image was abandoned when the "Pact of Pacification," signed August 2 by Mussolini and representatives of the PSI, quickly backfired and opened still wider the breaches within the fascist ranks. While careful not to underestimate the fascists, Gramsci's response was his most sustained probe at that time into the historical sources of the "two fascisms."[21]

The early, war-generated *fasci di combattimento*, he recalled, were essentially of petty bourgeois orientation given their support base in the various associations of ex-servicemen. This made them hostile to the PSI which was, of course, working class in orientation and had opposed the Italian intervention in the war. Their anti-socialism gained the *fasci* some support among "the capitalists and the authorities" but also, and primarily, among the "agrarians," i.e., the small and medium farmers and large latifundists—everyone except the landless peasants. Fascism's problem was that its class origin ultimately went counter to the direction of its expanding strength which was predominantly in the northern cities where those attracted to it ("the *ceti medi* [middle strata], employees, and small businessmen and industrialists") were more parliamentary and collaborationist in orientation. Discomfort with the political style of fascism's rural wing was also evident among the capitalists who gave the movement financial backing and even among the local authorities who looked the other way during outbursts of fascist violence.

To guarantee his political future, the always alert Mussolini had recognized early the necessity of building ties with at least some industrial capitalists. "The reality of the world," he was fond of saying, "is capitalist."[22] Yet, as Gramsci clearly perceived, Mussolini could not take such ties for granted.[23] If the industrialists feared

---

[20] *S.F.*, 187; cf. also *S.F.*, 247-48, 257-59 (1921).

[21] *S.F.*, 297-99 (1921). See also S.F. 544-46 (1921) for an argument about the political repercussions of the past.

[22] Quoted in *S.F.*, 301 (1921). Gramsci's early perception of the division within fascism between its largely petty bourgeois mass base and its financial backing by big business is confirmed by the recent study of Roland Sarti, *Fascism and the Industrial Leadership in Italy, 1919-1940* (Berkeley and Los Angeles, 1970), 113.

[23] *S.F.*, 301 (1921).

fascism's instability, Mussolini and his cohorts were uneasy among the industrialists and, or so it appeared to Gramsci, incapable even of understanding the nature of their new industrialism. Mussolini's economic conceptions remained mired in the "pre-war years, the period before the 'trusts' and the concentration of industrial capital in banks."[24]

Yet despite all these weaknesses, Gramsci's proletariat-to-the-rescue scenario became steadily less plausible over the fall and winter of 1921-22. Gradually Mussolini managed to patch over the schisms within the movement and to restore its vitality, while at the same time the fortunes of the PCI continued to wane amidst incessant bickering with the PSI and a prevailing disillusion among the urban working classes. Gramsci himself became increasingly embittered and despondent in his *Ordine Nuovo* articles, and his health, habitually poor, declined rapidly under the strain. In the spring, as a fascist seizure of power seemed all but a matter of time, it was decided that Gramsci should take a rest cure in a Russian sanatorium. His last article of May 23 spoke darkly of those who will "pay in person for having disgraced themselves with crimes" of "opposition to proletarian unity" and "vain compromise."[25]

While in Russia, Gramsci had the opportunity to reflect on events in Italy from a more detached standpoint, and his article for the Fourth Congress of the International in November 1922 marks his first effort to come to grips with the broad historical origins of the now governing fascist movement.[26] As in his later, more extended discussions of these origins in the "Lyon Theses" (1926), the essay on the "Southern Question" (1926), and his prison discussions of 1930,[27] Gramsci found his starting point in the character of the Italian Risorgimento. Unlike France and Britain, Italy had never really experienced a bourgeois, democratic revolution. The Risorgimento was

---

[24] *Ibid.;* cf. also Angelo Tasca's discussion in his *Rise of Italian Fascism, 1918-1922* (London, 1938), 134, where Mussolini is quoted as saying, "We must abolish the collectivist state that the war forced on us, and return to the Manchester state." These perceptions tend to undercut those recent attempts by Gregor and others to assimilate Mussolini's fascism to movements of "modernization." Cf. Gregor, *op. cit.*, and more recently "Fascism and Comparative Politics," *Comparative Political Studies* 9: 2 (July 1976), 207-22. For a recent critique of this position which argues that Mussolini simply did not think in these terms, see Charles S. Maier, "Some Recent Studies of Fascism," *Journal of Modern History*, **48**: 3 (Sept. 1976), 518-21.

[25] *S.F.*, 494 (1922). [26] *S.F.*, 528-30 (1922).

[27] *C.P.C.*, 488-513, 137-58 (1926); the latter are most extensively reported in Athos Lisa, *Memorie: In carcere con Gramsci* (Milan, 1973), 81-103. In the *Prison Notebooks*, Gramsci goes back even further and connects fascism with the larger groups of petty bourgeoisie formed by the disintegration in the early modern era of those smaller cities of the northern Italian interior dubbed by D'Annunzio the "cities of silence"; cf. *S.P.N.* 131 (1932).

a revolution from above, successful largely because of Cavour's skillful diplomacy, and the resulting political system, though parliamentary in form, was in practice based on a system of inter-elite collaboration known as *trasformismo*. While they had some input into this collaboration, bourgeois elements were in no position to "defend the unity and integrity of the state against the repeated attacks of the reactionary forces, represented above all by the alliance of the great landowners with the Vatican."[28]

This weakness was exacerbated by the tumult of the war. Though a strengthened, left-wing, populist opposition, led by the PSI and in 1919 by the Catholic Partito popolari, also emerged from the war crisis, its leadership was never properly consolidated. Thus the revolutionary moment which existed in Italy above all in 1919 was missed, and the groundwork was laid for a powerful right-wing reaction. 1920 saw the formation of a centralized organization of industrialists, *Confindustria*, which crushed the Turin labor movement in every encounter, and the rapid expansion of the *fasci di combattimento*. Given the disarray on the left and the loss of all confidence in parliamentarism, the fascists, Gramsci now seemed to suggest, were the only political force capable of filling the vacuum.

The upshot of this account is that Gramsci already explicitly rejected any identification of fascism as the "agent" of the bourgeoisie. Moreover, the thesis that fascism is a form of "Bonapartism" is rejected as well, at least as it was propounded by Thalheimer and others a decade later in Germany.[29] Fascism is not the product of a standoff between bourgeoisie and proletariat, but of the proletariat's outright defeat in a political setting where the bourgeoisie is dominant despite the intrinsic weaknesses of its political institutions. In prison Gramsci will use the concept of hegemony to develop this insight into a highly original theory of fascism as a form of "Caesarism."

Two other points should also be clear from the development of Gramsci's account of fascism through 1922. First, he defined fascism, above all in its manifestations as a political party. Like all political parties, the fascists were seeking to build a mass base. Gramsci's interest was in the character and makeup of this base, which he analyzed in class and regional terms, and in the tensions between its various constituent parts. At first he thought these tensions would

---

[28] *S.F.*, 528-29 (1922).

[29] Cf. Martin Kitchen, "Thalheimer's Theory of Fascism," *JHI* **34**: 1 (Jan.-March 1973), 67-78. For a later statement clearly linking fascism's victory in 1922 with the proletariat's defeat in 1920, see *C.P.C.*, 495. Nicos Poulantzas, who in *Fascism and Dictatorship* (60-61) clearly and correctly distinguishes Gramsci's interpretation from Thalheimer's nonetheless fails to perceive Gramsci's concession of the Italian proletariat's defeat. His criticism of Gramsci on this point is thus wide of the mark.

182 WALTER L. ADAMSON

prevent a fascist victory; even when it became necessary to revise this judgment, however, he still insisted on the sharp internal cleavages within fascism. Unlike Trotsky and Thalheimer, whose important analyses date from the 1930s and who therefore confronted fascism as a constructed and fully operative edifice, Gramsci dealt with it as a project under construction, subject to delays and reversals in support as well as to some brilliant spurts of growth.

Secondly, Gramsci was also concerned with fascism as a mass movement reflecting the general character of Italian society and cultural life in the wake of four years of war and a string of proletarian defeats. This, in part, is why he could not reduce it to a reflection of its class supports, however complex and mediated. Yet Gramsci did not push the social-psychological analysis of fascism very far. The irrational character he imputed to it was explained strictly as a result of the extraordinary circumstances which had surrounded its birth, and his general commitment to an implicit model of politics as a product of essentially market rational behavior was never for a moment questioned. Had he done so, he might have achieved a keener insight into the nature of the fascist appeal and a more synthetic understanding of fascism as party and as social movement; as it is, the two levels are never successfully integrated. Thus he was still unable to explain if, and in what sense, fascism had "solved" the post-war crisis.

II. The news of the March on Rome reached Gramsci while he was still in temporary exile in the Soviet Union. The magnitude of the defeat this represented for the PCI, together with the imminence of the Comintern Fourth Congress, thrust the question of PCI strategy and tactics onto center stage. Despite the intense opposition of the Comintern, Gramsci had largely supported Bordiga's narrowly sectarian and anti-united front positions in 1921-22. The only significant concession to the united front idea he made then was the support he at one point voiced for the cross-party, anti-fascist defense groups known as *arditi del popolo*.[30] After the March on Rome, however, his strategic thinking shifted dramatically. While there exist no documents which would allow us to reconstruct the course this reconstruction took, it is clear that by late 1923 he was voicing strong criticism of Bordiga and equally strong support for the Comintern-

---

[30] For Gramsci's support of the *arditi del popolo,* see S.F., 542 (1921). A discussion of Gramsci's relation to Bordiga in this period and of the reasons behind the changes in his strategic thinking from 1922-24 are included in my "Towards the *Prison Notebooks:* The Evolution of Gramsci's Thinking on Political Organization, 1918-1926," *Polity* (1979). Most of the documents relevant to the latter point are included in Palmiro Togliatti, *La formazione del gruppo dirigente del partito comunista italiano nel 1923-1924* (Rome, 1962).

backed united front proposal. Given his position in exile, it is doubtful that this shift resulted directly from a reappraisal of fascism, beyond the obvious fact that it was now in power. What it did appear to reflect were certain historically contingent factors (e.g., the need for closer ties with the Comintern) and one still undeveloped, theoretical insight: that the form revolution might take in the west, given the far greater development of its political and cultural superstructures, was necessarily different from the form it had taken in Russia.

As he suggested to Togliatti in a letter of Feb. 9, 1924, the *Ordine Nuovo* movement which they had jointly guided in 1919-20 had been misled by the Bolshevik example.[31] Fascism had since demonstrated in practice that the bourgeois state had chameleon-like qualities of adaptability which could extend the capitalist crisis far beyond what tsarism had been capable of. If this could not be explained theoretically, fascism's successful tactics could at least be identified and countered—or mimicked where appropriate—by the proletariat. So, for instance, since fascism sought to gain the support of the same loose coalition of great landowners and large capitalists which had undergirded Giolitti's liberalism, it would probably have difficulty in formulating an adequate policy on the Southern Question; the PCI must therefore seek to establish stronger bases in and programs for the south.[32] Since fascism seemed incapable of attracting much support among poor peasants and workers, the PCI must seek to build a united front centered around these classes. Since fascism sought ties with the Vatican, with influential intellectuals like Croce, and with traditional legitimating symbols in order to build a solid consensual basis for its rule, the PCI must launch a counter-hegemonic strategy in response.[33]

Gramsci had already developed many of these ideas in letters from abroad before returning to Italy on May 12, 1924. Yet like everyone else on the Italian left, he was strategically unprepared for the especially acute crisis phase into which fascism was plunged a month later by the assassination of opposition deputy Giacomo Matteotti. Almost immediately he could see that fascism's support among the urban

---

[31] *S.F.*, 197 (1924). This insight is later linked to a theory of fascism as "Caesarism" from which a proletarian counterstrategy of "war of attrition" is derived.

[32] This point is most fully developed in the essay on the "Southern Question"; see *C.P.C.*, 137-58. Among the specific measures advocated were alliances with servicemen's committees and support for "small and medium reviews." The former is especially indicative of Gramsci's effort to overcome fascism by learning from it.

[33] The concept of "hegemony," which becomes central in the *Notebooks* and is first extensively employed in the essay on the "Southern Question," first appears in 1924; cf. *L'Ordine Nuovo*, March 1924, p. 4, reprinted in *L'Ordine Nuovo* (Milan, 1966).

184 WALTER L. ADAMSON

petty bourgeoisie and middle classes was evaporating; fascism's legal facade was crumbling, and its inner essence as an "armed dictatorship" was being revealed. By early July he was arguing that the regime was in danger of collapse.[34] Throughout the summer and into the fall he sought to fortify the PCI and to build bridges to the peasantry. What went relatively neglected were bridges to those more middle-class political groups, like the Aventine parliament, which had become disillusioned with the regime. By November he recognized that once again a revolutionary moment had passed; embittered, he sought to blame "the influence of democrats and social democrats."[35] Only later would he recognize that the real problem was his own insufficient initiative in organizing a broad constituent assembly.[36] This failure was not accidental; it was the logical, if not inevitable, result of Gramsci's prior failure to grasp the nature of fascism's rational and irrational appeal to its constituencies. Without this grasp he could hardly be expected to make a successful counter-appeal, even if he had chosen to do so.

While in prison he did read one book by Freud,[37] yet he never developed the socio-psychological tools necessary for approaching fascism as a political movement. What he had learned from the Matteotti Crisis, however, was that whatever the nature of fascism's appeal, it was somehow unstable, and the level of support for fascism could be expected to fluctuate widely. In his most interesting and fully developed analyses, during his tenure as PCI chairman, he probed for the sources of the fluctuations in the cleavages of the fascist party and in the relations between party and regime.[38]

After Jan. 3, 1925 when Mussolini assumed dictatorial power, Gramsci thought that tensions between the regime and the party were becoming increasingly manifest. The tendency within the regime, typified by its Internal Affairs Minister Luigi Federzoni, was to advocate liquidating the party as a political organism and incorporating it within the state apparatus. Here the prevailing attitude was one of *realpolitik* and moderation—close collaboration with the Crown, majority rule, and the incorporation of some Catholic and even some ex-Aventine factions. The tendency within the party, however, especially after Roberto Farinacci was appointed its general secretary early in 1926, was to adopt a more extreme and more fragmented policy.

---

[34] *C.P.C.*, 25-28 (1924).   [35] *Ibid.*, 210.

[36] *C.P.C.*, 122 (1926) and according to the Lisa memoirs, 89.

[37] Freud's *Introduction à la Psychanalyse*, trans. S. Jankélévitch (Paris, 1922); see *Q.C.*, 2467.

[38] See, e.g., *C.P.C.*, 113-24 (1926), 495-99 (1926), 517-22 (1923), 541-45 (1924), 550-52 (1925).

Gramsci perceived a split, first of all, between the party's predominantly petty bourgeois mass base (which understood the party structure to be the main instrument of its self-defense as a class and hence supported it with religious fanaticism) and the party's major financial bases which were generally much cooler towards that structure. The financial supporters were themselves divided between big industry and big agriculture; their interests often directly conflicted on issues like taxes, import duties, and state fiscal policies.[39] Between these rival groups lay broad middle strata whose loyalties, as was apparent from the Matteotti Crisis, tended to vacillate between reaction and liberal opposition. Now Gramsci expanded on the vacillation: he argued that in the two years prior to the March on Rome fears of the proletariat among these strata had led them in a reactionary direction, but beginning in 1923 "the most active elements of the middle classes" had shifted towards the left, eventually providing the backbone of the Aventine opposition.[40] New fears of proletarian extremism, however, soon drove them back towards the regime, and they tended to support Mussolini's assumption of dictatorial power. Uncomfortable with this by 1926, the middle classes seemed to be swinging back towards liberalism, or so at least Gramsci perceived, and he held out great hope that they might now become allied with a more disciplined and pragmatic proletarian left into a viable counter-fascist bloc.

How was this oscillation to be explained? The closest Gramsci could come to a direct answer was based on fascism's appeal to a "fear of the proletariat." Yet he managed to develop another more interesting, though still partial, answer by formulating a comparative analysis of European regimes.[41] A tendency towards middle-class fluctuations roughly similar to those in Italy could also be discerned, he suggested, in the parallel politics of Spain, Portugal, Poland, and the Balkans. These parallels might be explained by the fact that all these states had a "peripheral" status within the structure of international capitalism. Since in more advanced states like Czechoslovakia and France one found instead a much greater continuity in the left bloc, it seemed to follow that Italy's peripheral status and the vacillating political allegiances of its middle classes were somehow related.

Gramsci nowhere pursued the inner logic of this connection, but his focus on the concept of a "peripheral state" did lead to a line of inquiry which later proved crucial to his entire political theory. What peripheral states shared, in terms of social structure, were certain "intermediate strata" within their middle classes who seemed to exercise a mediating function between the regime and its peasant and rural worker constituencies.[42] These intermediate strata were

---

[39] Cf. *C.P.C.*, 496 (1926).   [40] *C.P.C.*, 122 (1926).   [41] *Ibid.*   [42] *Ibid.*

mostly of the older petty bourgeois and/or rural type which had been conserved or even expanded because of what would now be called the "uneven development" of the peripheral state. Yet instead of attempting a deeper analysis of the political economy of uneven development, Gramsci focused on the mechanisms through which the intermediate strata carried out their mediating function. Very likely it was this consideration which led him to his first close examination of the concept of hegemony in his essay on "The Southern Question." His major concern in that essay, however, was less with theoretical elaboration of any sort than with the implementation of strategy. Its central thrust was to reformulate the notion of a counter-fascist bloc in terms of an alliance between a disciplined and pragmatic PCI and the "democratic intellectuals" of the mediating strata in Italy's rural areas.[43]

In retrospect, this strategic program appears as a tragic manifestation of Gramsci's self-proclaimed "optimism of the will"; his arrest, just as the essay was apparently nearing completion, and his later imprisonment would isolate him almost totally from political practice of any sort. His efforts at a proletarian counter-hegemony became reduced to writing an "anti-Croce" (he regarded Croce as one of the "great figures of Italian reaction"[44]) and to conducting prison classes at Turi in 1930, which, if anything, seem to have been counter-productive.[45] What his forced isolation did produce, however, was an extended theoretical exploration of some of the issues in a Marxist interpretation of fascism as well as the emergence from this analysis of a new understanding for Marxism of the relationship between politics and economics as partial factors within a cultural whole.

III. If, as we have seen, Gramsci's analysis of fascism led him indirectly to the concept of hegemony, the latter was only fully formulated in the *Prison Notebooks*. In his "Southern Question," hegemony had been defined in a rather restricted way as "the social basis of the proletarian dictatorship and the workers' state."[46] In this sense, hegemony referred to two concrete requirements: a level of proletarian class-consciousness adequate to ensure the consensual basis for its self-rule and, since in Italy the proletariat was far from a majority, a class alliance which "succeeds in obtaining the consent of the large peasant masses."[47] Gramsci already understood that to gain such a hegemony meant at least in part to deprive fascism of its consensual basis, "to break up the intellectual bloc which forms the flexible but very resistant armor of the agrarian bloc."[48] Yet only in the *Prison Notebooks* is the latter idea theoretically clarified. There

---

[43] *C.P.C.*, 150-58 (1926).   [44] *C.P.C.*, 150 (1926).   [45] See Lisa, *op. cit.*, 90-103.
[46] *C.P.C.*, 139-40 (1926).   [47] *Ibid.*, 140.   [48] *Ibid.*, 158.

hegemony becomes a double-edged concept: it is used in opposition to both a mere "economic-corporative" stage of consciousness on the part of the proletariat and to "domination" as a form of ruling-class control. In the former sense (roughly the 1926 usage), hegemony represents the proletariat's historical achievement of a higher stage of "class consciousness" in which its world outlook has been unified and solidified in its own cultural forms. In the latter sense, hegemony refers to the consensual basis of any given political regime within civil society, i.e., roughly what Weber meant by legitimation, though with a greater sensitivity to the interweaving of consent and culture. Hegemony in this sense is nothing less than the conscious or unconscious diffusion of the philosophical outlook of a dominant class in the customs, habits, ideological structures, political and social institutions, and even the everyday "common sense" of a particular society.[49]

Did the fascist movement exercise such a hegemony over Italy? Gramsci's analysis of the vacillating allegiances of the middle classes under fascism already suggested a negative answer, confirmed by his continued insistence that, despite the March on Rome, fascism had never "solved," but had only extended and perhaps attenuated, capitalism's post-war crisis. Indeed, as he wrote in April 1924, prior to the Matteotti Crisis, "fascism has actually created a permanently revolutionary situation."[50] Certainly he did not mean this in some narrow economic sense: fascism had put Italy back to work and its trains did run on time. This was even truer by 1930. How he was able to persist in this claim can be understood only in connection with the conceptual compound he concocted in the *Prison Notebooks*: the "hegemonic crisis."[51]

One source of a political phenomenon like fascism, Gramsci now proposed, might be the detachment at a certain moment of all, or the most important, social classes from the political parties with which they have previously been associated. His suspicion here was that a systematic relationship can be established between social classes and political parties as their representatives, though not in any simple, mechanical way.[52]

If a probably illicit borrowing from Thomas Kuhn may be admitted, such relationships are especially evident during "normal politics." Detachments, on the other hand, occur during "revolutionary politics." Revolutionary politics are brought on by a hegemonic crisis which itself "occurs either because the ruling class has failed in some major political undertaking for which it has requested, or forcibly

---

[49] E.g., for the two usages: *S.P.N.*, 57 (1934-35), 181-82 (1932).
[50] Letter to Zino Zini (April 2, 1924), reprinted in *Rinascità*, April 25, 1964.
[51] *S.P.N.*, 210 (1933).   [52] *Ibid.*, cf. also S.P.N., 227 (1930).

extracted, the consent of the broad masses (war, for example), or because huge masses (especially of peasants and petit-bourgeois intellectuals) have passed suddenly from a state of political passivity to a certain activity, and put forward demands which taken together, albeit not organically formulated, add up to a revolution."[53]

One of two outcomes then becomes likely. An "organic solution" to the crisis may emerge in the form of a single party which marshals the troops of many previous parties and creates the political basis for a new hegemony. Had the PSI organized itself properly as a collective will in 1919, it might have produced such an outcome.[54] When such a party is missing or fails in its efforts, the political field becomes open to a second possibility, a violent solution led by "charismatic 'men of destiny.'"[55] Such a solution has the effect of restoring a "static equilibrium," which means only that no other group, neither progressive nor traditionalist, is able to muster a formidable challenge. As an outcome of this type, fascism nonetheless did not "solve" the Italian crisis; a "static equilibrium" never involves a true hegemony. Yet through its ruthless domination and its partial but unstable consensual basis in civil society, fascism was generally able to contain that crisis.

Such is the essence of Gramsci's theory of fascism as propounded in the *Notebooks*. Yet its richness and complexity are only fully understood in relation to three more general concepts he developed in conjunction with it: "Caesarism," "war of attrition," and "passive revolution." If fascism is a species, Caesarism is its genus.[56] Caesarism refers to a political intervention by some previously dormant or even previously unknown political force capable of asserting domination and thus of restoring a static equilibrium during a hegemonic crisis. As such it may have variants which are progressive (Caesar and Napoleon I) and some which are reactionary (Napoleon III and Bismarck). It may be the sudden creation of a single heroic figure, or it may be the gradual and institutionalized outcome of a coalition government.[57] But whatever its specific nature and source in a particular instance, Caesarism always seeks to strengthen itself by

---

[53] *Ibid.*

[54] *S.P.N.*, 228-29 (1930). A party which successfully fulfills this function is, in the lexicon of the *Notebooks*, a "Jacobin" party.

[55] *S.P.N.*, 210 (1933).

[56] *S.P.N.*, 219-23 (1933). It seems likely that Gramsci chose the term Caesarism as a way of speaking indirectly about fascism, for a parallel between Caesar and Mussolini was quite common in the Italy of this era; cf. *Q.C.*, 1924 (1933).

[57] *S.P.N.* That Caesarism is not necessarily tied to the great heroic figure and sometimes uses the mass organizations of modern political life is one of the ways Gramsci means to distinguish it from Bonapartism. The other, referred to above, is that it results not so much from an equilibrium of rival class forces but from the defeat of one and the intrinsic weakness of the other.

building up the level of its hegemony to match that of its domination, thus rendering the latter less evident and less necessary. Likewise, the efforts of rival political forces to weaken it are best waged amidst the complex superstructures of civil society where Caesarism's fragile hegemony can be further eroded and challenged by a counter-hegemony. Though its intensity may vary considerably, Caesarism always involves a perpetual struggle for the hearts and minds of the population beyond that usually associated with processes of legitimation in "normal politics."

Gramsci referred to such a struggle as a "war of attrition."[58] Fascism was a particularly intense, institutionalized waging of this war which, however, it was unlikely ever to win given its apparently insuperable antagonism towards the working classes (and of them towards it). Yet in this respect fascism was only one manifestation of the sort of politics which, for Gramsci, had become characteristic of western societies. "War of attrition" was his metaphor in the *Notebooks* for the form taken by the class struggle in the complex superstructures which had become characteristic of the west and which he had noted at least as early as his February 1924 letter to Togliatti. As such it is to be contrasted with a "war of movement," the seizure of power through military confrontation in the strict sense, as in the Bolshevik coup of November 1917. Such politics, as fascism had helped to show, were now outmoded. In the current "culminating phase" of a "political-historical situation" the war of position "once won"—whether by incumbents or insurgents—is by itself "decisive definitively."[59]

Gramsci's third concept in his analysis of fascism, that of "passive revolution," in certain ways comprehends the other two. If fascism is a Caesarism because of its imbalance between domination and hegemony, and if it is a war of attrition because of the perpetual struggle this imbalance touches off, it is a "passive revolution" because, despite the constraints of imbalance and perpetual struggle, it manages to play a historically progressive role.[60] Passive revolutions are progressive political or cultural mass movements which, like wars of attrition, do not launch frontal attacks but "molecular" and subterranean ones. They are constrained to operate in this fashion because they possess either substantial hegemonic force without a capability for domination or, like Caesarism, a capability for domination without a substantial hegemonic force. The passive revolution of Christianity under the Roman Empire was an example of the first type; the

---

[58] See *S.P.N.*, 229-43 (1929-23) and *Q.C.*, 1088-89 (1932).

[59] *S.P.N.*, 239 (1931).

[60] *Q.C.*, 1088-89 (1932); for an analysis of fascism's progressive role, see the discussion of "black parliamentarism"; *S.P.N.*, 254-57 (1933).

Italian Risorgimento was an example of the second. Fascism was a passive revolution, indeed a passive revolution peculiarly suited to the twentieth century, because it allowed the restructuring of the economy away from the individualism and anarchic competition of the liberal marketplace and towards an organized and reformist, state-guided system of capitalist enterprise. And like many though not all passive revolutions, fascism was progressive in a defensive fashion since it was designed to curb a still more progressive political force. Its peculiar feat was to have promoted the development of a progressive economic system without the radical cataclysm of a proletarian revolution.

Together, the various modes through which Gramsci analyzed fascism in the *Notebooks* provided him with a provocative and reasonably comprehensive theory of its source, nature, and developmental tendencies as well as a coherent answer to a most vexing problem: how had Italian capitalism been able to survive despite an unresolved and apparently permanent crisis? An answer to this question could not fail to have more general implications for Gramsci's "philosophy of praxis." The central one, to which we may now turn in concluding this paper, concerns the relation of politics and economics as "moments" or partial factors within a larger cultural whole.

As early as 1926 Gramsci had maintained that "in advanced capitalist countries the dominant class possesses political and organizational reserves which were not found, for instance, in Russia. This means that even the gravest economic crisis will not have immediate repercussions in the political domain. Politics always follows and follows far behind economics."[61] By 1930, when Gramsci had fully absorbed the impact of the Sixth Comintern Congress's adoption of a "social fascism" line and its "turn" away from the politics of united front towards a proletarian political offensive, his earlier conviction could only have been strengthened. In stooping to the basest of economisms, Stalin's Comintern was not only disastrously wrong in its analysis of a concrete situation (or "conjuncture") but wholly insensitive to those features of politics which required theoretical consideration of it as an "autonomous science."[62]

This view distinguished Gramsci's position from those of other dissidents within the Third International like Trotsky and Thalheimer. Though their reaction to fascism was similar to Gramsci's in its stress on the distance between political and economic elites, they implied that fascism was some kind of exception. Neither of them had superseded the view long ago articulated by Engels that

[61] *C.P.C.*, 121 (1926).
[62] Cf. *S.P.N.*, 136-43 (1932-33). For Gramsci's critique of the "turn," see Lisa, *op cit.*, Ch. 5.

most states were merely executive committees of ruling classes.[63] If fascism was a ''Bonapartism'' because, as a form of politics based on class compromise, it was relatively free from class struggle, it was also for this very reason an exceptional state and not one capable of being used as a model for contemporary politics. Or to resort to an earlier metaphor, if single-class dictatorship was ''normal politics,'' Bonapartism was one possible manifestation of ''revolutionary politics.'' Gramsci's analysis was necessarily more radical than this, for when he combined his analysis of fascism with his comparative analysis of superstructures in Russia and the west, he was led to conclude that ''revolutionary politics'' had become the west's new ''normal politics.'' Fascism was only the clearest single example of the politics of hegemonic struggle which had become characteristic of post-war bourgeois society in the west.

Whatever its merits as an historical assessment, Gramsci's view had the undoubted advantage of pushing him towards a reconsideration of the nature of the state and the relation of politics to economics. Consider, for instance, the following assertions:

Politics becomes permanent action and gives birth to permanent organizations precisely insofar as it identifies itself with economics. But it is also distinct from it, which is why one may speak separately of economics and politics, and speak of ''political passion'' as of an immediate impulse to action which is born on the ''permanent and organic'' terrain of economic life but which transcends it, bringing into play emotions and aspirations in whose incandescent atmosphere even calculations involving individual human life itself obey different laws from those of individual profit.[64]

This is an extraordinary statement for a lifelong Marxist and communist revolutionary to have made in 1932. Its inspiration derives less from Marx than from a reading of Machiavelli who had justified the autonomy of politics in a way sufficiently profound to provide, for Gramsci, a complement to Croce (who denigrated and feared politics) in a general recasting of Marxism as a ''philosophy of praxis'' adequate to the new age of monopoly capital, imperialism, and fascism. Politics, Gramsci was saying, is autonomous because it has its own principles and ''laws of tendency''[65] distinct from those of economics as well as from morality and religion; politics is, as Machiavelli had seen so fully, human activity par excellence.[66]

---

[63] Cf. Friedrich Engels, ''On the Origin of the State,'' in *The Marx-Engels Reader* ed. Robert Tucker (New York, 1972), 653-54.

[64] *S.P.N.*, 139-40 (1932).

[65] The concept of a ''law of tendency'' is adapted from Antonio Labriola; cf. *S.P.N.*, 428.

[66] No doubt Gramsci's move towards a Marxist *political* theory was influenced as well by his reading of more recent Italian writers like the elite theorists of Mosca, Pareto, and Michels. Though intensely critical of Michels, for example, he devoted considerable space to his views in the *Notebooks*; cf. *Q.C.*, 239 (1930).

192 WALTER L. ADAMSON

Gramsci was never more theoretically daring than when he set out the elements of an autonomous science of politics. He included for instance: (1) the "primordial fact" that "there really do exist rulers and ruled, leaders and led";[67] (2) the idea that democracy therefore exists in practice "to the extent that the development of the economy and therefore the legislation which expresses that development hold open the channels for the ruled to enter the ruling group";[68] (3) the idea that it is possible to specify a set of universally necessary conditions for the formation of a "collective will";[69] (4) the proposition that parties are the most effective institutional mechanisms for developing leaders;[70] and (5) the charge of inadequacy against "bureaucratic centralism" and even the claim that a "theorem of fixed proportions" might be useful in analyzing the internal relations of political groups.[71] Eventually, Gramsci intended to write a book entitled *The Modern Prince* which would have analyzed and grouped these and other elements of politics into a systematic treatise.

Yet Gramsci's analysis does not deny that political activity is only *relatively* autonomous in the sense that it is connected to the economic factor, though by a long and complex chain of mediations, e.g., an evolving human nature, moral norms and rules, ideological systems, and the general character of social relations.[72] Together with politics and economics, these related factors form a rapidly shifting and interpenetrating cultural whole. Politics and the state are therefore not determined, even distantly, by the economic factor, nor do they serve merely as neutral mediators between economy and society. Politics is relatively autonomous in the sense that those who participate in it have margins of maneuverability, given the multiple and complex relations between economic and political elites and the fact that political relations have their own independent logic.

The critical question then becomes how relative is the relative autonomy of politics? In most of the passages, such as the one quoted above, in which Gramsci discusses the interrelation of the economic, political, and military moments,[73] the suggestion is that the economic factor is a crucial determinant of the starting point for political action. By studying the "fundamental data" of the economic structure, "it is possible to discover whether in a particular society there exist the necessary and sufficient conditions for its transformation, in other words, to check the degree of realism and practicability of the various ideologies which have been born on this terrain. . . ."[74] The economic

---

[67] *S.P.N.*, 144 (1933). [68] *Q.C.*, 1056 (1932).
[69] *S.P.N.*, 130 (1933) and 194 (1932). [70] *S.P.N.*, 146 (1933).
[71] *S.P.N.*, 185-92 (1933). Gramsci had the beginnings of a powerful critique of bureaucracy, but he seems to have been hamstrung by his desire to uphold "democratic centralism" at all costs. In any case, he did not pursue his critique very far.
[72] Cf. *S.P.N.*, 133-34 (1933).
[73] See, e.g., *S.P.N.*, 175-85 (1932). [74] *S.P.N.*, 181 (1932).

factor sets the parameters of action, so to speak, but once these are established, political action advances entirely with its own internal logic.

This makes sense, one might agree, as an answer to the specific question of the conditions for revolutionary action, the question Gramsci seems to have in mind in the passage just quoted. Yet what about the conditions for state action? How independent are government elites from business pressure in a capitalist society? Gramsci never dealt with these questions directly, yet some elements of possible answers can be gleaned from his writings. Certainly he would never have answered categorically, for the nature and degree of a government's autonomy depend on a host of contingent factors. In 1926 Gramsci's typology of European states suggests that one such factor is the regime's position—advanced, transitional, or peripheral—within the structure of international capitalism. His essay on "The Southern Question" suggests a second parallel factor operating at the national level. Both factors set limits upon, and promote certain directions of, governmental action. Among other obvious contingent factors is the magnitude of a regime's hegemony and domination; as they increase, one would expect the regime to be relatively more powerful and, roughly speaking, to have the capacity for a greater degree of autonomy.

In the case of Italian fascism Gramsci seems to have perceived a relatively high degree of autonomy; it was, after all, primarily this movement which had first alerted him to the relative importance and independence of western superstructures. Fascism had arisen at war's end as an independent, even chaotic and unguided, political movement. Under Mussolini's direction it had gradually established closer ties with major Italian corporations, but Gramsci recognized that many industrialists remained confirmed Giolittian liberals long after the March on Rome. Moreover, he always treated fascism's major responses to crises, such as that of January 3, 1925, as due entirely to the decisions of Mussolini and his inner coterie. Mussolini never violated the essential interests of capitalism because they were his interests too, so the sources of his political strength in general lay elsewhere: an evident decisive source was Mussolini's effective manipulation of parliament. On that basis Gramsci predicted a "long life" for the regime even though he denied that it would "constitute an epoch."[75] As it turned out, he was probably right even though fascism's partial epoch outlasted his own life by a little over half a decade.

Emory University.

[75] *S.P.N.*, 256 (1933).

X

CHARCOT'S RESPONSE TO FREUD'S REBELLION

By Toby Gelfand

In the voluminous scholarship on Freud, Jean-Martin Charcot occupies a modest yet respectable and secure niche. Charcot, Freud's teacher in Paris, typically fills the role of precursor. For it was Charcot, the master of neurology and the "Napoleon of the neuroses," who in the fall and winter of 1885-86 revealed to the twenty-nine-year-old visiting physician from Vienna exciting new possibilities for the psychological interpretation of hysteria and for the use of hypnosis for experimental intervention or even treatment. Freud, the standard accounts agree, arrived in Paris a bright young neurologist but returned to Vienna a pioneer in psychopathology.[1] This Freudocentric perspective presents Charcot in the role of a John the Baptist to Freud's Jesus, someone who anticipated the gospel of psychoanalytic truth but, as a result of various limitations, not least of which his own untimely demise, had to leave the actual mission of revelation to his disciple. Charcot profoundly "influenced" Freud, who then proceeded to eclipse his teacher.[2]

I thank Drs. Marvin Silverman and Ian Musgrave for encouraging this work and the Social Sciences and Humanities Research Council of Canada and the Hannah Institute (Toronto, Canada) for financially supporting the research. Earlier versions were read to the Forum for Independent Research in Science and Technology Studies, Cambridge, Massachusetts on July 16, 1988, organized by Joy Harvey and to a psychoanalytic study group in Ottawa led by Dr. A. Fayek. I thank the participants for their comments. I have also benefitted from numerous recent conversations with Peter J. Swales on this subject and related Freudiana.

[1] See James Strachey, "Editor's note," *The Standard Edition of the Complete Psychological Works of Sigmund Freud*, tr. and ed. James Strachey (London, 1966), I, 3-4, hereafter cited as *S.E.*; Ernest Jones, *The Life and Work of Sigmund Freud* (New York, 1953), I, 207-12, 226-28, 232-34; Henri F. Ellenberger, *The Discovery of the Unconscious. The History and Evolution of Dynamic Psychiatry* (New York, 1970), 439-44, 484-89; Frank J. Sulloway, *Freud, Biologist of the Mind* (New York, 1979), 30-35. The fullest discussions of the relationship between Charcot and Freud are Ola Andersson, *Studies in the Prehistory of Psychoanalysis* (Norsteds, Sweden, 1962), 28-103; Leon Chertok, "Freud à Paris: Etape décisive. Essai psychobiographique," *l'Evolution psychiatrique*, 34 (1969), 733-50; Julian A. Miller *et al*, "Some aspects of Charcot's influence on Freud," *Journal of the American Psychoanalytic Association*, 17 (1969), 608-23.

[2] Peter Gay, *Freud, A Life for Our Time* (New York, 1988), 48-53, exemplifies the tendency to assess Charcot mainly through Freud's glowing eulogy of his master. In an earlier study, Gay wrongly credited Charcot with anticipating Freud's rejection of degeneration theory (*Freud and other Germans* [New York, 1978], 73) and (59) misreads Freud's Charcot eulogy as "Freud had played Adam to Charcot's God," whereas Freud in fact likened Charcot's taxonomic achievement in neuropathology to Adam's naming the animals. For a telling critique of a cursory effort to reduce Freud to Charcot's "influence," see Elizabeth Roudinesco, *La Bataille de cent ans. Histoire de la psychoan-*

194

Such a picture strikes me as fundamentally flawed, since it falls prey to the anachronistic (and Whiggish) fallacy of the historical inevitability of psychoanalysis and then projects it backward in time on to Freud's teacher. Charcot was primarily and always a neuropathologist. His interest in hysteria, intensive though it became in the 1880s, never took him beyond the conceptual framework of other diseases of the central nervous system.[3] Second, the implication that Charcot, had he lived, would have applauded Freud's revision of hysteria is not only gratuitous and speculative but inherently doubtful. To be sure, Freud himself later recalled that the Frenchman had displayed an intuitive appreciation of the invariable presence of underlying disordered sexuality (*la chose génitale*) in hysterics even though he could not bring himself to acknowledge, much less develop, this insight. One must, however, view this along with Freud's other historical reconstructions with caution.[4]

In any case, Charcot's sudden death in 1893, just as Freud was beginning to extend his thinking on the etiology of hysteria in independent directions, has always been taken to rule out the possibility of significant dialogue between the two men concerning Freud's new ideas. This is in fact not the case. New evidence dating from about a year before Charcot's death shows that Charcot did respond, and it offers an answer to the intriguing question of how the French master countered Freud's earliest criticism of his doctrines.

On 30 June 1892 Jean-Martin Charcot addressed a letter to his translator and former student, Sigmund Freud. This letter, running to seven manuscript pages, forms part of a recently published correspondence from Paris master to Viennese disciple extending over the years 1888 to 1893.[5] The Charcot letters were mentioned in passing by Jeffrey M. Masson, who singled out that of 30 June 1892 as evidence of Charcot's

---

alyse en France, I (Paris, 1982), I, 74-76, on R. Laforgue and H. Codet, "L'influence de Charcot sur Freud," *Progrès médical*, 30 (1925), 801-2.

[3] Freud "Charcot," *S.E.*, III, 21: "He treated hysteria as just another topic in neuropathology."

[4] *S.E.*, III, 199. Freud here states that Charcot (and Breuer) "had a personal disinclination" toward a sexual etiology of hysteria, thus contradicting the later and better-known account in *S.E.*, XIV, 13-14, in which Freud recalled Charcot's exclamation, ". . . c'est toujours la chose génitale, toujours . . . toujours . . . toujours." On Freud's reconstructions, see the example discussed by Peter J. Swales, "Freud, Katherina, and the First 'Wild Analysis,' " Paul E. Stepansky (ed.), *Freud. Appraisals and Reappraisals. Contributions to Freud Studies*, III (Hillsdale, N.J., 1988), 81-164.

[5] See T. Gelfand, " 'Mon Cher Docteur Freud': Charcot's Unpublished Correspondence to Freud, 1888-1893, Annotation, translation, and commentary," *Bulletin of the History of Medicine*, 62 (1988), 563-88. The Charcot correspondence to Freud is deposited in the Freud Archives in the Library of Congress, Washington, D.C.

"receptiveness to Freud's newly emerging ideas."[6] In fact, as I shall demonstrate, the letter reveals striking disagreement between the two men on matters of etiological doctrine.

Charcot held that hysteria, along with the vast majority of neurological and mental diseases and many other chronic diseases, was essentially the result of familial inheritance. He had defended this view on numerous occasions over the years and particularly in his famous *Leçons du Mardi*, the Tuesday clinical discussions of neurological out-patients at the Salpêtrière hospital, which Freud had attended during his Paris studies in 1885-86. Most of the Charcot-Freud correspondence in fact deals with the business arrangements attendant upon Freud's translation of the *Leçons* into German.[7] It was in this German translation that Freud took the opportunity to add to the original text numerous footnotes, several of which were sharply critical of Charcot's emphasis on hereditary etiology.[8]

In the letter of 30 June 1892, written upon his receipt from Freud of the first installment of the translation, Charcot responded to his student's objections. Masson, unfortunately, quoted only Charcot's opening exclamation: "By the way, I am delighted with the notes and criticism which I found at the bottom of the pages of my *Leçons*. It is perfect: long live liberty, as we say here in France."[9] This might indeed give the impression of a satisfied Charcot, but Masson failed to take notice of the subsequent eighty-three lines of the letter in which the chief of the Salpêtrière left no doubt of his vigorous disagreement with Freud. A full reading indicates that Charcot's opening remark is simply rhetorical;

[6] *The Complete Letters of Sigmund Freud to Wilhelm Fliess 1887-1904*, tr. and ed. Jeffrey Moussaieff Masson (Cambridge, Mass., 1985), 20. Masson made an elusive earlier reference to "previously unknown" letters from Charcot to Freud "in a large black cupboard outside Anna Freud's bedroom" (in her house at Maresfield Gardens), Masson, *The Assault on Truth. Freud's Suppression of the seduction theory* (New York, 1984), xvi; see also Janet Malcolm, *In the Freud Archives* (New York, 1985), 34 (originally published in *The New Yorker*, 1983).

[7] In his letter of 13 November 1891, Charcot wrote: "Je serai enchanté de vous voir traduire mes *Leçons du Mardi*." This and subsequent letters of 15 November 1891, 23 November 1891, 27 January 1892, and March 1892 concern business arrangements relating to the translation.

[8] *S.E.*, I, 137-43. *S.E.* contains only thirteen of the total of sixty-two footnotes that Freud added. See Jones, *Sigmund Freud*, I, 228.

[9] Masson, *Letters*, 20. Masson's translation as well as his omission of punctuation may be faulted. The French text reads "c'est parfait! vive la liberté!!, comme on dit chez nous." This may better be rendered as "that's fine! Long live liberty!!, as we say here." Freud also sent a copy of the first installment to his friend Fliess on 28 June 1892 with the comment that it "is on the whole successful" except for several errors in French words and punctuation. *S.E.*, I, 131. Evidently, Freud sent already published texts to Charcot and Fliess.

indeed, it is immediately followed by: "after this declaration, I shall ask the same [liberty] from you. . . ."[10]

In his footnotes to the *Leçons du Mardi* Freud, for the first time in print, had expressed serious reservations about the hereditary determination of nervous and a variety of other metabolic diseases that Charcot and other French authors had grouped under the rubrics of nervous and/ or arthritic diatheses and evocatively labelled *la famille névropathique*. This latter term had been coined in 1884 by Charcot's *chef de clinique* and secretary, Charles Féré, to refer to the tendency of nervous and mental diseases to transform into one another as they were transmitted from one generation to the next.[11] Like the patients in whom they appeared, these diseases could be regarded as a "family" deriving or, to use the scientific shibboleth of the day, evolving from a common ancestral form, probably some kind of lesion or taint in the nervous system.

While Freud had initially accepted the notion of *la famille névropathique* and while he never entirely abandoned a role for heredity in the etiology of the neuroses, by 1892 he was beginning to consider acquired factors and, in particular, disorders in sexuality as the crucial or necessary cause.[12] In two articles published in 1896, one of which appeared in a Paris journal, Freud boldly declared that childhood sexual trauma caused the later development of hysteria and other neuroses, this in open defiance of "the disciples of J.-M. Charcot . . . and the etiological theory of the neuroses transmitted to us by our master."[13] With the master in his grave since 1893, Freud, like other dissenters, evidently felt freer to elaborate his skepticism about *la famille névropathique*, a skepticism that had surfaced in the footnotes to the *Leçons* and even crept into his otherwise lavishly complimentary obituary notice of Charcot.[14]

---

[10] Charcot to Freud, 30 June 1892.

[11] Charles Féré, *Archives de neurologie*, 7 (1884), 1-43, 171-91; Charcot himself defined *la famille névropathique* as "celle de toutes ces maladies nerveuses qui se transmettent par voie d'hérédité directe ou indirecte. Elle est l'alliée intime de la famille arthritique, qui comprend les migraines, certaines migraines du moins, le diabète, la gravelle, la goutte, le rhumatisme articulaire," *Leçons du mardi à la Salpêtrière Policliniques, 1887-1888. Notes de Cours de M M. Blin, Charcot et H. Colin* (Paris, 1887), I, 4. Subsequent references to the *Leçons* are to the second edition of vol. I (1892), which is the one Freud translated, unless otherwise indicated.

[12] *S.E.*, I, 139, 142. These first comments on the sexual as opposed to hereditary etiology of phobia and neurasthenia occur in Freud's notes to the *Leçons*. On Freud's earlier commitment to hereditary over sexual etiology, *S.E.*, I, 50, and his subsequent reversal of emphasis, *S.E.*, I, 177-78, 196-97. See Larry Stewart, "Freud before Oedipus: Race and heredity in the origins of psychoanalysis," *Journal of the history of biology*, 9 (1976), 215-28.

[13] *S.E.*, III, 143-56, first published as "L'hérédité et l'étiologie des névroses," *Revue neurologique*, 4 (1896), 161-69; "The etiology of hysteria," *S.E.*, III, 191-221.

[14] *S.E.*, III, "Charcot," 11-33. Freud's footnotes explicitly rejecting the notion of *la famille névropathique* are near the end of his translation (I, 404, 417) and therefore did

The Charcot letter of 1892 thus takes on unique significance because it contains Charcot's only direct response to the early signs of Freud's revolt. Many historians have discussed Freud's break with hereditarian or degeneration theory in psychiatry. Likewise, much has been written on Charcot from Freud's perspective or on Charcot as a precursor of Freud's psychoanalytic revolution.[15] In what follows I pick up the neglected reciprocal side of the relationship. How did Charcot respond to Freud's challenge to *la famille névropathique*? How did the master of the Salpêtrière defend hereditarian against environmental etiology? Within this fundamental debate, Charcot, as we shall see, repeated a specific argument or evidentiary claim—that Jews had a marked predisposition toward *la famille névropathique*—which he had made frequently at his Tuesday talks. Although one can here only speculate, it is plausible that the alleged Jewish clinical example may have contributed at some level to Freud's doctrinal rift with Charcot. Despite the fact that neither Charcot, an anti-clerical Catholic, nor Freud, an assimilated Jew, formally adhered to the religious faiths into which they were born, both men identified strongly with different ethnic backgrounds during a period of intensifying anti-Semitism in France as in Europe generally.[16] Finally, I consider briefly how the Charcot to Freud correspondence illuminates the Paris master's attitude toward German medical science and his personal rapport with Freud.

From at least the time of the mid-nineteenth-century founders of degeneration theory, etiological thinking in mental pathology had made hereditary explanations central to a scientific psychology and psychopathology. Charcot here followed a tradition established in France by the alienists Prosper Lucas, B.-A. Morel, and J.-J. Moreau de Tours and continued by the psychologist Théodule Ribot, and the chief alienist at the Sainte Anne asylum, Valentin Magnan. Ribot's writings on heredity influenced Charcot and the psychologist in turn attended the neurologist's lessons at the Salpêtrière. Magnan, perhaps the leading spokesman for

---

not appear until after Charcot's death. See *S.E.*, I, 131. On the negative critique of Charcot following his death, see Ellenberger, *The Discovery of the Unconscious*, 100-101.

[15] On Freud and degeneration theory see Sander L. Gilman, "Sexology, Psychoanalysis and degeneration," *Difference and Pathology* (Ithaca, N.Y., 1985), 191-216; and Jean-Claude Beaune, *Le Vagabond et la Machine: essai sur l'automatisme ambulatoire; médecine, technique et société en France, 1880-1910* (Seyssel, 1983), 149, 240-41. On Freud and Charcot, see above n. 1 and 2 and William J. McGrath, *Freud's discovery of psychoanalysis. The politics of hysteria* (Ithaca, N.Y., 1986), 150-62.

[16] See Steven Wilson, *Ideology and Experience: Antisemitism in France at the Time of the Dreyfus Affair* (East Brunswick, N.J., 1982); McGrath, *Freud's discovery*, 160-62, 175-78, 212-13, Jan Goldstein, "The wandering Jew and the problem of psychiatric anti-semitism in fin-de-siècle France," *Journal of Contemporary History*, 20 (1985), 521-51; Peter Gay, *A Godless Jew. Freud, Atheism, and the Making of Psychoanalysis* (New Haven, Conn., 1987), 121-27, 138-39.

degeneration theory in France during the last decades of the century, collaborated with Charcot on several publications.[17]

By endorsing the concept of *la famille névropathique*, Charcot lent his considerable authority and prestige to the extension of hereditary causality beyond frank mental pathology to a spectrum of other diseases of the central nervous system as well as to a seemingly disparate collection of chronic so-called constitutional ailments known as diatheses. Depending upon whose classificatory scheme was followed, the diatheses included syphilis, cancer, tuberculosis and scrofulous diseases, arthritic conditions, gout, diabetes, renal and gall stones, and various skin diseases.[18] Diatheses were disease states or, more precisely, predispositions of patients to an ensemble of chronic ailments assumed to be acquired by heredity. A given diathesis might be transmitted from one generation to the next as the same clinical manifestation or, as seemed to be more often the case, it might express itself in another form. Similarly, variable rules governed other aspects of the hereditary transmission: a generation might be skipped or a peculiar gender susceptibility might be evident.

The various diatheses possessed an underlying unity in their assumed common origin in the nervous system. These diverse but interconvertible pathological entities also shared a special epistemological status. As complex clinical manifestations of inborn personal, familial, and racial characteristics, they were essentially independent of causal explanation in environmental terms. Unlike acute infections, toxic ailments, or obviously external traumas, diatheses seemed to originate spontaneously from within the individual. They remained with the victim for life, an intrinsic part of his or her identity, and were transmissable in one form or another to progeny. Moreover, a diathesis was, for all practical purposes, resistant to replication on experimental animals in the physiological or pathological laboratory and thus could not be accounted for in the language of reductionist science.[19] Except for the aid of pathological anatomy and

---

[17] See Ian Dowbiggin, "French Psychiatry, Hereditarianism and Professional Legitimacy, 1840-1900," *Research in law, deviance and social control*, 7 (1985), 135-65; Robert Nye, *Crime, Madness, and Politics in Modern France. The Medical Concept of National Decline* (Princeton, N.J., 1984), 97-131. Jean Borie, *Mythologies de hérédité au XIXe siècle* (Paris, 1981).

[18] See Maurice Raynaud, art. "Diathèse," *Nouveau dictionnaire de médecine et chirurgie pratique*, XI (Paris, 1872), 410-62, and E. H. Ackerknecht, "Diathesis; the word and the Concept in Medical History," *Bulletin of the History of Medicine*, 56 (1982), 317-25.

[19] J.-M. Charcot, *Clinical Lectures on Senile and Chronic Diseases*, tr. William S. Tuke (London, 1881), 19. Charcot cited the authority of Germain Sée who in *Leçons de pathologie experimentale* (Paris, 1866), 11, had pronounced the diatheses an exception to reproduction on experimental animals. Although sympathetic in general to experimental pathology, Sée stated: "...le propre de la diathèse, c'est précisément de se développer spontanément, indépendamment des circonstances extérieures, ou sous l'influence mystérieuse de l'hérédité."

histology, only clinical methods (including history taking and genealogical research) could be brought to bear on the investigation of a given diathesis or, collectively, *la famille névropathique*.

Charcot, a self-proclaimed defender of the French clinical medical tradition stemming from the Paris "hospital school" at the outset of the century, might be anticipated to be sympathetic to the concept of diathesis and to the methods of investigation it implied. Such was indeed the case, as can be seen from his early work on gout and articular rheumatism, his persistent references to the nervous-arthritic diathesis, and his frequent recourse to diagrams of familial disease genealogies.[20] While earlier generations of French clinical investigators tended to regard the ultimate causes of diseases as unknowable, Charcot and his contemporaries embraced hereditary etiology. For Charcot, as for his psychiatrist colleagues, this position had the attributes of scientific respectability and at the same time kept the methodology of experimental science subordinate to conventional clinical and anatomical modes of investigation.

The hereditarian strategy summed up in *la famille névropathique* denied any primary etiological role to external acquired factors, such as the pathogenic microbes identified by Pasteur, Koch, and others. By the closing decades of the century, bacteria responsible for many infectious diseases had been isolated and their role as necessary causes rigorously proven. The young Freud, as Codell Carter has noted, made implicit and at times explicit use of analogies between germ theory and his proposed scientific sexual etiology of hysteria and other neuroses.[21] It was widely believed that discoveries in microbiology would ultimately reveal the causes of many more pathological entities; in the meantime, statistical and epidemiological evidence strongly suggested causal links between infectious (presumably microbial) and various chronic diseases.

An outstanding example of this sort was the work of the syphilographer, Alfred Fournier of Paris, suggesting that syphilis was responsible for subsequent diseases of the central nervous system, in particular locomotor ataxia or tabes dorsalis and general paralysis of the insane. By the mid-1880s Fournier's thesis, ably seconded by Wilhelm Erb, a Heidelberg neuropathologist, had captured a considerable following among students of nervous and mental disease. A heated controversy ensued between the supporters of the Fournier-Erb etiological position and those who denied that syphilis was the specific and necessary cause of tabes and general paralysis. Championing the latter point of view were Charcot and his psychiatrist colleague, Magnan, who along with many of their

[20] J.-M. Charcot, *Goutte asthénique primaire* (thesis; Paris, 1853). *Leçons sur les maladies des veillards et des maladies chroniques* (Paris, 1868). *Leçons du Mardi*, passim. See my "Reflexions sur Charcot et *la famille névropathique*," *Histoire des sciences médicales*, 21 (1987), 245-50.

[21] Codell Carter, "Germ Theory, Hysteria, and Freud's Early Work in Psychopathology," *Medical History*, 24 (1980), 259-74.

followers adhered to the hereditary etiology of these diseases in conformance with their membership in the *famille névropathique*.[22]

Charcot, as we have suggested, vigorously denied a primary causal action to external factors in neuropathology. Infectious diseases such as syphilis or typhoid fever, toxic substances such as lead or mercury, alcoholism, physical or emotional trauma might be associated with subsequent disease of the central nervous system. But, Charcot insisted, this spectrum of environmental insults should not be mistaken for authentic causes; such factors functioned rather as *agents provocateurs*, to use Charcot's favorite label, agents which merely provoked the manifestation of latent pathological states to which patients were already predisposed by their heredity. To confuse *agents provocateurs* with true causes would be to posit an obviously false conclusion, namely, that each agent produced a different type of hysteria (or other nervous disease). In fact, Charcot believed he had demonstrated that hysteria (or tabes or any other member of *la famille névropathique*) conformed to a characteristic pathological form which was fundamentally the same regardless of the provoking agent.[23]

Perhaps Charcot's opposition to environmental etiological explanations reflected a concern to keep medical theory and nosography, or the classification of disease based on clinical and anatomical changes within the human body. Here he would have shared a perspective held by leading medical scientists of his generation who, like Rudolf Virchow (1821-1902), did not welcome the emphasis on external pathogens fostered by germ theory.[24] Clinical medicine and pathological anatomy were the fields Charcot considered fundamental. Relying upon them since the beginning of his career at mid-century, he, more than any other individual, had virtually created the objects of knowledge and methods of investigation of modern neuropathology. On this view, Charcot's etiological stance can be understood, at least in part, as a defense of the autonomy of his discipline.

Such territorial concerns would not be as compelling for neuropathologists of Freud's generation. On the other hand, those whose maturation as medical men was contemporaneous with germ theory had an incentive

---

[22] See F. Raymond, art. "Tabes dorsalis," *Dictionnaire encyclopédique des sciences médicales* (Paris, 1885), XCIV, 290-98; Jacques Postel, "La Paralysie générale," *Nouvelle histoire de la Psychiatrie*, ed. J. Postel and C. Quetel (Paris, 1983), 322-33, esp. 330-31. Tabes dorsalis or locomotor ataxia is a disease of the spinal cord producing progressive motor incoordination and lightning-like joint pains among other symptoms; general paralysis or general paresis of the insane, a disease of the brain, has symptoms of motor weakness, partial paralysis, and progressive dementia; both neurological conditions are now viewed as tertiary complications of syphilis.

[23] *Leçons du mardi*, I, 7, 31, 93, 179; II, 95. Protesting that he was not a "reactionary," Charcot noted that he acknowledged that syphilis did cause certain diseases of the central nervous system. But in the case of tabes, it was only an *agent provocateur. Ibid.*, 7.

[24] See E. H. Ackerknecht, *Rudolf Virchow* (Madison, Wis., 1953), 106-8.

to keep their field abreast of innovations in general pathology.[25] Thus, even within the Salpêtrière school at least one of Charcot's inner circle of disciples, Pierre Marie (1853-1940), dared to question the sufficiency of hereditary etiology.[26] Freud cited Marie's unorthodox views on the causal role of infectious diseases in neuropathology shortly after their publication in 1887, and he appreciated their dissonance with Charcot's doctrine.[27] Whether Freud was emulating this specific precedent—he had met Marie during his Paris studies in 1885 and had been favorably impressed[28]—or had arrived at a similar conclusion by other means, he began his own criticism of the master in Charcot's *Leçons du mardi* by breaking with the doctrine of the hereditary etiology of tabes and general paralysis and declaring his conversion to the Fournier-Erb syphilitic explanation.[29] And, it was on this controversial issue, with general implications for etiology in neuropathology, that Charcot, when he saw Freud's offending comment, launched his counterattack.

In his letter of 30 June 1892 Charcot reaffirmed his long-standing position that prior infection with syphilis was not the cause of tabes and general paralysis of the insane. Even if one were to accept claims as high as 90% prior infection with syphilis, "what," Charcot queried, "do you do with the other 10%?"[30] In effect Charcot had cleverly turned against Freud the logic of Koch's first postulate for establishing the necessity of

---

[25] Carter, "Germ theory, hysteria, and Freud's early work," 266-68, for discussion of two examples, Adolf Strümpell (1853-1925) and P. J. Möbius (1854-1907).

[26] "Note sur l'étiologie de l'epilepsie," *Le Progrès médical*, 15 (1887), 333-34. Marie concluded this article in which he opposed attributing epilepsy primarily to "l'hérédité néuropathique" with a reference to syphilis as the necessary cause of general paralysis. In his *Leçons sur les maladies de la moelle* (Paris, 1892), 318, (based on Marie's course at the Paris medical Faculty in the summer of 1891 and dedicated to Charcot), Marie declared: "le tabes est toujours d'origine syphilitique."

[27] Freud to Fliess, 24 Nov. 1887, *The Origins of Psychoanalysis*, ed. Marie Bonaparte, Anna Freud, and Ernst Kris, (New York, 1954), 51-52; *Polyklinische Vorträge von Prof. J.-M. Charcot*, tr. Sigmund Freud (Leipzig, 1892-93), 386n. Freud later quoted Marie's article on the etiology of epilepsy (note 26) at length in Sigmund Freud, *Infantile Cerebral Paralysis*, tr. Lester A. Russin (Coral Gables, Fla., 1968), 328-29 (first published in 1897).

[28] *Letters of Sigmund Freud*, ed. Ernst L. Freud and tr. Tania and James Stern (New York, 1960), 175-76 (21 October 1885).

[29] *Polyklinische Vorträge*, 8n. In this extensive note, Freud explains that he began his practice as a follower of Charcot's teaching that "syphilis is an *agent provocateur* of tabes" but that his own experience compelled him to turn to a recognition of syphilis as the decisive cause of tabes and general paralysis. Freud's subtle alteration in translation of the title of the first lesson from "syphilis, ataxie locomotrice progressive . . ." to "Ein Fall von Tabes . . . nach Syphilis" reflected his difference with Charcot. This first patient in Charcot's first lesson suffered from both syphilis and tabes, but Charcot denied that the former caused the latter. *Leçons du mardi*, I, 4-10 (case of 15 Nov. 1887).

[30] Charcot to Freud, 30 June 1892, probably making a snide reference to the clinical statistics of Fournier, Erb, and others that reached as high as 90%. See also *Leçons du mardi*, I, 7.

a causal agent. The suspected agent (for Koch, a microbe, for Freud here syphilis and, shortly thereafter, by analogy, sexual factors as causes of the neuroses) had to be present invariably in all cases of the disease.[31]

For Charcot heredity remained the primordial cause underlying the production of all members of *la famille névropathique*. He informed Freud that he had a "very beautiful collection" of genealogies of tabetic families that he was thinking of publishing in the near future.[32] This method of familial research suggested that acquired factors, like syphilis, should be considered merely occasional causes or *agents provocateurs*. Charcot's enormous clinical experience with tabes permitted him to state with confidence that he had personally observed cases without any history of syphilis. Completing the argument with a counterproof, Charcot pointed out "the absolute uselessness and even the danger of the therapy indicated by this [syphilitic] etiological theory. Every day I see tabes develop in the midst of a vigorous anti-syphilitic treatment."[33]

Charcot pursued his defense of hereditary etiology by citing a second clinical example, diabetes. He declared that he was currently "mounting a campaign" to show by means of family trees the hereditary nature of this "most distinguished member of the arthritic family." Diabetes, along with urinary gout and true asthma, constituted solid clinical evidence of the validity of the conception of families of arthritic diseases within families of patients. If there were any doubt, Charcot reminded Freud to look at Jewish families ("the exploration is easy, especially in Jewish families"), and he would see inherited arthritic diseases alongside ataxia, general paralysis, and epilepsy: "those diseases [the arthritic] appear at the same time as the members of *la famille névropathique*...."[34]

Charcot hoped that this array of clinical examples would convince Freud of the etiological primacy of heredity and that "the *phantom* of syphilis that seeks to invade everything would gradually fade away and

[31] See Carter, "Germ Theory" and the same author's "Koch's postulates in relation to the work of Jacob Henle and Edwin Klebs," *Medical History*, 29 (1985), 353-74 for the concept of necessary causes. See e.g., *S.E.*, III, 137 for Freud's analogy in 1895 between the specific etiology of tuberculosis by Koch's bacillus and that of anxiety neurosis by a "sexual factor."

[32] Charcot to Freud, 30 June 1892. See below, n. 34.

[33] *Ibid.* See *Leçons du mardi*, I (Paris, 1887, lithograph ed.), 8: "A quoi bon cette notion de l'ataxie syphilitique puisque le traitement n'y fait rien, tel a toujours été mon avis." The argument on therapeutic grounds obviously weighed heavily in Charcot's rejection of syphilitic etiology together with the non-universalist argument, a further clinical argument over length of incubation period, and, finally, his conviction that heredity was a sufficient causal explanation.

[34] Charcot to Freud, 30 June 1892. In an article "Association de tabes avec le diabète sucré," first published in *Archives de neurologie*, in October 1891 and March 1892, Charcot's students, Guinon and Souques, included 40 genealogical tables, of which nearly a third were "familles israélites," *Clinique des maladies du système nerveux*, ed. G. Guinon (Paris, 1893), II, 289-348.

204   TOBY GELFAND

so reassume the secondary role assigned to it by nature, *agent provocateur and that's all.*"[35] Passing to his professorial tone, Charcot reminded Freud of his doctrine by quoting at length from his own preface to the French translation of Althaus's "rather mediocre book" on *Diseases of the Spinal Cord* published at Paris in 1885.[36] Here Charcot had stated his objections to syphilis being the cause of locomotor ataxia (tabes), conceding only that statistics showed it probably to be "a very active and powerful agent provocateur." He then peremptorily closed the discussion:

voilà mon opinion, j'y suis, j'y reste—in spite of the 90 percent—and *"prevalebit"* one day or another—while waiting, I spare the poor tabetics, and I think it's for their welfare, the "horrors" of the rigorous specific treatment, and still better, the general paralytics.[37]

In the final analysis Charcot invoked his unparalleled clinical and therapeutic experience to counter Freud's opposing etiological views, which were based upon statistics and recourse to analogy with other diseases and medical sciences, notably the infectious diseases and bacteriology.

    In addition to the central debate over etiology, Charcot's rivalry with German medical science is revealed in his letter to Freud. On several occasions the Frenchman had displayed open hostility toward the victors of 1870.[38] Here, however, the spirit was one of collegial competition, an eagerness to gain via Freud's translation a greater exposure for his work in German-speaking medical circles.[39] Charcot in fact begins his letter by thanking Freud "heartily" for procuring him a "true pleasure" in translating the *Leçons* into German. To the future interpreter of dreams, Charcot confides his own reveries on reading the first installment of the *Leçons* "from one end to the other:"

I seemed to hear myself speaking in German and lecturing in some Germanic university: I don't know which one, at Vienna, perhaps: they listened to me very attentively and I think I was persuading them; the language was beautiful; that didn't surprise me since I was listening to you speak, repeating everything

---

[35] Charcot to Freud, 30 June 1892 (emphasis in original). Charcot's notion of "agents provocateurs" received wide currency in the thesis by his student G. Guinon, "Les agents provocateurs de l'hystérie" (Paris, 1889).

[36] *Ibid.* Althaus defended the syphilitic etiology of tabes.

[37] *Ibid.* See also, *Leçons du mardi*, I, 8 (lithograph ed.): "Et je porte sur ce point un défi à la doctrine contraire à la mienne."

[38] See Georges Guillain, *J.-M. Charcot 1825-1893. His life—his work*, ed. and tr. Pearce Bailey (New York, 1959), 26-27.

[39] Charcot's delight with the prospect of a German translation (see letters to Freud, 13 Nov., 15 Nov., 23 Nov. 1891, and 27 Jan. 1892 in Gelfand, " 'Mon Cher Docteur Freud' ") indicate his conviction that the *Leçons* accurately mirrored his clinical concepts and teaching.

that I was receiving from you through my eyes. It was like a dream, a pleasant dream.[40]

Charcot's affection and admiration for Freud are evident in this passage. Freud appears in the role of personal emissary, the conduit between Charcot and the "Germanic university," and the conveyor of the message of the Salpêtrière to foreign, perhaps skeptical ears. Earlier letters in the correspondence make clear that Charcot, at least in some measure reciprocated Freud's respect and affection.[41] But the master-disciple bond depended on Freud's doctrinal allegiance. Significant deviation might strain this kind of relationship, particularly given Charcot's paternalistic style and his belief that he had converted Freud into a German proselyte. Such concerns may account for Charcot's aggressive tone when, after referring to his notion of the "arthritic family" of diseases, he continues: "arthritic? you say, that means nothing to us Germans. Possibly! But what do your colleagues and compatriots think of diabetes, of urinary gout, of true asthma—are not these things concrete?"[42] Charcot immediately follows this challenge with the reference to Jewish families, a remark that he underlines for emphasis, thereby reminding Freud in a personal letter of a racial corollary of *la famille névropathique*, one with which Freud was acquainted and which he could not have failed to notice in Charcot's frequent allusions to Jews in the *Leçons* as he translated the text.[43]

Although Charcot's letter to Freud remained cordial and his reaction might be read as a friendly polemic, it was nonetheless a serious rebuttal on a fundamental issue of etiology, the master's strong response to a deviant disciple. Written a little more than one year before Charcot's death, the letter of 30 June 1892 apparently was his final lengthy com-

[40] Charcot to Freud, 30 June 1892.

[41] See Charcot to Freud, 23 January 1888 (Charcot sends regards to Madame Freud et "embraces" Freud's daughter); 26 Sept. 1888 (Charcot compliments Freud on treatment of patient whom both men have seen); 17 Feb. 1889 (Charcot expresses hopes that Freud will gain university post, which would provide leisure for his research work and in turn be "heureux pour notre art"); 13 Nov. 1891 (Charcot thanks Freud for two studies which he holds "en grande estime" and plans to use often in his lessons); 23 Nov. 1891 (Charcot compliments Freud's translations of his work, calling him "un interpret aussi distingué et aussi compétent").

[42] Charcot to Freud, 30 June 1892. Freud, *PolyKlinische Vorträge*, 4n., had commented that the notion of an arthritic family of diseases "will appear somewhat strange to many a German reader."

[43] See *Letters of Sigmund Freud*, 210 (10 Feb. 1886). Virtually all of Charcot's published references to Jews appear in the *Leçons du Mardi* rather than in his more formal lessons. Even in the supposedly informal Tuesday lessons (faites au jour de jour, Charcot to Freud, 23 Nov. 1891), Charcot typically used the polite "Israélite" or the scientific "sémite" rather than the vulgar "juif" used in the letter to Freud.

206   TOBY GELFAND

munication to Freud,[44] whose own half of the correspondence has, unfortunately, disappeared. In any case Charcot's previously unknown response to Freud's rebellion makes clear the master's categorical disagreement with his translator's critical footnotes, his spirited defense against Freud's challenge to hereditary etiology, and his own firm and continuing commitment to that explanatory framework. This was both less and more than a conflict between the personalities of master and disciple. At stake were two medical generations' different etiological paradigms. In that broader sense, the debate over etiology in psychiatry has never ceased while the hereditary position appears in the ascendant in contemporary neuropathology.

Afterword: Freud's "revolt."

I have concentrated on Charcot rather than Freud in part simply because of the gross disproportion in the opposite sense in the historical literature on the relationship between the two men. My aim has not been to write a retrospective history of psychoanalysis but to explore a fissure in the fin-de-siècle paradigm of hereditary pathology. Second, it is not often that one has the opportunity to examine an older generation's response (as opposed to the revolt of the young) on an issue of fundamental theoretical importance. In this case, perhaps not atypically, the master talked largely past the erstwhile disciple.

In closing, however, I cannot altogether resist the temptation to make a few observations about Freud's revolt. First, I think it unlikely that Freud responded in his turn to Charcot's letter of 30 June 1892. Freud had already stated his position in the dissenting footnotes to the first installment of the *Leçons du Mardi*, and he would go on to use the notes in this fashion until and after Charcot's death.[45] In some respects this was an audacious thing to do. Despite his disclaimer in the preface to the *Leçons* that he was not "trying in any way to set my views above those of my honored teacher," this was precisely what Freud had done in the text of the master's own cherished *Leçons*, not in an independent review, as he suggested was common practice.[46] It would have been gratuitous to reply further to Charcot in a personal letter and ungracious as well, given that Freud had drawn heavily on the prestige of being Charcot's student over the preceding seven years. He may no longer have needed that source of patronage as much as earlier (perhaps one reason

[44] Charcot's final letter to Freud (undated but internal evidence indicates that it was written in June 1893) was simply a one-page acknowledgment of receipt of Freud's comparative study of hysterical and organic paralyses.

[45] Freud's initial installment, which probably consisted of the first four lessons, contained critical notes on pp. 4, 8, 9, 26, 37, 52, and 56, none of which are translated in *S.E.*

[46] *S.E.*, I, 136.

for his temerity), now that he had consolidated a working relationship with Breuer and had begun to develop an intimate collegiality with his Berlin friend, Wilhelm Fliess; but it still would have been foolish to risk further direct offense to Charcot.[47]

In other respects, however, the revolt was cautious, even timid. In the case of the Fournier-Erb model for tabes and general paralysis, Freud aligned himself with a respectable and increasingly plausible alternative to hereditary etiology, one which, as we have seen, even some in Charcot's own circle had adopted. This was scarcely revolutionary, and Freud took pains in his long critical note on syphilitic etiology not to extend the example to a global rejection of degeneration theory in favor of acquired causes. On the contrary, in that note, he still speaks of "cerebrospinal neurasthenia" as a "degenerative disease of the nervous system" and a familial disease par excellence (in contrast to tabes and paralysis).[48]

In a subsequent note to the *Leçons*, however, Freud extended acquired etiology to encompass the neuroses. Here, probably for the first time in published form, Freud asserts that "abnormalities in sexual life" as opposed to heredity are more frequently the cause of phobias. Freud's next note categorically charged "Charcot's etiological theory" with ignoring acquired causes, overestimating heredity, and failing to distinguish neuroses from organic nervous diseases. This is clear revolt, and we are now on familiar ground in Freud scholarship (these two notes are translated in the *Standard Edition*).[49] But as I have sought to show in this paper, the process of open dissent began in mid-1892 with a note (not published in the *Standard Edition*), on a subject of purely organic nervous disease, namely, Freud's objection to the hereditary etiology of tabes dorsalis and general paralysis.

Precisely how Freud came to his revolt is difficult to say, but it seems reasonable to suggest that the very process of meticulous line-by-line

---

[47] Freud finally completed the task begun under Charcot seven years earlier, the comparative study of organic and hysterical motor paralyses, and it was published in Charcot's *Archives de neurologie* (July 1893). But he evidently withheld a manuscript on the "theory of the hysterical attack," this despite the fact that Charcot had in his letter of 30 June 1892 enthusiastically accepted the piece for the *Archives*. It subsequently appeared as part of his and Breuer's "preliminary communication" to the *Studies on Hysteria* in the *Neurologisches Centralblatt* (January 1893). Freud, returned to his differences with Charcot in his *éloge* and the two articles of 1896 (see above n. 13 and 14). In the article published in the *Revue neurologique*, 162, Freud in fact referred to "une lettre privée du maître [Charcot]" in which Charcot remained "en stricte opposition contre la théorie de Fournier [on the syphilitic origin of tabes and general paresis]," doubtless the letter of 30 June 1892. Finally, in 1901, Freud alluded to footnotes he had added to a translation "without asking the author's permission" as an "arbitrary action" that had probably displeased the author. *S.E.*, VI, 161.

[48] *Polyklinische Vorträge*, 8n.

[49] *S.E.*, I, 139. The location of these notes in *Polyklinische Vorträge*, 224, 237, indicates that they were written before July 1893; i.e., while Charcot was still alive.

reading required for the translation of the *Leçons du Mardi* may have crystallized growing differences with Charcot, and these differences could well have involved more than etiological doctrine. As we have seen, Charcot repeated his views about the Jewish race as a paradigm for the study of neuropathology several times in the *Leçons*, including once in the controversial first lesson on syphilis and tabes.[50] When Charcot advised Freud in 1892 to look at Jewish families, the teacher's admonition was in a sense gratuitous. Ever since 1886, when Freud returned from Paris to begin practice in Vienna, his clientele had been composed of little else but Jews. Unlike the master and many of his disciples at the Salpêtrière, Freud made clear that he did not find the concept of familial degeneration at all useful in understanding these hysterics.[51]

Ironically, Freud's little noticed initial revolt may have required more hubris (perhaps *chutzpah* might be more appropriate in this context) on the level of personal confrontation with Charcot than his better known divergence over the sexual etiology of hysteria and other neuroses. In the first instance, dealing with a disease of the spinal cord, a comparative novice faulted his teacher and the world's leading authority on his own terrain. In the case of hysteria as with hypnotism, Charcot's views had never been more than provisional constructs awaiting further investigation and revision.

University of Ottawa.

[50] *Leçons du mardi*, I, 6. In his capacity as translator, Freud did not have much of a choice over where to begin his critical commentary. But Charcot did, and I think his selection of a case of tabes and syphilis suggests the importance of the former disease and its independence of the latter in his concept of neuropathology.

[51] Joseph Breuer and Sigmund Freud, *Studies in Hysteria, S.E.* II, 87, 104, 161, 294. See also Peter J. Swales, "Freud, his Teacher and the Birth of Psychoanalysis," *Freud, Appraisals and Reappraisals, Contributions to Freud Studies* (Hillsdale, N.J., 1986), I, 16-17, 28, 48; Goldstein, "The Wandering Jew and the Problem of Psychiatric Anti-Semitism in Fin-de-siècle France," and n. 34 above.

XI

BERGSON AND JUNG

By Pete A. Y. Gunter

1. To date there has not been an extensive analysis of the parallels between Henri Bergson's philosophy and Carl Gustav Jung's analytical psychology. Such an analysis can prove useful. The parallels between Jung and Bergson are thoroughgoing and can cast a revealing light on the thought of each. There is, moreover, a line of influence running from Bergson's philosophy to Jung's dynamic psychiatry. The psychiatrist was able to use models developed by the philosopher to help shape and broaden his own ideas. This should not be surprising, for Bergson intended philosophy to be a fruitful, catalytic agency, not a sterile scholastic game. It is highly instructive that in Jung's case Bergson was able to have such a fruitful, constructive effect.

2. It has been a long while since Bergson's *L'Evolution Créatrice* (Paris, 1907) made him world-famous overnight, calling forth an enthusiastic public response such as is rarely encountered by a philosopher. (When he came to Columbia University to lecture in 1913, Bergson through his popularity created what one authority describes as the first traffic jam in the history of the new world.)[1] The eclipse of the Bergsonian movement after World War I and the diversion of philosophy into quite different channels have, however, caused the impact of his ideas in the first two decades of this century to be largely forgotten.

Basic to the philosophy of Bergson is his distinction between time as spatialized and time as experienced. "Spatialized" time is mathematical, a "clock time" all of whose parts are alike and all of whose instants are static. When analyzed, such a time turns out to be not time at all but a "fourth dimension of space."[2] By contrast, experienced time is a qualitative duration, no new parts of which are identical or capable of being repeated. In his first book (*Essai sur les données immédiates de la conscience* (1889), translated as *Time and Free Will; an Essay on the Immediate Data of Consciousness* (1910), Bergson limits duration to the human stream of consciousness: "Pure duration is the form which the succession of our conscious states assumes when our ego . . . refrains from separating its present state from its former states." (*TFW*, 100.) In such circumstances we form ". . . both the past and the present states into an organic whole, as

---

[1] Geraldine Jonçich, *The Sane Positivist: A Biography of Edward L. Thorndike* (Middletown, Connecticut, 1968), 334.

[2] Henri Bergson, *Time and Free Will*, authorized translation by F.L. Pogson (London, 1950), 109. (Hereafter *TFW*.)

210   PETE A. Y. GUNTER

happens when we recall the notes of a tune, melting, so to speak, into one another." (*Ibid.*) Duration is thus experienced as a melodic continuity, a flow. Unfortunately, Bergson complains, our ordinary thought breaks up this organic becoming into atomized fragments.

This is, in fact, the essential function of a spatialized, mathematical time. It presents us with a fixed, stable, neatly segmented world in which we can safely go about our practical affairs. But while such a schema is useful, it is liable to prejudice the philosopher and the psychologist who may forget what it leaves out. While an atomized, fragmented world contains nothing that should not be, in principle, predictable, the experienced world of "inner duration" exhibits the emergence of novelty: the appearance of the really surprising, the ontologically new. In other words, for Bergson inner duration provides a paradigm of creativity; spatialized time provides a paradigm of predictable repetition.[3]

As Samuel Alexander said, Bergson was perhaps the first philosopher to "take time seriously." While to take time seriously[3a] may be to make a distinction between duration and space, there are problems connected with this distinction. Bergson sometimes speaks as if inner duration and spatialized time constitute two entirely distinct worlds. Thus, it seems as if he has created a new dualism every bit as radical as the Cartesian dualism which preceded him. While numerous passages in *Time and Free Will* might be called on to support this Cartesian interpretation, Bergson's second book, *Matière et Mémoire* (1896) dispenses with sharp dualisms. In this work, so difficult and yet so central to Bergson's philosophy, duration is renamed and also partially reconceived as "memory," while memory is shown to be in constant and fertile interaction with matter. In exploring this interaction Bergson develops a theory of the unconscious and of mental pathology which was to have a significant effect on subsequent dynamic psychiatry.

In Bergson's psychological duration there is no clear-cut distinction between present and past: the past shades into the present without precise boundaries. It is only a slight extension of this idea to conclude that there is no clear-cut distinction between our present and the *totality* of our past, that is, between our present state and the totality of our personal memory. Thus, Bergson (like Freud) postulates that all of our memories are conserved and make up our uncon-

---

[3] *Time and Free Will* did produce, however, an anticipation of Jung's person-persona contrast. Bergson states (*TFW*, 231): "Hence there are finally two different selves, one of which is, as it were, the external projection of the other, its spatial and, so to speak, social representation." This social self may be "parasitic" upon the fundamental self. "Many live this kind of life, and die without having known true freedom" (*TFW*, 166).

[3a] S. Alexander, *Space, Time and Deity* (New York, 1950), I, 44.

scious mind.[4] It is this unconscious mind which constitutes the basis of our character and nourishes our free acts:

The whole of our past psychical life conditions our present state, without being its necessary determinant; whole also, it reveals itself in our character, although no one of its past states manifests itself explicitly in character. (*MM*, 191)

It may appear that in recollection we return in thought from the present to the past, but the truth is quite different: in recollection our memories return to us, often involuntarily. Our brains operate so as to screen out most of this forgotten background, else we would be inundated by reminiscences. As it is, our lives are a sort of dialectical tension between our unconscious, perpetually seeking expression, and our present, practically-oriented action which, thanks to the focal power of our neural system, enables us to "attend to life."

In *Creative Evolution* the psychology of *Matter and Memory* becomes a metaphysics on the grand scale. The contrast between memory and matter is transformed into the contrast between life and entropy: life proceeding toward higher and higher levels of creativity, matter receding toward thermodynamic dissolution and, in the process, opposing the upward thrust of evolution.[5] Just as in human consciousness contemporary states interpenetrate, so in evolution, Bergson holds, each of the three main directions in which life has diverged (vegetative, instinctive, intelligent) contains aspects of the others. Man, the most "intelligent" vertebrate, possesses unsuspected "instinctive" capacities; social insects, though instinctive, possess vestigial capacities for intelligence. Vertebrates and insects both possess the plant's capacity to ingest and store energy, and plants (as the behavior of climbing vines and insectivorous plants testifies) can mimic animal behavior. (*CE*, 108-09)

The preceding is a highly schematic picture of Bergson's evolutionism. It omits consideration of the life force (*élan vital*) that he describes as impelling evolution on its course. That consideration will arise in comparison with the Jungian notion of *libido*. It also fails to mention the concept of *intuition* which Bergson describes as a refinement of "instinct," a way of grasping the flux of duration "from within."

For our purposes the important thing to note in all this is that with *Creative Evolution* the human unconscious becomes suprapersonal. There is in each of us the memory of a biological past which far antedates our individual lives. Though Bergson does not speak of a

---

[4] Bergson, *Matter and Memory*, authorized translation by W. Scott Palmer and Nancy Margaret Paul (London, 1950), 94-95. (Hereafter *MM*.)

[5] Bergson, *Creative Evolution*, authorized translation by Arthur Mitchell (New York, 1911), 246-51. (Hereafter CE.)

PETE A. Y. GUNTER

human collective unconscious, his search for supraindividual elements in man's unconscious mind will certainly appear remarkably familiar to students of Jung.

3. Ascribing intellectual influence is often tricky. Did Freud, or Pierre Janet, or Charcot create the concept of the unconscious? Or should we reach further back to Edouard Hartmann and Arthur Schopenhauer, to Benedict Spinoza, Gottfried Leibniz—even to Plato? One thing is certain: the complex of assumptions referred to by historians of ideas as "dynamic psychiatry"[6] was very much in the air around the turn of the century. The climate of opinion beginning to precipitate itself in Zurich, Paris, and Vienna contained many ideas which might plausibly be ascribed to Jung, Bergson, Janet, Adler, Freud, or others. Luckily, Jung had much to say about Bergson. It is to Jung's own assertions, therefore, that we must turn.

Jung has stated clearly the similarities he perceived between his views and Bergson's. In 1914, he confided:

I realize that my views are parallel with those of Bergson, and that in my book (*The Psychology of the Unconscious*) the concept of the libido which I have given is a concept parallel to that of *élan vital*; my constructive method corresponds to his intuitive method. I, however, confine myself to the psychological side and to practical work. When I first read Bergson a year and a half ago I discovered to my great pleasure everything which I had worked out practically, but expressed by him in consummate language and in wonderfully clear philosophical style.[7]

The date of this admission is important because it locates Jung's acquaintance with Bergson at the time he was struggling to free himself from his collaboration with Sigmund Freud. As is widely known, it was the libido-concept which increasingly divided the two: for Freud, libido was primarily sexual, but Jung increasingly insisted that sexuality is only one component of psychic energy.

Was Bergson's *élan vital* really similar to Jung's post-Freudian *libido*? E. A. Bennet denies it:

Mental energy is a much-debated concept in psychology and philosophy. Bergson's *élan vital*, for instance, is a specific theory of mental energy and is different from Jung's view. It is mentioned here because the two have been confused. Those who seek a complete exposition of Jung's viewpoint are referred to his paper "On Psychic Energy". . . .[8]

---

[6] Henri Ellenberger, *The Discovery of the Unconscious (New York, 1970), 932.*

[7] *Carl Gustav Jung, "The Content of the Psychoses, Part II, 1914," trans. M.D. Elder* in *Collected Papers on Analytical Psychology (authorized translation)*, ed. C.E. Long (London, 1922), 351.

[8] E.A. Bennet, *C.G. Jung* (London, 1961), 31. For a similar opinion, cf. Thomas F. Graham, *Parallel Profiles: Pioneers in Mental Health* (Chicago, 1966), 147.

But when we turn to Jung's "On Psychic Energy" (begun 1912-1913, completed 1927), we discover that *Jung himself draws a parallel here between élan vital and Jungian libido*.[9] Nor was this his last such comparison. In "On Psychoanalysis" (1913)[10] and "A Contribution to the Study of Psychological Types" (1913)[11] the parallel is again extended. In "The Content of the Psychoses: Part II" (1914)[12] and "Psychological Understanding" (1914)[13] the equation is restated *twice in each essay*. The comparison in question lost no significance for him, for Jung proposed it again twenty years later in "The Meaning of Psychology for Modern Man" (1934).[14]

A detailed comparison of Bergson's and Jung's notions of life-energy would not be without interest. It would reveal a nucleus of agreement as well as peripheral differences. I suggest, however, that comparisons be cut short by simply admitting that Jung, who was certainly in a position to know, was right about the close similarity of the two ideas. If he did not think so, it would have been strange indeed for him to say so, in print, at least nine times.[15]

Parallelism, however, is not influence. Did Bergson's conception of *élan vital*, a life-force containing sexuality as only one of its expressions, aid Jung? The answer depends in part on when Jung first encountered Bergson and, equally, on when he began to diverge from Freud.

[9] Jung, "On Psychical Energy," in *Contributions to Analytical Psychology*, trans. H.G. and Cary F. Barnes (New York, 1928), 32.

[10] Jung, "On Psychoanalysis," in *Collected Papers on Analytical Psychology*, 230-31.

[11] Jung, "A Contribution to the Study of Psychological Types," trans. C.E. Long, in *Collected Papers on Analytical Psychology*, 293.

[12] Jung, "The Content of the Psychoses, Part II, 1914," 348, 351.

[13] Jung, "On Psychological Understanding," *Journal of Abnormal Psychology*, 9, (1914-1915), 396, 399.

[14] Jung, "The Meaning of Psychology for Modern Man," *Collected Works*, 2nd ed., eds. Herbert Read, Michael Fordham, Gerhard Adler, and William McGuire, trans. R. F. C. Hull (Princeton, N.J., 1960-79), X, 147. Jung includes Aristotle's *hormé* here as another possible candidate, and denies that any such notion (even, apparently, his own) can fully explain mental dynamics.

[15] Jung's paralleling of his libido and Bergson's *élan vital* is accompanied after 1920 by previously unstated reservations. Translations of passages concerning Bergson are also changed in Jung's collected works so as to distance Jung from Bergson. In "On Psychic Energy" (completed in 1928) the paralleling of Jungian libido with *élan vital, hormé*, and (Schopenhauer's) will is followed by a demurrer: "From these concepts I have borrowed only the concrete character of the term, not the definition of the concept. The omission of the detailed explanation of this in my earlier book is responsible for numerous misunderstandings, such as the accusation that I have built up a kind of vitalistic concept." (Jung, *Collected Works*, VIII, 30.) But Jung, prior to the 1920s, was in a position to express himself accurately and to examine carefully the work of his English-language translators. The *meaning* of statements made concerning Bergson by Jung and translated prior to 1920 is often not consistent with later versions of the same statements.

214   PETE A. Y. GUNTER

The dates of Jung's conclusive divergence from Freud have been amply documented. Liliane Frey-Rohn concludes:

Although the first hints of a new concept of energy could already be seen in *The Psychology of Dementia Praecox*, the breakthrough to an abstract concept of energy took place only in the years 1911-1913.[16]

By 1906 Jung was familiar with certain of Bergson's basic ideas. A reader of the *Journal of Abnormal Psychology*, he would probably have come across J. W. Courtney's brief discussion (August 1906) of Bergson's theory of false recognition.[17] Jung's *The Psychology of Dementia Praecox*, written in 1906, refers to Bergson's theory of dreams.[18] More significantly, it contains numerous references to Pierre Janet's *Les Obsessions et la psychasthénie* (1903) which contains references to and important quotes from *Matter and Memory*. The relations between Janet Bergson, and Jung are interesting subjects for speculation, and I shall discuss them again near the end of this study.

In the 1909-1910 issue of *The Journal of Abnormal Psychology*, James Jackson Putnam published an article, which Jung and Freud both read, titled "Personal Impressions of Sigmund Freud and His Work."[19] Putnam was an avid Bergsonian who persisted in trying to convert Freud to certain of Bergson's views. In his journal article Putnam mentions Bergson's account of the part played by memory in perception and his theory of the role played by memories as living forces in our daily lives.

Putnam was not the only source from which Jung might have learned about Bergson. Ernest Jones noted that Jung had completed the first part of "*The Psychology of the Unconscious* by June, 1910.[20] In this work (*Wandlungen und Symbole der Libido*, referred to below as *Wandlungen I* and *II*), Jung refers to Bergson's concept of creative

---

[16] Liliane Frey-Rohn, *From Freud to Jung* (New York, 1974), 158.

[17] J.W. Courtney, "Review of 'A Propos de Déjà vu' by Pierre Janet," *Journal of Abnormal Psychology*, 1 (August 1906), 149-50.

[18] Jung, "The Psychology of Dementia Praecox," in *Collected Works* III, 66n. Bergson is referred to here in conjunction with Edouard Claparède though Bergson's "Le Rêve" is not included in Jung's bibliography. Claparède's "Esquisse d'une théorie biologique du sommeil" (*Archives psychologique de la Suisse Romande*, IV [1904-1905], 245-349) is footnoted.

[19] James Jackson Putnam, "Personal Impressions of Sigmund Freud and His Work, *Journal of Abnormal Psychology*, 4, (1909-1910), 293-310. Cf. 297-98 for Putnam's remarks on Bergson. Jung's comments on the article are contained in a letter to Sigmund Freud (Jan. 10, 1910); Freud's mention of Putnam's article appears in a letter to Jung (Jan. 13, 1910). *The Freud/Jung Letters*, ed. William McGuire, trans. Ralph Manheim and R.F.C. Hull (Princeton, 1974), 286.

[20] Ernest Jones, *The Life and Work of Sigmund Freud*, Vol. II: *Years of Maturity* (New York, 1961), 143.

duration in a footnote to a passage in which Jung describes "the driving force of the libido."[21] In this footnote Jung briefly thanks Dr. Adolph Keller of Zurich, whom he had known for several years, for calling his attention to this idea. In March 1909, he had mentioned to Freud that Keller (who later published a study of Bergson[22]) was "busily at work in psychoanalysis."[23]

In 1911 Jung again was in a position to ponder the ideas, if not of Bergson, then at least of Bergsonians. Beatrice M. Hinkle, converted to dynamic psychiatry through a reading of Breuer's and Freud's *Studies in Hysteria* and "a book by Bergson,"[24] set out for Europe in 1911 to see Bergson and Jung. She was to be present at the Third Psychoanalytic Congress in September 1911, as were Keller and Putnam whose ideas Freud asked Jung to probe during Putnam's stay.[25] Jung need not have troubled himself. Putnam's paper ("A Plea for the Study of Philosophic Methods in Preparation for Psychoanalytic Work")[26] does not mention Bergson, but its reiteration of the place of creativity in evolution and in human life are thoroughly Bergsonian. Nor is it likely that Jung would have failed to learn of Putnam's philosophical sympathies through Freud.

In *Wandlungen II*, written in 1912, Jung uses Bergson's *durée* to describe creation through time. His description appears in the context of a mythological investigation:

In the Egyptian Book of the Dead, Tum is even designated as a he-cat, because as such he fought the snake, Apophis. The encoiling also means the engulfing, the entering into the mother's womb. This time is defined by the rising and setting of the sun, that is to say, through the death and renewal of the libido. The addition of the cock again suggests time, and the addition of implements suggests the creation through time. ("Durée créatrice," Bergson.) Oromazdes and Ahriman were produced through Zrwanakarana, the "infinitely long duration."[27]

The purely formal concept of time is, Jung concludes, expressed in mythology by transformations of the creative libido.

---

[21] Jung, *Psychology of the Unconscious*, Part I, authorized translation and introduction by Beatrice M. Hinkle (New York, 1965), 295-96.

[22] Adolph Keller, *Eine Philosophie des Lebens* (Jena, 1914), 46.

[23] Jung, "Letter to Sigmund Freud, March 7, 1909," *The Freud/Jung Letters*, 209.

[24] John C. Burnham, *Psychoanalysis and American Medicine: 1894-1918, Medicine, Science, and Culture* (New York, 1967), 131-32.

[25] *The Freud/Jung Letters*, 444-45. Cf. Sigmund Freud, "Letter to Carl Gustav Jung, September 1, 1911," in *ibid.*, 441-42.

[26] James Jackson Putnam, "A Plea for the Study of Philosophic Methods in Preparation for Psychoanalytic Work," *Journal of Abnormal Psychology*, **4**, (Oct.-Nov. 1911), 249-64.

[27] Jung, *Psychology of the Unconscious*, 314.

By 1910, then, Jung had connected Bergson's concept of creative duration with the concept of libido. Two years later he had restated the connection, extending it to include symbolic expression. Can we go further? To answer this question we would have to know either how extensive were Jung's conversations with Adolph Keller or exactly when he read Bergson (presumably *Creative Evolution*). *Wandlungen II* — which Jung had great difficulty finishing — was completed in September 1912.[28] If Jung were writing in *early* 1914 when he reported having read Bergson a year and a half before, this would push back the reading of *Creative Evolution* to the middle months of 1912 — early enough to aid him in broadening his concept of psychic energy and with time to provide him with positive reinforcement in his struggle with Freud.

Although these factors are not conclusive, there are three arguments which indicate that something more than parallelism was at work. The first is the essential convergence of the two concepts, as Jung describes them. Coincidences certainly do occur in the history of ideas, but the more convergence becomes identity, the more we ought to consider the possibility of influence. (Basic agreements of the two thinkers on the concept of life-energy will become more apparent as we proceed.) The second is the language which Jung uses in describing the positive force of libido. When he speaks of an "onward urging, living libido"[29] or of an "active fructifying (upward striving) form of the libido,"[30] we find ourselves in the presence of an *élan* not to be found in Freud, Schopenhauer, or even Nietzsche.

Finally, orothodox psychoanalysts saw Bergson's influence at work in Jung's defection. Thus, Ernest Jones confides:

As early as 1909 Jung was complaining to Freud about his difficulty in explaining to his pupils the concept of libido and begged him for a fuller definition. Freud tersely replied that he could give no clearer one than he had already. Only two years later Jung equated the concept with Bergson's *élan vital,* with life energy in general, and thus robbed it of its distinctive sexual connotation.[31]

Freud evidently perceived Jung's apostasy similary. Writing to Putnam in 1915 he complained:

What I have seen of religious-ethical conversion has not been inviting. Jung, for example, I found sympathetic so long as he lived blindly, as I did. Then came his religious-ethical crisis with higher morality, "rebirth," Bergson and at the same time lies, brutality and antisemitic condescension towards me.[32]

---

[28] Ernest Jones, *The Life and Work of Sigmund Freud*, II, 143.

[29] Jung, *Psychology of the Unconscious*, 335.   [30] *Ibid.*, 416.

[31] Ernest Jones, *The Life and Work of Sigmund Freud*, II, 383.

[32] Sigmund Freud, "Letter to James Jackson Putnam, July 8, 1915," trans. Judith Bernays Heller, in Nathan G. Hale, Jr., ed., *James Jackson Putnam and Psycho-*

One would like to know more about Freud's view of Bergson's influence. Unfortunately, the published record says little more on this point.

If the period 1911-13 marks the emergence of Jung's new psychiatry and his break with Sigmund Freud, the years 1913-20 have been called his "fallow period." Henri Ellenberger points out, however, that in this period, which culminated in Jung's *Psychological Types* (1920), his system of psychological analysis achieved definitive form.[33] In *Wandlungen II* one finds anticipations of concepts for which Jung was later to become famous, but anticipations are not yet doctrines. Jung's reading of Bergson in mid-1912 to mid-1913 occurred at a time when important components of Jung's conceptual scheme were still taking form. During the period 1913-20 Jung specifically equates Bergson's ideas with his own concepts of instinct,[34] intuition,[35] the (limited) function of the human intellect,[36] reaction-formation,[37] and introversion-extroversion.[38] His treatment of mechanism and finalism during these years is notably similar to Bergson's (though here the common source is probably Kant),[39] as is his closely-related insistence that the difficulties of the present, and not of the past or future, are the key to mental illness.[40] Nor can it be purely a matter of accident that Jung includes the intuitive personality among his four basic psychological types and, like Bergson, connects intuition with future-oriented speculation.[41] There can be no question, then, that the philosophy of creative evolution had by 1913 become an integral part of Jung's reflections. One can easily imagine that it played a role in the development of such Jungian concepts as the archetypes, individuation, the collective unconscious, and intuition. I shall argue that this likelihood becomes increasingly strong as one moves from the first of these concepts (the archetypes) to the last (intuition).

The concept of the unconscious developed by Bergson in *Matter and Memory* (1896) is limited, as we noted above, to the individual's experience. On this point Bergson agreed with Freud: there is nothing

---

analysis (Cambridge, Mass., 1971), 188-91. This passage was omitted from previously published versions of Freud's letter (191n.).

[33] Henri Ellenberger, *The Discovery of the Unconscious*, 698-703.

[34] Jung, "Instinct and the Unconscious," *Contributions to Analytical Psychology*, 274.   [35] *Ibid.*, 274.   [36] *Ibid.*, 275.

[37] Jung, "On Some Crucial Points in Psychoanalysis," *Collected Papers on Analytical Psychology*, 274-75. This insight is contained in a letter of March 1913.

[38] *Ibid.*, 293.

[39] Jung, "The Psychology of Dreams," *Collected Papers on Analytical Psychology*, 309-10. Prepared in 1914, this talk was given after World War I.

[40] Jung, "On Psychoanalysis, "*ibid.*, 229.

[41] Jung, *Psychological Types,* trans. H. Godwin Baynes (New York, 1944), 461-67, 508-13, 567-69.

218 PETE A. Y. GUNTER

in the unconscious that was not first in the conscious mind. In *Creative Evolution* (1907) this position is revised through the inclusion in man of the memory of his evolutionary past:

Is it not plain that life goes to work . . . exactly like consciousness, exactly like memory? We trail behind us, unaware, the whole of our past; but our memory pours into the present only the odd recollection or two that can in some way complete our present situation. Thus the instinctive knowledge which one species possesses of another on a certain particular point has its roots in the very unity of life, which is, to use the expression of an ancient philosopher, a "whole sympathetic to itself." (*CE*, 167)

This passage demonstrates the analogy and the connection between the individual unconscious and what I call Bergson's collective "biological unconscious." Each living creature, he holds, contains within itself dormant potentialities, "memories" of a common past which it shares with all other living creatures. We thus share *via* an inherited and universal unconscious what Bergson claims are unsuspected capacities for the understanding of modes of life other than our own. Other creatures are also endowed with such capacities which, however, they use in very practical, if often unedifying, ways. A wasp like the sphex seems to have an almost *a priori* instinctive knowledge of its prey, the cricket, and is able to sting the cricket precisely on the three nerve centers which paralyze its legs, transforming it into a suitable living meal for the sphex's larvae.[42] We will return to the sphex when we consider Bergson's concept of instinct in connection with the Jungian archetypes.

Man is not, on Bergson's terms, primarily an instinctive animal. He is a vertebrate, hence a creature of intelligence. In man, however, can be found potentially compensatory instinctive capacities which, if extended and made reflective, might give us the key to many puzzles. These insights Bergson calls "intuitions." Unlike the primitive substratum from which they are drawn, intuitions are "disinterested, self-conscious, capable of reflecting upon [their] object and enlarging it indefinitely" (*CE*, 176). But, however disinterested and reflective

---

[42] Critics have held that Bergson drew an unwarranted conclusion from Henri Fabre's (1823-1915) research by suggesting that the sphex's attack on the cricket is unerring. (See Jean Henri Casimir Fabre, *The Mason-Wasps*, trans. Alexander Teixeira de Mattos [New York, 1919].) Whether Bergson in fact committed this error is a matter that deserves a lengthy and careful analysis that cannot be undertaken here. It should be noted, however, that in the same passage in which he describes the behavior of the sphex Bergson also describes errors made by wasps which result in killing rather than paralyzing their prey. Like intelligence, he concedes, instinct is "fallible" (C 172-173). For more recent treatments of this issue see Raymond Ruyer, "Bergson et le sphex ammophile," *Revue de Métaphysique et de Morale*, **64** (1959), 165-179; Loren Eisely, "The Coming of the Giant Wasps," *Audubon Magazine*, **77** (September, 1975), 36-39.

they may become, for Bergson our intuitions have their roots in modes of knowledge and action of which we are ordinarily unaware.

This all too brief résumé of Bergson's concepts of biological memory, instinct, and intuition provides the basis for a comparison with Jung's notions of the collective unconscious, archetypes, and intuition. In *Creative Evolution* (1907) Bergson does not discuss his collective unconscious in terms of anthropology and myth, although he does so specifically in *The Two Sources of Morality and Religion* (1932). Rather, he applies that concept to biological problems. Jung was cautious in dealing with the natural sciences but was quite capable of approaching the unconscious from a biological viewpoint. In "Instinct and the Unconscious," a talk delivered in July 1919, he begins by criticizing the neo-Darwinian account of instinct:

But such an explanation is far from being satisfactory. Bergson's philosophy suggests another way of explanation, where the factor of "intuition" comes in. Intuition, as a psychological function, is also an unconscious process. Just as instinct is the intrusion of an unconsciously motivated impulse into conscious action, so intuition is the intrusion of an unconscious content, or 'image' into conscious apperception.[43]

Instinct and intuition are analogous but by no means identical: instinct, an impulse toward action, and intuition, an unconscious apprehension, are "counterparts." The one is no less difficult to understand than the other. But Jung cautions in language which is almost a direct quote from *Creative Evolution:*

. . . we must never forget that things we call complicated or even miraculous are only so for the human mind, whereas for nature they are just simple and by no means miraculous. We always have a tendency to project into things the difficulties of our understanding and to call them complicated, while in reality they are very simple and do not partake of our intellectual difficulties. Intellect is not always an apt instrument; it is only one of several faculties of the human mind.[44]

A few pages further on he credits the French intuitionist with having rediscovered an archetype in his "durée créatrice."[45]

The family resemblance between Jung's collective unconscious and Bergson's collective biological memory is thus undeniable. Even so, it might be thought that the *contents* of these two universal memories differ completely. The Bergsonian collective unconscious would

---

[43] Jung, "Instinct and the Unconscious," *Contributions to Analytical Psychology,* 274. This passage is retranslated in Jung's *Collected Works* so as to distance Jungian from Bergsonian intuition. As late as 1928, however, Jung published it unchanged.

[44] *Ibid.*, 274-75; cf. *Creative Evolution*, 89-91, 217.

[45] Jung, "Instinct and the Unconscious," in *Contributions to Analytical Psychology*, 280. Jung reiterated this claim in 1935. *Collected Works*, XVIII, 121.

appear to contain the amorphous flux of the life-force with its inter-mingled potentialities, while Jungian racial memory would appear to contain a set of fixed, clearly distinguishable forms (archetypes). Un-questionably the two men chose to present their ideas in those terms; under closer examination, however, the contrast is attenuated.

Jung regarded his archetype or "primordial image" as a "crystal-lized form": a crystallization of the libido which lacks the libido's pregnant dynamism.[46] For Jung dynamic life-energies are the ultimate source of the primordial images. The underlying "dynamis" must be cast in the form of a fixed symbol. We experience, Jung explains: ". . . an ever-growing resistance against the purely shapeless and chaotic character of sheer *dynamis* . . . the unquenchable need for reform and law. The soul, which dives into the stream, must also create the symbol, which embraces, maintains, and expresses this energy."[47] Such is the task of the poets and artists "whose chief creative source is the collective unconscious,"[48] but the artist's ul-timate source is the stream, not the crystallized contents, the raw developmental potential and not the finished symbol. Similarly, the mystic's insights derive from a common basis:

. . . the primordial foundation of primitive mentality, with its primitive ener-getic notion of God, in which the impelling *dynamis* has not crystallized into the abstract idea of God.[49]

When a mystic or an artist is "seized by an archetype" we do not have to conceive him in the grip of an abstract form. Rather, he is grasped by fundamental energies *which it is his task to express in novel forms*. Like Bergson, then, Jung describes creativity as the crystallization of an underlying psychic flux or stream.

It can be argued that though one can find an *élan* in Jung's arche-types, one can find nothing like an archetype in Bergson's evolu-tionism, but this is not true. There are specific developmental poten-tials in Bergson's *élan vital*. Evolution by no means excludes the emergence of distinguishable types or even a sort of preexistence of these types in the original evolutionary thrust. Hence, the capacity of the sphex to recognize the basic structure of its prey lies in a biological memory which the sphex retains long after having developed along a quite different evolutionary path. Bergson gives several examples of such biological memories: the sitaris bettle, which utilizes the life cycle of the anthrophora (a bee) as if it were a learned entomologist (*CE*, 146-47); the scolia, which stings the motor ganglia of the rose

---

[46] Jung notes that Bergson also uses the term "crystallization" to "illustrate the essence of intellectual abstraction." Jung, "A Contribution to the Study of Psycho-logical Types," *Collected Papers on Analytical Psychology*, 293.

[47] Jung, *Psychological Types*, 318.   [48] *Ibid.*, 318-39.   [49] *Ibid.*, 316.

beetle so as to cause paralysis but not death (*CE*, 172); the ammophila hirsuta, which, stinging the nine nerve centers of its caterpillar, then squeezes its head so as, again, to cause not death but paralysis (*CE*, 172). Such instinctive behavior, Bergson contends, involves not complicated reflexes but a kind of knowledge,[50] and this knowledge depends upon a biological memory which is remarkably specific. Just how specific this memory is becomes even clearer when we recall Bergson's example of the human eye and that of the pectin, a shellfish whose eye is almost identical with our own even to the point of having an inverted retina. In this case, Bergson holds, biological memory is specific enough to produce identical organs in very different organisms on widely divergent evolutionary pathways.

It is surprising that the similarity between Jung and Bergson at this point has rarely, if ever, been stressed. For both thinkers, possibility is not "ahead of" us in a set of clearly marked ideal characteristics, a view rejected by both thinkers as an unrealistic form of "finalistic" teleology. Rather, for Jung and Bergson, possibility is "behind us" in biological conditions stemming from the past. When we meet, Bergson says, ". . . . on one line of evolution, a recollection, so to speak, of what is developed along other lines, we must conclude that we have before us dissociated elements of one and the same original tendency." (*CE*, 118) When Bergson stresses the manner in which these tendencies originally "coalesce" (*CE*, 117), "interpenetrate" (*CE*, 135), or are "blended" (*CE*, 99), he is emphasizing their internal relatedness in an un-Jungian manner. But in stressing the reality of a collective unconscious and its specific developmental potentials, Jung and Bergson are speaking very nearly in the same voice. Nor was this near identity lost on Jung who liked to refer to his archetypes using the Bergsonian phrase "les éternels incréés."[51]

A similar agreement emerges when Jung's notion of differentiation is compared with Bergson's concept of evolutionary divergence. Like the concept of the archetype, the concept of differentiation is not explicitly worked out in *Wandlungen I* and *II*, though it is implicit in Jung's account of the individual's journey toward self-realization through the struggle with the "mother-libido" and his analysis of the concept of The Hero. In *Psychological Types*, however, the concept of differentiation is made into a technical term and used to explain individuation[52] which, Jung holds, is differentiation since by means of it the individual is more and more separated from the mass of his fellows. With characteristic optimism, he sees the human race, like

---

[50] For a recent account of the instincts of the paralyzing wasps, see Loren Eiseley, *loc. cit.*, see note 42 above. *All the Strange Hours* (New York, 1975), 243-54.

[51] Jolande Jacobi, *Complex/Archetype/Symbol in the Psychology of C.G. Jung*, trans. Ralph Manheim (Princeton, 1959), 52.

[52] Jung, *Psychological Types*, 534-40.

the human individual, as engaged in this process which separates man from his archaic past while rendering him truly civilized.

We have already seen that Bergson lays great emphasis on evolutionary differentiation or divergence. He thus differs from, for example, Pierre Teilhard de Chardin for whom convergence, not divergence, is the essence of evolution.[53] For Bergson, however, the end result of these evolutionary "divergent directions" (*CE*, 101, 135) is the creation of distinct species and ultimately distinct individuals. While individuality is never perfect, life ". . . manifests a search for individuality, as if it strove to constitute systems naturally isolated, naturally closed." (*CE*, 14-15.) Bergson uses the human process of individuation as a metaphor for evolutionary divergence. Life, he teaches, is tendency:

. . . and the essence of a tendency is to develop in the form of a sheaf, creating, by its very growth, divergent directions among which its impetus is divided. This we observe in ourselves, in the evolution of that special tendency which we call our character. (*CE*, 99-100)

Self-realization is for Bergson differentiation, the divergence from shared traits to the development of traits uniquely defining an individual. Like Jung, Bergson sees human history as a process of differential self-realization:

Man, then, continues the vital movement indefinitely, although he does not draw along with him all that life carries in itself. On other lines of evolution there have traveled other tendencies which life implied, and of which, since everything interpenetrates, man has, doubtless, kept something, but of which he has kept only very little. *It is as if a vague and formless being, whom we may call, as we will,* man *or* superman, *had sought to realize himself, and had succeeded only by abandoning a part of himself on the way.* (*CE*, 266)

Implicit in this description is the belief—also found in Jung—that a compensatory move toward intuition is needed in the modern world if man is to realize himself as a complete being.

In developing his concepts of the archetypes and the collective unconscious, Jung would have found it helpful to utilize Bergson's similar ideas with their broad background of biological and philosophical reflections. He certainly would have been encouraged by Bergson's conclusions. But when it comes to the concept of intuition, Bergson's influence is decisive. Jung is the first psychologist to introduce the "intuitive" person as a distinct character type. Intuition, to be sure, has meant different things to different thinkers. Throughout

[53] Nicholas Core, *Pierre Teilhard de Chardin: His Life and Spirit* (New York, 1960), 10.

the history of Western philosophy it has traditionally connoted recourse to eternal forms: the meaning of Alfred North Whitehead's claim that Western philosophy is just so many footnotes to the philosophy of Plato. Bergson, however, denied the Platonic concept of intuition. Where for Plato direct knowledge (intuition) has as its object timeless forms, for Bergson intuition probes the dynamics of reality. Plato's "knowledge" of change is at best opinion, but Bergson inverts this claim, contending that "knowledge" of static forms is merely "symbolic." It is clear that Jung's intuitive type stands in the Bergsonian, and not in the Platonic, tradition. By equating intuition with future-oriented speculation, by finding its substratum in the dynamic unconscious, Jung transforms our notion of intuition into a species of dynamism.

Jung shows a curious ambiguity toward Bergson's notion of intuition. In *Psychological Types* he is at pains to explain that it is Nietzsche, not Bergson, who truly understands intuition.[54] German philosophy, Jung asserts, grasped the notion of intuition in the late nineteenth century, well before the philosopher across the Rhine.[55] Jung's denial is remarkably weak, however. Leaving aside his barely veiled nationalism, there is the odd fact that less than a year before, in "Instinct and the Unconscious," Jung himself had equated his concept of intuition with Bergson's. This sudden about-face is nowhere explained. It is equally hard to square the position which Jung takes in *Psychological Types* with his remarks in 1916 at the Zurich School for Analytical Psychology:

Special thanks are due to Bergson for having broken a lance for the right of the irrational to exist. Psychology will probably be obliged to acknowledge and to submit to a plurality of principles, in spite of the fact that this does not suit the scientific mind.[56]

Only in this way, Jung concludes, can psychology be saved from shipwreck.

There is an element of conjecture in the suggestion that Bergson's ideas on psychic energy played a role, at a crucial time, in separating Jung from Freud. (The evidence here is admittedly circumstantial.) There is a less pronounced element of conjecture in the assertion that the Jungian concepts of the archetypes, the collective unconscious, and individuation were broadened and, in part, crystallized through a reading of *Creative Evolution*. That Jung should have taken up intuition, in his special sense, as a fundamental way of viewing reality and a fundamental character-type, is a move clearly influenced by Berg-

---

[54] Jung, *Psychological Types*, 398-99.   [55] *Ibid.*, 400.

[56] Jung, "The Conception of the Unconscious," *Collected Papers on Analytical Psychology*, 464.

son, though there is certainly room for conjecture about the exact manner in which Bergson's influence made itself felt. There is another point of influence, however, about which there can be little doubt but about which Jung was probably not aware. It stems from the work of Pierre Janet.

Like Bergson's philosophy, Janet's psychological analysis has gone into eclipse. Around the turn of the century Janet was the acknowledged leader of dynamic psychiatry. Jung studied for a semester with him in Paris in 1900[57] and took from him several key ideas which can be traced to later, post-Freudian features of Jung's psychology. Two of Janet's central concepts clearly worked their way into Jung's thought: "fonction du réel" and "tension psychologique." The hardest conceivable task, Janet held, is that of coping with present reality. This effort he termed the function of reality—renamed the ego by later psychiatrists. "Psychological tension" is closely related to the function of reality. In a healthy mind psychological tension is maintained and developed, and the function of reality is sustained. But when, through the encounter with insuperable obstacles, the tension of personality is broken, we have regression, "l'abaissement du niveau mental." In *Wandlungen II* and in *Psychological Types* Jung returns repeatedly to these ideas, reshaping them in terms of his own theory of psychological energy, using them against Freudian theories of the self.[58] Janet terms the activity through which the function of reality is made effective by confronting the present (*présentification*). Jung recurs to this notion repeatedly, insisting against Freud that mental illness often springs from a failure to deal with *present* problems and that the iliness can by no means be traced simplistically to early childhood traumas. He recurs often also to the decay of psychological tension and its accompanying regression, insisting that regression in many cases results from the fear of life, not from crippling childhood conflicts. It can also, he holds, result from an injury to the ego itself.

The extent to which Janet's concepts of "attention to life" and "psychological tension" were derived by him from Bergson's *Matter and Memory* ought to be more widely known to historians of psychology. In 1911, in an introduction written for the English translation of *Matter and Memory*, Bergson states that these two concepts, at first

---

[57] "I studied with Janet in Paris and he formed my ideas very much. He was a first-class observer, though he had no dynamic psychological theory. It was a sort of physiological theory of unconscious phenomena, the so-called *abaissement du niveau mental*, that is, a certain depotentiation of the tension of consciousness." *C.G. Jung Speaking: Interviews and Encounters*, ed. William McGuire and R.F.C. Hull (Princeton, 1977), 283.

[58] Present in abundance in *The Psychology of Dementia Praecox*, they remain largely "repressed" during Jung's collaboration with Freud.

considered paradoxical, were found indispensable by Pierre Janet in developing a theory of "psychasthenic" mental illness[59] (which Jung would later term "introverted schizophrenia"). Bergson refers to Janet's major work *Les Obsessions et la psychasthénie* (1903), citing passages in the first volume (474-502) as verification for his claim.[60] One does not find in these pages an explicit admission by Janet of the influence of Bergson's ideas, but Janet's phrase "psychological tension" is precisely the phrase used by Bergson in *Matter and Memory*, while the manner in which Janet employs it is scarcely distinguishable from Bergson's usage. The similarity between Bergson's "attention to life" and Janet's "function of reality" is conspicuous. When Jung, therefore, uses these and other closely related concepts to distinguish his dynamic psychiatry from Freud's, he owes (probably without being aware of it) a real debt to Bergson. Perhaps had he been aware of this, certain similarities which he later discovered between analytical psychology and the philosophy of creative evolution would have appeared less surprising to him.

There is no attempt here to deny Jung's creativity or to hold that he "derived his dynamic psychiatry from Bergson." What I have tried to establish is, first, that there is an extraordinarily close agreement between these two thinkers on many basic points—an agreement historians of ideas have overlooked. This fundamental agreement should be useful in understanding creativity in Jung's thought. But a second point is that there is a line of influence running from Bergson's thought to Jung's analytical psychology. As a rule this function appears to have been "catalytic" in a special way, that is, it helped Jung in directions in which he was already going. In the case of indirect influence (exerted through the person and writings of Pierre Janet), Bergson's ideas were almost certainly more decisive in providing Jung with root assumptions. But the credit here must be shared with Janet, not only because he applied the philosopher's insights to specific cases, and thus developed ("crystallized") them, but because in other respects Bergson was indebted to Janet.[61] Theirs was a complex, problematic, and highly fruitful collaboration.

4. I conclude by posing a general question suggested by the content and conclusions of this paper: Does Jung really have a concept of creativity, or does his recourse to a fixed set of timeless archetypes

---

[59] Bergson, *Matter and Memory*, xix. The other of Janet's chief works is *L'Automatisme psychologique* (Paris, 1889).

[60] Pierre Janet, *Les Obsessions et al psychasthénie*, (Paris, 1903), I, 474-502.

[61] See esp. Claude M. Prévost, *Janet, Freud et la psychologie clinique* (Paris, 1973). On 203n. Prévost calls for a systematic study of the relationships between Janet and Bergson, a study which will be extremely difficult.

limit him to a cyclic, repetitive concept of man and of history? Many of Jung's assertions would support this conclusion. Thus, in *Psychological Types* he states concerning the human knowing process:

These adjustments are not merely accidental or arbitrary happenings, but adhere to strictly preformed conditions, which are not transmitted, as are perception-contents, through experience but are *a priori* conditions of apprehension. . . . This explains why even fantasy, the freest activity of the mind, can never roam in the infinite (albeit, so the poet senses it), but remains bound to the preformed possibilities, the *primordial images or archetypes*. (378)

If, as James A.C. Brown and others have noted, there is a "generally static impression conveyed by the Jungian system,"[62] the priority of the archetypes would be its source.

But in *Psychological Types*, at least, Jung is ambivalent on precisely this point. While there are, he intimates, a fixed set of archetypes, these archetypes achieve new, creative expression and can thus be said to evolve. Thus there is room in Jung's thought during this period for a static, Kantian rendering of the archetypes as sheer *a priori* determinants of thought and behavior as well as for a dynamic, process-oriented explanation of the archetypes as specific tendencies toward development. However, the second, more Bergsonian tendency in Jung's thought provides a more fruitful, and hopeful, beginning.

North Texas State University.

[62] James A.C. Brown, "Assessments and Applications," *The Freudian Paradigm*, ed. Md. Mujeeb-ur-Rahman (Chicago, 1977), 379.

XII

WITTGENSTEIN'S "WONDERFUL LIFE"

By Peter C. John

> ... Theodorius was not wrong in his estimate of your nature. This sense of wonder is the mark of the philosopher. Philosophy indeed has no other origin, and he was a good genealogist who made Iris the daughter of Thaumas.　　　Socrates to Thaetetus[1]

> For it is owing to their wonder that men both now begin and at first began to philosophize.　　　Aristotle, *Metaphysics* 982b[2]

In *The Illusion of Technique*[3] William Barrett asserts that the experience referred to in the well-known passage at 6.44 in the *Tractatus*, "Not how the world is, but that it is is the Mystical," was of life-long significance for Wittgenstein. Its importance for him at the time it was composed is clearly seen in his letter to the publisher Ludwig von Ficker.[4] Barrett claims, however, that the experience to which the words at 6.44 refer is potently present and influential throughout his life. "It circulates from beginning to end through his later *Philosophical Investigations*, present but not announced—not even by way of a thunderous declaration of silence, as in the earlier work."[5] While Barrett correctly, albeit intuitively, appreciates the importance of this experience for Wittgenstein's life and work, he nevertheless insists that this sense of wonder at the fact that anything at all exists, "is acknowledged explicitly, or almost explicitly, only once ..." and "after ... momentary contact (in the *Tractatus*) seems to drop out of view for Wittgenstein." I have cited Barrett's opinion because, regardless of how bold it may appear, the actual evidence compels us to an even broader interpretation of the importance this experience held for Wittgenstein. Wittgenstein mentioned his experience, which he most often described with the words, "I wonder at the existence of the world," to friends and colleagues and in many places throughout his written work. Whenever he spoke or wrote about it, he did so invariably with the greatest emphasis and passion. Despite his numerous attempts to say something about this experience, Wittgenstein was conscious that such attempts were futile and could at best convey only metaphorically what he felt. Nevertheless, he continued throughout his life to make reference to this experience, a habit which he did not condemn

---

[1] Plato, "Thaetetus," *The Collected Dialogues*, tr. F. M. Cornford (Princeton, 1973) 860.

[2] Aristotle, *Metaphysics*, tr. W. D. Ross (Oxford, 1966), book A, sec. 982, l. 12.

[3] William Barrett, *The Illusion of Technique* (New York, 1978).

[4] Ludwig Wittgenstein, *Briefe an Ludwig von Ficker* (Salzburg, 1969), 35-36.

[5] William Barrett, *The Illusion of Technique*, 160.

228 PETER C. JOHN

in himself or in others. His persistence we may take as evidence of the importance of this experience in the unfolding of his life and in the development of his work.

My emphasis upon this particular experience as a means of understanding Wittgenstein's philosophical accomplishments allies me with the revision in Wittgenstein scholarship begun by Janik and Toulmin,[6] who were the first to argue that the *Tractatus*, to be properly understood, had to be viewed in its Viennese cultural context and, more particularly, in its personal ethical context. As a work which invited others to consider more carefully the connection between this philosopher's values and his thought, *Wittgenstein's Vienna* was invaluable. At about the same time William Bartley offered quite a different sort of analysis of Wittgenstein.[7] His primary task was to understand how Wittgenstein's name and thought have managed to captivate us. Bartley relies heavily, in his first and later work, on Wittgenstein's alleged homosexuality for explaining the apparent mythological status that this individual has achieved. More in the tradition of Janik and Toulmin, Peter Munz has recently sought to understand Wittgenstein's thought by linking his strict bifurcation of the subjective and objective to the cultural and political conditions of *fin-de-siècle* Vienna.[8] Munz illustrates through Klimt, and with a quick glance at Hofmannsthal and Musil, the failure of that culture to reconcile the subjective and objective. The implication is, of course, that Viennese culture is unique not in its failure but in being among the first moderns to struggle for such a reconciliation; and Wittgenstein is an early response to its failure. At best, Munz claims, life and art, life and poetry, objectivity and subjectivity "could be reconciled only in terms of . . . unclarity . . ." (*Verschwommenheit*).[9] He concludes, "If subjectivity and objectivity could only be linked in *Verschwommenheit*, Wittgenstein's austere puritanism and his passion for clarity forced him to sever the *verschwommene* link between the two." He sums up Wittgenstein's inevitable course of action by echoing Englemann's conviction that "he could not deny to himself the passionate truth of subjective feeling, of 'what really mattered in life. . . .' " This very interesting, though somewhat hasty explanation of the genesis of Wittgenstein's philosophy ignores, however, the very issue of "what really mattered" to Wittgenstein and what it was he was trying to enshrine and protect in his act of bifurcation. It is this issue that I wish to discuss.

The *Notebooks, 1914-1916* offer one of the first written mentions of

---

[6] Allan Janik and Stephen Toulmin, *Wittgenstein's Vienna* (New York, 1973).

[7] William Bartley, *Wittgenstein* (Philadelphia, 1973) and "Wittgenstein and Homosexuality," *Salmagundi*, No. 58-59 (1983), 166-96. The new edition of Bartley's *Wittgenstein* (LaSalle, 1985) combines these two works.

[8] Peter Munz, "Bloor's Wittgenstein or The Fly in the Bottle," *Philosophy of the Social Sciences*, 17 (1987), 67-96.

[9] *Ibid.*, 89-90.

his experience. Dated October 20, 1916, the passage reads, "Das künstlerische Wunder ist, dass es die Welt gibt, dass es das gibt, was es gibt."[10] Rendered in English this reads, "The aesthetic miracle is that the world exists, that what exists does exist."

We find an analogous remark in the *Tractatus*, which he completed during the war, just after the period embraced by the *Notebooks*. At proposition 6.44 we read, "Nicht wie die Welt ist, ist das Mystische, sondern dass sie ist." "Not how the world is, is the mystical, but that it is." Although the obvious point here is Wittgenstein's astonishment that anything at all exists, he uses, in these passages, two different terms in an effort to convey his meaning. "Wunder" and "Mystische," miracle and mystical, are apparently being used in an effort to point to something. We are given some clue as to what is being pointed to when we look at 6.432. Here "das Mystische" points to what is "higher" (*das Höhere*); perhaps this is even meant as a synonym for God. It moves counter to the function of these words to try to articulate precisely what they point to. For Wittgenstein these terms were significant to the degree that they pointed not to but away from the "hows" and "whys" of our existence. Miracle and mystical are markers for that which cannot be explained; both words serve their function in directing the reader away from the explicable toward the inexplicable and ineffable.

It may be objected that although this experience is mentioned in the *Tractatus*, it apparently holds no special status among all the other numbered propositions, except perhaps for the fact that it is near the end, which Wittgenstein recognized as significant in itself, in that it was the only portion of the work likely to be understood. But the accessibility of this passage does not by itself argue for its importance. What does, however, argue for the primacy of this proposition in our understanding of the work and its author is Wittgenstein's self-confessed purpose in composing the *Tractatus*.

As is now widely recognized, Wittgenstein's letter to his friend and prospective publisher, Ludwig von Ficker, states in unequivocal terms the meaning the *Tractatus* held for its author. Explaining his intent in composing his work Wittgenstein states:

The book's point is an ethical one. I once meant to include in the preface a sentence which is not in fact there now but which I will write out for you here, because it will perhaps be a key to the work for you. What I meant to write, then, was this: My work consists of two parts: the one presented here plus all that I have not written. And it is precisely this second part that is the important one. My book draws limits to the sphere of the ethical from the inside as it were, and I am convinced that this is the ONLY *rigorous* way of drawing those limits. In short, I believe that where *many* others today are just *gassing*, I have

[10] *Notebooks, 1916-1918* (Oxford, 1969), 86.

230 PETER C. JOHN

managed in my book to put everything firmly into place by being silent about it.[11]

Although Wittgenstein purports to explain in this passage his purpose in writing the *Tractatus*, it tells at best only half the story. To say that the point of any work is an "ethical one" without more specific qualification does not illuminate the matter. What, we must ask, does Wittgenstein intend by the "ethical"? In his *Lectures on Ethics*, delivered at Cambridge in late 1929 or early 1930, Wittgenstein explains what he means when he employs expressions such as "absolute good" and "ethical value." "In my case," he says, "it always happens that the idea of one particular experience presents itself to me. . . ." "I believe the best way of describing it is to say that when I have it *I wonder at the existence of the world* [italicized in the original]. And I am inclined to use such phrases as 'how extraordinary that anything should exist' or 'how extraordinary that the world should exist.' "[12]

Ethical value for Wittgenstein, it appears, was singularly informed by the experience referred to in his *Notebooks*, in his Cambridge lecture, and most notably in the passage at 6.44 in the *Tractatus*. As his *Lecture on Ethics* makes abundantly clear, if the notion of ethics had significant meaning for Wittgenstein, his sense of wonder that anything should exist was an essential component of that meaning. We may sensibly conclude upon the basis of his remarks to von Ficker, therefore, that the "book's point" is inextricably linked to Wittgenstein's sense of wonder.

This is, however, but a preview of the role that this experience played in shaping Wittgenstein's life and work. In 1929, we see Wittgenstein making reference to his particular experience, this time in the company of the Vienna Circle. In a rare conversation on the subject of religion, Wittgenstein endeavors to clarify his thoughts on the matter by saying, "The facts of the matter are of no importance for me. But what men mean when they say that '*the world is there*' is something I have at heart." [13] In another discussion recorded by Waismann, this time between Wittgenstein and Schlick on the subject of Heidegger, Wittgenstein suggests something very important about the connection between this experience and his work as a philosopher. He is recorded by Waismann to have said,

Man feels the urge to run up against the limits of language. Think for example of the astonishment that anything at all exists. This astonishment cannot be expressed in the form of a question, and there is also no answer whatsoever. Anything we might say is *a priori* bound to be mere nonsense. Nevertheless we

---

[11] *Briefe an Ludwig von Ficker* (Salzburg, 1969), 35-36. Translation quoted from William Bartley's *Wittgenstein* (New York, 1973), 56-57.

[12] "Lecture on Ethics," *Philosophical Review*, 74 (1965), 3-12.

[13] Friedrich Waismann, *Wittgenstein and the Vienna Circle* (Oxford, 1967), 118.

do run up against the limits of language. Kierkegaard too saw that there is this running up against something and he referred to it in a fairly similar way (as running up against paradox). This running up against the limits of language is *ethics*. I think it is definitely important to put an end to all the claptrap about ethics—whether intuitive knowledge exists, whether values exist, whether the good is definable. In ethics we are always making the attempt to say something that cannot be said, something that does not and never will touch the essence of the matter. It is *a priori* certain that whatever definition of the good may be given—it will always be merely a misunderstanding to say that the essential thing, that what is really meant, corresponds to what is expressed.... But the inclination, the running up against something, *indicates something*.[14]

In this passage, while offering yet another reference to his experience, Wittgenstein suggests where his work as a philosopher stands in relation to such matters of value. A task he feels is "definitely important" we may view as his task as a philosopher, that is "to put an end to all the claptrap," to undermine "attempt[s] to say something that cannot be said...." What is achieved as a result is an avoidance of the "misunderstanding" that "the essential thing" (for Wittgenstein, what he attempts to convey with words describing a sense of wonder) somehow "corresponds to what is expressed."

We can begin to see the inextricable relation of Wittgenstein's "one particular experience" and his activities as a philosopher as we look closer at his work. Take, for example, his brief reflections on a work by Ernst Renan. After objecting in numerous ways to the presuppositions inherent in Renan's investigations, Wittgenstein announces emphatically, "Man has to awaken to wonder...." He proceeds to broaden his criticism of Renan into a general critique of science. "Man has to awaken to wonder," he insists, and objects that "Science is a way of sending him to sleep again."[15]

Wittgenstein's values, implied in his hostility toward the prejudices displayed in the work of Renan, are echoed in his observations on James Frazer's *The Golden Bough*. Frazer, for example, explains that ancient man found the resemblance between fire and the sun impressive because it was for him mysteriously inexplicable. Wittgenstein exclaims in response, "how could fire or fire's resemblance to the sun have failed to make an impression on the awakening mind of man? But not 'because he can't explain it' (the stupid superstition of our time)—for does an 'explanation' make it less impressive?"[16] Here Wittgenstein attacks Frazer's anthropological approach but, more importantly, attacks a tendency that for him Frazer only exemplifies. Wittgenstein is hostile to the notion that explanation should be thought to dispel mystery. That it can and

[14] *Ibid.*, 68-69.
[15] *Culture and Value* (Oxford, 1973), 5e.
[16] *Remarks on Frazer's* Golden Bough (Retford, 1979), 6e.

232 PETER C. JOHN

does dispel wonder at the mystery of things occurs in significant degree because individuals like Frazer believe it can. Wittgenstein intimates that fire's resemblance to the sun should in fact be impressive to us still. The fact that we have theories and formulas which endeavor to explain this resemblance should not, in his view, make the resemblance less impressive or wonderful. Certainly, he was quite aware that explanations do indeed seem to undermine an individual's capacity for wonder, thus his unflagging hostility toward theories and other forms of explanation.

This can be brought into sharper focus if we return to some further comments he made on Renan. Renan offers an explanation of a primitive response to natural phenomena analogous to that offered by Frazer. Wittgenstein quotes the *History of the People of Israel*: "Birth, sickness, death, madness, catalepsy, sleep, dreams, all made an immense impression and, even nowadays, only a few have the gift of seeing clearly that these phenomena have causes within our constitution."[17] Again, Wittgenstein reacts sternly to the idea that explanation, causal or otherwise, should imply that one cannot be impressed or filled with wonder. He goes on to insist that there is nothing necessarily "primitive" about the capacity to wonder. Wittgenstein states that for people to "suddenly start to wonder at" natural phenomena such as those mentioned above "has nothing to do with their being primitive. Unless it is called primitive not to wonder at things, in which case the people of today are really the primitive ones, and Renan himself too if he supposes that scientific explanations could intensify wonderment."[18] Returning to his remarks on Frazer, Wittgenstein believes that it is "the stupid superstition of our time" that we endeavor always to explain and thereby convince ourselves, perhaps unwittingly, that the mystery of things is somehow no longer there. Wittgenstein objects to Frazer and Renan on the same grounds that he criticizes the use of dogmatic or rigid concepts in science or mathematics. As soon as one adopts a matter-of-fact, explanatory posture toward the phenomena under investigation, whether in the form of a law or an inviolable theory, one often sacrifices the capacity to be in awe of those phenomena.

Such criticisms are part of a consistent and discernible appraisal, developed by Wittgenstein, of a form of human inquiry that best epitomizes our age, that is, science. His remarks in the *Tractatus* on the proper place of facts, laws, and theories were only the beginning of a life-long denigration of the means man employs to undermine his own capacity to wonder. He speaks of science as a source of "impoverishment" because "one particular method elbows all others aside." As a consequence, "They all seem paltry by comparison, preliminary stages at best."[19]

[17] *Culture and Value*, 5e.
[18] *Ibid.*
[19] *Ibid.*, 60e.

Wittgenstein believed that one should endeavor to go "right down to the original sources so as to see them all side by side, both the neglected and the preferred." The result, he believed, would be "enrichment" through the multiplication of "fertile new points of view."

Wittgenstein's remarks on science accord remarkably with his devotion to his sense of wonder. "Enrichment" in science is not the outcome of an endless refinement of technologies or the constant displacement of unsuitable theories by superior ones; Wittgenstein's criticism of modern science is indicative of his criticism of a wide range of matters and implies that enrichment or progress arises out of an openness to a multiplicity of points of view. Wittgenstein's quotation from Nestroy, at the beginning of the *Investigations*,[20] intends to suggest just this, that progress is not the product of transcending the old but grows from the appreciation of perspectives, new and old.

As should be expected, Wittgenstein's thoughts on the philosophy of mathematics show a marked similarity to his thoughts about science. In 1947, by which time he had recorded the ideas that now constitute his *Remarks on the Foundations of Mathematics*, Wittgenstein exclaimed that a mathematician "too can wonder at the miracle . . . of nature. . . ." "But," Wittgenstein wonders, "can he do so once a problem has arisen about what it actually is he is contemplating? Is it really possible as long as the object that he finds astonishing and gazes at with awe is shrouded [*verschleiert*] in a philosophical fog?"[21] We may immediately note two very revealing features of this passage. Wittgenstein, first of all, assumes in this passage that "wonder" is something naturally to be desired, and second, he implies that the path to it necessarily requires the dissipation of "philosophical fog."

What causes this "fog" and what, in Wittgenstein's view, could dissipate it? The answer to the first part of the question is implied in the passage itself. The "fog" arises "once a problem has arisen about what it actually is [one] is contemplating." Wittgenstein argues elsewhere that mathematicians, like other investigators, become confused and forsake their capacity for wonder when they concern themselves with the *actual* foundation of their discipline. "What a mathematician is inclined to say about objectivity and reality of mathematical facts, is not a philosophy of mathematics, but something for philosophical *treatment*."[22] What needs to be avoided, for the sake of evoking a sense of wonder, is an

---

[20] Wittgenstein's quotation from Nestroy at the beginning of the *Investigations* reads: "Überhaupt hat der Fortschritt das an sich, dass er viel grösser ausschaut, als er wirklich ist." Malcolm, in his *Memoir* (Oxford, 1984), 51, renders this, "It is the nature of every advance, that it appears much greater than it actually is." If we translate "Fortschritt" simply as "progress," this passage bears comparison to Wittgenstein's opening remarks to his *Philosophische Bemerkungen* (*Philosophical Remarks*) (Oxford, 1975).

[21] *Culture and Values*, 57e.

[22] *Philosophical Investigations* (New York, 1953), #254.

234   PETER C. JOHN

inquiry into what knowledge, in any of its forms, actually consists of. One expression of this tendency is the conviction that mathematical technique must necessarily conform to certain rules.

> We say: "If you really follow the rule in multiplying, you *must* all get the same result." Now if this is only the somewhat hysterical way of putting things that you get in university talk, it need not interest us overmuch.
> It is however the expression, which comes out everywhere in our life. The emphasis of the *must* corresponds only to the inexorableness of this attitude both to the technique of calculating and to a host of related techniques.
> The mathematical Must is only another expression of the fact that mathematics forms concepts.
> And concepts help us to comprehend things. They correspond to a particular way of dealing with situations.
> Mathematics forms a network of norms.[23]

For Wittgenstein the mathematical "must" seems to have been of the same species as the scientific "explanation." Both harbor the pretense of not obeying the limits of a form of knowledge; thus both are antagonistic to the mystery which persists beyond the forms of knowledge.

What can dissipate the philosophical fog? For Wittgenstein what seemed to be required was the awareness that mathematics, like other areas of knowledge, was a human technique, formed of "concepts [that] help us comprehend things." They are formal and limited "way[s] of dealing with situations." To achieve this, he seems to indicate, requires battling against the supposition of the "objectivity and reality" of our forms of knowledge. What he battled against was the desire for an absolute or "god's eye" view, which he appears to have felt still captivates our scientific and philosophical investigations of the world.

> What harm is done ... by saying that God knows *all* irrational numbers? Or: that they are already all there, even though we only know certain of them? Why are these pictures not harmless? For one thing, they hide certain problems.
> Suppose that people go on and on calculating the expansion of π. So God, who knows everything, knows whether they will have reached "777" by the end of the world. But can his *omniscience* decide whether they *would* have reached it after the end of the world? It cannot. I want to say: even God can determine something mathematical only by mathematics. Even for him the mere rule of expansion cannot decide anything that it does not decide for us.[24]

More than just concealing certain "problems" though, such an assumption, Wittgenstein intimates, divorces one from the sense of wonder which is evoked with the realization that complete knowledge or a complete explanation does not reside anywhere, not even with God.

Wittgenstein's views on mathematics embody in encapsulated form

---

[23] *Remarks on the Foundations of Mathematics* (Oxford, 1956), V, #46.
[24] *Ibid.*, V, #34.

many of the assumptions and techniques of his entire later philosophy. A fundamental assumption for him, as I have indicated, was that wonder is valuable in its own right and something to be desired. In addition it was his conviction that there is something in the way we look at things, in our "picture" of things, that inhibits our capacity to wonder. His technique as a philosopher was specifically designed for the removal of what stood between him and the capacity of wonder. To see how this worked in his later philosophy in particular and his philosophical work in general, we must briefly return to some propositions of the *Tractatus*.

At 6.44 Wittgenstein states what for him is mystical and what, we later discover, is a fundamental criterion for what he feels is absolutely good and valuable, that is, his sense of wonder. At 6.45, however, he indicates what technique is required in order to evoke his mystical sense of wonder. To see and feel the world as a "limited whole—it is this that is mystical." To evoke his sense of wonder Wittgenstein sought a view of things as a "limited whole." On the basis of these propositions and the evidence showing his devotion to his sense of wonder, it appears that interpreting Wittgenstein's philosophical corpus as an "ethical deed" (to use Janik and Toulmin's phrase) or as a *"single work* of thinking" (to use James Edwards's) means interpreting it as a protracted endeavor to view things as a "limited whole."

We may clarify this a bit more by considering some remarks from his *Notebooks*. Seeing the world as a "limited whole," Wittgenstein equated with viewing the world *sub specie aeternitatis*. At 6.45 we read, "To view the world *sub specie aeternitatis* is to view it as a whole—a limited whole." In a remark dated 7/10/16, which comes after a month of passages recounting Wittgenstein's struggle to identify something he could classify as *good* in an ethical sense, he writes, "the good life is the world seen *sub specie aeternitatis.*" I find this an uncommonly significant statement for anyone wishing to understand Wittgenstein's philosophical and personal objective for the simple reason that ethical declarations of this kind are so rare in his corpus and in the record of his spoken words; and what it indicates is that Wittgenstein consciously equated his capacity for wonder, that is, for achieving the "good," with his capacity for seeing things as a "limited whole."

We discover with what deliberate intent Wittgenstein sought a view of the "limited whole" in his later philosophy as well when we look at the proposed preface to his *Philosophical Remarks*, which, more than the *Brown Book*, signals the beginning of his later philosophical investigations. He writes,

Our civilization is occupied with building an ever more complicated structure ... even clarity is sought only as a means to this end, not as an end in itself. For me on the contrary clarity, perspicuity are valuable in themselves. I am not interested in constructing a building, so much as in having a perspicuous view

236 PETER C. JOHN

of the foundations of possible buildings. So I am not aiming at the same target as the scientists and my way of thinking is different from theirs.[25]

This interesting confession from a one-time architect provides us with one of Wittgenstein's few explicit declarations of what he was actually trying to achieve in his later work, particularly in the *Investigations*. This passage suggests that the later work is a protracted exercise in which he traces, to borrow Engelmann's metaphor, the island of objective fact, so as to clearly distinguish it from the ocean of boundless mystery. But as Engelmann has observed, "When he nevertheless takes immense pains to delimit the unimportant, it is not the coastline of that island which he is bent on surveying with such meticulous accuracy, but the boundary of the ocean."[26]

It is at that boundary, I believe, that Wittgenstein encountered a sense of wonder. The important thing was for Wittgenstein clearly and repeatedly to witness that our knowledge, as he later suggests, is located within a particular form of life, and that beyond our forms of knowledge all is mystery. Wittgenstein's ambition in the *Tractatus*, for a view of the facts of the world as a "limited whole" and through a description of how all facts are represented, is transformed in his later work into a description of how particular facts achieve significance within particular language-games. In his early work he desired to view the world of facts *sub specie aeternitatis*; beginning with the *Remarks*, he begins to grope after the same, but now usually termed *Übersichtlichkeit*, a clear, perspicuous, and "synoptic" view of the facts. He complains that it is the "chief trouble with our grammar" that it does not give us such a point of view. In an uncommonly poetic description of his own activity as a philosopher, Wittgenstein announces the relation of his sense of wonder to his philosophical effort to see a limited whole.

But it seems to me too that there is a way of capturing the world *sub specie aeterni* other than through the work of the artist. Thought has such a way— so I believe—it is as though it flies above the world and leaves it as it is— observing it from above, in flight.[27]

This passage tells us several things, one of which is indicated by the metaphor that is employed. This remark, which was made near the

---

[25] *Culture and Value*, 7e. Peter French has recently written an essay which asserts that the notion of limits "more than anything else characterizes Wittgensteinian philosophy." (Peter A. French, "Wittgenstein's Limits of the World," *Ludwig Wittgenstein, Critical Assessments*, 1 [London, 1986]). His focus is upon proposition 5.6 ("The limits of my language mean the limits of my world") and in the later work upon the concept of "form of life"; beginning with these he proffers an integrated interpretation of Wittgenstein's philosophy.

[26] Paul Engelmann, *Letters from Wittgenstein*, (Oxford, 1967), 97.

[27] *Culture and Value*, 5e.

beginning of Wittgenstein's later philosophical endeavors, eschews the limitations imposed by his earlier metaphor, the ladder. What he is here setting out to achieve is not to be achieved only once, but repeatedly; he wishes continually to recapture the world as a limited whole. Moreover, his choice of metaphors, early and late, tells us that he can only do this from "above" by acquiring a synoptic overview. Most importantly, this passage indicates not only the end but also the means with which to achieve it, which is to say, *thought*.

Wittgenstein, late in life, wrote a letter to his long-time friend Arvid Sjögren in which he discussed in unusually frank terms the value he placed upon thinking.[28] Ostensibly the letter is a discussion about religion, which stemmed from a disagreement between Wittgenstein and Arvid's wife over a passage from Wilhelm Kügelgen's *Lebenerrin eines Alten Mannes*. At the beginning of the letter Wittgenstein outlines two possible paths to religion, as he views it. One of them leads through a concept or a particular understanding ("durch eine Art von Philosophie"). Another leads through actions and deeds to the point where religious words begin to actually mean something but not to a point which brings one within the vicinity of a philosophy ("der Andere auf einem Weg, der ihn nicht einmal in der Nahe einer Philosophie"). Wittgenstein does not attempt to argue for the superiority of one or the other path but merely wishes to equate himself with the latter path. His identification with this path, the path of deeds, is achieved, however, in a very peculiar manner. In explaining this identification to Arvid, his emphasis is upon thought, not what we commonly regard as deeds; as a result, Wittgenstein's assumed devotion to the belief that *Am Anfang war die Tat* appears diminished, and his stated preference for action, as in his letter to Arvid, may seem insincere. But it is clear from what has been observed that Wittgenstein never considered philosophical thought to be an end in itself or a deed. Thought was an activity he was engaged in for getting past "a concept or a particular understanding" or form of knowledge which would otherwise stand between him and the performance of a deed. Thought was not his goal; it was his path. He writes to his friend, "I am myself, like you, a *thinker*. The natural way for me, which, at first, had likewise led me astray, leads *through* [my emphasis] thinking." Again, Wittgenstein immediately disclaims that his is a better way and instead refers to it simply as a "roundabout way" ("den Weg von aussenherum").

Thinking which brought with it fresh, innocent points of view, perceptions of things as if seen for the first time, totally original ways of tackling problems, the capacity to undermine stultifying theories and to wonder anew at the things of this world without regard to skeptical doubt

---

[28] *Sein Leben in Bilden und Texten*, ed. M. Nedo and M. Ranchetti (Frankfurt am Main, 1983), 245.

238   PETER C. JOHN

or matter-of-fact explanations—these were some of Wittgenstein's paths
to a meaningful and valuable existence. His golden path, however, was
the ability to capture through thought a vision of things as a "limited
whole."

This use of thought as the means of achieving what for him was most
valuable, gives substance to a remark he once made to his friend Drury.
Wittgenstein stated, "I am not a religious man," but, he added, "I cannot
help seeing every problem from a religious point of view."[29] I take this
to imply that the foundation of Wittgenstein's religion was a profound
sense of mystery about the existence of the world and of oneself and of
God's relation to these things. As I have endeavored to argue, Wittgenstein's work as a philosopher was singularly oriented toward resurrecting
in himself a sense of wonder and mystery, particularly by isolating by
means of thought the "limited whole" of what is known. In practicing
his philosophy, he was performing a religious deed in his effort to direct
his attention and the attention of others to the profound mystery of life.

For one who practiced this form of religion, nothing was more crippling than the cessation of thought. Such a cessation occurred for a
prolonged period only once in his life, and it was in this period that he
was most desperately suicidal; I refer to the period after the completion
of the *Tractatus*, to which, I surmise, Wittgenstein also refers in his letter
to Arvid with the statement that his "way" had "at first . . . led astray."
In a myriad of ways Wittgenstein announced his fear, often mortal, of
whatever might bring thought to an end. Late in life his letters and words
to Malcolm express in all seriousness his preference for death should he
no longer be able to think productively. To Moore he praised fertility
and derided conclusions. To members of the Vienna Circle he insisted
that theory gave him nothing, that for him it was "without value." To
Russell he praised the science of logic because it was, to him, a science
that was infinitely strange; and later on, when he was expounding new
thoughts about language, he again confronted Russell with a vision of
language that was protean and infinitely strange. For Renan, Frazer,
Eddington, Jeans, and their likes, who, in his view, endeavored to explain
mysteries or simplify complexities, he offered nothing but the harshest
criticism.

In revealing the importance of Wittgenstein's "particular experience"
for his work and the simultaneous function of his work in the evocation
of his sense of wonder, I have thus far ignored the significance his sense
of wonder had for his everyday life. Norman Malcolm, one of Wittgenstein's closest friends from about 1938 through 1951, notes in his *Memoir*
the significance of Wittgenstein's experience. "I believe," Malcolm says,
"that a certain feeling of amazement that *anything should exist at all*
[Malcolm's emphasis], was sometimes experienced by Wittgenstein, not

[29] Norman Malcolm, *Ludwig Wittgenstein: A Memoir* (Oxford, 1984), 83.

only during the *Tractatus* period, but also when I knew him."[30] In the new edition of his *Memoirs* Malcolm confesses that he tended in his original memoir to overlook or not to have given due emphasis to Wittgenstein's preoccupation with such matters. This is an important confession from someone who emphasized, in the first place, the apparent significance a "feeling of amazement" had for Wittgenstein. Malcolm amends his original characterization of Wittgenstein as "fiercely unhappy." He notes Wittgenstein's numerous friendships that "were surely a source of richness in his life." In his consideration of the potential "richness" of Wittgenstein's life Malcolm's emphasis is not on friendships however. He emphasizes rather the good emotional effects arising from "prolonged and intensive intellectual work." Through philosophical work, Malcolm argues, Wittgenstein was "continually arriving at fresh insights, seeing connections between one region of thought and another, spotting false analogies, trying out new ways of tackling the problems that have kept philosophy in turmoil for many centuries."[31] Malcolm is convinced that this "activity of creation and discovery" gave Wittgenstein delight; I would go further and say that this activity produced in Wittgenstein the sense of things that he valued most highly. Malcolm's latest thoughts point out that it was in large measure because of philosophical work that Wittgenstein could experience "joy and much that was 'wonderful.'"

Wittgenstein's ethical value was, if anything, more conspicuously displayed in his behavior than in this work. Engelmann describes Wittgenstein reading passages from Möricke with "a shudder of awe" and tells how, upon hearing the sounds of a quartet, he was "carried away by passion."[32] Drury recalls attending a sermon with Wittgenstein during which Wittgenstein "leant over and whispered . . ., 'I am not listening to a word he is saying. But think about the text, that is wonderful, that is really wonderful.'"[33] Fania Pascal noted that "To watch him in a state of hushed, silent awe, as though looking far beyond what oneself could see, was an experience next only to hearing him talk."[34] She continued, "that there was nobody else who could . . . make you feel that your mind was stretched, thrown of its course, forced to look at matters it had never considered before."[35] What he appeared to seek was the "newly created piece of art or a divine revelation."[36]

---

[30] *Ibid.*, 58-59.

[31] *Ibid.*, 84 (Appendix, #4).

[32] P. Engelmann, *Letters from Wittgenstein*, 86 and 90.

[33] M' O. C. Drury, in *Ludwig Wittgenstein, Personal Recollections*, ed. Rush Rhees (Oxford, 1981), 146.

[34] Fania Pascal, in *Ludwig Wittgenstein, Personal Recollections*, 33-34.

[35] *Ibid.*, 42.

[36] Rudolf Carnap, in *Ludwig Wittgenstein: The Man and His Philosophy*, ed. K. T. Fann (New York, 1967), 34-35.

240   PETER C. JOHN

This desire is displayed in his attitude to the work of others. Russell recalls that Wittgenstein "spoke with intense feeling about the *beauty* of the [*Principia*]"; "he found it like music."[37] Pascal recalls him "picking up [a] volume of Grimm's tales and reading out with awe in his voice 'Ach, wie gut ist dass niemand weiss dass ich Rumpelstilzchen heiss.' " "Profound, profound," he exclaimed. She notes, "I liked *Rumpelstiltskin*, understood that the strength of the dwarf lay in his name being unknown to humans; but was unable to share Wittgenstein's vision."[38] About Tolstoy's *Hadji Murat* Wittgenstein wrote to Russell, "Have you read it? If not, you ought to for it is *wonderful* [Wittgenstein's emphasis]."[39] In another letter he commends Russell for having read the lives of Mozart and Beethoven because, he exclaims, "These are the actual sons of God."[40] Pascal even notes the expression of Wittgenstein's values in the manner of his gaze. He "showed me around the Fellow's Garden," she writes, "stood in awe before some plant saying 'You can almost see it grow hourly. . . .' "[41] And as is to be expected, Wittgenstein's ethical criterion expressed itself as he taught, a fact conveyed in the observations of Rudolf Carnap. Carnap observed that Wittgenstein's "point of view and his attitude toward people and problems, even theoretical problems, were much more similar to those of a creative artist than to those of a scientist; one might almost say, similar to those of a religious prophet or a seer."[42] Carnap also noted Wittgenstein's "internal struggle" when engaged in philosophical thought, a struggle "visible on his most expressive face." He continues: "When finally, sometimes after a prolonged arduous effort, his answer came forth, his statement stood before us like a newly created piece of art or a divine revelation. . . . [T]he impression he made on us was as if insight came to him as through a divine inspiration, so that we could not help feeling that any sober rational comment or analysis of it would be a profanation." A student expressed much of this in the succinct observation that "We have never *seen* a man thinking before."[43] Carnap's description is also captured in what C. van Peursen called Wittgenstein's style of "thinking aloud."[44]

The profoundly serious, which Carnap practically views as the "revelatory," nature of Wittgenstein's thought and speech conveyed itself to others. Frank Ramsey, who travelled from Cambridge to Austria during the early 1920s to engage Wittgenstein in discussion about the *Tractatus*, came to appreciate his seriousness. In 1924 he wrote to Keynes in an

---

[37] *Sein Leben in Bilden und Texten*, 74.
[38] F. Pascal, 33-34.
[39] *Letters to Russell, Keynes and Moore* (Cornell, 1974), 16.
[40] *Ibid.*, 15.
[41] F. Pascal, 42.
[42] R. Carnap, 34-35.
[43] Karl Britton, in *Ludwig Wittgenstein: The Man and His Philosophy*, 61.
[44] *Ludwig Wittgenstein: An Introduction to his Philosophy* (London, 1969), 11.

attempt to explain Wittgenstein's apparent reluctance to visit England: "To come to Cambridge and just to go out to tea and see people, is, he thinks, not merely not worthwhile, but positively bad because such intercourse would merely distract him from his contemplation without offering any alternative good."[45] Precisely the same sentiment was expressed by Wittgenstein to Norman Malcolm when Wittgenstein decided to visit the United States and was faced with the prospect of having to travel by car for several hours with someone whom he suspected would have attempted to engage him in chit-chat.[46]

It would be very easy to interpret Wittgenstein's behavior in this regard as sheer rudeness; but this would ignore entirely his persistent struggle to think, speak, and behave in a manner which was true to what he recognized as valuable. Wittgenstein sought to appreciate the world in a way that was not simply given but had to be striven for. Pascal recognized that he "was driven to distraction by the manner in which people spoke."[47] It was in an attempt to minimize the distractions of his world that Wittgenstein would often behave abruptly. We can see the same motivation in his choice of places to live and work. He has been characterized as arrogant, callous, and even mad; but when he is considered within the pattern of his entire life, his behavior appears no longer as aberrant but as deliberate attempts to achieve a certain goal.

What Wittgenstein sought upon successfully avoiding the perils of banality and matter-of-factness, was the "stretch[ing]," the "throw[ing] of course," that "forced [one] to look at matters it had never considered before." Wittgenstein sought in his own work and in the work of others, including the work of nature, the "newly created piece of art or a divine revelation." As Engelmann noted, what above all else had intellectual value for Wittgenstein was the "spontaneous idea." Ideas and understanding which came in a flash obliterating in an instant confusion and incoherence are what he esteemed.

Accordingly, he denigrated the tendency to mouth the teachings of others. He especially abhorred the thought that he himself should have followers, and so he never actually taught but merely thought and, if someone were willing, discussed. H. D. P. Lee recalls Wittgenstein's "insisting that (he) should think any problem out for himself."[48] Wittgenstein expressed surprise to Lee that one could be very interested in "other people's thoughts." He sternly berated G. E. Moore for lecturing upon Ward's views on psychology instead of Moore's own. Wittgenstein is paraphrased as having once said, "if we took a book seriously it ought to puzzle us so much that we would throw it across the room and think

---

[45] *Sein Leben in Bilden und Texten*, 191.
[46] N. Malcolm, Letters of 14/6/49 and 7/7/49.
[47] F. Pascal, 43.
[48] H. D. P. Lee, "Wittgenstein, 1929-1931," *Philosophia* (1979), 219.

about the problem for ourselves."[49] For his own part, Wittgenstein successfully avoided any formal training in philosophy; to the end of his days he managed never to have read Aristotle. But this was not done out of pride; he simply viewed one's own creation of a thought as much more valuable than one merely imbibed. He said of the *Tractatus* that its value would be if someone were to come along some day and create the entire work anew by their own efforts.[50]

Friedrich Waismann, noting in conversation with fellow member Moritz Schlick that Wittgenstein appeared to have the marvelous ability to look at things as if seeing them for the very first time,[51] describes this as if it were some innate talent. What he did not seem to realize is that this way of seeing was a skill Wittgenstein had struggled for and was to struggle for all of his life. Trying to see things as though for the first time was his deliberate means of struggling to resurrect in himself a sense of wonderment about that which exists.

Finally, what has long been a mystery to Malcolm and others who knew and cared about Wittgenstein, are the words he spoke just before his death in the house of a friend. Mrs. Bevan, the wife of the physician at whose house he was then living, records that shortly before he passed away Wittgenstein asked her, with supposed reference to his friends, to "tell them I've had a wonderful life."[52] These words struck Norman Malcolm, as "mysterious and strangely moving." The fundamental importance of wonder in Wittgenstein's life, however, should give us every reason to take his final words quite literally. That Wittgenstein should refer to his life as "wonderful" should be seen neither as pun nor as glib appraisal of his own life. On the basis of what we know of the man, his last words must be read as a profoundly sincere declaration of what he cherished above all else during his life.

What Wittgenstein sought in his life is identical to what he sought in his work. For a time, in his early years, these were at odds; but for the greater portion of his life Wittgenstein lived to wonder, and for this reason he lived to trace the limits of the known and thereby free himself to wonder at the mystery of what lay beyond.

University of California, San Diego.

---

[49] K. T. Fann, *Ludwig Wittgenstein: The Man and His Philosophy*, 58.

[50] See Ramsey's letter to his mother in Ludwig Wittgenstein, *Letters to C. K. Ogden* (Oxford, 1973), 78. Ramsey writes: "His idea of his book is not that anyone by reading it will understand his ideas, but that some day someone will think them out again for himself, and will derive great pleasure from finding in this book their exact expression."

[51] F. Waismann, 26.

[52] N. Malcolm, 81.

XIII

Hans-Georg Gadamer's "Correction" of Heidegger

Walter Lammi

Among the remarkable range of thinkers to have come under the influence of Martin Heidegger, the figure perhaps most deserving to be regarded as Heidegger's proper and faithful "heir" has been Hans-Georg Gadamer. Gadamer himself has always been quick to acknowledge the intellectual debt to his predecessor. Although the two men were only eleven years apart in age, their relationship to all appearances was very much one of master and pupil; never does Gadamer seem to take umbrage at being described as a "Heideggerian."[1] Indeed, he has characterized himself as a "student of Heidegger" who has "learned the craft of classical philology."[2]

However, Gadamer's reference to the classics in this connection raises an interesting question. Gadamer has also been known to say, quite flatly, "I am a Platonist."[3] How could this be possible? How could Gadamer consider himself a "Heideggerian" and a "Platonist" at the same time? At the least, the expression "Heideggerian Platonist" is an oxymoron that must refer to a strange sort of paradoxical figure.

We may add to this the puzzling difference simply in the surface of the two thinkers' work, in their writing styles. Although Gadamer has described his project in *Truth and Method*, his magnum opus, as following the later Heidegger's line of inquiry,[4] his straightforward discursive prose stands in marked contrast to the later Heidegger's "oracular" or quasi-poetic ruminations. Clearly language plays a central role to both thinkers—it is the "house of the truth of Being" to Heidegger, and according to a celebrated formulation by Gadamer, "Language is [that kind of] being

---

[1] See for example Leo Strauss's description of *Truth and Method* (henceforth *TM*) as the most important work by a "Heideggerian" (CG 5).

[2] Jürgen Habermas, *Philosophical-Political Profiles*, tr. Frederick G. Lawrence (Cambridge, 1983), 190.

[3] "Gadamer on Strauss: An Interview," *Interpretation*, 12 (1984), 10.

[4] "On the Problem of Self-Understanding," in *Philosophical Hermeneutics*, tr. David E. Linge (Berkeley, 1976), 50.

244   WALTER LAMMI

which can be understood."[5] Consequently, this "surface" difference is unlikely to be superficial.

The difference has led commentators to posit that Gadamer is in a sense domesticating Heidegger. Jürgen Habermas in a well-known *laudatio* to Gadamer describes the effect as "urbanizing the Heideggerian province."[6] In Habermas's view, the extreme radicality of Heidegger's thought creates a gulf between himself and his readers, an isolation that calls for a "bridge" to render his insights accessible. Gadamer's great achievement, then, has been to effect a kind of taming that nonetheless succeeds in following Heidegger "far enough to promote his thought productively and on a sound basis."[7]

But given the centrality of language to both thinkers, could such a change in style take place without decisively affecting substance? Could not one argue, on the same grounds on which Habermas praises Gadamer, that Gadamer has on the contrary rendered Heidegger familiar and acceptable at the cost of trivializing his thought?[8] As indicated by the poetic stylistic development of Heidegger's own work after *Being and Time*, the "divine madness" of the philosopher translates rather poorly into a scholarly medium.[9]

In reality, it will be argued here, Gadamer's "translation" of Heidegger also offers a fundamental corrective to Heidegger's thought. The corrective is connected, in turn, to Gadamer's "Platonism" and to his embrace of the "craft of classical philology." To grasp the nature of this corrective, it is necessary to sort out the rather complicated relationship between Gadamer and Heidegger (both the "early" Heidegger and the "late"). Of special importance are four issues: (1) the link between Gadamer and the early Heidegger on the question of "truth"; (2) the different postures assumed by Gadamer and Heidegger toward phenomenology ("method"); (3) the special significance for Gadamer of the late-Heidegger essay, "The Origin of the Work of Art"; and, most critically, (4) the two thinkers' different treatments of time, particularly in relation to (a) the importance of continuity versus discontinuity and (b) orientation toward the future versus orientation toward the past. At the end of this exploration we will discover that Gadamer is indeed in a sense a Platonist, having turned from a Heideggerian to what is arguably a more Platonic understanding

---

[5] *Sein, das verstanden werden kann, ist Sprache*, often but somewhat obscurely rendered as "Being that can be understood is language." The sentence is italicized in the original although not in the translation (*TM*,432; *WM*,450). We will return to this statement below.

[6] Habermas, *Profiles*, 190.

[7] *Ibid.*, 190-91.

[8] Robert Bernasconi offers this critique of Gadamer in "Bridging the Abyss: Heidegger and Gadamer," *Research in Phenomenology*, 16 (1986), 4.

[9] See Stanley Rosen, *Hermeneutics as Politics* (New York, 1987), 94: "Philological sobriety is a very admirable quality, but it pales into historical insignificance in the face of philosophical madness."

of reason, and of the relation between reason and experience, or reason and revelation.

I. The Question of Truth

It could be said that the the title of Gadamer's magnum opus *Truth and Method* is a misnomer because the book contains no theory of truth and is not about method.[10] The failure of *Truth and Method* to provide any explicitly developed theory of truth[11] has been cited as a prime example of how Gadamer rests the entire edifice of his thought on appeals to Heideggerian grounds.[12] Indeed, Gadamer does not hesitate to acknowledge his debt to Heidegger in regard to his approach to the meaning of "truth."

This debt involves both the early Heidegger, whose work culminated in *Being and Time*, and the later Heidegger following the experience of the "turn," or *Kehre*. It is of some interest in examining the influence of Heidegger on Gadamer to sort out the effects of the two. Gadamer himself professes primary identification with the later Heidegger. He has described *Truth and Method* as an attempt to express "within the hermeneutical consciousness itself" Heidegger's line of inquiry following the *Kehre*;[13] and, in context of both "truth" and what we may tentatively term the "way" of hermeneutics, he makes particular reference to Heidegger's groundbreaking essay, "The Origin of the Work of Art."[14]

However, it is also the case that the concept of truth in Gadamer's philosophical hermeneutics is based on Heidegger's radicalization of "hermeneutics,"[15] with his concept of the hermeneutical circle in *Being and*

---

[10] Although this argument is true enough as far as it goes, ultimately it lacks force because it misses the point of *Truth and Method*. Briefly put, that point is to describe how we find truth, which is not at all through any "theory of truth." As for "method," we will see that while Gadamer's hermeneutical approach to truth is relevant to judging the limitations of any formal method of gaining knowledge, including the "scientific," it is itself simply descriptive as opposed to "methodological."

[11] "Gadamer himself seldom mentions truth directly and nowhere formulates a coherent characterization of it in his own terms." Francis J. Ambrosio, "Dawn and Dusk: Gadamer and Heidegger on Truth," *Man and World*, 19 (1986), 39. A list of critics who have fastened on this lacuna in *Truth and Method* is provided by Brice R. Wachterhauser, "Must We Be What We Say? Gadamer on Truth in the Human Sciences," in *Hermeneutics and Modern Philosophy*, ed. Brice R. Wachterhauser (Albany, 1986), 220 and n. 7, 238.

[12] Bernasconi, "Bridging the Abyss," 3.

[13] Gadamer, "On the Problem of Self-Understanding," 50.

[14] See Gadamer's description of the deep impression this work made on Heidegger's students in "Heidegger's Later Philosophy (1960)," in *Philosophical Hermeneutics*, 216-17.

[15] Earlier "hermeneutics" referred usually to interpretation of the Bible; but not until Heidegger was it universalized to refer to the very structure of human being-in-the-world. See Josef Bleicher, *Contemporary Hermeneutics: Hermeneutics as Method, Philosophy and Critique* (London, 1980), 11-26.

Time.[16] The hermeneutical circle *per se* is limited to the early Heidegger, although the concept reappears in altered form in Heidegger's later thinking. In fact, after the *Kehre* Heidegger abandoned use of the very term "hermeneutics," an abandonment that Gadamer considers to have been a mistake.[17]

The hermeneutical circle had a fundamental role in the early Heidegger's thought. In *Being and Time* the circle describes Dasein's privileged access to Being by way of an intrinsic forestructure of understanding. To Heidegger the issue is not whether the circle is "vicious" but where and how we enter into it. That entry, Dasein's understanding of the truth, is always a temporal event.

In similar fashion the hermeneutical circle is the basis for human understanding in Gadamer's work. To Gadamer, as to Heidegger, understanding is an ontologically based mode of human being and not at all an "'act' of subjectivity." It is still to be conceived of dynamically[18]—it is always an "event"—but this event cannot accurately be characterized as a subject's becoming conscious of something as an object.[19] Gadamer is entirely in agreement with Heidegger's analysis of the forestructure of understanding, which he calls the "reading of what is there."[20] But to Gadamer the circle is primarily or paradigmatically to be understood as the *movement* between interpreter and text, in which the forestructure consists of the expectations or "prejudices" with which the interpreter necessarily begins his reading.[21] Thus in Gadamer's hermeneutical circle, as in Heidegger's, everything stands under anticipations so that there can be no object of understanding that is simply "there."[22]

In other words there is no pure perception or perfect objectivity that allows us to separate objects of knowledge from acts of interpretation. The minds of real people can never be likened to a "blank slate," and the anticipations that color our perceptions are shaped by personal experience. Gadamer adds that while the goal of textual interpretation is unquestionably to understand an author "in his sense," the expression "in his sense"

---

[16] Hans-Georg Gadamer, "Text and Interpretation," in *Hermeneutics and Modern Philosophy*, 378-79.

[17] *Ibid.*, 380.

[18] See Theodore Kisiel, "The Happening of Tradition: The Hermeneutics of Gadamer and Heidegger," in *Hermeneutics and Praxis*, ed. Robert Hollinger (Notre Dame, 1985), 9: ". . . understanding is an undergoing."

[19] See, for example, Hans-Georg Gadamer, "The Philosophic Foundations of the Twentieth Century," *Philosophical Hermeneutics*, 125.

[20] *TM*, 239.

[21] Roy J. Howard, *Three Faces of Hermeneutics: An Introduction to Current Theories of Understanding* (Berkeley, 1982), 147.

[22] At issue, Gadamer points out, is the "astounding naiveté of the subjective consciousness," which approaches a text with a sense of certainty that "that is what is written here!" ("Philosophical Foundations," 121).

GADAMER'S "CORRECTION" OF HEIDEGGER 247

is not to be taken as referring only to the author's intentions as subjective acts of meaning.[23]

Consideration of such influences has led to the criticism that Gadamer, his protestations to the contrary notwithstanding, is fundamentally an "early Heideggerian."[24] To buttress this conclusion, one need merely refer back to the question of how the two thinkers express themselves. Gadamer's discursive style bears much closer relation to the speculative Heidegger of *Being and Time* than to the quasi-poetic Heidegger of the works written after the *Kehre*. Furthermore, Gadamer's view of philosophy as a "natural" human inclination[25] seems to accord not with the later Heidegger's "end of philosophy" but with Dasein's intrinsic desire for understanding the truth of Being in *Being and Time*.[26]

The force of this criticism is that if in these crucial respects Gadamer is in fact an "early Heideggerian," it is hard to see how he avoids falling into the same linguistic and conceptual limitations of the traditional "metaphysics of presence" that led Heidegger to what Gadamer himself has called the "dead-end street"[27] of *Being and Time*. The early Heidegger believed that philosophical problems remain constant due to the "constancy of human nature,"[28] and in his earlier works he attempted to provide answers to those problems by way of scholarly analysis. Since *Being and Time* reflected both of these assumptions, there was no reason to finish the book if they were wrong. Heidegger believed that the errors of *Being and Time* were not at all personal but reflected the fundamental failure of post-Platonic Western metaphysics. This failure, summed up in the phrase "metaphysics of presence," consists of viewing truth not as the temporal *occurrence* of unconcealedness but as the *constant presence* of eternal objects.[29]

[23] *Ibid.*, 121-22. Between Heidegger's hermeneutic circle and Gadamer's addition or "radicalization" (122) is the decisive impetus of the "universalization" from Heidegger's "The Origin of the Work of Art." See below, Part III, 11ff.

[24] Bernasconi, "Bridging the Abyss," 12.

[25] Hans-Georg Gadamer, "On the Natural Inclination of Human Beings Toward Philosophy," in *Reason in the Age of Science*, tr. Frederick G. Lawrence (Cambridge, 1984), 139-150.

[26] Bernasconi, "Bridging the Abyss," 12.

[27] Hans-Georg Gadamer, "Heidegger's Paths," tr. C. Kayser and G. Stack, *Philosophical Exchange* 2 (1979), 87.

[28] Quoted from the beginning of Heidegger's *Habilitationsschrift* by Otto Pöggeler in *Martin Heidegger's Path of Thinking*, tr. Daniel Magurshak and Sigmund Barber (Atlantic Highlands, 1987), 13.

[29] Heidegger's critique of the "metaphysics of presence" is clearly explained in his seminal essay "Plato's Doctrine of Truth," tr. by Joan Stambaugh in W. Barrett and H. D. Aiken (eds.), *Philosophy in the Twentieth Century* (New York, 1962), 251-270. Gadamer's agreement with the later Heidegger's emphasis on temporality does not imply endorsement of Heidegger's Platonic scholarship, which has been subjected to devastating criticism by a number of scholars. (See, for example, William A. Galston, "Heidegger's Plato: A Critique of *Plato's Doctrine of Truth*," *The Philosophical Forum*, 13 [1982], 371-84. The

248   WALTER LAMMI

The transformation, and ultimate elimination, of the question of truth in Heidegger's later writings has influenced Gadamer in a different and more subtle direction. This will be taken up after discussion of the question of method because it involves a thematic collapse of the two questions in Gadamer's treatment of the philosophical tradition—a treatment that, it will be argued, ends up by departing from Heidegger in an important way.

II. Phenomenology and the Question of Method

That *Truth and Method* fails to address issues of methodology is stressed by Gadamer himself. In no way is that book intended to provide a method in the sense of normative rules of procedure for the human sciences or *Geisteswissenschaften* parallel to the methodologies of the natural sciences, and in the foreword to the second edition Gadamer takes care to correct a common misapprehension to the contrary.[30] His concern is instead solely with what we actually do when we seek understanding, whether of texts, works of art, or the world, whether we are aware of what we are doing or not.[31] The scope of hermeneutics as developed by Gadamer is intended to be universal,[32] and consequently he insists that hermeneutics underlies the natural as well as the human sciences.[33] Hermeneutics "only describes what always happens whenever an interpretation is convincing and successful." This means that it is nothing other than—philosophy.[34] Hermeneutics is "practical philosophy," by which Gadamer means "a theoretical attitude toward the practice of interpretation."[35]

Thus the "method" of *Truth and Method* itself is descriptive or, as Gadamer puts it, "phenomenological." While granting that this may seem paradoxical, inasmuch as his hermeneutics is avowedly based on Heidegger's "turn" away from the last vestiges of transcendental phenomenology,[36] Gadamer nonetheless believes that it is possible to retain a meaningful sense of "phenomenology" from both Husserl and the early

---

history of scholarly criticism is discussed in Robert J. Dostal, "Heidegger's Plato," *Journal of the History of Philosophy*, 23 [1985], 71-98.)

[30] *TM*, xvi-xvii.

[31] Kisiel, "Heidegger and Gadamer," 5.

[32] See, for example, "Aesthetics and Hermeneutics," in *Philosophical Hermeneutics*, 103.

[33] *TM*, 432-33.

[34] Hans-Georg Gadamer, "Hermeneutics as Practical Philosophy," *Reason in the Age of Science*, 111.

[35] *Ibid.*, 112.

[36] Gadamer has described the *Kehre* as precisely Heidegger's attempt to "reshape his own project so as to dissociate it completely from the Husserlian model. . . ." "Heidegger and the History of Philosophy," 437.

Heidegger's hermeneutical "theory of the real experience that thinking is."[37]

In the late 1950s Heidegger visited a seminar conducted by Gadamer, in the course of which he asked the students what the connection was between Husserl's analysis of internal time-consciousness[38] and his own study of time in *Being and Time*. Rejecting every attempted answer, he finally explained: There was none![39] Gadamer tells this anecdote to illustrate the decisiveness with which the later Heidegger rejected the entire approach of his teacher Husserl's phenomenology—a decisiveness that is hardly historically justified as applied to the Heidegger of *Being and Time*.[40]

Gadamer is not in accord with this attitude.[41] However, he is also unwilling to grant "phenomenology" a univocal meaning, in recognition of Husserl's failure to establish it as a "strict science." In philosophy, he says, there can be no such thing as an objective "methodological technique": "One's own philosophical standpoint always shines through [one's] description of the basic meaning of phenomenology."[42] This is consistent with his refusal to supply any method in *Truth and Method*; but it leaves unclear what Gadamer means by characterizing his own procedure as phenomenological, other than the vague or tautological meaning of "descriptive."

This issue can be clarified by looking at specific insights that Gadamer in various writings says he has appropriated from Husserl and the phenomenological movement. For the purposes of the present discussion two of these are of particular importance: the phenomenological concept of "horizon" and the phenomenological analysis of the "intentional object," particularly in regard to the "thing-in-itself."

The concept of "horizon" in phenomenology was not originally Husserlian but appropriated from Friedrich Nietzsche. The concept of "horizon" plays an important role in Nietzsche's thought. It is a limiting concept in that human beings cannot see beyond their historical or cultural horizons. Yet this limitation is a prerequisite for health, and ultimately for life itself. Nietzsche formulates this as a "general law": "Every living

---

[37] *TM*, xxiv.

[38] Heidegger was the editor of the published portions of Husserl's voluminous studies of internal time-consciousness.

[39] Gadamer, "Heidegger's Paths," 83.

[40] To simplify somewhat, Heidegger's analysis in *Being and Time* retains Husserl's notion of intentionality but reapplies it from "consciousness" to Dasein's entire being-in-the-world (Jitendra Nath Mohanty, *The Concept of Intentionality* [St. Louis, 1972], 129).

[41] He speaks of the "phenomenological craftsmanship" that was "all too quickly forgotten by the scholarship of the time." Hans-Georg Gadamer, "Heidegger and the Language of Metaphysics (1967)," *Philosophical Hermeneutics*, 230.

[42] Hans-Georg Gadamer, "The Phenomenological Movement (1963)," *Philosophical Hermeneutics*, 143.

250   WALTER LAMMI

thing can become healthy, strong and fruitful only within a horizon . . ."
Everything depends on a person's ability to "forget at the right time as
well as to remember at the right time."[43] According to this perspective,
the term "historicism" means insight into the essential relativity of all
horizons. Historicism for Nietzsche is a great but life-destroying truth
because it takes away our ability to believe absolutely in anything. Nothing
is meaningful in itself, yet it is essential that we believe in something—
which can apparently be almost anything—for in freeing ourselves from
"the tyranny of capricious laws" by recognizing that they are capricious,
we end up destroying the source of cultural vitality.[44]

The concept of "horizon" is also fundamental to Husserl, not so much
in the sense of overall cultural limitations as on the level of personal
experience, where implicit horizons of before and after require focusing
on one thing at a necessary cost of forgetting or ignoring an infinity of
others. However, in Husserl's investigation, which ultimately concerned
the inner experience of time-consciousness, the horizons of one experience
flow into those of another so that in the continuum of experiences there
is a constant flux of horizons. "Horizon," then, to Husserl as opposed to
Nietzsche, is in no way a static concept.[45]

From Husserl's studies Gadamer developed the concept of "horizon"
for hermeneutical purposes of his own. In so doing he reexamined
Nietzsche's concept and arrived at what amounts to a fundamental critique of the assumption that knowledge is relative to temporal or historical
conditions. On the one hand Gadamer, like Nietzsche, understands "horizon" to denote the finite limitations of any particular perspective at any
particular time.[46] However, he interprets Nietzsche as believing that a
horizon can be simply "closed," which in Gadamer's judgment constitutes
a "romantic reflection, a kind of Robinson Crusoe dream,"[47] because just
as no individual exists without others, no cultural or historical horizon
exists in static and total isolation from others.[48] Horizons, most particularly the horizon of the past that we call "tradition," are always in motion
just as human life is always in motion.[49] There is no historical consciousness in the sense of Nietzsche's "historicist insight" that sets the horizons
into motion; all historical consciousness does is make that motion aware

---

[43] Friedrich Nietzsche, "On the Advantage and Disadvantage of History for Life," tr.
Peter Preuss (Indianapolis, 1980), 10.

[44] See Friedrich Nietzsche, *Beyond Good and Evil*, tr. Walter Kaufmann (New York,
1966), 100-102 (aphorism 188).

[45] Cf. *TM*, 216.

[46] *TM*, 269.

[47] *Ibid.*, 271.

[48] Gadamer's interpretation of Nietzsche is problematic on this point. Whether or not
his critique is on target, however, Gadamer's positive argument for the dynamic concept
of "horizon" remains cogent.

[49] *Ibid.*, 217.

of itself.[50] The awareness that our horizons are fluid, rather than teaching that nothing is true, makes it possible to find new truths—to "expand our horizons," as the saying has it.

Thus the self-awareness of historical consciousness, far from being a "deadly truth" about the relativity of all values, is for Gadamer the key for reaching beyond or behind a given horizon to confront the possibility that there is truth to be learned from the past. "I am convinced of the fact that, quite simply, we can learn from the classics," Gadamer concludes.[51] Nietzsche's historicism is true in the sense that time and place set limits: "To exist historically means that knowledge of oneself can never be complete."[52] But it fails to understand temporal distance as a positive aid to discovering truth,[53] which is the way Gadamer understands the interpreter's hermeneutical situation once it is brought to self-consciousness. This self-consciousness is what he terms "consciousness of the history of influence,"[54] and to Gadamer the whole point of historical studies is to trace concepts back through the history of their influence to the point of awakening their "real, living, evocative meaning."[55] At that point, the interpreter has achieved the before-mentioned "fusion of horizons." Gadamer views the "central problem" of hermeneutics, which he calls the "problem of application," as precisely the task of that tracing—the task, in other words, of "consciousness of the history of influence" to bring about the interpretive understanding[56] of a text's claim to truth, which is what constitutes a "fusion of horizons."[57]

It is clear that this sort of historical study departs fundamentally from Husserl's approach to phenomenology as pure ahistorical description of experience[58] despite its debt to his concept of "horizon." The purpose here is to explicate Gadamer's self-termed "phenomenological" approach from its roots in the phenomenological movement, not to conflate and thereby confuse the two.

The second "methodologically" important concept that Gadamer appropriates from phenomenology concerns the "intentional object." This

---

[50] *Ibid.*, 271.

[51] *Ibid.*, 490.

[52] *Ibid.*, 269.

[53] Cf. Howard, *Three Faces of Hermeneutics*, 148.

[54] The German terms *Wirkungsgeschichte* and *wirkungsgeschichtliches Bewusstsein* are misleadingly translated throughout the English translation of *Truth and Method* and elsewhere as "effective-history" and "effective-historical consciousness." Here they will be rendered more accurately as "history of the influence" and "consciousness of the history of influence" respectively. (I am indebted to Professor George L. Kline at Bryn Mawr College for both pointing out this problem and suggesting the solution.)

[55] "Philosophical Foundations," 127.

[56] Understanding to Gadamer always involves interpretation. See, for example, *TM*, 274: "Interpretation is the explicit form of understanding."

[57] *TM*, 274.

[58] "Philosophical Foundations," 127.

252 WALTER LAMMI

is the object of consciousness as temporally constituted in consciousness. Gadamer's is also a highly selective appropriation. Gadamer agrees with Heidegger's rejection of the notion of a pure consciousness characterized by intentionality,[59] but nonetheless he sees merit in the notion that any object, i.e., something that is "out there," only exists for us via our perspectives on it. This does not mean that the object is simply relative to our (historically conditioned) perspectives; Gadamer does not deny its reality as itself—as, that is, the "thing-in-itself." But he follows Husserl's approach to the "thing-in-itself," which is to say that phenomenologically speaking, it is "nothing other than the continuity with which the shades of the various perspectives of the perception of objects pass into one another."[60] To turn this point around, in every perspective on the world the existence of a "world-in-itself" is implied. The presence of many world-views does not relativize the world that is being viewed.

This is why Gadamer can say in the Foreword to the second edition of *Truth and Method* that "the idea of a work-in-itself, divorced from its constantly renewed reality of being experienced, always has something abstract about it." This means that while it is quite possible and may even be necessary for the interpreter to intend or seek to understand the work as it is in itself—that is, definitively—that goal is in reality unattainable. Gadamer's principle that understanding necessarily involves interpretation[61] means that while on the one hand understanding can never be arbitrary or merely subjective behavior toward the given "object," on the other hand the claim to a definitive understanding is necessarily a "dogmatic solution."[62]

In light of the above discussion, it becomes clearer why Gadamer should choose to call his approach "phenomenological" despite his Heideggerian roots. This bears directly on the issue, which has been raised but not resolved, of Heidegger's influence on Gadamer, particularly of the relative influence of the early and late Heidegger. There are two ways to look at the matter. One is to view this debt to phenomenology, which is largely in accord with *Being and Time*, as further evidence that despite Gadamer's own belief that his work is primarily based on the post-*Kehre* Heidegger, he is really just an early Heideggerian who is consequently entangled anew in the perennial "metaphysics of presence." The other is to take Gadamer at his word, in which case his phenomenology may indicate not so much a dependence on the early Heidegger as an independence from Heidegger altogether. To resolve this issue it is necessary to examine first, Gadamer's claimed debt to the later Heidegger, and second,

---

[59] Cf. Mohanty, *The Concept of Intentionality*, 129-32.
[60] *TM*, 406.
[61] *Ibid.*, 274.
[62] *Ibid.*, xix.

his relation to the tradition and understanding of the "metaphysics of presence."

III. Legacies of the Later Heidegger: The Work of Art

In "The Origin of the Work of Art," Heidegger discusses a number of themes that are central to his later, post-*Kehre* thinking. For Heidegger the work of art originates not, as "common sense" and nineteenth-century aesthetics would have it, from the artist or his "genius" but rather from the "essence" of art, which is its truth.[63] The work of art, that is, the "great" work of art, is not merely a manifestation of truth, but an "event" in which truth comes to be as something "standing in itself" that "opens up its own world."[64] In the creation of the work of art the happening of truth shows its historicity by virtue not of entering, but of "making" history anew. The founding of a political state is another such event. A thinker's essential questioning provides yet another.[65]

In all of these events, for which the work of art is paradigmatic, the accomplishment is an historical event whose meaning consequently stands quite apart from the subjective intentions of the artist, statesman, or thinker. Heidegger's essay effectively extends the hermeneutical analysis of Dasein's truth and Being in *Being and Time* into the realm of art,[66] and behind the experience of art appears "the whole universality of the hermeneutic experience."[67] The distinction between the meaning of the work of art and its creator's subjective intentions underlies Gadamer's hermeneutical principle that understanding a text is independent of "what the author meant."[68]

The idea that the work of art brings its own world with it leads directly to Gadamer's focus on the relation between the work and our encounter with it; this relation to Gadamer, as to Heidegger, has priority over its relata. The relation is nothing other than the previously discussed "fusion of horizons."[69] Thus Gadamer's use of the concept "horizon" is developed

---

[63] Heidegger, "Origin," 57 ff. The issue of "genius" in the theory of aesthetics is discussed in Part I of *TM*.

[64] Gadamer, "Heidegger's Later Philosophy," 222.

[65] Heidegger, "Origin," 62.

[66] Richard E. Palmer, *Hermeneutics* (Evanston, 1969), 159. The circle also reappears in aesthetics: we can know what the work of art is only from the essence of art; yet we must infer the essence of art from works of art. Heidegger, "Origin," 18.

[67] Hans-Georg Gadamer, "Martin Heidegger and Marburg Theology (1964)," *Philosophical Hermeneutics*, 201.

[68] *Ibid.*, 210.

[69] "Editor's Introduction" to Hans-Georg Gadamer, *The Relevance of the Beautiful and Other Essays*, ed. Robert Bernasconi (Cambridge, 1986), xiii. Cf. *TM*, 273: "Understanding . . . is always the fusion of these horizons which we imagine to exist by themselves."

not only from the phenomenology of Husserl and the early Heidegger but also and more directly from the transformations of Heidegger's *Kehre*.

It is now generally acknowledged that the *Kehre* did not constitute a "reversal" in Heidegger's thought.[70] Even the characterization of it as representing a shift in perspective from Dasein's understanding of the meaning of Being to the truth of Being (and eventually to what Heidegger calls the "topology of Being")[71] appears in the present context not exactly wrong but overly simplistic. The question is, what does such a "shift in perspective" mean? The later Heidegger's abandonment of such terms as "Dasein," "hermeneutics," and even "truth" itself does not mean that he simply abandoned the concepts represented by those terms. It is rather the case that he reassessed and reworked them again and again, so that to convey the "way" of his thought he was forced to find new means of linguistic expression.

For example, the elimination of "Dasein" in the effort of the later Heidegger to think "Being" without beings by no means calls for a concept of "Being" as somehow disembodied. It means rather that the manifestations of Being in different "epochs" take on varied significance, so that there is no single, univocal sense of "There-being" to warrant the term "Dasein." The "history of Being" is no less essentially tied to human being.[72] While Gadamer's refusal to follow the path of the later Heidegger's quasi-poetic expression remains to be satisfactorily explained, it is now possible to understand how he could claim to be expressing the thought of the *Kehre* in *Truth and Method* while retaining key terms of the early Heidegger. It has become clear with the concepts of "hermeneutics," "horizon," and the "meaning" of the work of art that the issue is whether and how his appropriation and development of terms found in the early Heidegger reflect the transformations of the *Kehre*.

In light of these considerations, it is useful to return to the discussion of Gadamer's notion of truth as it relates to the later Heidegger. The transformation of "truth" in "The Origin of the Work of Art" may be summed up as "putting truth to work."[73] In the work of art truth is established in an absolutely unique way, as the "bringing forth of a being

---

[70] This is the thrust of Heidegger's letter to Richardson in the Foreword of *Through Phenomenology to Thought*. See also David Krell, "Nietzsche in Heidegger's *Kehre*," 198-99, and Calvin O. Schrag, "The Transvaluation of Aesthetics and the Work of Art," *Thinking About Being*, 123.

[71] The "topology of Being" is among the late Heidegger's most opaque and poetic concepts. To explain it would be beyond the scope of this essay, as well as the competence of its author. A simplistic summary is that Heidegger attempts poetically to "locate" Being by bringing its traces "home" in language.

[72] David Farrell Krell, *Intimations of Mortality: Time, Truth, and Finitude in Heidegger's Thinking of Being* (University Park, 1986), 103.

[73] Cf. Heidegger, "Origin," 39.

such as never was before and will never come to be again."[74] The origin of the work of art concerns that truth "from which an openness of beings can first actually show itself."[75]

From the uniqueness of art's manifestation of truth, Gadamer concludes that philosophy cannot subsume art. As much as commentary and interpretation can facilitate the experience of the work of art, they cannot exhaust its claim to truth. Art, Gadamer says, "resists pure conceptualization."[76] This is not to deny that it can be understood. There is a "language of art,"[77] the understanding of which requires a combination of historical or hermeneutical consciousness and openness to the work's claim to truth as it "addresses us directly as if it showed us ourselves."[78] In Gadamer's formulation the inexhaustibility or ultimate resistance to translation of meaning in the work of art shows an "excess of meaning" that is present in each work of the "language of art."[79]

What, then, "is" this truth that is being claimed? Here, once again, the question "what it is" becomes inseparable from "how it is." Truth in the origin of the work of art comes to be as an interplay or "dialectic"[80] of truth and untruth, or *a-lētheia* and *lēthē*. In this context Heidegger introduces the concept of "earth," which with the term "world" constitutes a preliminary formulation of the "fourfold" of his later development of the concept "truth" (and abandonment of the term) in the previously mentioned "topology of Being" (in which the term "Being" is also eventually abandoned).

Gadamer views the concept of "earth" as the "new and startling" element in the "Origin of the Work of Art."[81] The concept of "world" had been developed in *Being and Time* as the horizon of Dasein's forestructure of knowledge, but "earth" added an essentially poetic note, a "mythical and gnostic" counterpart to "world."[82] The truth of art as self-presentation of Being comes to presence through the struggle of "world" and "earth" in which a "clearing" (*Lichtung*) or open space is created for the event of truth. "Earth" represents self-concealment as "world" does openness. It is that out of which the self-presentation arises, and into which it disappears.[83] Every genuine work of art carries with it

---

[74] *Ibid.*, 62.

[75] Pöggeler, *Path*, 107.

[76] Gadamer, "The Relevance of the Beautiful," *Relevance* 37.

[77] *TM*, 432.

[78] *Ibid.*, 11.

[79] Gadamer, "Aesthetics and Hermeneutics," *Philosophical Hermeneutics*, 102.

[80] C. D. Keyes, "Truth as Art: An Interpretation of Heidegger's *Sein und Zeit* (Sec.44) and *Der Ursprung Des Kunstwerkes*," in Sallis (ed.), *Heidegger and the Path of Thinking*, 70-71.

[81] Gadamer, "Heidegger's Later Philosophy," 217.

[82] *Ibid.*

[83] *Ibid.*, 223.

an "incomplete history" of simultaneous concealment and unconcealment so that its very finiteness displays the infinite variability or "unfathomable depth" of truth.[84] In the tension of world and earth is the abiding or repose of that self-presentation, alongside of which the beholder must also tarry.[85] Thus it is only a step beyond Gadamer's own explanation to interpret the import of the struggle and interconnection of "earth" and "world" as a matter of *time*.

As the *"becoming and happening of truth,"*[86] art is an event not only in its origin but in every instance of genuine interpretation or understanding. Thus an essential element of the truth of art is its representation,[87] and in each of its eventful occasions we to whom it is represented experience the presence of its truth as sudden and unfamiliar. In these closely related aspects of the work of art we come to the center of Heidegger's analysis.

The sudden arrival of meaning in the work of art combined with the necessity of tarrying alongside its abiding self-presentation characterize the critical elements of discontinuity and continuity within temporality. Since the work of art is history in the "essential sense that it grounds history,"[88] at issue is the nature of historical discontinuity and continuity.

The element of discontinuity is expressed in a concept that Heidegger appropriates from his study of early or "primordial" Christianity, the *kairos*.[89] The *kairos* is time reckoned not in linear fashion but according to significant events, in the first instance the coming of Christ. Thus the *kairos* reflects how history is made and made anew in a way that cannot be calculated in advance but appears as a sudden arrival, "as a thief in the night."[90]

Heidegger's analysis of the work of art represents a decisive development of the *kairos* not simply as the suddenness of novelty in the historical moment but as a present dependent upon a future toward which there is a gathering of the past in "fulfilled" time.[91] This is the "abiding" or "tarrying" within the tension of world and earth in the work of art. The strangeness of truth happens in the "intimacy of the battle"[92] of this abiding of world and earth.

---

[84] Pöggeler, " 'Historicity' in Heidegger's Late Work," 63.

[85] Gadamer, "Heidegger's Later Philosophy," 222-23.

[86] Heidegger, "Origin," 71. Emphasis in the original.

[87] *TM*, 104. Gadamer goes on to characterize this representation as "play": "We started from the position that the work of art is play, i.e., that its actual being cannot be detached from its representation and that in the representation the unity and identity of a structure emerge" (109).

[88] "Origin," 77.

[89] See the discussion of Heidegger's relation to primordial Christianity in Pöggeler, *Path*, 24-31.

[90] I Thess., 5.

[91] Pöggeler, "Historicity," 60.

[92] Heidegger, "Origin," 77.

To explicate the concept of "abiding," Gadamer refers to the historical origins of art in religious dance and festivals. In the performance of dance and, more clearly, the re-creation of festival, the events are joined not simply "in" time, but take on a time of their own. "Festival time" is not just a span of hours or days, but a special kind of time with a special mood (*Stimmung*)—that is, a special way of being. Fulfilled time is autonomous time, that is, time that stands apart from the ongoing temporal movement of external nature.[93] In the special way that we have to learn how to tarry with the work of art in order to experience it, Gadamer finds a kind of temporality that is "perhaps the only way that is granted to us finite beings to relate to what we call eternity."[94]

In order to understand Heidegger's rejection of transhistorical and atemporal truth, the critical question becomes: what sort of discontinuity and continuity does this special sort of time imply? "Real knowledge," Gadamer has written, "has to recognize the *kairos*."[95] But for Gadamer, above all it is "precisely continuity that every understanding of time has to achieve, even when it is a question of the temporality of a work of art."[96] For Heidegger, as we see in the next section, this is not so clear.

IV. Continuity vs. Discontinuity

The substantively most apparent and perhaps also most fundamental difference between Heidegger and Gadamer, which bears on their contrasting modes of expression, is between Gadamer's orientation toward the historical past versus Heidegger's orientation toward the future. For Gadamer the primary task may be described as one of remembrance, which requires an "unceasing conversation" with the tradition. For Heidegger conversation with the tradition is only instrumental toward the thinking of Being, so remembrance always remains a secondary task.[97] In a well-known passage Gadamer himself articulates this difference:

Heidegger, who first described the idea of understanding as the universal determinateness of There-being [*Dasein*], means the very projective character of understanding, i.e., the futural character of There-being [*Dasein*]. I shall not deny, however, that within the universal context of the elements of understandings I have emphasized the element of the assimilation of what is past and handed down. Heidegger also, like many of my critics, would probably feel the lack of an ultimate radicality in the drawing of [my] conclusions. . . . When science . . . brings on the "cosmic night" on the "forgetfulness of being," the nihilism that Nietzsche prophesied, then may one look at the last fading light of the sun that

[93] Gadamer, "The Relevance of the Beautiful," 42.

[94] *Ibid.*, 45.

[95] Gadamer, "Hermeneutics as a Theoretical and Practical Task," *Reason in the Age of Science*, 121.

[96] *TM*, 109.

[97] Francis J. Ambrosio, "Dawn and Dusk: Gadamer and Heidegger on Truth," 47.

has set in the evening sky, instead of turning around to look for the first shimmer of its return?[98]

In this description Gadamer seems to be expressing no more than a preference, a difference merely of emphasis rather than of substance. It is fair to accuse Gadamer of being disingenuous if his preference turns out to have substantive implications. To the extent that Gadamer's view of the history of philosophy differs from that of Heidegger, this difference of temporal focus will magnify the importance of their disagreement. Is Gadamer being less than forthright about the depth of his disagreement with Heidegger?

Such in fact seems to be the case. It is no mere conflict of taste that Gadamer sees in history or the tradition[99] an essential continuity where Heidegger finds an irreducible element of discontinuity. This distinction is assumed in Habermas's *laudatio* to Gadamer, with its contrast of Heidegger's radical break and Gadamer's attempt to build a bridge.[100]

This argument goes to the heart of Gadamer's intellectual relation to Heidegger. One way to conceptualize Heidegger's view of historical discontinuity is in terms of his formulation of "epochs" of Being:

The history of Being means destiny of Being in whose sendings both the sending and the It which sends forth hold back with their self-manifestation. To hold back is, in Greek, *epoche*. Hence we speak of the epochs of the destiny of Being [*Seinsgeschick*]. . . . The sequence of epochs [cannot] be calculated as necessary. . . . The epochs overlap each other in their sequence so that the original sending of Being as presence is more and more obscured in different ways.[101]

The sequence cannot be calculated as necessary because it is not simply continuous. What is "sent" in the history of Being that in an essential sense "holds back," yet nonetheless sends itself, can be described (insofar as the matter—the "mystery"—permits description at all) as an "excess" of Being. In this case "any attempt to understand that history as continuous expels the excess of Being," thereby denying Heidegger's "central insight."[102]

Thus epochal events are those in which the overlapping epochs of Being have been "sent" to found the epochs of history, which culminate in the "greatest danger" of the modern age of technology. That Gadamer agrees at least to some extent with this view is indicated by his mention of the "cosmic night" of the "forgetfulness of Being"; with Heidegger, he

---

[98] *TM*, xxv, translation slightly revised.

[99] The close relationship of "history" and "the tradition" is expressed in Gadamer's work by the concept of "consciousness of the history of influence," to which we return below (*TM*, 416).

[100] Cf. Bernasconi, "Bridging the Abyss," 5.

[101] Heidegger, "Time and Being," 9.

[102] Bernasconi, "Bridging the Abyss," 5.

thinks that modernity is defined "quite unequivocally" by the emergence of modern science.[103] That is Heidegger's grand view, in which the *kairos* is the epochal sending of Being as the delimitation of temporal truth. In order to understand what will turn out to be a subtle but ultimately important correction of this view by Gadamer, it is helpful to turn to another sense or "level" of the *kairos*, also suggested by the Biblical reference: "[T]hen sudden destruction cometh upon them, as travail upon a woman with child,"[104] or as the ever-unexpected arrival of our own death.

Heidegger grants priority to the future in the temporal constitution of Dasein in *Being and Time*. This priority is consistent with the epochal gifts of Being: "the origin always comes to meet us from the future."[105] This consistency provides another reminder of the element of continuity in Heidegger's thought after the *Kehre*; as Heidegger himself has stressed, the orientation after the *Kehre* is only possible on the basis of the existential analytic of *Being and Time*.[106] The reason for Dasein's future-orientation turns out to be its ultimate possibility—its *"ownmost* potentiality-for-Being"—which is nothing other than death.[107] Dasein's discovery of how to live authentically depends upon an anxious and resolute being-toward-death, and consequently toward the future.[108]

On this issue Gadamer takes specific exception to Heidegger's analysis. He points out that being-toward-death is unnecessary for establishing the essential temporality or finiteness of Dasein, since its basic constitution of being-in-the-world as "care" (*Sorge*) already establishes that finiteness. Indeed, after *Being and Time* Heidegger himself "never again placed the problematic of death at the center of his thought."[109] Thus while Heidegger retained his sense of the priority of the future after the *Kehre*, in respect to its original basis in the temporal analytic of Dasein it becomes to Gadamer highly questionable.

Probably because of Gadamer's general reluctance to take issue with Heidegger, as well as the relative prominence of his more gentle affirmation of difference in the Foreword to the second edition of *Truth and*

---

[103] Gadamer, "Science and Philosophy," *Reason in the Age of Science*, 6.

[104] I Thess.: 5,3.

[105] Heidegger, "Dialogue on Language," 10.

[106] Heidegger, "Letter to Richardson," xvi-xx.

[107] Martin Heidegger, *Being and Time*, tr. John Macquarrie and Edward Robinson (New York, 1962), 307, emphasis in the original.

[108] Cf. *Being and Time*, 311 (*Sein und Zeit*, 266): "[A]nticipation reveals to Dasein its lostness in the they-self, and brings it face to face with the possibility of being itself, primarily unsupported by concernful solicitude, but of being itself, rather, in an impassioned *freedom towards death*—a freedom which has been released from the illusions of the 'they,' and which is factical, certain of itself, and anxious." The entire passage is italicized in the original, with the phrase "freedom towards death" boldfaced for added emphasis.

[109] Gadamer, "Heidegger's Paths," 85-86.

Method, this point of disagreement has not generally been remarked upon despite Gadamer's characterization of its "urgency" to him.[110] Yet its importance is difficult to overemphasize because it shows that there is a serious substantive basis for what otherwise appears as a mere preference against Heidegger's granting of priority to the future.

There is another interesting way in which Gadamer's departure from Heidegger's assigning priority to the future can be seen to have substantive foundation. Gadamer suggests that understanding, far from consisting of the act of a subject, involves a momentary "loss of self."[111] In terms of human knowledge, he consequently concludes that there is a kind of priority of the past. "It is not really we ourselves who understand: it is always a past that allows us to say, 'I have understood'."[112]

On the level of the work of art and consequently of history, for Gadamer the *kairos* of fulfilled time is seen as consisting of an "absolute present" in which is gathered the past in readiness for the future.[113] Hence the equivocation in describing Gadamer as granting a "kind of" priority to the past. Nevertheless the difference of emphasis from Heidegger and its substantive basis remain clear. The question, then, is how this difference bears on the issue of historical continuity and discontinuity.

There is a certain lack of clarity in Heidegger's view of history that is brought out with some force by Gadamer. The element of discontinuity in Being's epochs or "fate" (*Geschick*) is crucial for the possibility of Heidegger's own fateful "step back" out of metaphysics into the "other thinking" which alone can await the "saving power." This is a matter not at all of Heidegger's own effort, but of what Being has allotted to man. Its appearance is the unforeseeable *kairos*. Yet on the other hand, Heidegger ascribes to history "a kind of inner consequentiality" in that it represents a process of the increasing forgetting of Being. Gadamer's conclusion is summed up in two rhetorical questions: "Does not history always present a continuity? Coming to be in passing away?"[114]

Clearly this conclusion is not simply contrary to Heidegger. It represents a choice of one tendency within Heidegger over another, conflicting tendency. Yet it amounts to a decisive correction of Heidegger's thought. In part its substantive basis has proven to be a difference of emphasis in the existential analytic of Dasein as well as in the phenomenological description of the act of understanding. Also, however, the corrective is dictated as a matter of straightforward, careful scholarship and consequently of what could be viewed as Gadamer's intellectual honesty.

---

[110] *Ibid.*, 86.

[111] "On the Problem of Self-Understanding," 51.

[112] *Ibid.*, 58.

[113] Cf. "Aesthetics and Hermeneutics," 104.

[114] Gadamer, "Hegel and Heidegger," *Hegel's Dialectic: Five Hermeneutical Studies*, tr. P. Christopher Smith (New Haven, 1971), 109.

Gadamer's argument for continuity-within-discontinuity becomes clear in his own commonsensical description of what it can possibly mean to speak of time in terms of "epochs." He starts by looking for elements of genuine discontinuity in the course of events. He finds four. First, there are certain historical events that so change the face of the world as to deserve being called "epochal"; the release of atomic power is the example he gives. Second, he considers the experience of time within our lives. While this happens gradually, there comes a point when incremental changes add up to qualitative ones, such as when we say of someone, "she is no longer a child," or "he is an old man now." Third, the transition from one generation to another may signify an epochal time-span, as we can see clearly in the transition of rulers in changing dynasties. And fourth, there are what he calls "absolute epochs" in events from which historical time is measured, such as the *kairos* of the birth of Christ. While the latter usually refers to religious events, Gadamer also includes the possibility of absolute epochs in terms of the history of ideas.[115]

In support of Heidegger and as opposed to the Greek view that only the ahistorical constants of human life are genuinely real,[116] Gadamer finds the reality of history in the experience of transition, which to him is what constitutes "fate" or "destiny" (*Geschick*). To this extent, then, he grants primacy to the discontinuity of the *kairos*. Yet it is quite obvious that this discontinuity, even—or especially—in the case of "absolute epochs" is anything but absolute. To Gadamer, "discontinuity poses the question of in what sense it contains continuity."[117]

The answer is that there is an important kind of truth in remembered reality. This may appear in so simple a matter as the death of an acquaintance, which suddenly casts his life in a new light, perhaps idealized, but now and henceforth out of the stream of history, standing still. This sudden stillness or discontinuity "seems to help the truth to speak." Thus to Gadamer the sense in which continuity is contained within discontinuity is found in remembered reality. In the remembering of historical consciousness (the problem of "application" of the "history of the influence") the past—the tradition—is not turned into an object but understood afresh as an event of truth.

An important qualification must be added to this emphasis on remembering. Gadamer credits Heidegger with the "great insight" that the way that the past belongs to human reality is not primarily in memory, but in forgetting. That which is transitory is forgotten. Memory is the mode of preservation amidst everything that is constantly sinking away in forgetfulness. Therefore history is not simply continuous; its continuity cannot

---

[115] Hans-Georg Gadamer, "The Continuity of History and the Existential Moment," tr. Thomas Wren, *Philosophy Today*, 16 (1972), 230-240.

[116] *Ibid.*, 235.

[117] *Ibid.*, 237.

262   WALTER LAMMI

be taken for granted but constitutes a human task of renewal.[118] Gadamer
has appropriated from Heidegger the structure—the "how it is" of truth
that we have seen as unconcealment (*alētheia*) arising from and in tension
with concealment (*lēthē*). The difference between them is that where
Heidegger seeks direct insight into the truth of Being (or Being of truth),
Gadamer looks for help in conversation with the tradition. This very
much resembles Socrates's "flight into the *logoi*" from Plato's *Phaedo*.[119]

The basic form in which the past is handed down is language. Gadamer
shares the later Heidegger's emphasis on the importance of language. A
detailed comparison of the relation between the two in this regard would
require a full-length study of its own. However, their difference may be
succinctly summed up in Gadamer's statement, quoted at the beginning
of this article, that "language is [that kind of] being which can be understood." To Heidegger, the understanding of Being is the "Event of Appropriation" (*Ereignis*), which involves an instantaneous "flash" of insight
that is ultimately wordless. To Heidegger, then, it seems that speech is
based on silence.[120] "Hermeneutics," says Gadamer to the contrary, "may
be precisely defined as the art of bringing what is said or written to speech
again."[121] He has described the later Heidegger's quasi-poetic writings as
"sometimes more expressive of a linguistic need than of its overcoming."[122]

It would be easy to exaggerate this difference. In Gadamer's thinking
there is also a place for the instantaneous, as we have seen in his description
of the momentary "loss of self" in the act of understanding, and he
describes knowledge as intuition, which at least in the case of perception
involves "direct givenness of what is known."[123] In no way does the
statement "language is [that kind of] being which can be understood"—
despite the appearance of its more common English rendition, "Being
which can be understood is language"—imply that Gadamer is a nomi-
nalist. He explains that this should not be taken as a metaphysical assertion. It is only intended to explain the universal scope of hermeneutics:
In every word of language is implied an infinity of meaning at the same
time that each word appears at the expense of all others, thereby exempli-
fying ineluctable finitude. Gadamer explains his point with a saying of
Goethe's that "everything is a symbol," which means that any given thing
is related to and hence implies everything else that there is. The assertion
is not about the "what is" of each being, but rather about "how it encounters man's understanding."[124]

Nonetheless, with all caveats taken into account there remain impor-

[118] *Ibid.*, 239-40.
[119] cf. *TM*, 414.
[120] See Stanley Rosen, *Nihilism: A Philosophical Essay* (New Haven, 1969), 87ff.
[121] Gadamer, "Hermeneutics as a Theoretical and Practical Task," 119.
[122] Gadamer, "The Heritage of Hegel," *Reason in the Age of Science*, 57.
[123] Gadamer, "The Phenomenological Movement," 132.
[124] Gadamer, "Aesthetics and Hermeneutics," 103.

tant differences between Gadamer and Heidegger. It is instructive to note the conceptualization of art as containing an excess of meaning. In one sense these represent the same thought. The meaning of the work of art is to Gadamer its truth, self-contained in its advent as *kairos* but of inexhaustible depth; the "excess" of Being as what Being "sends" is to Heidegger also the truth of art, and the "sending" can also be understood in terms of the *kairos*.

Yet behind the difference of perspective, in Heidegger's case from Being and in Gadamer's from the work of art, rests a fundamental difference between the two. Heidegger's approach is "grandly speculative" where Gadamer's is merely "commonsensical"—or "phenomenological." Heidegger can be understood as basing his entire way of thought on an ultimately experiential foundation[125] or, which amounts to the same thing, not on "reason" but on "revelation."[126] Gadamer, on the contrary, abstains from faith with a kind of determined sobriety that neither starts from nothing nor ends in the infinite. In so doing, he can be seen as reviving the Greek understanding of reason, which by virtue neither of dogmatically denying nor of affirming matters about which it is necessarily ignorant, "remains at most just open to revelation."[127]

The American University in Cairo.

---

[125] See, for example, Grimm's Introduction to Pöggeler, "Being as Appropriation," 146.

[126] Michael Allen Gillespie, "Martin Heidegger," *History of Political Philosophy*, ed. Leo Strauss and Joseph Cropsey (Chicago, 1972), 903.

[127] Frederick Lawrence, "Gadamer and Lonergan: A Dialectical Comparison," *International Philosophical Quarterly*, 20 (1980), 31. Lawrence's point seems to be that the avoidance of dogmatism in the Greek understanding of reason entails a kind of agnosticism: Reason permits of revelation "in principle," so to speak, even though as "beyond reason," revelation is ultimately "unreasonable."

XIV

Metaphors for Mankind: The Development of Hans Blumenberg's Anthropological Metaphorology

David Adams

> Alle diese Gleichnisse wollen eigentlich nur sagen, dass das
> Unfassbare unfassbar ist, und das haben wir gewusst.
> —Franz Kafka

Hans Blumenberg appears to be more prolific now, forty-five years into his career, than ever before.[1] This means that an assessment of his "metaphorology" could prove premature, but he has given us little reason to expect any fundamental changes in his position. In the past he has remained quite consistent as he has developed and extended his ideas. In any case we need not speculate about his future course; we can begin to measure the distance he has come without considering where he will end up. To indicate his point of departure and provide a context for his accomplishment, I shall begin with a brief discussion of the confrontation between Ernst Cassirer and Martin Heidegger in 1929 in Davos, Switzerland. The Davos debate, which survives in the form of "minutes" taken by students, gives succinct expression to the two philosophers' striking differences on a variety of interrelated issues. It allows us to see the challenge that "metaphysics" (Heidegger) had presented to "philosophical anthropology" (Cassirer) before Blumenberg took up the cause of the latter.

Cassirer and Heidegger in Davos

On most questions, Cassirer and Heidegger face in opposite directions. One adopts the forward-looking stance of the Enlightenment, interpreting the history of civilization as an advance from *mythos* to *logos*; the other is a deeply Romantic thinker, always reaching back towards the origin of language, of civilization, and

---

[1] For a comprehensive bibliography of Blumenberg's work, including English translations, see Peter Behrenberg and David Adams, "Bibliographie Hans Blumenberg: Zum 70. Geburtstag," *Zeitschrift für philosophische Forschung,* XLIV (1990).

264

of history. At one point in the debate Heidegger accurately summed up this essential difference in their orientations: "With Cassirer the terminus a quo is completely problematical. My position is the opposite: the terminus a quo is the central problematic that I develop. The question is: is the terminus ad quem so clear for me?"[2] The one focusing on the products of civilization has trouble accounting for their origin, Heidegger charges, but he seems to realize that the argument is easily reversed: perhaps one striving to uncover the origin has trouble dealing with the products?[3]

The debate over the termini of civilization is closely tied to the question of totalization. Both philosophers try to explain man's connection to phenomena beyond his experience: what ties him to transcendental, infinite, or absolute truths? What gives a mortal creature intuitions of eternity? Cassirer argues that mankind's way to infinity is "through the medium of form," form that is created by man himself. Infinity, he explains, is "the totality, the fulfillment of finitude itself. But precisely this fulfillment of finitude constitutes infinity. Goethe: 'If you want to stride into the infinite, just walk to all sides of the finite.' "[4] For Heidegger, on the other hand, "man, as a finite being, has a certain infinitude in the ontological. Man is never infinite and absolute in creating the existent [*Seienden*] itself, rather he is infinite in the sense of understanding Being [*des Verstehens des Seins*]." The temporality of *Dasein* and the fact that "an inner transcendence lies in the essence of time" make possible this understanding of Being prior to all culture or philosophy of culture. This "transcendence of *Dasein*" consists of "the inner possibility of this finite being to relate to the totality of the existent."[5] In spite of and because of the different vocabularies employed by the two philosophers, the radical difference between their views of the absolute is apparent: for Heidegger it is found at the terminus a quo, prior to civilization and internal to *Dasein*; Cassirer associates it with the terminus ad quem, the culmination of civilization and the externalizations of *Dasein*.

The final exchange in the debate demonstrated that Cassirer was prepared to accept the irreconcilable differences while Heidegger pushed for a decisive victory. "I do not want to try to make Heidegger abandon his position," Cassirer explained, warning against thinking that rational argument can "coerce" someone to start out from a new position. His perception of a multitude of world-views and symbolic forms—of "Being, which proceeds from manifold functional determinations and meanings"—made him more inclined to accept dissenting opin-

---

[2] "Davoser Disputation zwischen Ernst Cassirer und Martin Heidegger," appendix to Martin Heidegger, *Kant und das Problem der Metaphysik*, 4th ed. (Frankfurt am Main, 1973), 260.

[3] Heidegger provided an answer to the question about the terminus ad quem four years after the Davos encounter, in his infamous Rector's speech: "the beginning . . . lies not *behind us* as what is long past, rather it stands *ahead of us*. . . . It stands there as the distant command to us to gather in its greatness again" (*Die Selbstbehauptung der deutschen Universität* [Frankfurt am Main, 1983], 12-13). Cassirer analyzes National Socialism in terms of its distance from the terminus ad quem in *The Myth of the State* (New Haven, 1946).

[4] "Davoser Disputation," 258.

[5] *Ibid.*, 252, 254, 256-57.

266   DAVID ADAMS

ions.[6] Heidegger, determined to get to the one "idea of Being" behind the "manifold modes of Being," could not afford to be so ecumenical. He warned against adjusting to the diversity of positions found among "philosophizing people." "The one thing" he wanted the audience to take away from the debate was a readiness to turn to "the central question of metaphysics"—the question of the meaning of Being.[7] His message hit home: the consensus among contemporaries was that Heidegger prevailed at Davos. The debate contributed to the decline of neo-Kantianism.

Although signs of renewed interest in the Davos debate and neo-Kantianism suggest that Cassirer is now getting a second hearing, Blumenberg has already completed the task of redeeming philosophical anthropology, in part by immunizing it against Heidegger's attacks. In 1974 Blumenberg received the Kuno Fischer Prize and delivered an acceptance speech that reveals the depth of his affection for the work of Cassirer, the prize's first recipient. He refers in the speech to Cassirer's *Substance and Function* (1910) as a "work that, in my opinion, is still not exhausted and is unjustly largely forgotten."[8] This is the work where Cassirer develops the concept of "function," arguing that the function of symbolic forms is as important as their substance and that relations among things are as important as the things in themselves. The concept of function has proven particularly fruitful in Blumenberg's hands. In fact it may be his single most important inheritance; it is an integral part of all his work, forming the basis of his diverse achievements.

Cassirer claims that only a "will to logic" fuels the functioning of symbolic forms.[9] Blumenberg has given the concept of function more power by lifting it out of this neo-Kantian context. He has turned Cassirer's philosophical anthropology around so that, like Heidegger's metaphysics, it is facing back in the direction of the terminus a quo; and this has enabled him to develop an understanding of the temporality of *Dasein* that rivals Heidegger's. The parallel to Heidegger should not be exaggerated, however. For Blumenberg the terminus a quo is inaccessible and repulsive; the meaning of Being is found in the process of removing ourselves from it. " 'History' means that the reasons ruling at the origin do not determine the process of becoming and what finally comes to be," he argues, trying to unmoor us from the terminus a quo. "Meaning is no constant in history."[10] He

---

[6] *Ibid.*, 264, 266. "Symbolic forms" is Cassirer's general term for all forms of culture, all modes of consciousness. In borrowing it in this essay, I often fail to distinguish among the wide variety of forms of expression and representation because I am focusing here on what they have in common: their function. Metaphor, myth, rhetoric, and symbol; concept, reason, and science; symbolic forms, civilization, systems of knowledge, and "answers": all these perform the function of satisfying curiosity, meeting needs, responding to "questions," "occupying positions."

[7] *Ibid.*, 267-68.

[8] Blumenberg, "Ernst Cassirers gedenkend bei Entgegennahme des Kuno-Fischer-Preises der Universität Heidelberg 1974," *Wirklichkeiten in denen wir leben* (Stuttgart, 1981), 164.

[9] Cassirer, *Substance and Function, and Einstein's Theory of Relativity*, tr. William Curtis Swabey and Marie Collins Swabey (Chicago, 1923), 319.

[10] Blumenberg, "Weltbilder und Weltmodelle," *Nachrichten der Giessener Hochschulgesellschaft*, 30 (1961), 70. Delivered at the University of Giessen, this speech can be read as an indirect commentary on Heidegger's Rector's speech.

refuses to consider the process of history either as decay or as progress toward a goal; he refuses, for example, to interpret the modern age as either an advance or decline in relation to preceding ages, and he thereby overcomes the Enlightenment-romanticism antithesis. Both Cassirer and Heidegger want to approach *toward* one of the termini; Blumenberg concentrates on removal *away* from them.

The core of Blumenberg's achievement has been a theory of metaphor describing the process by which man gives a total, tangible form to his experience. Absolutes, according to this theory, are always mediated, if not created, by metaphor. He studies these metaphors from within an expanded *Begriffsgeschichte*,[11] a method that brings out both their historicity and the pragmatic effects of their use. These features of Blumenberg's work have remained constant. What has changed is his understanding of the role of metaphor in his own thought. In his earliest major work, "Paradigms for a Metaphorology" (1960), he attempted to exclude the question of absolutes by avoiding the use of absolute metaphors. He quickly became aware, however, that the question of the terminus a quo, asked with such insistence by Heidegger, could not so easily be ignored. In subsequent work Blumenberg has increasingly embraced the use of metaphor to satisfy the irrepressible desire for absolute knowledge. He seems to have realized that metaphor not only produces the illusion of presence when taken literally but also can have the opposite effect, reminding us of the absence of its object when it is used with self-awareness. In other words, by mediating between *Dasein* and the whole of reality, metaphor not only establishes a relation but it also preserves distance, blocking direct contact between mankind and the absolute.

The next section of the present essay focuses on difficulties in "Paradigms for a Metaphorology," where, in trying to retreat from absolutes by limiting the use of metaphor, Blumenberg in fact ends up using metaphors unknowingly to name the termini a quo and ad quem, to outline, in other words, the whole of human experience. The third and fourth sections show how he has slipped out of this bind in subsequent work by developing anthropological metaphors that name a distant or absent terminus a quo; section three focuses on his elaboration of an anthropological terminus a quo and section four on his growing awareness of the rhetorical nature of this elaboration. The essay's fifth and final section considers the possibility that, having confronted the question of absolutes from the perspective of philosophical anthropology, he may now be exploring more sophisticated means of forgetting this question.

The Paradigm Metaphor

"What is the world?" "What part does mankind have in the totality of truth?"[12] These are examples from "Paradigms for a Metaphorology" of questions

---

[11] *Begriffsgeschichte* is perhaps best translated as "history of concepts": in Germany this discipline has been defined more narrowly than the analogous "history of ideas" in America, which explains why Blumenberg has had to argue for expanding it to include metaphor. Cf. Melvin Richter, "*Begriffsgeschichte* and the History of Ideas," *JHI,* 48 (1987), 247-63.

[12] "Paradigmen zu einer Metaphorologie," *Archiv für Begriffsgeschichte,* 6 (1960), 20, 13.

268   DAVID ADAMS

that Blumenberg tries *not* to answer in his attempt to avoid naming or defining absolutes. He tries to resist the desire for this kind of answer, which invariably takes the form of a metaphor: absolute metaphors "represent the totality of reality, which can never been seen or experienced."[13] To believe one has direct access to the totality of reality is to be fooled by metaphor. The closing lines of the essay announce his campaign against this mistake: "The absolute metaphor . . . springs into a void, projects itself on the *tabula rasa* of what cannot be fulfilled by theory; here it has taken the place of the no-longer living absolute will. Metaphysics often proved itself to us to be metaphorics taken literally; the disappearance of metaphysics calls metaphorics back to its place."[14]

Yet Blumenberg's essay unwittingly illustrates the difficulty of renouncing the illusion of absolute knowledge. He provides just this kind of knowledge, paradoxically, in a brief passage about the source of our desire for such knowledge: "absolute metaphors 'answer' those supposedly naive, principally unanswerable questions whose relevance lies quite simply in the fact that they cannot be eliminated because we don't *ask* them, but find them *asked* in the foundation of existence [*Daseinsgrund*]."[15] This idea is the seed out of which his philosophical anthropology will grow. At this point, however, it introduces a contradiction. At the moment he addresses the question about metaphor's terminus a quo, he provides the kind of knowledge he is trying to renounce: he defines our curiosity, our "questions," as an unchanging, intersubjective aspect of existence—one thing that lies behind all civilization.

This conflict between intention and execution in "Paradigms for a Metaphorology" is reflected in Blumenberg's understanding of the relationship between reason and rhetoric. In the introduction he rejects Descartes's anticipation, in *Discourse on Method*, of a final state of philosophy in which everything would be defined with clear, precise, unchanging concepts. The un-Cartesian view of history is inherent in the concept of the absolute *metaphor*—we have seen that such metaphors provide a type of knowledge that resists translation into univocal terminology. In fact, they make up "the substructure of thought, . . . the underground, the nutrient of systematic crystallizations." This is a "catalytic sphere, from which indeed the world of concepts continually enriches itself, but without thereby transforming or consuming this supporting material."[16] Yet he uses the *concept* of absolute metaphor to delimit and limit this type of knowledge, revealing an interest and optimism in the ability of reason to intrude further into the realm of rhetoric. He asserts the impropriety of using metaphors to give structure to his project: "as practitioners of metaphorology, we have already robbed ourselves of the possibility of finding 'answers' in metaphors to those unanswerable questions."[17] The essay is made up of histories of absolute metaphors that have been

---

[13] *Ibid.*, 20. For further definitions of the term see also page 9 (where "absolute" refers to metaphor's resistance to translation into concepts, and not specifically to the issue of totalization), page 108, and the following passage, from page 123: the absolute metaphor gives "an orienting hold for the question, not answerable through theoretical investigation, about the position of man in the universe of the existent."

[14] *Ibid.*, 142.

[15] *Ibid.*, 19.

[16] *Ibid.*, 10-11.

[17] *Ibid.*, 19.

carefully chosen to serve as "paradigms." The resulting "typology of histories of metaphors"[18] is intended to circumscribe the realm of metaphor, clearly distinguishing it from other modes of consciousness: the rational, the mythic, the symbolic. The very title of the work—"for" or "toward [zu] a metaphorology"—implies a Cartesian trajectory towards greater rationality in human activity, a trajectory towards a science (*logos*) of metaphor.

Despite Blumenberg's assertion that practitioners of metaphorology may not find answers in metaphors, one metaphor, "paradigm," appears in this essay frequently without being an object of study. It is this linguistic metaphor that allows him to map out the full range of mankind's relation to the absolute; it gives structure and unity to the other metaphors in the essay. Its success in performing this task is the very quality that makes it absolute. The completeness of the typology is a sure sign that the typology is not complete—one metaphor has necessarily escaped to provide the ground on which the typology is constructed.[19] The purpose of the paradigms is to lead to the rule of reason, and yet this reason is dependent on rhetoric—the paradigm metaphor—for its power. "Paradigms for a Metaphorology" is a title dramatizing the manner in which rhetoric always reasserts itself most forcefully at the very moment when reason tries to increase its autonomy.

Blumenberg's implicit devaluation of metaphor in relation to concept derives from the view of history in which reason displaces myth, and this arises from inattention to what the two realms share: the terminus a quo. (Later, in *Work on Myth*, we find Blumenberg applying the same criticism to Cassirer.) Although Blumenberg already defines metaphor in terms of its function in this early work, his understanding of that function will grow more profound once he articulates more fully the terminus a quo, or *Daseinsgrund*.

The contradictions in "Paradigms for a Metaphorology" indicate the difficulty, if not the impossibility, of its ambitious project: it is not easy to leave unsatisfied the desire for certain kinds of knowledge. Blumenberg later acknowledged that when metaphors lose their effectiveness, "they leave behind them the corresponding questions, to which then new answers become due when and because it is not possible to destroy the question itself critically."[20] A philosophy of symbolic forms may have no intrinsic need to articulate the terminus a quo; but the "accomplishment and establishment of the reoccupation," in which one

---

[18] *Ibid.*, 84.

[19] Cf. Jacques Derrida's comments on the "impossibility" of a "metaphorology of philosophy": "If one wished to conceive and to class all the metaphorical possibilities of philosophy, one metaphor, at least, always would remain excluded, outside the system" ("White Mythology: Metaphor in the Text of Philosophy," *Margins of Philosophy*, tr. Alan Bass [Chicago, 1982], 219-20 and *passim*). On the metaphor "paradigm," see Anselm Haverkamp, "Paradigma *Metapher*, Metapher *Paradigma*—Zur Metakinetic hermeneutischer Horizonte (Blumenberg/Derrida, Kuhn/Foucault, Black/White)," *Epochenschwelle und Epochenbewusstsein*, Poetik und Hermeneutik 12, ed. Reinhart Herzog and Reinhart Koselleck (Munich, 1987), 547-60, and also the discussion of "Observations on Metaphors," below.

[20] *The Legitimacy of the Modern Age*, tr. Robert M. Wallace (Cambridge, Mass., 1983), 66 (translation revised based on 1966 edition). The English translation is based on the three-volume revised edition (1974, 1973, 1976), but all of the passages I cite in this essay, unless otherwise noted, were already present in the first edition (1966).

DAVID ADAMS

answer, philosophy, or epoch replaces another, "are rhetorical acts"; and any philosophy that leaves questions unanswered is likely to be less compelling than its predecessors and competitors.[21] This was demonstrated in Davos, where Heidegger scored points by giving a better account than Cassirer of the terminus a quo. Addressing this question is necessary to maximize the persuasiveness of a philosophical position. Perhaps this explains why, when Blumenberg intentionally tries to avoid certain questions in this early essay, he unconsciously answers them with the "concepts" of "*Daseinsgrund*" and "Paradigm."

An Anthropological Terminus a Quo

The next twenty years of Blumenberg's career show him becoming increasingly aware and deliberate in providing answers to the question of the terminus a quo. In "Paradigms for a Metaphorology," as we have seen, he defined the terminus a quo in a single sentence: metaphor originates from questions placed in the *Daseinsgrund*. In *The Legitimacy of the Modern Age* (1966; revised 1973-76) he suggests that these questions are not constant but, like the answers, subject to history. The book defends the modern age against the attack of the secularization thesis, which suggests that modern thought (e.g., the idea of progress) consists of disguised and illegitimately appropriated material (e.g., Christian eschatology) from the Middle Ages. He argues that this "identity in the historical process" between the two epochs "is not one of contents but one of functions. It is in fact possible for totally heterogeneous contents to take on identical functions in specific positions in the system of man's interpretation of the world and of himself."[22] This model appears to be borrowed from *Substance and Function*, in which Cassirer argues that "the *meaning* of certain functions of experience is not affected in principle by a change in their material content." A transition in intellectual hypotheses "never means that the fundamental form absolutely disappears, and another absolutely new form takes its place. The new form must contain the *answer* to the *questions*, proposed within the older form."[23] But Blumenberg applies the model on a much grander scale, to epochal transitions, in an attempt to explain the source and the inherent legitimacy of the modern age's answers. Modern metaphors, different in "substance" from their theological predecessors, may appear similar since they are forced to respond to the same questions:

In our history this system [of man's interpretation of the world and of himself] has been decisively determined by Christian theology, and specifically, above all, in the direction of its expansion. Theology created new "positions" in the framework of the statements about the world and man that are possible and are expected, "positions" that cannot simply be "set aside" again or left unoccupied in the interest of theoretical economy. For theology there was no need for questions about the totality of the world and history, about the origin of man and the purpose of his existence, to be unanswerable. This explains the readiness with which it introduced titles into the budget of man's needs in the area of knowledge,

---

[21] "An Anthropological Approach to the Contemporary Significance of Rhetoric," tr. Robert M. Wallace, *After Philosophy: End or Transformation?*, ed. Kenneth Baynes, James Bohman, and Thomas McCarthy (Cambridge, Mass., 1987), 451.

[22] *Legitimacy of the Modern Age*, 64.

[23] *Substance and Function*, 268-69.

HANS BLUMENBERG'S ANTHROPOLOGICAL METAPHOROLOGY   271

to honor which was bound to be difficult or even impossible for any knowledge that did not appeal, as it did, to transcendent sources.[24]

This passage makes it clear that the questions Christian theology placed in our *Daseinsgrund* are the same ones answered by absolute metaphors. By focusing here on forms of curiosity added relatively recently to our framework of knowledge, Blumenberg's philosophical anthropology provides a partial account of the terminus a quo and still avoids absolutes and the temptation for totalization.

Yet implicit in this analysis is the belief that mankind always possesses questions or needs of some kind which are the terminus a quo of civilization. This implication is explicated in "An Anthropological Approach to the Contemporary Significance of Rhetoric" (1971). To date, Blumenberg's major work has addressed other topics—the genesis of the modern age, metaphor, myth—and the anthropological elements have remained in the background. "An Anthropological Approach to Rhetoric" is the only work devoted to the topic of concern to us here. In it he introduces a name for the animal with the expanding and shrinking "budget" of curiosity: the "creature of deficiency" (*Mängelwesen*). The concept is borrowed from Arnold Gehlen and a tradition in the philosophy of language stretching back to Johann Gottfried Herder, but in the context of Blumenberg's own development it must be viewed as a descendent of the concept of the *Daseinsgrund* in the "Paradigms" essay. Blumenberg sees rhetoric as the tool of a creature who must compensate for a deficiency of meaning. Unlike animals, man lacks sufficient instincts to determine his behavior in all situations, and rhetoric helps him survive these crises.

Man's deficiency in specific dispositions for reactive behavior vis-à-vis reality—that is, his poverty of instincts—is the starting point for the central anthropological question as to how this creature is able to exist in spite of his lack of fixed biological dispositions. The answer can be reduced to the formula: by not dealing with this reality directly. The human relation to reality is indirect, circumstantial, delayed, selective, and above all "metaphorical."[25]

Here the metaphorologist is not so quick to "rob" himself of the possibility of finding answers in metaphors. The risk of doing so is further suggested by his comments on "identity" near the end of the essay:

anthropological approaches to rhetoric converge on a central descriptive statement: Man has no immediate, no purely "internal" relation to himself. His self-understanding has the structure of "self-externality." Kant was the first to deny that inner experience has any precedence over outer experience; we are appearance to ourselves, the secondary synthesis of a primary multiplicity, not the reverse. . . . Man comprehends himself only by way of what he is not. It is not only his situation that is potentially metaphorical; his constitution itself already is.[26]

This passage echoes an insight of Cassirer's, expressed in the formula representation precedes presentation: we do not know things in isolation; rather we know

[24] *Legitimacy of the Modern Age*, 64-65.
[25] "Anthropological Approach," 439.
[26] *Ibid.*, 456.

272   DAVID ADAMS

primarily relations among things.[27] The formula, combined with Blumenberg's concept of the *Mängelwesen*, makes one hesitant to join Heidegger on the path back to the terminus a quo in *Dasein*. If we conceive of man, as Blumenberg suggests, as a creature with no predetermined, no "inner" understanding of himself or the world, then we recognize the danger of Heidegger's impatience with symbolic forms.[28]

With the development of this ontological terminus a quo in the concept of the *Mängelwesen*, Blumenberg set the stage to give a fuller account of the historical terminus a quo. *Work on Myth* (1979) adds this critical element to his philosophical anthropology. Specifically, it adds the concept of the "absolutism of reality": the phenomenon that the *Mängelwesen* must hold at a distance by means of myth and metaphor. The absolutism of reality is defined as the situation in which "man came close to not having control of the conditions of his existence and, what is more important, believed that he simply lacked control of them."[29] Myth is the means by which man responded to this situation and diffused the superior power of what is other than himself. This "division of powers" enables man to respond piecemeal to the overwhelming indeterminacy and ambiguity that the world possesses for him.

The "absolutism of reality," in conjunction with the *Mängelwesen*, describes a terminus a quo that repels: "Nothing wants to go back to the beginning that . . . we are speaking of here."[30] Hence there is a realization that seemed to be lacking in the "Paradigms" essay: "the antithesis between myth and reason is a late and a poor invention, because it forgoes seeing the function of myth, in the overcoming of that archaic unfamiliarity of the world, as itself a rational function."[31] Like metaphor and the "answers" of the modern age, myth is defined in terms of its function. But in *Work on Myth* Blumenberg reaches farther back into history—and deeper into the *Mängelwesen*—to find the minimum of identity for all civilization, instead of just two epochs.[32] By considering what function is shared by all symbolic forms, he is able to imagine their common origin.

The task performed by symbolic forms is never finished; mankind never enjoys an "absolutism of images and wishes" characterized by the "supremacy of the subject."[33] The continuing fluctuation between these absolutes—between "real-

[27] Cf. *Substance and Function*, 284.

[28] Cf. Hans Blumenberg, "Der Parteibeitrag: Heidegger und der Nationalsozialismus: Im Hinblick auf eine 'Neue Philosophie des Geldes,' " *Neue Zürcher Zeitung*, 12 Feb. 1988, Fernausgabe, 43. While defending Heidegger from those who find it significant that he paid his party tax for so long, this article also attacks him for underestimating the importance of symbols. The article is interesting also for the fact that the reclusive Blumenberg discloses personal information here: he alludes to his experience during the war as an "unregistered chamberlain" (*ungemeldeter Kammerherr*), a punning reference to the fact that he was forced to go into hiding.

[29] *Work on Myth*, tr. Robert M. Wallace (Cambridge, Mass., 1985), 3-4.

[30] *Ibid.*, 21.

[31] *Ibid.*, 48.

[32] Cf. *Legitimacy of the Modern Age*: "the concept of 'reoccupation' designates, by implication, the minimum of identity that it must be possible to discover, or at least to presuppose and to search for, in even the most agitated movement of history" (p. 466). This passage first appeared in the revised edition.

[33] *Work on Myth*, 8-9.

HANS BLUMENBERG'S ANTHROPOLOGICAL METAPHOROLOGY 273

ity" and imagination, helplessness and control, question and answer, indeterminacy and plenitude of meaning—is what we call "history." To preserve this process Blumenberg concerns himself with removal away from rather than approach toward these extremes: to stay between them one must avoid arriving at either one.

Metaphorical Anthropology

The development of an anthropological terminus a quo for metaphorology has coincided with a growing recognition of the metaphorical nature of philosophical anthropology. Blumenberg's early attempt to avoid answers about things never experienced or seen has given way to imaginative speculation reaching far beyond experience and sight. In *Work on Myth*, for example, he increases the rhetorical force of the "absolutism of reality" concept by filling it with narrative content:

Whatever may have been the appearance of the prehuman creature that was induced, by an enforced or an accidental change in the environment it inhabited, to avail itself of the sensory advantage of raising itself upright into a bipedal posture and to stabilize the advantage in spite of all its internal disadvantages in the functioning of organs—that creature had, in any case, left the protection of a more hidden form of life, and an adapted one, in order to expose itself to the risks of the widened horizon of its perception, which were also those of its perceivability. . . . [This move] was a situational leap, which made the unoccupied distant horizon into the ongoing expectation of hitherto unknown things. What came about through the combination of leaving the shrinking rain forest for the savanna and settling in caves was a combination of the meeting of new requirements for performance in obtaining food outside the living places and the old advantage of undisturbed reproduction and rearing of the next generation, with its prolonged need for learning, now in the protection of housing that was easy to close off from the outside.[34]

"Is grander speculation imaginable?"—this is the understandable response to this passage from a critic who observes that "Blumenberg, despite his peremptory dismissal of the quest for origin, does not himself forsake the quest."[35] But Blumenberg's quest is not so much for origin *per se* as for an account of origin that satisfies our need for such stories. *Work on Myth* calls attention to its own rhetorical foundation in speaking of the absolutism of reality as a "limit concept" pointing back toward the "archaic" or the "past's past" (*Vorvergangenheit*, plu-

---

[34] *Ibid.*, 4.

[35] Robert A. Segal, "Blumenberg as Theorist of Myth," *Annals of Scholarship*, 5 (1987), 93. See also Robert Wallace, "Translator's Introduction," *Work on Myth*, xvi-xix. Blumenberg may avoid describing the origin of the contents of individual myths, but he certainly does not avoid giving "content" or "substance" to his idea of the origin of the function of myth as a whole. The emphasis on function does not free one from the need to deal with "contents," but makes one more conscious of *how* one does so, i.e., of one's own dependence on myth.

perfect); in other words, back toward an inaccessible realm.[36] The reader of *Substance and Function* will once again recognize the influence of Cassirer, who proposes the use of such "limit concepts" as a way to account for the totality of reality without resorting to metaphysics. As an extrapolation from empirical knowledge, a limit concept serves the function of formation, bringing out the relations among things.[37] But Cassirer, as we have seen, never attempts such an extrapolation in the direction of the terminus a quo and therefore never fully appreciates the importance of myth and metaphor in creating and transmitting such limit concepts.

The self-consciousness with which Blumenberg now accomplishes this extrapolation transforms the contradictions and "dead" metaphors in "Paradigms for a Metaphorology" into effective paradoxes and vital metaphors. Blumenberg now realizes that " 'carryings-over' [*Übertragungen*, metaphors] are things that have to be performed, but that must not be taken literally."[38] His philosophical anthropology answers questions that are both unanswerable and unavoidable. Its metaphors are necessary and necessarily provisional, and his mature anthropology embraces both necessities, providing answers without taking them literally. This awareness of the function of his own rhetoric brings together the form and content of his work, creating harmony between his assertion that the function of ideas is more important than their content, and the manner in which he makes this assertion.

"Observations on Metaphors" (1971) is a minor work, but shows Blumenberg developing this self-awareness.[39] In Section IV, "Paradigm, Grammatical," he discusses "paradigm" as a metaphor. (In his usual oblique manner, he makes no reference here to his earlier essay in which this word played such an important role.) The title "Observations on Metaphors" reflects the informality of this essay, which contrasts with the more systematic approach of the "Paradigms" essay. The title also indicates one of his growing interests: to locate the position of the observer of metaphors, who is never fully "outside" or free of metaphors himself. One object of study here is a topos that helps locate the observer: the metaphor of the shipwreck witnessed by a spectator.

Blumenberg's interest in the shipwreck metaphor has found its fullest expression so far in *Shipwreck with Spectator: Paradigm of a* Dasein *Metaphor* (1979), where he traces its history from antiquity to the present. The talk is now of a *Daseinsmetapher* rather than the *Daseinsgrund*, a development anticipated by the claim in "An Anthropological Approach to Rhetoric" that mankind's constitution is potentially metaphorical. The shipwreck metaphor seems to describe its own fate and Blumenberg's study of it: he observes its disintegration through history as its various components fall away—land, ports, spectator, even the ship

---

[36] *Work on Myth*, 3, 21. *Legitimacy of the Modern Age* also points to its own metaphorical basis: the talk of the "reoccupation" of "positions" in the "budget" of man's knowledge is "only a heuristic principle" (p. 464), as he reminds us by repeatedly placing these terms in quotation marks himself. "Paradigms for a Metaphorology," in contrast, contains no such references to its rhetorical structure; "paradigm" and "*Daseinsgrund*" function subversively.

[37] *Substance and Function*, 228-29.

[38] *Work on Myth*, 7.

[39] "Beobachtungen an Metaphern," *Archiv für Begriffsgeschichte*, 15 (1971), 161-214.

HANS BLUMENBERG'S ANTHROPOLOGICAL METAPHOROLOGY   275

and its wreck. The story arrives at Jacob Burckhardt's reflection that "we would like to know the waves in which we are floating, but we are these waves themselves."[40] The final lines of Blumenberg's account ask a question that the book in a small way has already answered: "obviously the ocean contains other material than that already used in building. From where can it come, in order to give courage to those beginning anew? Perhaps out of earlier shipwrecks?"[41] Blumenberg has given the metaphor new life by making himself—and the reader—the spectators of this metaphor's shipwreck. Inside and outside, subject and object are confused: this is a "paradigm" for a "metaphorology" practiced with a consciousness and acceptance of the fact that metaphors not only are the objects of analysis but also give form to the subject performing this analysis. By setting himself adrift on the sea of metaphor, Blumenberg avoids the illusion of being anchored to the absolute.

In the past decade Blumenberg's rate of publication of such histories of metaphor has increased. Throughout these works there is the double movement found in *Shipwreck with Spectator*: towards distance *and* immediacy in relation to the metaphors. On the one hand each history of an absolute metaphor seems to be complete, total—a rounded off object set off from the historian. On the other hand each work emphasizes the extent to which the observer and the act of observation are themselves metaphorical and constituted by the very metaphors being studied. The ambiguity of the position of the author and reader of these works and the preoccupation with the concept of the observer—whether as *Betrachter, Beobachter, Zuschauer, Anschauer,* or *Leser*[42]—indicate the self-consciousness of Blumenberg's attempts to describe and to create his relation to the past. How "new" is his anthropological metaphorology? Might he be straddling the threshold to the next epoch, partly "inside" and partly "outside" modern metaphors? How much can and should one attempt to influence such an epochal transition by altering the answers and perhaps even the questions?

Forgetting a Question Intentionally?

Blumenberg shares—and heightens—Cassirer's ecumenicalism. For Blumenberg every manifestation of culture is fundamentally valuable in helping to distance the terminus a quo, at which human life is threatened. This does not mean that all "answers" are equally valid at all times: each must display convincing supporting evidence and satisfy our prior internal expectations for knowledge. But presumably two or more contradictory interpretations can function equally well. The concepts "absolutism of reality" and "Mängelwesen" accommodate this fact by granting *every* epoch and mode of expression—even those that explicitly contradict these concepts—a fundamental legitimacy as part of the ongoing

[40] Quoted in *Schiffbruch mit Zuschauer: Paradigma einer Daseinsmetapher* (Frankfurt am Main, 1979), 66.

[41] *Schiffbruch mit Zuschauer,* 74.

[42] See *Die Lesbarkeit der Welt* (Frankfurt am Main, 1981), *Das Lachen der Thrakerin* (Frankfurt am Main, 1987), *Matthäuspassion* (Frankfurt am Main, 1988), *Höhlenausgänge* (Frankfurt am Main, 1989), and his extensive work on cosmological metaphor, the most important example of which is *The Genesis of the Copernican World,* tr. Robert M. Wallace (Cambridge, Mass., 1987).

276 DAVID ADAMS

process of self-preservation. Of course there are other interpretive systems capable of matching this ecumenicalism, finding reasons of their own to grant philosophical anthropology legitimacy.[43]

Blumenberg often gives expression to the radical ecumenicalism justified by his concepts, arguing that the products of every culture, every epoch, every individual should be preserved, however obsolete they may seem at present. He speaks of "the elementary obligation not to give up for lost anything that is human," or claims that "noteworthy [*denkwürdig*, worthy of thought] is anything people have ever thought."[44] Elsewhere he extends the obligation to remember to the "questions": "Philosophy represents only a more general condition in each culture: that of the irrepressibility of its elemental needs and questions despite attempts to overcome them. Culture also means respecting the questions that we cannot answer"—and this includes Heidegger's question of the meaning of Being.[45] Every time a piece of history falls victim to oblivion, our understanding of what it means to be human, and hence our range of possibilities, is narrowed. Thus an ecumenical memory contributes to the cause of self-preservation.

Yet the advice Cassirer passed on from Goethe at Davos is not easy to follow: we lack the time to "walk to all sides of the finite." Obviously we cannot give equal life to all past forms; we must attribute various degrees of significance to them. Self-preservation also means being selective. The most ecumenically inclined person (or culture) cannot respond to all questions and answers with equal enthusiasm, but whether and how we can influence the questions that claim our attention remains problematic. Take, for example, the question about the subject of history. This "position" in our framework of knowledge was "reoccupied" in the modern age, transferred from God to man: "the most daring metaphor, which tried to embrace the greatest tension, may have accomplished the most for man's self-conception: trying to think the God absolutely away from himself, as the totally Other, he inexorably began the most difficult rhetorical act, namely, the act of comparing himself to this God."[46] Blumenberg's attitude towards the modern age is ambiguous: he has repeatedly pointed to the excesses of this conception of man, however "legitimate" the reoccupation may have been. Man simply does not have the means to answer the larger questions inherited from Christianity, and the struggle to do so often obscures many smaller questions and answers; ecumenicalism and self-preservation may not be best served by the question about the subject of history.

So how does Blumenberg deal with this inheritance? Is he succeeding in backing away from this "position," in beginning to forget the question? Consciousness of the aesthetic nature of a particular category of answers is a sign that the need they are satisfying is beginning to lose its urgency and can be dealt

[43] Blumenberg's ecumenicalism was first pointed out to me by Allen Mandelbaum. For another view of the problems of newness and totalization, see his " 'Taken From Brindisi': Vergil in an Other's Otherworld," *Vergil at 2000*, ed. John Bernard (New York, 1986), 225-39.

[44] "Ernst Cassirers gedenkend," 170 and *passim*; *Lesbarkeit der Welt*, 409.

[45] "Pensiveness," tr. David Adams, *Caliban*, 6 (1989), 54; see also "Being—A MacGuffin: How to Preserve the Desire to Think," tr. David Adams, *Salmagundi* (forthcoming 1991).

[46] "Anthropological Approach," 456.

HANS BLUMENBERG'S ANTHROPOLOGICAL METAPHOROLOGY   277

with more circuitously. The greater rhetorical freedom Blumenberg is allowing himself in the discussion of absolutes is an indication of his growing distance from the question of absolutes. The question about the subject of history has grown less insistent when one can recognize that "the singular form of 'history' is itself an absolute metaphor."[47] How dependent is Blumenberg's metaphorology on this metaphor—do his various histories of individual metaphors collectively make up one unified history? Leaving this question in the background has allowed the individual histories to thrive. They do not delimit or limit the realm of metaphor, but they do seem to be accomplishing one of the aims of the "Paradigms" essay with slightly different means: the need for absolutes is becoming less memorable, more distant, more "metaphorical."

Can one deliberately encourage this process? Talk of intentionally forgetting something is, admittedly, a self-defeating activity. Kant must have experienced this futility when, upset by the memory of his former servant, he wrote a note to remind himself that "the name Lampe must now be completely forgotten." The humor of this anecdote reminds us that techniques for forgetting are not as simple as those for remembering, but it reminds us also that our talk of "forgetting" is itself metaphorical: in contrast to Kant's desire to let go of a piece of consciousness, "forgetting a question" involves letting go of a need at the root of consciousness. For these reasons it is not easy to determine to what extent Blumenberg's conscious intentions have contributed to his growing distance from the question of absolutes. But he does seem to have found a method for dealing with this question less and less directly. Robert Wallace has summarized the process in discussing *Legitimacy of the Modern Age*: "by questioning the nature of our own questioning, we alter the dynamic of our curiosity not by fiat, by proscribing questions, but by extending it to and satisfying it on another level."[48] The most concise example I have found of this process appears on the first page of *The Legibility of the World*, where Blumenberg offers sequels to the great questions put forward by Kant. Kant's question, "What can we know?" is echoed by Blumenberg's "What was it that we wanted to know?" And Kant's "What may we hope?" is replaced by Blumenberg's "What was it that we might have hoped for?"[49] The surrogate questions push their predecessors into the background, undermining our expectations and our need for knowledge.

As the problem of absolutes begins to recede into the background, Blumenberg is branching out into other areas. In the past decade he has begun to experiment with new genres: short prose pieces such as newspaper essays, "imaginary anecdotes" which take off from obscure historical facts, and "glosses" on fables in which he often provides more adaptation than commentary.[50] The turn to this more overtly literary work seems appropriate for a philosopher becoming more conscious of the metaphorical structure of his own thought. But these literary productions remain enigmatic; they confuse the boundaries between the imagi-

[47] "Beobachtungen an Metaphern," 168.

[48] Robert M. Wallace, "Translator's Introduction," *Legitimacy of the Modern Age*, xxviii.

[49] *Lesbarkeit der Welt*, 9.

[50] These literary pieces have been appearing regularly in *Frankfurter Allgemeine Zeitung, Neue Zürcher Zeitung*, and *Akzente; Die Sorge geht über den Fluss* (Frankfurt am Main, 1987) is a collection of such pieces.

nary and the historical, the peripheral and the central, the significant and the insignificant, and the universal and the particular. Perhaps they can be understood as another step in the attempt to ignore a big question and to develop on the site of that ignorance many smaller questions and possibilities, old and new. Blumenberg, in other words, continues to find new ways to distract himself and us from whatever it was that we thought we wanted to know. He continues to learn ignorance, to remember oblivion.

Queens College and The Graduate School of The City University
of New York.